Artificial Intelligence and Natural Algorithms

Edited by

Rijwan Khan

Department of Computer Science and Engineering
ABES Institute of Technology,
Ghaziabad (U.P.), India

Pawan Kumar Sharma

Department of Applied Science
Dronacharya Group of Institutions,
Gr. Noida (U.P.), India

Sugam Sharma

Senior Systems Analyst
Center for Survey
Statistics & Methodology,
Iowa State University, USA

&

Santosh Kumar

Department of Mathematics,
College of Natural and Applied Sciences,
University of Dar es Salaam,
Tanzania

Artificial Intelligence and Natural Algorithms

Editors: Rijwan Khan, Pawan Kumar Sharma, Sugam Sharma and Santosh Kumar

ISBN (Online): 978-981-5036-09-1

ISBN (Print): 978-981-5036-10-7

ISBN (Paperback): 978-981-5036-11-4

need for a court order if at any point you breach any terms of this License Agreement. In no event will any delay or failure by Bentham Science Publishers in enforcing your compliance with this License Agreement constitute a waiver of any of its rights.

3. You acknowledge that you have read this License Agreement, and agree to be bound by its terms and conditions. To the extent that any other terms and conditions presented on any website of Bentham Science Publishers conflict with, or are inconsistent with, the terms and conditions set out in this License Agreement, you acknowledge that the terms and conditions set out in this License Agreement shall prevail.

Bentham Science Publishers Pte. Ltd.
80 Robinson Road #02-00
Singapore 068898
Singapore
Email: subscriptions@benthamscience.net

BENTHAM SCIENCE

CONTENTS

PREFACE

This book is based on Applications of Artificial Intelligence and Nature Inspired Algorithms in different areas of Computer Science. Artificial Intelligence (AI) encompasses by means of computers to do things that customarily need human intelligence. It also includes acting on data, learning from new data, and improving over time, just corresponding to a small human kid growing up into a smarter human adult. Nature-inspired algorithms are a set of original problem-solving practices and approaches and take enticing substantial consideration for their respectable act. Typical examples of nature-inspired algorithms contain evolutionary computing (EC), artificial neural networks (ANN), swarm intelligence (SI), and fuzzy systems (FS) and they have been useful to resolve several actual problems. Even with the fame of nature-inspired algorithms, several tests endure, which need extra research efforts. In this book, we focus on Artificial Intelligence (AI) and optimization algorithms for data analytical processes. Each chapter in this book is written by topic experts on applications of Artificial Intelligence (AI) and nature-inspired algorithms in data science.

Rijwan Khan
Department of Computer Science and Engineering
ABES Institute of Technology,
Ghaziabad (U.P.),
India

List of Contributors

Agnik Guha	Department of Computer Engineering, Faculty of Engineering and Technology, Jamia Millia Islamia, New Delhi-25, India
Ajay Kumar Yadav	Department of Computer Engineering, Faculty of Engineering and Technology, Jamia Millia Islamia, New Delhi-25, India
Amit Kumar Singh	Department of Instrumentation and Control Engineering, Dr. B. R. Ambedkar NIT Jalandhar, India
Amreen Ahmad	Department of Computer Engineering, Faculty of Engineering and Technology, Jamia Millia Islamia, New Delhi-25, India
Anand Singh Rajawat	Deptartment of CS Engineering, Shri Vaishnav Vidyapeeth Vishwavidyalaya, Indore, India
Anil Kumar	Department of Mathematics, Swami Vivekananda Subharti University, Meerut (UP), India
Ankita R. Angre	Department of Computer Engineering, Modern Education Society's College of Engineering, SPPU Pune, India
Archana P. Kale	Department of Computer Engineering, Modern Education Society's College of Engineering, SPPU Pune, India
Arvinda Kushwaha	Department of Computer Science and Engineering, MIET Meerut, India
Asfia Aziz	School of Engineering Science and Technology, Jamia Hamdard, New Delhi, India
Ashish Kumar Chakraverti	Department of Computer Science and Engineering, School of Engineering and Technology, Sharda University, Gr. Noida, India
Bharti Suri	MSIT, USICT, New Delhi, India
Bhaskar Singh	EC, RITS, RGPV, Bhopal, India
Chanchal Kumar	Department of Computer Engineering, Faculty of Engineering and Technology, Jamia Millia Islamia, New Delhi-25, India
Devika Bihani	Computer Science Engineering, Shri Vaishnav Vidyapeeth Vishwavidyalaya, Indore, India
Dhanashree V. Paranjape	Department of Computer Engineering, Modern Education Society's College of Engineering, SPPU Pune, India
Divakar Singh	CSE, BUIT, Bhopal, India
Harsh Pratap Singh	CSE, SOE, SSSUTMS, Sehore, India
Harshit Bhadwaj	Department of Computer Science and Engineering, MIET, Greater Noida, India
Harshit Jain	Computer Science Engineering, Shri Vaishnav Vidyapeeth Vishwavidyalaya, Indore, India
I. Kumar	Graphic Era Hill University, Dehradun, India
J. Rawat	Graphic Era Hill University, Dehradun, India
Jyoti Kumar	Department of Design, Indian Institute of Technology, Delhi, India

Kanishk Barhanpurkar	Deptartment of CS Engineering, Sambhram Institute of Technology, Bengaluru, Karnataka, India
Krishna Kumar	Department of Computer Science and Engineering, MJPRU, Bareilly, India
N. Mohd	Graphic Era Hill University, Dehradun, India
Nahid Sami	School of Engineering Science and Technology, Jamia Hamdard, New Delhi, India
Nishtha Jatana	Research Scholar, USICT and Assistant Professor, MSIT, USICT, New Delhi, India
Piyush Bhushan Singh	Department of Information Technology, Pranveer Singh Institute of Technology, Kanpur UP, India
Rakesh Ranjan	Department of Information Technology, Pranveer Singh Institute of Technology, Kanpur UP, India
Rashmi Singh	MIS Head Trident Group, Hosangabad, India
Romil Rawat	Deptartment of CS Engineering, Sambhram Institute of Technology, Bengaluru, Karnataka, India
S.P. Singh	Graphic Era Deemed to be University, Dehradun, India DIT University, Dehradun, India
Samia Chehbi Gamoura	EM Strasbourg Business School, Strasbourg University, HuManiS (UR 7308), Strasbourg, France
Saransh Sharma	Computer Science Engineering, Shri Vaishnav Vidyapeeth Vishwavidyalaya, Indore, India
Saty Prakash Yadav	Department of Instrumentation and Control Engineering, Dr. B R Ambedkar NIT Jalandhar, India
Shashwati P. Kale	Department of Computer Engineering, Modern Education Society's College of Engineering, SPPU Pune, India
Shefali P. Sonavane	Department of Computer Engineering, Modern Education Society's College of Engineering, SPPU Pune, India
Shivam	Graphic Era Deemed to be Universituy, Dehradun, India
Sugandha Chakraverti	Department of Computer Science and Engineering, Greater Noida Institute of Technology, Gr. Noida, UP, India
Sunil K. Singh	Department of Computer Science & Engineering, CCET, Chandigarh, India
Taranjeet Singh	Department of Computer Science and Engineering, IFTM University, Moradabad, India
Upasana Pandey	Department of Computer Sciences & Engineering, (AI) ABES Institute of Technology, Ghaziabad, India
Vani Kansa	Department of Computer Science & Engineering, Guru Kashi University, Bathinda, India
Vaseem Naiyer	MIS Head Trident Group, Hosangabad, India
Vinay Singh	CSE, SISTEC Gandhinagar, Bhopal, India

Wade Aditi R.   Department of Information Technology, Walchand College of Engineering Sangli, The Bishops Education Society, Pune, The Kaushalya Academy, Latur, India

CHAPTER 1

Data Computation: Awareness, Architecture and Applications

Vani Kansal[1,*] and **Sunil K. Singh**[2]

[1] *Department of Computer Science & Engineering, Guru Kashi University, Bathinda, India*

[2] *Department of Computer Science & Engineering, CCET, Chandigarh, India*

Abstract: There has been a tremendous revolution in computing technologies to handle the vast amount of data in recent years. Big data is the large-scale complex data in which real-time data is available and mushrooms the development of almost every field. In recent years, the demand and requirement of big data produced an opportunity to replace traditional data techniques due to their low efficiency and low accuracy. It shows adequate responsiveness, absence of versatility, execution, and precision for meeting the convolution of Big Data challenges. As an outcome, this created different dispersions and innovations. Big data does not mean that the data is humongous but additionally excessive in range and speed. This factor makes them tough to deal with the usage of conventional gear and techniques. Decision-makers read the extension and expansion of big data to understand and extract valuable information from rapidly varying data using big data analytics. In this chapter, we can analyze big data tools and techniques useful for big data. This chapter presents a literature survey covering various applications and technologies that play an indispensable role in offering new solutions dealing with large-scale, high-dimensional data. By summarizing different available technologies in one place from 2011 to 2019, it covers highly ranked international publications. Further, it extends in the context of computing challenges faced by significant Data Healthcare, Clinical Research, E-Commerce, Cloud Computing, Fog computing, Parallel Computing, Pervasive Computing, Reconfigurable Computing, Green Computing, Embedded Computing, Blockchain, Digital Image Processing and IoT and Computing Technology. The survey summarizes the large-scale data computing solutions that help in directing future research in a proper direction. This chapter shows that the popularity of data computing technology has steeply risen in the year 2015, and before 2011, the core research was more popular.

Keywords: Big Data, Big Data Analytics Applications, Challenges, Data Computation, Decision Making.

* **Corresponding author Vani Kansal:** Department of Computer Science & Engineering, Guru Kashi University, Bathinda, India; E-mail: ervanikansal@gku.ac.in

Rijwan Khan, Pawan Sharma, Sugam Sharma and Santosh Kumar (Eds.)

INTRODUCTION

Data refers to bits or chunks of information represented in a digital format in the computational world. This data is available in multiple forms, such as text, symbols, numbers, *etc.*, that are formatted peculiarly (refer to Fig. **1**). It is considered an element for modelling or representing real-world events, such as a line segment representing the location of a road. Data represents a binary format for interpreting the process and converting computer data into meaningful information during its transfer. According to Michener, the concept of meta-informatics describes the context, content, structure, accessibility, and quality aspects of the data [1]. Computing covers the activities that require a computer to perform any task, such as processing, managing, transferring, or communicating a piece of information. Here, the concept of hardware and software came into existence.

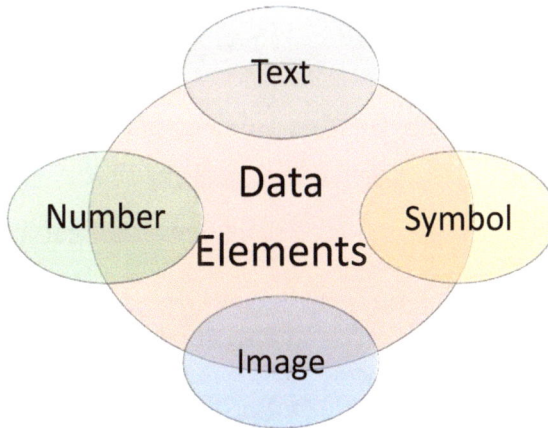

Fig. (1). Data Elements.

With the emergence of the latest revolutionized tools and technologies, Darmont described the advancement of data-centric computing compared to earlier times [2]. Data analytics and large-scale data mining attracted the interest of various researchers, which led to the existence of a cost-effective solution for online and offline data storage and manipulation, as shown by Sandor *et al.*, while addressing mobile clouds. They proposed "Multi-Authority-based Encryption" to solve the "Key Escrow Problem" in authority-based encryption [3]. From cloud technology and online computing solutions to data storage techniques, all these inherit the risk of threats and attacks. The necessity of data security and privacy has also grown on these grounds. In the last few decades, data has risen to many folds in each field, whether it is dealing with Online Social Media [4], E-Commerce [5], Internet-of-Things [6], Cloud, Healthcare, Bio-Research, or Clinical Data [7]. These big data analytics are characterized by proper data management strategies with supporting architecture to offer better visualization, user interaction, and the development of models. The present review provides a survey of the approaches to deal with the enormously growing demand for a higher level of data computing. Highly cited research articles and relevant research studies are accessed and mined during the process. The work covers the literature supporting applications and approaches based on various technologies to deal with vivid kinds of massive data.

The survey is divided into five sections, including an introduction. Section 2 discusses the survey strategies and provides the application-wise literature review about various approaches; Section 3 provides a descriptive analysis of the work, and Section 4 enumerates the data computing challenges. Finally, the paper summarizes and concludes in Section 5.

SURVEY STRATEGIES

The study design involves intensive data mining, which is related to research articles published from 2011 to date in journals and indexed in PubMed, Science Direct, IEEE, Google Scholar, Scopus, SCI with reputed publishers such as Springer, Elsevier, Taylor & Francis, *etc*. The keywords like "Data Computing", "Big Data", "Massive Data", "Healthcare", "E-Commerce", "Cloud", "Image Processing", "Biomedical", "IoT", "Clinical" are useful with and without "applications", "tools", technologies", "solution", "approaches", "analytics" and "server". The section includes Social Networking, Biomedical Research, E-Commerce [8], Internet-of-Things [9], Online Media, NGS Technologies [10], and Education Sector [11], which is continuously adding up to the data volume and variety. This has irresistibly flooded the network with organized and unorganized data types. Here, the computing framework has revolutionized various data mining, analysis, and visualization strategies. It has also reduced manual efforts. Cloud environment strengthened by fog and parallel computing offers an interesting platform to deal with large-scale multifaceted computing challenges. The technology eradicates the necessity of maintaining the costly computing hardware required to perform various tasks. Moreover, it also effectively addresses software and space requirements. Recent time has seen a tremendous increase in the big data technologies touching the medical and informatics field. We can use data mining by selecting the most recent and relevant research papers in this area. The paper is selected based on variously defined approaches:

- Published papers must be in the English language.
- The publication year should lie between 2011 and 2019.
- The paper should discuss the design, approach, or application to deal with extensive data.
- The paper should evaluate the performance of data computing applications.

Initially, 160 papers were mined between 2011 and 2019. Furthermore, while employing various inclusion and exclusion criteria, 90 papers were selected. Finally, 73 papers were selected by reading and analyzing the paper content for the study. This is followed by comparing the literary work that is further analyzed regarding data computing applications.

Big Data

The advent of data-based computing architectures has added pace to the research aspects and resulted in a large-scale data generation with extraordinarily high dimensions and pace. Here, the data is referred to as "Big Data" which is featured by the large volume, veracity, variety, velocity, and value representing larger data sets with complex, massive, and diverse data [12]. The big data revenue forecast published by Shanhong in Statistics 2019 (refer to Fig. **2**) predicts that at the end of 2027, the size of the market will hike up to103 billion dollars, which is nearly double the market size of 49 billion dollars in 2019 [13].

A comprehensive survey conducted by Oussous *et al.* summarized the various aspects of big data computing technology to deal with enormously rising structured and unstructured data with high-tech designs. They also compared big data technology according to their distinct layers like "Data Storage Layer", "Data Processing Layer", "Data Querying Layer", "Data Access Layer" and "Management Layer" [14]. Usha and Aps observed that in the last few decades, Apache Hadoop and Map-Reduce have emerged with the instrumental capability to run a query on terabyte sized data in a couple of seconds that traditional query technologies process in minutes [15]. In this regard, HBase was developed by George that is strengthened by Hadoop technology for high-speed queries from billions of records [16], while Hydra was developed by Lewis *et al.* as a search engine based on the distributed computing architecture of Hadoop [17].

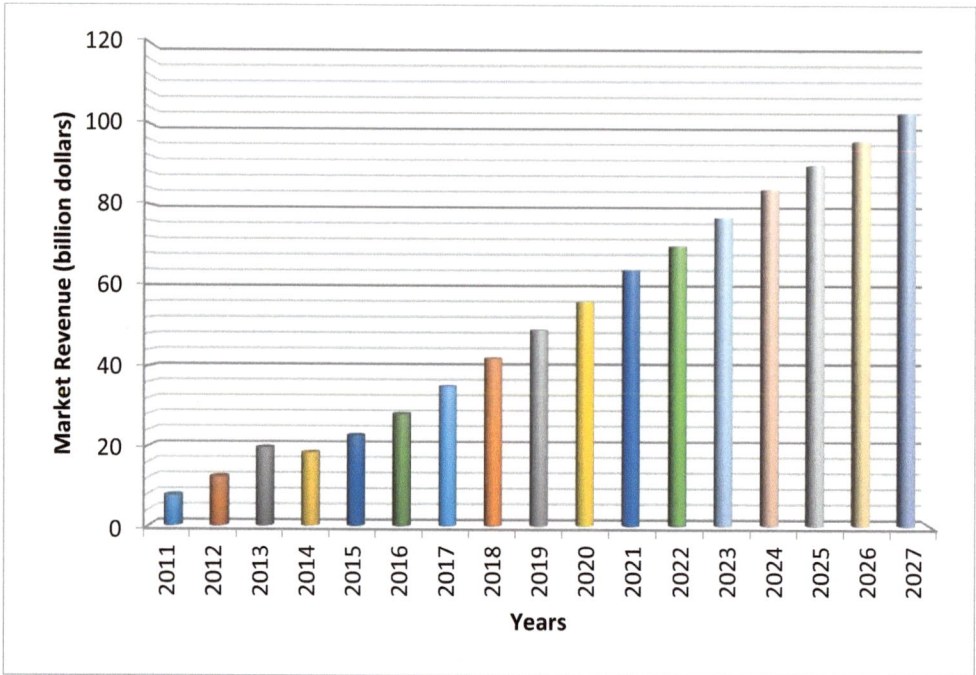

Fig. (2). Worldwide Big Data Market Revenue Prediction [13].

Cloud Computing

Cloud offers a robust computational environment and storage space for outsourcing data. The flooding of large-scale data on the network has led to the channelization of data to various cloud servers. These days, cloud storage has been popularly used by both individuals and enterprises. When an individual is sharing data in a public cloud environment, he or she should check for privacy and security aspects. Myrna was developed by Langmead *et al.* for large-scale cloud computing. Myrna is a tool based on a cloud computing environment used to determine genes in a large dataset of RNA-sequences [18]. Nellore *et al.* address the privacy protection of cloud data with "Rail-dbGap (Database of Genotypes and Phenotypes)" [19]. "CloVR (Cloud Virtual Machine)" was developed by Angiuoli *et al.* to address cloud computing environments from the desktop. It is used to manage the data transfer between the desktop and cloud servers. It also improves the performance for processing large datasets using cloud computing resources [20], and a high-performance query system, "Hadoop GIS" was developed using Map Reduce by Wang *et al.* [21].

Pervasive Computing

Pervasive computing, also considered ubiquitous computing, aims to create an environment packed with all kinds of built-in and portable computing devices that communicate with users' wireless technologies as they move through this environment. As early as 2006, Shuxin had presented a trust model to deal with the pervasive computing environment [22]. Authors established pervasive computing for creating a revolution by providing services that satisfy user expectations and desires using the information of nearby physical sites. Furthermore, Youssef (2013) has summarized the practicability of pervasive computing regarding cloud services and their adjoining applications. It was found that the cloud environment presents effective communication through devices such as PDAs, mobile phones, and wireless sensors to offer vivid services and facilities [23]. One of the most important features of pervasive computing systems over traditional computing is that it hides out the complex computing functions from the users who are unaware of the computing environment.

Reconfigurable Computing

Reconfigurable computing is a structural design intended to fill the gap between hardware and software. Koren *et al.* (2018) offer potentially much higher performance than software while retaining a greater degree of flexibility of hardware components [24]. Earlier in 2002, the author had described Reconfigurable devices, including Field-Programmable Door Arrays (FPGAs). There are several computational elements that are defined by the programmable configuration bits. Campton *et al.* examined that these elements, often known as logic blocks, are linked by means of a collection of programmable routing resources [25].

Green Computing

Green Computing refers to the efficient use of computers and other technologies while respecting the environment through energy-efficient peripherals, environmental protection, and reducing electronic waste. Mishra *et al.* (2018) demonstrated that these goals not only make resources more effective but, at the same time, enhance the overall performance of the system [26]. Naji *et al.* (2017) summarised that green computing had been described in two ways [27]:

- Software Technology: The main goal is to create techniques to improve software, storage, and energy efficiency.
- Hardware Technology: The goal is to reduce energy consumption without presenting expertise that can create economically efficient technology assisted

with the concept of recycling.

EMBEDDED COMPUTING

"Embedded System" is an acronym representing "Embedded Computer System" that embodies the system product or electronic device in which a computer has been incorporated. Furuichi *et al.* (2014) presented "Internal system" as a general term for any electronic device that includes any system, product, and computer [28]. Jakoyljevis examined the "Embedded Systems" consisting of a series of software and hardware modules designed to support and sustain manageable and certifiable integration and hosting of various control and maintenance functions [29].

Parallel Computing

It is one of the advanced computing technologies that have recently been implemented to deal with enormous data volumes. CloudBurst is one of the parallelized computing models that facilitate the genome mapping process developed by Schatz, and for "Short-read mapping" process. It uses multiple nodes to parallelize the execution of processes using the "Hadoop Map Reduce" framework [30]. Keckler *et al.* (2011) detailed the salient features of implementing a high-throughput architecture that is based on GPU. They also considered the parallel computing challenge with its potential effects on the research community [31]. Zhang *et al.* (2019) postulated various parallel computing-based solutions to deal with the modelling of multidimensional statistical analysis of the Markov Chain Random Field model. In the methodology, Multicore Processor Parallel Computing, GPU-based Nearest Neighbour Searching (GNNS) Parallel Computing, and Multicore Processor-based GNNS were also used. Simulation analysis employed both CPU and GPU during the execution of computing solutions. The results demonstrated that the proposed parallel computing designs were 1.8 units faster [32].

Fog Computing

Many applications are available that are hybrid approaches involving various technologies together to improve the technology outcomes. Tortonesi *et al.* (2019) proposed a "new information-centric" and "Value-based service" model designed as "SPF Fog-as-a- Service Platform" which can be used to tackle the important challenges in a smart city *i.e.*, to process a massive amount of raw data generated in a smart city. They established that fog computing is a wiser combination of WSN, IoT, mobile, and edge computing technology. The concept proved to be well suitable for smart city concepts. Various applications related to business and civil service can also be run on "Fog Computing" platform. The authors described how fog computing governs the location, time-sensitive, and context-based applications covering sensitive information of both consumers and producers to offer a reasonably cost-effective platform [33]. For instance, Fog computing architecture is an enhanced cloud computing platform combining designs for enhancing IoT based applications in the industry. This proposed work by Jang *et al.* (2019) summarized the design of smart factories for the future. The technology-driven intelligent, self-monitoring and self-organizing design proved to be nearly autonomous to adapt to the factory's manufacturing design. The system was successfully evaluated against a permission-based fog computing system that was inspired by decentralized technology [34]. Communication and computation are the essential aspects of Fog Computing. The rush of vehicles increases in downtown during working hours and most vehicles are parked in the parking areas and on the roadside for a long time. Thus, these movable and immovable transports can be used as resources for communication and computing. Ergo Hou *et al.* proposed a "Vehicular Fog Computing" in which they used vehicles as an infrastructure to forge the better usage of these automobiles' conveyance and calculations [35]. Laun also considers Fog computing as the best solution for providing exemplary mobile services to users at any place with proper usage of resources and for better service of mobile traffic when they use location-based services of the mobile devices [36].

Internet of Things and Computing Technology

Internet-of-Things (IoT) has also shown wide data computing applications developed across wider domains, including Production, Occupation, Shipping, Health Protection, and Households. For instance, Breidenbacher *et al.* presented HADES-IoT in the year 2019 as a "Tamper-Proof" host-based anomaly detection design for IoT devices to protect them from malware devices. They offer the last line defence mechanism for installing a range of IoT devices advantaged with Linux platform. The design is 100% effective in detecting IoT, Reaper, and VPN Filters while utilizing nearly 5% of the memory [37]. Yun designed one M2M as a standardised IoT platform for assisting the sensing capabilities of one M2M-defined web-based application. The design successfully dealt with the heterogeneous hardware interfaces of IoT devices [38]. Dimitrov (2016) focussed their study on various MIoT "(Medical Internet of Things)" devices and big data for computing data related to healthcare facilities offered by hospitals and various government and private organizations. A new category of "Digital Health Advisors "will help their clients avoid illness related to their diet, improve their mental health, and achieve a better lifestyle. There are so many devices and mobile apps like "Myo", "Zio patch", "Glaxo", "Novartis" that are used for smart healthcare. People have started using mobile apps and IoT devices to monitor their health, remember their appointments, calculate the calories they burnt while walking or running, and easily communicate with their doctors [39]. Bhattacharyya *et al.* (2018) designed an exciting and interactive gaming app in Visual Studio (IDE) using user's "myoelectric signal" to aid in the rehabilitation of patients recovering from heart diseases, stroke, depression, surgery and design and control of orthotics, prosthetics, *etc.* It offers an "MYO armband" that needs to be tied to the recovering patient to recognize various gestures of hand movements and uses the in-built "EMG (Electromyography)" electrode for data retrieval [40]. Liu *et al.* (2018) dedicated their research to designing IoT based "patch-type ECG monitor "applications to offer real-time monitoring apps and used to measure the heartbeat of patients fighting with "cardiovascular disorders" [41]. The rising demand for encryption in every field has led to the emergence of novel ideas to deal with privacy and security aspects. Singh *et al.* (2019) proposed an IoT-based smart home design using decentralization technology of blockchain and cloud computing. To achieve confidentiality and integrity in block chain technology, they use encryption and hashing algorithms. Smart home security aspects were dealt with while monitoring the network traffic to establish a correlation between network traffic and traffic features so that they can use the "Multivariate Correlation Analysis (MCA)" identification technique to measure the flow of smart network traffic. This helps to categories the association between the features of traffic [42]. The blockchains offer the most efficient solution to IoT based design.

Blockchain

Blockchain offers a kind of one-time design and creation of databases that can only be read without any scope of removal or modification. It offers decentralized data accessible by the owner with the help of private keys. Kaye *et al.* (2015) designed a dynamic patient consent system that worked as a personalized communication interface. This interface helps user-centred decision making, where participants can securely share their data with third parties in an encrypted form and offers a single platform for intermingling their interests and concerns [43]. Blockchain inspired design offers encryption of sensitive data when the records and samples are shared. Globally, blockchain has shown potential applications in maintaining Electronic Medical Records to aid in the apt functioning of the Food and Drug Administration. Cyran (2018) had designed a blockchain-based solution that was inspired by the microservices framework [44].

The design offered an independently secured encapsulation of different services customizable to meet individual hospital needs. The core design covered interaction among nodes, cryptographic security, extensive data file sharing facilities, and integration of logical business sharing using smart contracts [45]. Dimitrov (2019) published his research focussing on the applications inspired by blockchain architecture. He was mainly concerned about offering solutions to data management issues faced by healthcare centres [46]. Field exhibiting tremendous data computing applications are shown in Fig. (3) and Table 1.

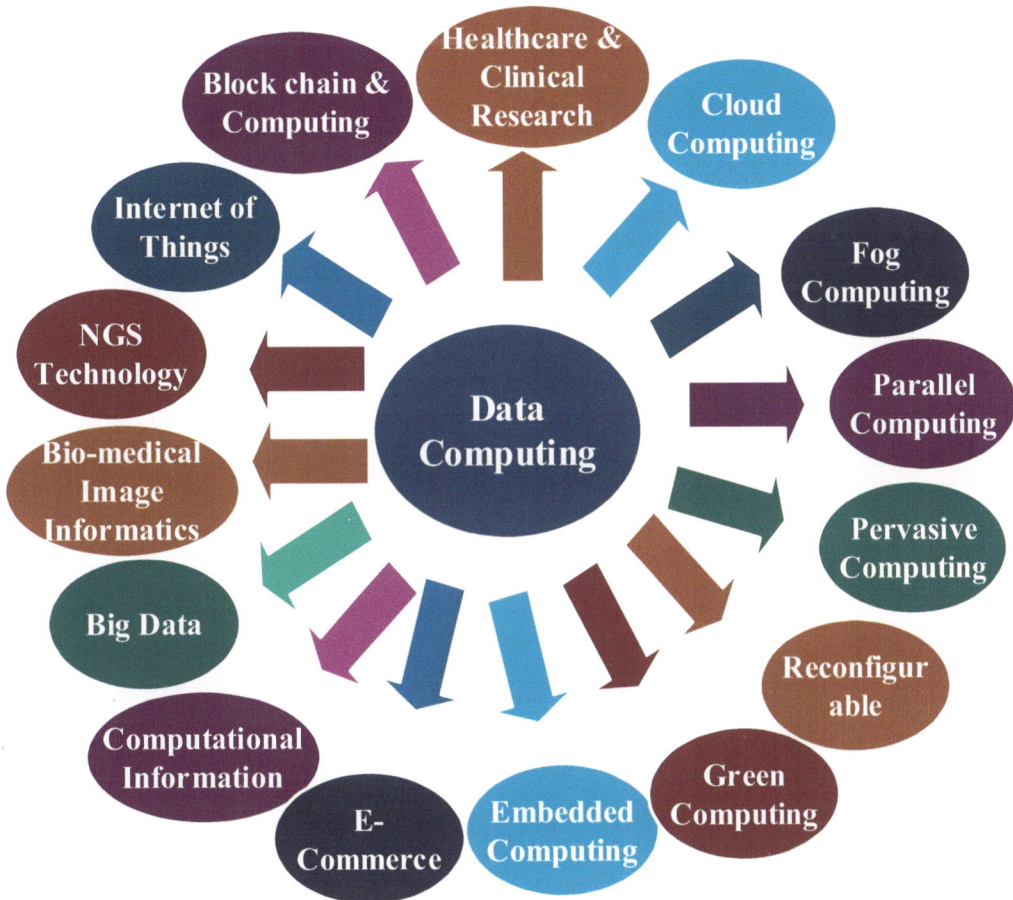

Fig. (3). Data Computing Applications in Various Fields.

Table 1. Some of the Data Computing Applications.

Application	Technology Used	Reference
BlueSNP	A genome-wide study using R-package for statistical testing	70
CloudBurst	Parallel computing design for mapping genome	30
Cloudwave	Clinical data processing using Hadoop	67
CloVR	The virtual machine on cloud computing for automated analysis	20
DistMap	Conducts mapping based on short-read mapping on a Hadoop cluster	71

(Table 1) cont.....

Application	Technology Used	Reference
Electronic Medical Records (EMR)	Microservices and blockchain-inspired service	53
HADES-IoT	anaomaly detection of IoTs	37
Hbase	Hadoop based query platform	16
Hydra	Software package based on Hadoop-distributed computing	17
MedCloud	Hadoop with HIPAA to deal with security aspects of patients data	66
MYO	Rehabilitation therapy app based on visual studio.	40
Myrna	Cloud computing for large expression data	18
oneM2M	IoT platform to assist sensing applications	38
Rail-dbGap	Privacy protection of cloud data	19
SeqPig	Enhanced Apache Pig involving Hadoop-BAM	73
SparkSeq	Software package taking advantage of Apache Spark and Hadoop-BAM library.	72

NGS-Throughput

Schuster published an article in which he established that the rising interest in the new generation of "Non-Sanger-based Sequencing" technology, *i.e.*, Next-Generation Sequencing, transformed the traditional design of genomic and expression analysis [47]. For instance, NGS technology could process billions of DNA sequence data in a day and gives maximum throughput than existing methods, as demonstrated by the study published by Knetsch *et al.* in 2019 [48]. Recently, in 2019, Seth *et al.* had also discussed the big data tools and technologies that majorly focussed on effectively addressing issues related to data storage, data retrieval, data analysis, data integration in the vivid platform, and detecting elements raising errors. Security has always been the main concern while storing data on the cloud. Hence, they proposed a mechanism for efficient storage of data using fog computing as an extended version of cloud computing [49]. Critical analysis of various achievements and hurdles for the transformation from Landscape Genetics" to "Landscape Genomics" was presented by Cushman *et al.* in his published study focussing on NGS data [50].

Digital Image Processing

The concept of Data Computation has an inevitable role in digital image processing applications in vivid fields like biometrics and medicine. For instance, in 2017, Ghazali *et al.* had addressed the problem of colour image processing with specific applications to weed classification [51]. In this work, they achieved higher classification accuracy by combining both colour and texture information of weed images. For preprocessing, a task colour filtering algorithm was used and the proposed technique and known as the extracted green colour. The two feature extraction algorithms, Gray level co-occurrence matrix (GLCM) and Fast Fourier Transform (FFT), were used for classification. Colour-based method is better than the gray scale for better classification results. Hassan *et al.* (2019) described novel methods used for detecting and classifying the external defects of olive fruits based on texture analysis and texture homogeneity [52]. The proposed technique distinguished the defected and healthy olive fruits and was further used to identify and recognize the real defected region. The outcomes were compared with image processing techniques such as Canny, Otsu, local binary pattern algorithm, K-means, and Fuzzy C-means algorithms, demonstrating the highest accuracy achieved by the proposed technique. Mia *et al.* (2018) proposed an efficient approach based on Linear Discriminant Analysis (LDA) for initial image segmentation by an unsupervised method [53]. The proposed method was capable of automatically separating and combining the clusters whenever required. The proposed method outperforms various cluster-based image segmentation methods, such as the k -means algorithm, the SOFM and LDA segmentation method, and the LDA and K-means based segmentation. The authors established that the performance of the proposed algorithm can be improved by using machine learning algorithms. These are important for the segmentation of natural images and medical images. In 2019, Trivedi *et al.* discussed image informatics as more related to the various aspects of medical image processing used in relation to "Digital Imaging and Communications in Medicine (DICOM)" format images, including tissue scans [54]. The concept for improvement of the quality of medical diagnosis has raised the interest in computer-based biomedical image processing and analysis. Radiology imaging provides depth visualization of various complex biological systems, tissues, and organs. In this area of research, Saba *et al.* had implemented Deep Learning (DL) Technology to analyse radiology data. With the proper use of technology, the value of the radiologist is enhanced with the dormant of DL in the conveyance of healthcare. It was conducted by upgrading the patient's results with minimal cost. They also discussed three fundamental challenges viz. "Safety", "Privacy", "Legality" in the diagnosis of radiology data [55]. Image diagnostics are widely available in the form of MRI, CT and X-Ray scans performed to distinguish benign and diseased tissues visually. The process is governed by implementing various Artificial Intelligence approaches to create intelligent systems to mimic the human brain. To achieve this, various Machine Learning approaches powered by image optimization strategies are implemented. For instance, Higaki *et al.* used Deep Learning Architecture for improving the quality of images in different expertise as "noise and artifact reduction", "super-resolution" and "image acquisition and reconstruction". They developed a deep learning-based "denoising convolutional neural network" to remove noise from the image [56]. Gyftopoulos *et al.* used artificial intelligence [57] and DeSouza *et al.* used multimodality imaging techniques [58]. Here, another important aspect is intelligent data selection or region selection from the whole image scan.

Kagadis *et al.* (2013) discussed cloud computing as a practical solution that offers resource reconfiguration of platforms, applications, and virtual environments in a very cost-effective manner. The researchers and clinicians have been inspired by the vital role being played by cloud computing and cloud storage facilities. The authors have majorly focussed on biomedical imaging technology, taking advantage of computing platforms [59]. Ali *et al.* (2018) described innovative designs to offer technology-driven services to the healthcare sector. The work involved a rigorous evaluation of the cloud data computing environment to cover applications, issues and offered opportunities for the emergence of cloud computing in healthcare. The study showed that cloud computing enhanced the quality that led to decision-making, security, and privacy [60].

E-commerce

Various E-commerce websites are also constantly generating a large volume of business data. The enterprises also extend their services to customers by learning individuals' interests. To avoid wasteful data searching, opinion and sentimental mining had shown great prospects. Kansal and Kumar have proposed financial sentiment analysis on social network data from financial markets, Facebook, Twitter, and news using artificial intelligence and Cuckoo search [61]. Derindag *et al.* (2019) presented an analytical study covering the technologies to address e-governance and e-commerce. They also critically analysed the impact of the revolution on the economic sector with various growth indicators [62]. Kansal and Kumar have also developed a stock market forecasting system that demonstrated 94.44% accuracy for emotion-based text categorization. The designed stock price forecasting system has implemented a cuckoo search with neural networks to obtain instrumental prediction results [63].

Healthcare Informatics and Clinical Research

The recent revolution in technologies has added pace to the research aspects of healthcare informatics, biomedical data analysis and resulted in large-scale data generation related to biological research with extraordinarily high dimensions and pace. The current section moves around analytics, majorly covering biomedical research about clinical informatics, including diagnostics. Chandana *et al.* in 2018 defined that healthcare informatics addresses the tools and techniques that are used to estimate and offer solutions to the breakout of the most hazardous infectious diseases. The proposed combined model "Convolutional Neural

Network" using "Naive Bayes", "Random Forest" and "Linear Regression" on "Hadoop platform" to forecast lung diseases at the beginning stage of the health service group [64]. Tavazzi in 2019 stated that clinical informatics deals with clinical trials and intelligent decision making to benefit patients in the light of knowledge and evidence [65]. The rising trends of personalized medicine have produced massive data covering large data sets. Mass patient selection, designing protocols, mass evaluation, and conducting various levels of clinical trials has become feasible with computing technologies. Therefore, storing an amount of electronic medical records efficiently is itself a great challenge. Software solutions like MedCloud based on HIPAA [66] and Cloudwave [67] were developed by Sobhy *et al.* and Jaypndian *et al.* to manage clinical data. Online data management has resulted in easy channelization of information that needs to be shared with patients, volunteers, drug industry, pharmacists, doctors, and professionals. Nipp *et al.* figured out various facts to enlighten individuals with many misconceptions and thereby encouraging higher patient recruitment under various trials [68].

SURVEY OUTCOMES

The review has shown that data computing has not only explored informatics related fields like cloud, IoT, social networks, enterprise, and industrial networks. Further encouragement proceeds with potential computing solutions to answer large-scale data computing issues of the biological world dealing with big genomic data, practical aspects of medical research, disease prognosis, and diagnosis. The strategies like patient participation, enrolment, and clinical trials have also been positively changed with the help of online data management assays with the help of blockchain-based secure cloud storage. Fig. (**4**) summarizes the relationships among various computing technologies along with their applications in various fields. It has also been observed that the various data computing technologies cannot be isolated, and to harvest the best computing results, secure storage space and communication channels are an essential part of data computing approaches.

The year-wise distribution of the publications considered for conducting the present study is shown in Fig. (**5**). It is observed from the pie chart that very few instances for applications of data computing are seen from 2011 to 2017, which corresponds to 8% to 15%. It is also observed that 57% of the total publications used in the survey have been published between 2017 and 2019. This means that data computing has been a recent technology that has shown its impact in dealing with larger volumes of diverse data. Overall, it can also be summarized that 75% of the survey covers the data computing applications that were published not before 2013. Hence, it can be said that from the year 2017, a new era of revolutionized data computing technology has started.

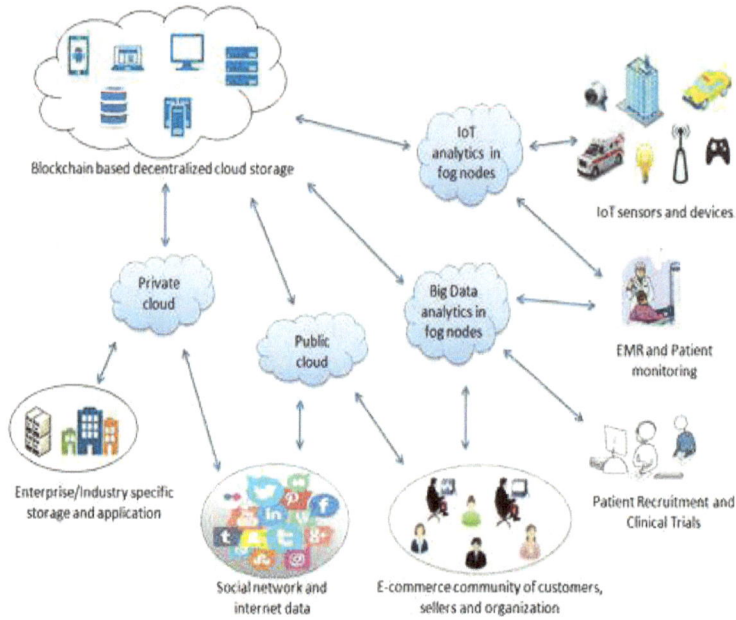

Fig. (4). Data Computing Architecture.

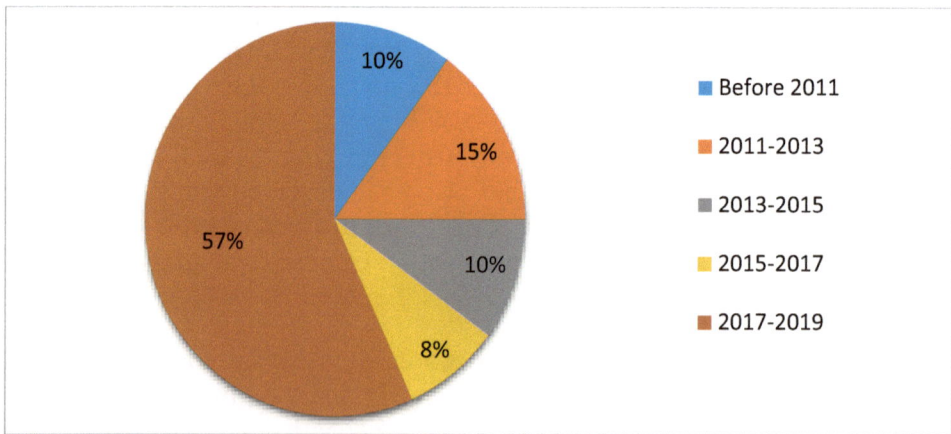

Fig. (5). Publications Referred in the Survey.

Application wise distribution of publications covered in the current survey is shown in Fig. (**6**). The data computing applications from 2011 to 2019 are plotted on the Y-axis with the number of publications used in surveys on the Y-axis. It is observed that maximum data computing applications deal with large-scale data applications, namely, IoT and Big Data analytics, followed by cloud computing, computational informatics, Digital Image Processing, healthcare and Clinical Research. The trend is further followed by the latest emerging technologies like blockchain, NGS, e-commerce, parallel computing, and fog computing that may surpass the popularity of the existing data computing applications in the coming years.

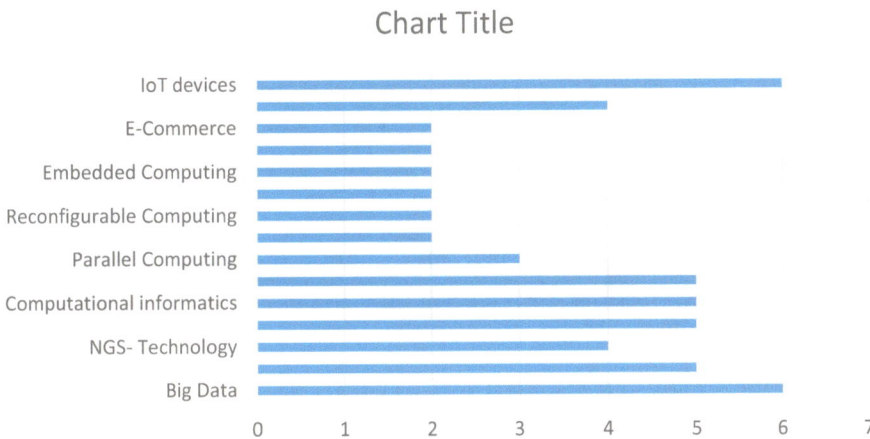

Fig. (6). Data Computing Applications from 2011 to 2019.

DATA COMPUTING CHALLENGES

Revolutionizing data computing technologies is constantly raising challenges regarding the variety and volume of data and that too at a very fast pace. This has subsequently challenged various aspects such as data availability, scalability, quality, security, privacy aspects, regulatory policies, and governance.

- Highly efficient large-scale data management strategies are required to deal with scalability concerns. In this regard, G-store was introduced by Das *et al.* offering key based structured data storage and retrieval with easy API [69].
- Data availability summarises the apt inputs, or the raw data should be constantly available as a resource for data computing technologies. Demand for a constant and high-quality resource needs to be addressed [70].
- Data integrity is another aspect of data resources that means that the data should remain unchanged or modified in any form during transfer, storage, or analysis. This aspect has been addressed with the standardisation of medical imaging in terms of DICOM and much more needs to be done in numerous fields [71].

- Large-scale computing usually results in unstructured or semistructured data. This data needs to be converted to structured data to aid further analysis. The challenge here lies in the data transformation strategies, as they should not alter data during the transformation process [72].
- Data security and privacy are indispensable needs of the current large-scale computing architectures. Data over the network or cloud environment is highly prone to theft and malicious attacks, exposing sensitive data fields to stealing, profiling, and loss of control. Vivid encryption strategies are available, including privacy preservation in the cloud, still, more customized security solutions are in high demand [73].
- Laws, rules, and regulations should safeguard sensitive data from unauthorised use. Adequate policies need to be developed to offer protection mechanisms and protect the enormously rising data volumes. Data governing policies, including monitoring, and monetizing information, should be developed to benefit the consumer and business sectors.

The nature of these challenges is constantly changing with the revolutionizing computing trends and technology advancements that need to be wisely addressed to harness the full advantage of the latest applications.

RELIABLE INDUSTRY 4.0 BASED ON MACHINE LEARNING AND IOT FOR ANALYZING

The authors provided a newly created intelligent approach for assessing the IoT smart system's dependability. A machine learning approach known as a decision tree is used to validate the data of the smart meter. The smart meter readings were regressed and classified using the decision tree approach into real and false types. In addition, the proposed system can identify data loss caused by erratic internet signals. The IoT platform's dashboard displays the system's online output, such as data loss, genuine and false data. Three scenarios have been used to assess the efficacy of the planned infrastructure. Scenario 1 demonstrates that the data is true and that there is no loss, and that the decision tree model is error-free. In scenario 2, it is demonstrated that the decision tree model can detect false data, allowing the user to secure and verify the smart meter. The traffic light has been changed to a red color to hint to the user about the abnormal case of fake data. The suggested infrastructure was tested in the final scenario to check for data loss and publish the findings on the IoT platform's dashboard, where it was determined that the network speed was insufficient for the smart system. In general, the suggested technique improves the dependability of smart IoT systems, which boosts industry 4.0 investment [74].

CONCLUSION

The survey showed that data volume is constantly rising with the revolutionized data computing technologies, data sensors, and mobile devices connected *via* the internet, offering diverse functionalities. Impossibility concludes to demarcate the big data from cloud computing and blockchain architecture. Additionally, further advanced data computing has been offered with the involvement of edge, fog, and parallel computing environments. Numerous applications have also been designed that use blockchain architecture to deal with the security and privacy aspects of cloud and IoT applications. In biomedical research, computing technology has revolutionized diagnostics and research protocols. Digital Imaging Processing has also been improved considerably, with data computing and data transfer of attributes related to the healthcare sector. In the education sector, data computing facilities have revolutionized the architecture of online classroom teaching and training based on Hadoop based online classes. Literature review from authenticated publication sources has shown that recent years from 2015 to 2019 have shown a tremendous rise in the development and deployment of computing solutions in every field. Hence, it can be summarized that data computing is a general term that has touched every aspect of life and is a popular area drawing the attention of the research community. However, there are rising instances of security attacks and privacy concerns that are being successfully addressed by computing technology. In light of the current computing survey, a highly revolutionized computing paradigm can be predicted in the near future.

CONSENT FOR PUBLICATION

Not applicable.

CONFLICT OF INTEREST

The authors declare no conflict of interest, financial or otherwise.

ACKNOWLEDGEMENT

The authors are thankful to the learned reviewers for their valuable comments.

REFERENCES

[1]   W.K. Michener, "Meta-information concepts for ecological data management", *Ecol. Inform.*, vol. 1, no. 1, pp. 3-7, 2006.
[http://dx.doi.org/10.1016/j.ecoinf.2005.08.004]

[2]   J. Darmont, "Data-Centric Benchmarking", In: *Advanced Methodologies and Technologies in Network Architecture, Mobile Computing, and Data Analytics*. IGI Global, 2019, pp. 342-353.

[3]   V.K.A. Sandor, Y. Lin, X. Li, F. Lin, and S. Zhang, "Efficient decentralized multi-authority attribute-based encryption for mobile cloud data storage", *J. Netw. Comput. Appl.*, vol. 129, pp. 25-36, 2019.

[http://dx.doi.org/10.1016/j.jnca.2019.01.003]

[4]   J. Reisman, V. Olazabal, and S. Hoffman, "Putting the "Impact" in Impact Investing: The Rising Demand for Data and Evidence of Social Outcomes", *Am. J. Eval.,* vol. 39, no. 3, pp. 389-395, 2018.
[http://dx.doi.org/10.1177/1098214018779141]

[5]   S. Ansari, R. Kohavi, L. Mason, and Z. Zheng, "Integrating e-commerce and data mining: Architecture and challenges", In: *Proceedings 2001 IEEE International Conference on Data Mining* IEEE, 2001, pp. 27-34.
[http://dx.doi.org/10.1109/ICDM.2001.989497]

[6]   C.C. Aggarwal, N. Ashish, and A. Sheth, "The internet of things: A survey from the data-centric perspective", In: *Managing and Mining Sensor Data.* Springer: Boston, MA, 2013, pp. 383-428.
[http://dx.doi.org/10.1007/978-1-4614-6309-2_12]

[7]   M.K. Hassan, A.I. El Desouky, S.M. Elghamrawy, and A.M. Sarhan, "Big Data Challenges and Opportunities in Healthcare Informatics and Smart Hospitals", In: *Security in Smart Cities: Models, Applications, and Challenges.* Springer: Cham, 2019, pp. 3-26.
[http://dx.doi.org/10.1007/978-3-030-01560-2_1]

[8]   F. Budiono, S. Lau, and W. Tibben, "Cloud Computing Adoption for E-Commerce in Developing Countries: Contributing Factors and Its Implication for Indonesia", *PACIS,* 2018.

[9]   Z. Zheng, W. Mao, F. Wu, and G. Chen, "Challenges and Opportunities in IoT Data Markets", In: *Proceedings of the Fourth International Workshop on Social Sensing* ACM, 2019, pp. 1-2.
[http://dx.doi.org/10.1145/3313294.3313378]

[10]   S.A. Cushman, A.J. Shirk, G.T. Howe, M.A. Murphy, R.J. Dyer, and S. Joost, "The least cost path from landscape genetics to landscape genomics: challenges and opportunities to explore NGS data in a spatially explicit context", *Front. Genet.,* vol. 9, p. 215, 2018.
[http://dx.doi.org/10.3389/fgene.2018.00215] [PMID: 29971091]

[11]   P.K. Paul, and M.K. Ghose, "A Novel Educational Proposal and Strategies Toward Promoting Cloud Computing, Big Data, and Human–Computer Interaction in Engineering Colleges and Universities", In: *Advances in Smart Grid and Renewable Energy.* Springer: Singapore, 2018, pp. 93-102.
[http://dx.doi.org/10.1007/978-981-10-4286-7_10]

[12]   B. Furht, and F. Villanustre, "Introduction to big data", In: *Big Data Technologies and Applications.* Springer: Cham, 2016, pp. 3-11.
[http://dx.doi.org/10.1007/978-3-319-44550-2_1]

[13]   "Big Data market revenue forecast worldwide 2011-2027", https://www.statista.com/statistics/254266/global-big-data-market-forecast/

[14]   A. Oussous, F-Z. Benjelloun, and A.A. Lahcen, "Big Data technologies: A survey", *Journal of King Saud University-Computer and Information Sciences,* vol. 30, no. 4, pp. 431-448, 2017.
[http://dx.doi.org/10.1016/j.jksuci.2017.06.001]

[15]   D. Usha, and A.J. Aps, "A survey of Big Data processing in perspective of Hadoop and MapReduce", *International Journal of Current Engineering and Technology,* vol. 4, no. 2, pp. 602-606, 2014.

[16]   L. George, *HBase: the definitive guide: random access to your planet-size data.* O'Reilly Media, Inc., 2011.

[17]   S. Lewis, A. Csordas, S. Killcoyne, H. Hermjakob, M.R. Hoopmann, R.L. Moritz, E.W. Deutsch, and J. Boyle, "Hydra: a scalable proteomic search engine which utilizes the Hadoop distributed computing framework", *BMC Bioinformatics,* vol. 13, no. 1, p. 324, 2012.
[http://dx.doi.org/10.1186/1471-2105-13-324] [PMID: 23216909]

[18]   B. Langmead, K.D. Hansen, and J.T. Leek, "Cloud-scale RNA-sequencing differential expression analysis with Myrna", *Genome Biol.,* vol. 11, no. 8, p. R83, 2010.
[http://dx.doi.org/10.1186/gb-2010-11-8-r83] [PMID: 20701754]

[19]   A. Nellore, C. Wilks, K.D. Hansen, J.T. Leek, and B. Langmead, "Rail-dbGaP: analyzing dbGaP-protected data in the cloud with Amazon Elastic MapReduce", *Bioinformatics,* vol. 32, no. 16, pp. 2551-2553, 2016.
[http://dx.doi.org/10.1093/bioinformatics/btw177] [PMID: 27153614]

[20]   S.V. Angiuoli, M. Matalka, A. Gussman, K. Galens, M. Vangala, D.R. Riley, C. Arze, J.R. White, O. White, and W.F. Fricke, "CloVR: a virtual machine for automated and portable sequence analysis from the desktop using cloud computing", *BMC Bioinformatics,* vol. 12, no. 1, p. 356, 2011.
[http://dx.doi.org/10.1186/1471-2105-12-356] [PMID: 21878105]

[21]   F. Wang, A. Aji, Q. Liu, and J. Saltz, "Hadoop-GIS: A high performance spatial query system for analytical medical imaging with MapReduce", *Center for Comprehensive Informatics, Technical Report,* 2011.

[22]   S. Yin, I. Ray, and I. Ray, "A trust model for pervasive computing environments", *Int. Conference on Collaborative Computing: Networking, Applications and Worksharing,* 2006.
[http://dx.doi.org/10.1109/COLCOM.2006.361880]

[23]   A. Youssef, "Towards pervasive computing environments with cloud services. International Journal of Ad Hoc", *Sensor & Ubiquitous Computing,* vol. 4, no. 3, pp. 1-9, 2013.
[http://dx.doi.org/10.5121/ijasuc.2013.4301]

[24]   K. Compton, and S. Hauck, "Reconfigurable computing: a survey of systems and software", *ACM Comput. Surv.,* vol. 34, no. 2, pp. 171-210, 2002. [csuR].
[http://dx.doi.org/10.1145/508352.508353]

[25]   Y. Koren, X. Gu, and W. Guo, "Reconfigurable manufacturing systems: Principles, design, and future trends", *Front. Mech. Eng.,* vol. 13, no. 2, pp. 121-136, 2018.
[http://dx.doi.org/10.1007/s11465-018-0483-0]

[26]   S.K. Mishra, D. Puthal, B. Sahoo, S.K. Jena, and M.S. Obaidat, "An adaptive task allocation technique for green cloud computing", *J. Supercomput.,* vol. 74, no. 1, pp. 370-385, 2018.
[http://dx.doi.org/10.1007/s11227-017-2133-4]

[27]   H.Z. Naji, M. Zbakh, and K. Munir, "A Review of Green Cloud Computing Techniques", In: *International Conference of Cloud Computing Technologies and Applications.* Springer: Cham, 2017, pp. 264-283.

[28]   T. Furuichi, and K. Yamada, "Next generation of embedded system on cloud computing", *Procedia Comput. Sci.,* vol. 35, pp. 1605-1614, 2014.
[http://dx.doi.org/10.1016/j.procs.2014.08.244]

[29]   M. Jakovljevic, C.C. Insaurralde, and A. Ademaj, "Embedded cloud computing for critical systems", *IEEE/AIAA 33rd Digital Avionics Systems Conference (DASC),* pp. 4A5-1, 2014.
[http://dx.doi.org/10.1109/DASC.2014.6979465]

[30]   M.C. Schatz, "CloudBurst: highly sensitive read mapping with MapReduce", *Bioinformatics,* vol. 25, no. 11, pp. 1363-1369, 2009.
[http://dx.doi.org/10.1093/bioinformatics/btp236] [PMID: 19357099]

[31]   S.W. Keckler, W.J. Dally, B. Khailany, M. Garland, and D. Glasco, "GPUs and the future of parallel computing", *IEEE Micro,* vol. 31, no. 5, pp. 7-17, 2011.
[http://dx.doi.org/10.1109/MM.2011.89]

[32]   W. Zhang, W. Li, C. Zhang, and T. Zhao, "Parallel computing solutions for Markov chain spatial sequential simulation of categorical fields", *Int. J. Digit. Earth,* vol. 12, no. 5, pp. 566-582, 2019.
[http://dx.doi.org/10.1080/17538947.2018.1464073]

[33]   M. Tortonesi, M. Govoni, A. Morelli, G. Riberto, C. Stefanelli, and N. Suri, "Taming the IoT data deluge: An innovative information-centric service model for fog computing applications", *Future Gener. Comput. Syst.,* vol. 93, pp. 888-902, 2019.
[http://dx.doi.org/10.1016/j.future.2018.06.009]

[34]   S.H. Jang, J. Guejong, J. Jeong, and B. Sangmin, "Fog Computing Architecture Based Blockchain for Industrial IoT", In: *International Conference on Computational Science* Springer: Cham, 2019, pp. 593-606.
[http://dx.doi.org/10.1007/978-3-030-22744-9_46]

[35]   X. Hou, Y. Li, M. Chen, D. Wu, D. Jin, and S. Chen, "Vehicular fog computing: A viewpoint of vehicles as the infrastructures", *IEEE Trans. Vehicular Technol.*, vol. 65, no. 6, pp. 3860-3873, 2016.
[http://dx.doi.org/10.1109/TVT.2016.2532863]

[36]   H. Luan Tom, Longxiang Gao, Zhi Liz, Yang Xiang, Guiyi Wey, and Limin Sun, "Fog Computing: Focusing on Mobile Users at the Edge", *arXiv:1502.01815v3*, 2016.

[37]   D. Breitenbacher, I. Homoliak, Y. L. Aung, N. O. Tippenhauer, and Y. Elovici, *HADES-IoT: A Practical Host-Based Anomaly Detection System for IoT Devices.*, 2019.
[http://dx.doi.org/10.1145/3321705.3329847]

[38]   J. Yun, I.Y. Ahn, J. Song, and J. Kim, "Implementation of Sensing and Actuation Capabilities for IoT Devices Using oneM2M Platforms", *Sensors (Basel)*, vol. 19, no. 20, p. 4567, 2019.
[http://dx.doi.org/10.3390/s19204567] [PMID: 31640134]

[39]   D.V. Dimitrov, "Medical internet of things and big data in healthcare", *Healthc. Inform. Res.*, vol. 22, no. 3, pp. 156-163, 2016.
[http://dx.doi.org/10.4258/hir.2016.22.3.156] [PMID: 27525156]

[40]   A. Bhattacharyya, O. Mazumder, K. Chakravarty, D. Chatterjee, A. Sinha, and R. Gavas, "Development of an interactive gaming solution using MYO sensor for rehabilitation", In: *2018 International Conference on Advances in Computing, Communications and Informatics (ICACCI)* IEEE, 2018, pp. 2127-2130.
[http://dx.doi.org/10.1109/ICACCI.2018.8554686]

[41]   S.H. Liu, J.J. Wang, C.H. Su, and T.H. Tan, "Development of a patch-type electrocardiographic monitor for real time heartbeat detection and heart rate variability analysis", *J. Med. Biol. Eng.*, vol. 38, no. 3, pp. 411-423, 2018.
[http://dx.doi.org/10.1007/s40846-018-0369-y]

[42]   S. Singh, I.H. Ra, W. Meng, M. Kaur, and G.H. Cho, "SH-BlockCC: A secure and efficient Internet of things smart home architecture based on cloud computing and blockchain technology", *Int. J. Distrib. Sens. Netw.*, vol. 15, no. 4, 2019.
[http://dx.doi.org/10.1177/1550147719844159]

[43]   J. Kaye, E.A. Whitley, D. Lund, M. Morrison, H. Teare, and K. Melham, "Dynamic consent: a patient interface for twenty-first century research networks", *Eur. J. Hum. Genet.*, vol. 23, no. 2, pp. 141-146, 2015.
[http://dx.doi.org/10.1038/ejhg.2014.71] [PMID: 24801761]

[44]   M.A. Cyran, *Blockchain as a Foundation for Sharing Healthcare Data.* Blockchain in Healthcare Today, 2018.
[http://dx.doi.org/10.30953/bhty.v1.13]

[45]   H.S.G. Pussewalage, and V.A. Oleshchuk, "Privacy preserving mechanisms for enforcing security and privacy requirements in E-health solutions", *Int. J. Inf. Manage.*, vol. 36, no. 6, pp. 1161-1173, 2016.
[http://dx.doi.org/10.1016/j.ijinfomgt.2016.07.006]

[46]   D.V. Dimitrov, "Blockchain Applications for Healthcare Data Management", *Healthc. Inform. Res.*, vol. 25, no. 1, pp. 51-56, 2019.
[http://dx.doi.org/10.4258/hir.2019.25.1.51] [PMID: 30788182]

[47]   S.C. Schuster, "Next-generation sequencing transforms today's biology", *Nat. Methods*, vol. 5, no. 1, pp. 16-18, 2008.
[http://dx.doi.org/10.1038/nmeth1156] [PMID: 18165802]

[48]   C.W. Knetsch, E.M. van der Veer, C. Henkel, and P. Taschner, "DNA Sequencing", In: *Molecular*

Diagnostics. Springer: Singapore, 2019, pp. 339-360.
[http://dx.doi.org/10.1007/978-981-13-1604-3_8]

[49]   B. Seth, S. Dalal, and R. Kumar, "Securing Bioinformatics Cloud for Big Data: Budding Buzzword or a Glance of the Future", In: *Recent Advances in Computational Intelligence.* Springer: Cham, 2019, pp. 121-147.
[http://dx.doi.org/10.1007/978-3-030-12500-4_8]

[50]   S. Manel, and R. Holderegger, "Ten years of landscape genetics", *Trends Ecol. Evol.,* vol. 28, no. 10, pp. 614-621, 2013.
[http://dx.doi.org/10.1016/j.tree.2013.05.012] [PMID: 23769416]

[51]   K Hawari Ghazali, M. Mustafa, and A Hussain, "Color image processing of weed classification: A comparison of Two feature extraction technique", *Proceedings of the International Conference on Electrical Engineering and Informatics,* 2007.

[52]   N.M.H. Hassan, and A.A. Nashat, "New effective techniques for automatic detection and classification of external olive fruits defects based on image processing techniques", *Multidimens. Syst. Signal Process.,* vol. 30, no. 2, pp. 571-589, 2019.
[http://dx.doi.org/10.1007/s11045-018-0573-5]

[53]   S. Mia, and M.M. Rahman, "An efficient image segmentation method based on linear discriminant analysis and K-means algorithm with automatically splitting and merging clusters", *Int. J. Imaging Robot,* vol. 18, no. 1, pp. 62-72, 2018.

[54]   D.N. Trivedi, N.D. Shah, A.M. Kothari, and R.M. Thanki, DICOM® Medical Image Standard., *Dental Image Processing for Human Identification.,* Springer: Cham, pp. 41-49, 2019.
[http://dx.doi.org/10.1007/978-3-319-99471-0_4]

[55]   L. Saba, M. Biswas, V. Kuppili, E. Cuadrado Godia, H.S. Suri, D.R. Edla, T. Omerzu, J.R. Laird, N.N. Khanna, S. Mavrogeni, A. Protogerou, P.P. Sfikakis, V. Viswanathan, G.D. Kitas, A. Nicolaides, A. Gupta, and J.S. Suri, "The present and future of deep learning in radiology", *Eur. J. Radiol.,* vol. 114, pp. 14-24, 2019.
[http://dx.doi.org/10.1016/j.ejrad.2019.02.038] [PMID: 31005165]

[56]   T. Higaki, Y. Nakamura, F. Tatsugami, T. Nakaura, and K. Awai, "Improvement of image quality at CT and MRI using deep learning", *Jpn. J. Radiol.,* vol. 37, no. 1, pp. 73-80, 2019.
[http://dx.doi.org/10.1007/s11604-018-0796-2] [PMID: 30498876]

[57]   S. Gyftopoulos, D. Lin, F. Knoll, A.M. Doshi, T.C. Rodrigues, and M.P. Recht, "Artificial Intelligence in Musculoskeletal Imaging: Current Status and Future Directions", *AJR Am. J. Roentgenol.,* vol. 213, no. 3, pp. 506-513, 2019.
[http://dx.doi.org/10.2214/AJR.19.21117] [PMID: 31166761]

[58]   M.A. De Souza, H.R. Gamba, H. Pedrini, Ed., *Multi-Modality Imaging: Applications and Computational Techniques.* Springer, 2018.
[http://dx.doi.org/10.1007/978-3-319-98974-7]

[59]   G.C. Kagadis, C. Kloukinas, K. Moore, J. Philbin, P. Papadimitroulas, C. Alexakos, P.G. Nagy, D. Visvikis, and W.R. Hendee, "Cloud computing in medical imaging", *Med. Phys.,* vol. 40, no. 7, p. 070901, 2013.
[http://dx.doi.org/10.1118/1.4811272] [PMID: 23822402]

[60]   O. Ali, A. Shrestha, J. Soar, and S.F. Wamba, "Cloud computing-enabled healthcare opportunities, issues, and applications: A systematic review", *Int. J. Inf. Manage.,* vol. 43, pp. 146-158, 2018.
[http://dx.doi.org/10.1016/j.ijinfomgt.2018.07.009]

[61]   V. Kansal, and R. Kumar, "A Hybrid Approach for Financial Sentiment Analysis Using Artificial Intelligence and Cuckoo Search", *2019 5th International Conference on Advanced Computing & Communication Systems (ICACCS),* pp. 523-528, 2019.
[http://dx.doi.org/10.1109/ICACCS.2019.8728495]

[62]   O.F. Derindag, M. Canakci, and R. Tsarev, "Information and communication technologies in e-commerce and e-governance", In: *Journal of Physics: Conference Series*, 2019.
[http://dx.doi.org/10.1088/1742-6596/1399/3/033110]

[63]   V. Kansal, and R. Kumar, "Optimized feature extraction based artificial 1301 intelligence technique for empirical analysis of stock market data", *Int. J. Innov. Technol. Exploring Eng*, vol. 8, no. 10, 2019.

[64]   H.S. Chandana, N. Kumari, R. Pallavi, V. Padmashree, and M. Jayashree, "Lung Disease Prediction over Big Data from Healthcare Communities", *Perspectives in Communication, Embedded-systems and Signal-processing-PiCES*, vol. 2, no. 9, pp. 214-217, 2018.

[65]   L. Tavazzi, "Big data: Is clinical practice changing?", *European Heart Journal*, vol. 21, no. Supplement_B, pp. B98-B102, 2019.
[http://dx.doi.org/10.1093/eurheartj/suz034]

[66]   D. Sobhy, Y. El-Sonbaty, and M.A. Elnasr, "MedCloud: healthcare cloud computing system", In: *2012 International Conference for Internet Technology and Secured Transactions*. IEEE, 2012, pp. 161-166.

[67]   C.P. Jayapandian, C.H. Chen, and A. Bozorgi, "Bozorgi, S. D. Lhatoo, G. Q. Zhang, S. S. Sahoo, "Cloudwave: distributed processing of "Big Data" from electrophysiological recordings for epilepsy clinical research using Hadoop", In: *AMIA Annual Symposium Proceedings* vol. 2013. American Medical Informatics Association, 2013, p. 691.

[68]   R.D. Nipp, K. Hong, and E.D. Paskett, "Overcoming Barriers to Clinical Trial Enrollment", *Am. Soc. Clin. Oncol. Educ. Book,* vol. 39, no. 39, pp. 105-114, 2019.
[http://dx.doi.org/10.1200/EDBK_243729] [PMID: 31099636]

[69]   S. Das, D. Agrawal, and A. El Abbadi, "G-store: a scalable data store for transactional multi key access sin the cloud", In: *Proceedings of the 1ˢᵗ ACM symposium on Cloud computing* ACM, 2010, pp. 163-174.
[http://dx.doi.org/10.1145/1807128.1807157]

[70]   H. Huang, S. Tata, and R.J. Prill, "BlueSNP: R package for highly scalable genome-wide association studies using Hadoop clusters", *Bioinformatics,* vol. 29, no. 1, pp. 135-136, 2013.
[http://dx.doi.org/10.1093/bioinformatics/bts647] [PMID: 23202745]

[71]   R.V. Pandey, and C. Schlötterer, "DistMap: a toolkit for distributed short read mapping on a Hadoop cluster", *PLoS One,* vol. 8, no. 8, p. e72614, 2013.
[http://dx.doi.org/10.1371/journal.pone.0072614] [PMID: 24009693]

[72]   M.S. Wiewiórka, A. Messina, A. Pacholewska, S. Maffioletti, P. Gawrysiak, and M.J. Okoniewski, "SparkSeq: fast, scalable and cloud-ready tool for the interactive genomic data analysis with nucleotide precision", *Bioinformatics,* vol. 30, no. 18, pp. 2652-2653, 2014.
[http://dx.doi.org/10.1093/bioinformatics/btu343] [PMID: 24845651]

[73]   A. Schumacher, L. Pireddu, M. Niemenmaa, A. Kallio, E. Korpelainen, G. Zanetti, and K. Heljanko, "SeqPig: simple and scalable scripting for large sequencing data sets in Hadoop", *Bioinformatics,* vol. 30, no. 1, pp. 119-120, 2014.
[http://dx.doi.org/10.1093/bioinformatics/btt601] [PMID: 24149054]

[74]   Mahmoud Elsisi, "Reliable industry 4.0 based on machine learning and iot for analyzing, monitoring, and securing smart meters", *Sensors,* vol. 21, no. 2, p. 487, 2021.
[http://dx.doi.org/10.3390/s21020487]

CHAPTER 2

Different Techniques of Data Fusion in Internet of Things (IoT)

Harsh Pratap Singh[1,*], Bhaskar Singh[2], Rashmi Singh[3] and Vaseem Naiyer[3]

[1] *CSE, SOE, SSSUTMS, Sehore, India*

[2] *EC, RITS, RGPV, Bhopal, India*

[3] *MIS Head Trident Group, Hosangabad, India*

Abstract: An IoT (Internet of Things) technology is a dynamic area of research, which has been growing at a remarkable rate for the last few years. The IoT is a mammoth network of associated things and people, which accumulates and shares data about how they are used and the environment around them. It is the discernment of connecting any device to the internet and other associated devices. When something is associated with the internet, it can propel or receive information, or both. This ability to propel and/or receive information makes things smart. IoT permits businesses and people to get more insights from the world around them and do more evocative higher-level work. Data fusion techniques are used to extract eloquent information from dissimilar IoT data. It ferocities dissimilar data from sensor sources to mutually find a consequence, which is more dependable, precise, and comprehensive. This chapter briefly designates the IoT by the characteristics of data procurement and data fusion.

Keywords: Bayes rule, Data Fusion, IoT, Markov model, Multi-sensor, Real-time data processing.

INTRODUCTION

The Internet of Things (IoT) novel technology has almost completely expanded the internet to computers and smartphones to a wide range of other objects, processes, and environments. Those compatible items are used to trim, send data back, or both. IoT transforms dumb devices into intelligent ones by providing them with an online data connection, allowing the device to connect with people and additional IoT-enabled devices. Compact devices in a smart home are some of the best examples of IoT. Fire-powered firefighters, thermostats, and security

* **Corresponding author Harsh Pratap Singh:** CSE, SOE, SSSUTMS, Sehore, India;
E-mail: drharshprataps@gmail.com

Rijwan Khan, Pawan Sharma, Sugam Sharma and Santosh Kumar (Eds.)

alarms create an interconnected hub where data is shared between mobile devices, and users can remotely control the objects in that hub (*i.e.*, control the temperature, open doors, *etc.*) *via* a mobile app or website. Far from being just a home block, many devices, industries, and settings can access the Internet of Things. From smart blackboards in classrooms to medical devices, IoT quickly makes the world smarter by connecting portable and digital gadgets with sensor-connected devices to the Internet of Things platform, which scans data from different devices and data analytics to address specific needs. IoT control platforms can pinpoint exactly what information is relevant and what is being overlooked. This information can familiarize you with commentary patterns, make recommendations, and comment on obvious problems before they occur. The insight provided by illuminated analytics makes processes more efficient. Smart systems and resources mean you can turn industrial operations quickly if this is tedious, labor-intensive, time-consuming, or dangerous. To separate the IoT concept, a real-life example can be taken. If I want to know which options are the most popular, then a device with the Internet of Things technology can automatically back up data. Compatible devices make smart decisions based on real-time information. In the Internet of Things (IoT), the process is organized into three stages:

Accumulating and Sending Information

This means the senses. Sensors can be temperature sensors, air quality sensors, moving sensors, light sensors, moisture sensors, *etc.* These senses, in turn, enable us to gather information from space, which in turn allows us to make more intelligent decisions. At the same time, as our vision, hearing, touch and hearing, smell, and taste allow us humans, to create the concept of the world, the senses allow machines to create the concept of the world [1]. In Grange, uncontrolled access to information about soil moisture can determine farmers where their crops are forcing irrigation. Instead of overirrigation (either over-irrigation and environmental degradation) or significantly reduced irrigation (which may be crop loss), the farmer can protect the plants from getting the right amount of water.

Receiving and Acting on Information

We are fully familiar with machines that receive data and operate it accordingly. For example, your printer prints the record on receiving the data, and your car gets the car key and opens the doors. It does not matter if the order is open or not; we can see that we can order equipment from afar. The real strength of the Internet of Things comes when things can do both things mentioned above. For example, it can collect and send data, besides receiving and tracking it.

Doing Both

Sensors can collect data about moisture content in the field and advise the farmer to irrigate the field. Also, these sensors can detect the moisture in the yield and provides information to the seller/buyer about the content of moisture without the need of a farmer. Instead, the structure of the water system may change differently, depending on the moisture content of the mud. You can do it again and again. In the event that the water framework receives weather data from its web organization, it can also detect when it will rain and choose not to irrigate the crops today because the rain will rain anywhere. And, not only that! This data about the humidity of contaminants, how well irrigation systems produce yields, and how well the crops grow can be collected and sent to supercomputers using sophisticated algorithms that can comprehend this data. Moreover, that is just one type of sensor. On installing various sensors such as light, air quality, and temperature, and these algorithms one can read these weather parameters in detail. With handfuls, many ranches collect this data, through these algorithms, which can create unusual pieces of information on how to create yields to improve the best, helping to take care of the developing world community [2].

Key Challenges of IoT

IoT can offer a wide range of novels to the Internet, document the widespread financial benefits, and pose some challenges [3, 4]. Selected from them are listed below:

1. *Unparalleled Identity Management:* IoT aims to connect millions and billions of information, which should be seamlessly distributed across the Internet. As a result, much-needed patent management is required to provide and fulfill specific terms for a wide range of mobile devices.

2. *Consistent and Efficient:* Sundry Wholesale is familiar with its devices with modified technologies unknown to everyone. There must be an unconventional approach to allow full interaction of physical and sensory devices.

3. *Confidentiality of Information:* IoT uses many identification technologies, such as RFID, 2D-barcode, *etc.* Since tolerance will enhance these identities, it is essential to obtain confidential information, which is why it prevents unauthorized access.

4. *Equipment Protection:* Items independent from premises deal with physical damage and unauthorized importations for ensuring their safety.

5. *Data Confidentiality:* Sensory devices transmit data to the data provisioning system that determines the transmission media. Sensors should check encryption methods that allow the integrity of the data in the data processing system.

6. *Network Security:* Data-sensing devices may be more than wireless or wireless transmission. The transfer unit must deal with this large amount of data that is not allowed to damage the information and must integrate strict procedures so that no external interference occurs.

DATA FUSION ARCHTECHTURE

Internet of Things (IoT) is associated with a wide range of wireless access networks through the interface and access to internet-connected objects. It can carry out investments in communication and can understand the relationship between articles and correspondence and exchange. The object focuses on the object, whereas data transmission is reliable and is good at preparing a dataset by combining items. Data fusion techniques are used to extract impressive data from available data for IoT data analysis. It integrates data in unity from mid-range to inclusive to get robust, straightforward, and complete results. Data integration is one of the most important developments in the web of things. On the web of things, radio duplicates are used to distinguish the proof gadget, the global landscape frame, the laser scanner and a variety of gadgets, the installed programs and frameworks, and the cutting and remote communication system, data management distribution, various gadgets, the installed programs and frameworks, the cutting and remote communication system, and data management distribution and much more innovation. Castanedo as a "Mix of copious sources to obtain less expensive and high-quality data or continuous active data" includes a combination of data. Data integration has been done in a variety of sensory areas from different evidence.

The Internet of Things (IoT) produces large amounts of raw data in a standard environment. WSN (wireless nerve networks) sets up a piece of IoT that detects environmental conditions and provides the employee with information. This data is also managed using data mining calculations on the part of the employee to get a general picture of what the conditions are, and after that, a controlled movement is performed. Often, the information provided by sensory centers is incorrect. Significant calculations should be performed on the data before extracting important data. The calculation must be done before the data mine can occur. Data mining is the last extraction of data. However, before the data can be mined, it must be in a good organization to obtain a known or unfamiliar pattern in the data. This process of data processing that joins and captures data from various sources is called fusion data.

It collaborates with real-time monitors, reviews, and collects program broadcasts from different natural or visual text regions, receiving material and material things, including people and objects of various communications. It is integrated with the Internet and forms a large data-based framework. Before the control of object systems, for example, the sensor organizes, to obtain precise information, it usually needs to pass a ton of sensory hubs to the position inside. To improve the overall accuracy of the system, the integrated data is stored at the center of the compact sensor hub. When the sensor is in high-density area or in the area where the object is placed or in the event of watching domains, then merge the sensor data with already received report data,, there will be a definite space connection. Like a comparable harp, the transmission is more than just passing over. If it is a chance that all hubs will look at the data sent to the meeting point, it could cause the system transfer speed to limit the misuse of resources. In addition, multiple data transfers simultaneously can also create a tourist struggle, reducing book performance. In addition, in the data transfer where the main variable is the power consumption of the hub, the excess data transfer will use the excess energy messengers from the location to shorten the pattern of the presence of the planned sensor. Data Fusion Architectures can be organized accordingly.

Centralized Fusion Architecture

In Centralized fusion architecture, crude information from multiple sensors is legitimately sent to a central fusion hub, which processes state gauges and settles on choices, as in Fig. (**1**). Albeit, nearby sensors may preprocess the information before transmitting it to the central hub. The term 'crude information' connotes sensor estimation or preprepared information without sifting or neighborhood fusion. Every sensor watches and gives estimations to the central framework where information is sifted and melded. If the information is effectively adjusted related, and there is no limitation on the correspondence data transfer capacity, the brought together fusion architecture yields a hypothetically ideal answer for state estimation. Be that as it may, preparing the data at a central hub presents different issues, for example, a large computational load on the central hub, considerable correspondence transmission capacity necessity, the chance of failure (because of failure of the central hub), and firmness to changes in architecture. In this engineering, the primary fusion place is situated in the central processor unit and all choices were taken from there. This architecture is shown in Fig. (**1**).

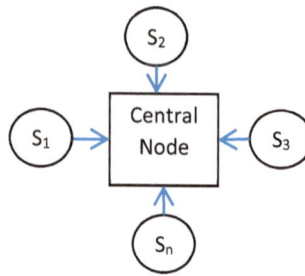

Fig. (1). Centralized Fusion Architecture.

Distributed Fusion Architecture

Advances in sensory and communication technology mean that each sensor node can independently process its sensor data to calculate local state estimates. In many systems, green data is difficult to calculate state estimates of a particular quantity of interest in terms of definition and covariance [5]. These measurements are then transferred between the sensory nerves and the central node to form a global scale. Compared to medium-sized construction, the distributed sensor network is excellent in many settings, *i.e.*, the potential for problem-solving in a collaborative model, tensile coverage, and greater durability in spatial resolution. Additionally, the local data processing means lower processing load on each node due to load distribution, lower communication costs, flexibility, and resilience to failures. However, the fusion structure is a separate area where the nodes operate independently, sharing information with each other outside of the central fusion node [6].

Unlike distributed or redistributed construction, the redevelopment of buildings somehow; each node compares the basic system and communicates. The motive for relying on reconstructed and distributed construction is the same. In addition, the local data processing means a lower processing load on each node due to load distribution, lower communication costs, flexibility, and resilience to failures. However, a fusion configuration is a shared space where nodes work independently, sharing information with each other outside of the central fusion node. In this structure, the estimated values of each sensor are processed and refined, and eventually, all useful information is sent to a central processor. The central processor then combined the information transmitted from the application used with other sensory data. This structure can be considered an improved form of central fusion construction. Its structure is shown in Fig. (**2**).

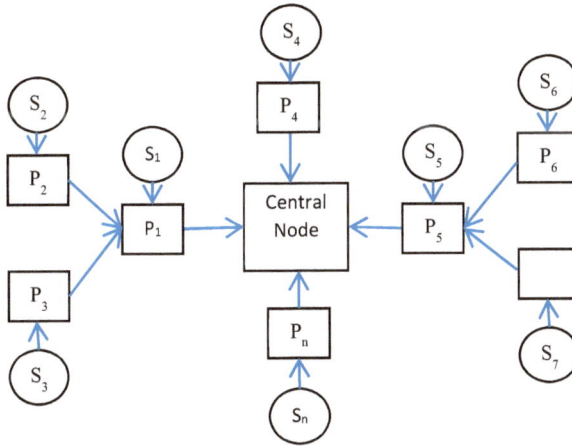

Fig. (2). Distributed Fusion Architecture.

Hybrid Fusion Architecture

By combining the two previous structures, a new structure is discovered, known as hybrid fusion architecture. In general, hybrid constructions have high accuracy in a variety of situations for any type of data. The structure is flexible, uses a variety of the algorithms and a variety of integrated and distributed structures are integrated, and new hybrid structures are being constructed. In Fig. **(3)**, the construction of a single hybrid structure is shown.

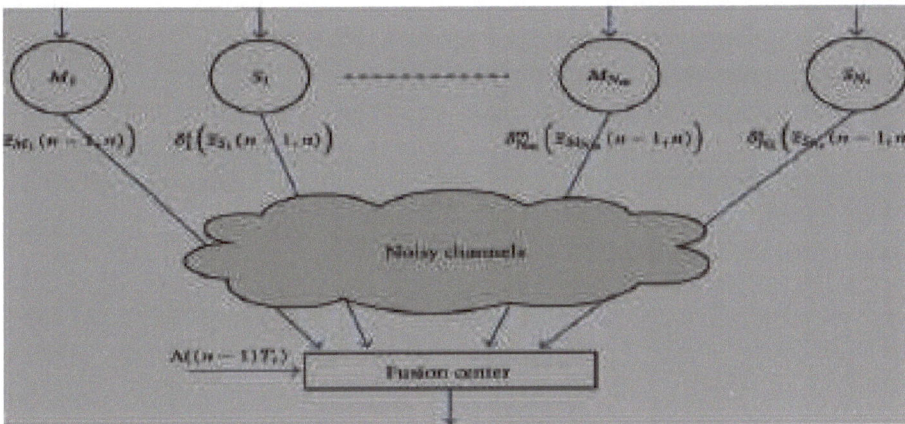

Fig. (3). Hybrid fusion Architecture.

LITERATURE REVIEW

There is a lot of research on IoT data integration techniques, which study data integration in Wireless Sensor Networks. These methods use advanced data fusion algorithms such as classical inference, Dempster - Shafer, Bayesian, and fuzzy logic methods to promote Internet of Things. There are various methods of data integration performed by various analysts. True Tactics serve as a way to deliver common and specially designed strategies such as Fuzzy Logic and Neural Network, Bayesian Methods, which are used to integrate multiple sensory data. The possibility of data aggregation data must be identified. There is research into developing a systematic vehicle storage framework using fluffy Multi-Sensor Data Fusion (MSDF) to reduce the risk of frustration. Two projects are mentioned here - Central Fusion and Distributed Fusion.

Alessandra De Paola *et al.* [7], proposed a system of self-preparation, context understanding, and flexibility in integrating sensory data based on the construction of three structures. Heterogeneous data collected by nerves at a very reduced level is integrated by a unique Bayesian network at the intermediate level, which also includes sensible data to filter the disruption process. At the highest level, the self-assembly process regenerates the tactile base by testing a set of sensors to reduce the energy consumption and increase the accuracy of the input. The Bayesian approach allows for the handling of touch-sensitive measurements due to environmental noise and think mechanical degradation [8] and presents basic philosophical research on the edge of the data. Data aggregation is a multiphase guided exploration field with a wide range of applications expected from regions, for example, security, mechanical technology, computer use, an intelligent framework system, and an example of consent [9, 10]. This has been and will continue to be a major backbone following the ever-increasing zeal of the experimental network in the advanced growth of data fusion algorithms and models. They have introduced scientific breakthroughs in data collection methods and investigated experimental concepts and related guessing networks and statistics available in all categories. In addition, a number of advanced test sites have been introduced to the data integration network.

Zheng et al. used a sensible approach to capture images from different nerves, to improve the perception of employment. With the help of vague rules and if membership functions are designed for image data setup, an obscure understanding approach [11] can model and link images to enhance the contrast of the integrated image. The Mamdani system is a type of trend that is used to combine images. Test results also show that subordinate testing deviates significantly from purpose from time to time [12]. *Padovitz et al.* developed a method characterized by a high-level utility hypothesis for sensory integration in a sensitive environment [13]. This approach is seen from the existing integration process that is useful for a variety of purposes. The strategy is designed to set logical applications and offers different points of interest in data integration in an area that understands the context. It is a vague notion of what constitutes a state of affairs: a state of affairs is referred to as the motto of the attributes within a permissible region of the state. They try to test using real sensors. *Paola et al.* showed that Bayesian Networks developed an effective data management tool before performing improved artificial thinking [14]. The Bayes network model incorporates a meta-level level taking into account the dynamic structure of the visual framework that provides evidence of possible assumptions. The additional meta-level represents both the accuracy of the system result and the cost of using the sensory infrastructure. It was planned to find the best balance between execution and cost by adjusting the operating system of the basic sensory device. Self-preparation of witnessed sites in the Bayesian network is done through on-line optimization [15]. The given model has shown that this proposed approach promises to overcome the challenges arising from the immeasurable reduction in the sensory balance, which allows achieving a more direct result while also reducing costs depending on energy consumption.

Zhang et al. have proposed a data integration system that relies on unique Bayesian networks to provide the power, power, purpose, and performance of data integration to reach a reliable conclusion in a timely manner with reduced devices [16]. The Dynamic Bayesian network as a fusion structure provides insight into and fully integrates the evolving structure for the expression, reconciliation, and acquisition of relevant data for a variety of processes at different levels of thought and represents a transcendental component. The proposed system is suitable for applications where elections are to be held with access to the most accessible information from a variety of sources. *Boulkaboul and Djenouri* proposed a tax on the methods of mixing decisions based on the concept of belief. It suggests an Internet of Things (DFIOT) data collection method based on the concept of Dempster - Shafer (D-S) and a weighted algorithm. It monitors the integrity of each device in the network and conflicts between devices when data is entered [17]. *Kumar and Pimparkar* used the Fuzzy Kalman Filter to measure the world, as well as the Dempster-Shafer method of mixing decisions to create a powerful system for understanding the context. The proposed design is also vulnerable to the high number of nodes in the network, which are not available for all applications. Research also provides design metrics that can be used to compare different data combinations [18]. *Jun Qi et al.* presented a systematic review, carefully examining PARM studies with a view to a collection of powerful IoT-based 3D functions and validation models. It summarizes the traditional techniques of modern data integration from three aircraft domains in the dynamic 3D model of IoT: devices, people, and timeline. This paper continues to identify some of the new research trends and challenges of data integration strategies in IoT-enabled I-PARS studies and discusses some key strategies for overcoming them [19].

MULTI-SENSOR DATA FUSION

The Data Fusion module proposed a dynamic Bayesian network capable of capturing the intensity of these observations, which looked at past provinces over current trends. There are many methods of data integration, including Markov's hidden model [20]. The Dynamic Bayesian network allows us to quantify the evidence that represents the visible manifestation of the hidden world over time. It provides a useful tool for performing data integration [9]. Here, the algorithm is designed for the Data Fusion module. Its main purpose is to present the state of the country, in the form of a given element of interest. It is represented by the hidden Xt variable. The set of sensory studies compiled by those sensors operating at time t, is represented by Et = (E1, ..., En), according to the Optimization Optra module. The context information, *i.e.*, Ct = (C1, ..., Ck), depends largely on the state of the application. The sensor model is defined by the distribution of opportunities P (Et, Xt), representing how sensory learning is affected by the current state of the system. The theory of the nature of a particular system in time t, is defined by Markov's first order as:

$$Bel\ (xt) = P((xt|E1{:}t, C1{:}t) \tag{1}$$

To obtain a practical formulation of our belief, Bayes rule is applied and expressed as follows:

$$Bel(xt) = P\ (xt|\boldsymbol{E}1{:}t, \boldsymbol{C}1{:}t) = P\ (xt|\boldsymbol{E}1{:}t-1, \boldsymbol{E}t, \boldsymbol{C}1{:}t)$$
$$= \eta \cdot P\ (\boldsymbol{E}t|xt, \boldsymbol{E}1{:}t-1, \boldsymbol{C}1{:}t) \cdot P\ (xt|\boldsymbol{E}1{:}t-1, \boldsymbol{C}1{:}t) \tag{2}$$

where η is a normalizing constant. After this, Markov assumption gives the value of the parent node Xt, by assuming that the sensor measurements are mutually conditionally independent:

$$P\ (\boldsymbol{E}t|xt, \boldsymbol{E}1{:}t-1, \boldsymbol{C}1{:}t) = P\ (\boldsymbol{E}t|xt, \boldsymbol{C}1{:}t) = P\ (\boldsymbol{E}t|xt) \tag{3}$$

where e^i is the specific value of the sensory reading gathered by the sensor i in the time slice t. Finally, this can be defined with the following recursive formula:

$$Bel(x_t) = \eta. \prod_{e_t^i} P\left(e_t^i \middle| x_t\right). \sum_{x_t-1} P\left(x_t \middle| x_{t-1}, C_t\right). Bel(x_{t-1}) \tag{4}$$

where α is integrated into the normalization constant η. Here n is the number of sensor nodes, and m is the number of possible values of Xt. Thus, the overall complexity of computing Bel(xt) for all values of Xt is O (m^2 + m · n). Using this equation, the inference can be performed, where the time and space required for updating the network belief are independent of the sequence length.

Fuzzy Logic-Based Data Fusion

This approach was introduced by the ruling system in 1965 [21]. This strategy is concerned with three phases: the first is the fuzzification input, the second is the use of fuzzy guides in information technology to obtain yields, and the end, is the use of fruit removal. As we use this incomprehensible approach to medical care information, the information provided by a complex framework is a large number of biological or environmental sensors or both. The results are a weak choice, which means the chances of a patient's collection condition. This framework does not indicate whether the client has been instructed to determine class status or not (complex selection). For example, when a patient suffers from heart failure, asthma, *etc.* However, it does indicate the potential for desire, or the patient may have a place in the category of ideas in each case. Ways to integrate unambiguous information are simple in terms of registering difficulties. It is flexible due to the reconciliation of the extra part of the sensor, and new guidelines can be added and modified to the framework over time. This provides an unusual opportunity to increase the accuracy of the frame and helps in reducing error.

Bayesian-based Technique

The Bayesian set-up fusion methodology is applicable in relation to the Bayes' hypothesis [22, 23]. This is not the case with any concept such as the abstract conceptual basis, with a Bayesian procedure used prior to data on clinical information and patient conditions to obtain the opportunity to explain new conditions. Therefore, a learning phase is required for this type of mixing method. The Bayesian vision is based on two possible types of work: previous opportunities, which are solved in terms of late plans. Another dependence opportunity depends on the new features of the collected sensor material. As a rule, the situation used for the opportunity test is possible:

$$p((C|A_1 \ldots \ldots \ldots \ldots A_n) = \frac{1}{Z} p(C) \prod_{i=1}^{n} p(A_i|C) \tag{5}$$

Where C is a condition to be defined, p (C) is the first chance of the class, and p (Ai | C) is the probability of existence. A1 using variable quality features collected from sensory data, where n is the total sensory information and Z is a measurement based on A1 to An. In [24], the makers proposed the SPHERE (Sensor Platform for Healthcare in Residential Environment) as a separate mode structure. The building forms a Bayesian model of application known as the multiclass Bayes point machine (BPM), which is illustrated by three models of various solutions. Then there is the weight and weight of the item and the medium-sized trading models that point and focus [24] on regional validation and strengthening of patient development.

Markov Process-based Technique

The Hidden Markov Model (HMM) is a breeding method used to make hidden lands from visible data. Using data collected from a variety of sensors (common sense sensors in the HMM space of a clinical research program indicating that the sensor can be turned on or off), it can be made into an incomprehensible Markov model. The model shows the continuity of normal patient activities where each function speaks to the status of the model. The idea is that the activities or parts of the patient are recorded and reported independently of the day for maintaining the end of the development / single region is the beginning of compliance. The model can be used to detect when a change is taking place in a game action plan step by step and expect a continuous view based on the current situation. This area and the desire for further development is a major factor when combined with other basic signal sensors and other general information for the ultimate purpose of an emergency and malicious ID case. The purpose of the structure in [25] is to identify the direct and prosperous changes of a person in a day-to-day routine that meets the wind by separating the constraints from consistent performance. Recognizing inconsistencies helps to make the disease clearer.

Demspter-Shafer Theory Based Technique

Demspter-Shafer (DST) speculation is a skilled strategy that looks at weaknesses in unverified models [26]. Applying DST as an integrated IoT strategy in clinical management can lead to a good decision or end with a preset number of sensory data while you have the option to combine various data. No matter how advanced the computer system is, it is a consistent strategy. In this method, data from sensor testing is converted into a structural vector.

$$m\theta A = [m(\bar{A}), m(A), m(\bar{A}, A)\,]$$ (6)

Where A represents the dynamic sensor, A nondynamic and (A, A) free. This is called the conviction mass breaking point vector. After the worth is extended by the consistency factor accomplishing the likelihood respect, a comparability relationship between various vectors (wellsprings of information) is looked at, for example, the vectors relating to a similar position are weaved. At last, in general, comprehended Dempster's standard of the mix is applied, and a choice is taken by the strategy utilized.

Thresholding Techniques and Others

Other sensor combination systems depend on thresholding calculations rather than model-based strategies. Despite how these proposed papers are cased and condition-based, they should be considered while assessing all mixed techniques of clinical organizations' applications. The producers' attempt to see a fall of the patient from the exercise of step-by--by-step living (ADL) is represented in research [27]. Combined arranging is performed after the information is sent from the wearable sensors, and the working relationship of the sensor focuses on the home to a base station. The wearable place construes a potential tumble to the transport layer through applying a thresholding figuring. The tally targets recognized four fundamental cases happening continuously. If every one of the cases is viewed as genuine, an information graph is dispatched off the base station. On the base station, the information from the work network is checked for acknowledging the fall as per the region of the patient announced by these sensors. A procedure is introduced in [28] for checking of the old enduring Alzheimer. The design can perceive strange conditions, likely falls, and getting area. For the fall affirmation, an educational methodology is utilized for picking the warning edges of the accelerometer exactly in an investigation place. Another figure is executed and portrayed for picking the domain.

APPLICATION OF IOT

The uses of IoT can be diverse from a little organization like family computerization to outsized organizations like cloud-based industry applications. Brief presentations about the endless use of IoT comparing ecological checking, home motorization, horticulture, hydroponics, medical care, transportation, and coordination have been given in this paper. The succeeding plan requirements must be tended to befittingly to advance a specific accommodation to have a consistent quality of costs and capabilities.

Smart Environment

Sensors and actuators coordinated or connected to family gear like coolers, lighting, and constrained air frameworks can screen the private house, plant or office environment. The igniting course of action of a house may change, as at the nightfall, most of the lights will be on while they will be off late around evening time. Considering the cognizance of an illness or a smoke caution sensor, a fire hesitation can be set off over and again. Such kind of usage is helpful for developing people free in the family. Considering the undertaking of inhabitants in the home, picking machines like entrance in the room can be conveyed; lights may be peculiar at late room, water centers will be open at the kitchen as demonstrated in Fig. (**4**).

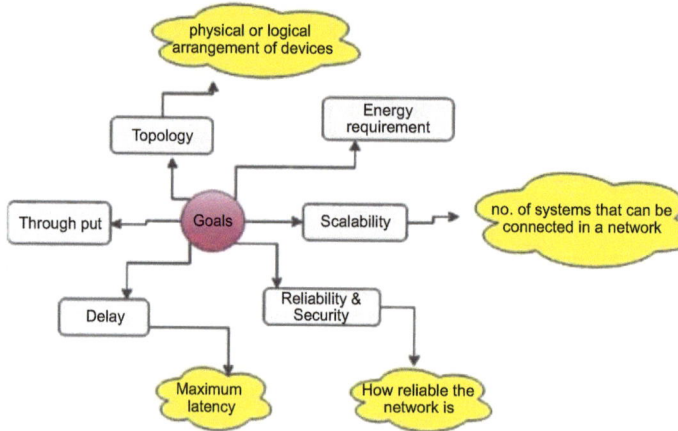

Fig. (4). Various design constraints for an IoT application.

Air-condition Fridge garment washers by and IoT-empowered and controlled over the Internet pursued to save dynamism. In the near future, a splendid tumbling ice chest will establish a connection with an assistance man who normally denies the customer's intervention. Present-day automation is improved by coordinating RFID marks with harvests. Creation improvement is assessed to confirm the differentiation of the item by satisfaction, unlike limit regard to sensors. IBM has dispatched Smart Home game plan [29], improved known as "Stratecast" to deal with the expense of organizations to customers permitting reliable correspondence between incalculable keen devices in the house, like clinical contraptions, PCs, mobiles, TVs, lighting, security or sound structure. IBM is assisting Verizon as a Communication administration has given (CSP) and Philips as a contraption sales rep in the course of executing the plan. Siemens, Cisco, Xerox, Microsoft, MIT, and various others are associated with this circle. They have set around 20 home labs consuming more than 30 home livelihoods, five association shows, and three Artificial Intelligence (AI) techniques [3, 4]. The Intel keen home stage plans affirmation of individual accomplices by voice or face and engravings within the home as demonstrated in Fig. (5). Intel bears the expense of IoT answers for more astute improvement to help personalization by controlling completed work environments/living environments, adaptability by connecting to chiefs to screen properties distantly and saving resources like energy, and water.

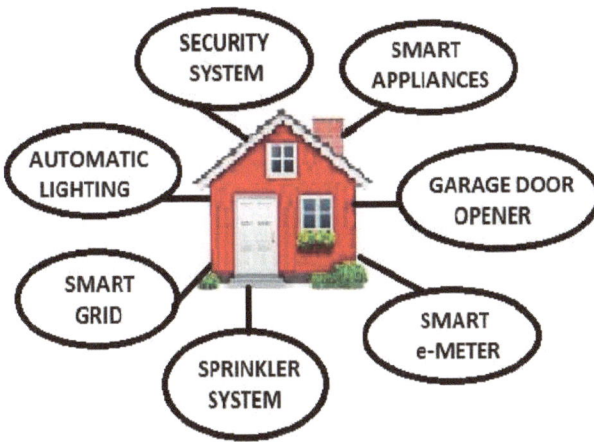

Fig. (5). Smart Home System [30].

Health Care

Most medical care frameworks in limitless countries are wasteful, moderate, and resolutely slanted to screw up. This can clearly be changed since the clinical benefits part relies upon consistent happenings and systems that can be electronic and expanded shut development. Additional advancement can smooth various moves like shoot sharing of various components and territories, most noticeable having a place and association medications, would go far in moving the clinical consideration territory [31, 32]. A large load of helps that IoT application suggestions in the clinical benefits division are most portrayed by seeking patients, staff, and articles, requesting, comparably approving individuals, and customized gathering of data and recognizing. Clinical center work cycle can be deliberately improved once the patients' stream is pursued. Additionally, attestation and documentation weaken entireties that may be perilous to patients, record insurance, and harder to track down cases of mismatching newborn children. Moreover, the modified data arrangement and transmission is basic, being created motorization, lessening of construction organization course of the occasion, mechanical procedure investigated similarly as a clinical stock organization. Sensor contraption license suggestions zeroed into patients, generally in diagnosing conditions and benefitting constant information about patients' prosperity pointers [33]. The employments of the Internet of Things (IoT) and the Internet of Everything (IoE) are further being broadened, finishing the epitome of the Internet of Nano-things (IoNT) [34]. The possibility of IoNT, as the name proposes, is being wangled by consolidating Nano-sensors in various (things) using nano organizations. Clinical application, as publicized in Fig. (**6**), is one of the large motivations for IoNT execution. Use of IoNT in the human body, for dealing with purposes, unravels permission to data from in situ parts of the body that were recently reachable to distinguish from or by eating up those clinical instruments bound along with large sensor size. Accordingly, IoNT will empower new clinical data to be accumulated, boss to new disclosures, and better diagnostics.

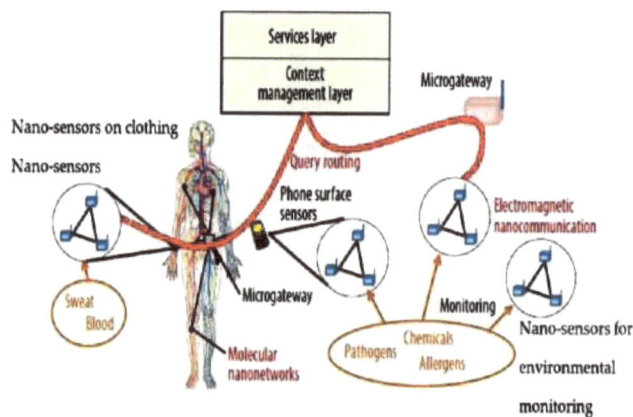

Fig. (6). The Internet of Nano-Things [35].

IoT in Agriculture

With the unremitting advancement of people of the world, the demand for food is enormously raised. Governments worldwide are plateful farmers to use unconventional procedures and investigation to reinforce food creation. Sagacious rustic is one of the speediest extending contributions which is used IoT in Fig. (**7**). Identifying for soil soddenness and supplements, planning water use for plant development, and proficient custom food are some clear businesses of IoT in agribusiness. The IoT underwrites strangely towards building up an agricultural system. Developing challenges provoked by people's progression and environmental change have made it one of the fundamental endeavors to use the IoT around here [30].

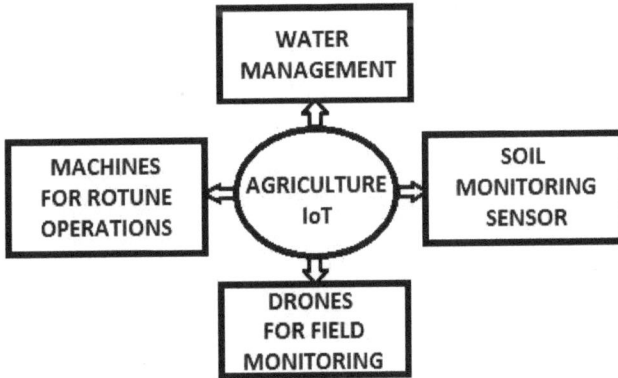

Fig. (7). Smart Agriculture System [30].

The mix of far-off sensors with adaptable agrarian applications and cloud stages helps in gathering unimaginable information affected to the natural conditions like temperature, precipitation, dampness, wind speed, bug interruption, other than others related with a woodland, can be used to broaden and modernize developing systems, take learned closures to propel quality and sum and decrease threats and wastes.

Associated Industry

The associated industry is the nebulous vision of a created climate where each machine can interface with all further machines athwart vegetal. The related business with IoT will interface, screen and rheostat by any means, some spot to bear the expense of operational throughput and productivity [34]. In tally, the mixing of IoT with sensor associations, distant organization, advanced hardware, and machine-to-machine correspondence will totally change the unadventurous motorization interaction of industry [36].

Smart Retail

For sellers, the IoT proposed unlimited openings to heighten store network productivity, advance novel conveniences, and modify the client's understanding. For representation, utilizes for seeking things, ongoing lists, data discussion among suppliers and merchants, and mechanized transport proficiencies will build up the exchange area [37, 38].

Smart Energy and Smart Grid

The IoT bears the cost of more information nearby the acts of force providers and buyers in a mechanized way to develop the energy feasibility. It similarly gives the trade a sharp organization of energy ingestion, for instance, energy meters, insightful occupations, and manageable force resources [39].

Traffic Monitoring

fpageSmart urban areas are the enormous errand of the web of things, and traffic noticing is an essential piece of the insightful city. To collection the structure self-reliable and to work wisely, traffic corner-to-corner metropolitan regions, either on commonplace roads or highway traffic, incorporate subbing information with each other. The stop-up on the expressway's will beginning stage is reasonable similarly to fuel incidents, which can be put away using canny information. The information concerning the blockage on the roads can be managed through the brief vehicles, so the inbound traffic on that approach can stay away from in an, unlike way. Such differences can be essential to propel the absolute structure. fpageA trap of things can be conveyed by far off sensor associations and endless unlike kinds of sensors that will instigate traffic IoT [40fpage]. Proper security moves should be made, so a couple of kinds of safety breaks, dread, and put together oppressor attacks with respect to the metropolitan networks can be avoided.

Smart Parking

Internet of things has shown up, and the withdrawal of vehicles by crediting boundless leaving sensors in leaving enormous to collection, which is more splendid. It serves to ably manage the halting locale, which makes the escort spare their time and fuel as the exact information nearby the free halting interstellar is provided for the driver and jam structure level. It is similarly reasonable to book for leaving intergalactic unswervingly from the vehicle, which will disregard time wastage and avoid the jams at the leaving districts [39].

CONCLUSION

In the Internet of Things, the data fusion can diminish networking traffic, reduce the energy feasting, and augment the accuracy of the consequences, optimizing the discernment of the network performance. This explores the present execution of data fusion approaches that will be deliberated in fact. Their hierarchical structure will be enlightened and related to standard parameters. By means of the upgradation in data fusion methods, the additional hierarchical resolution will be provided, and it will be associated with the prevailing methods. This research will outspread the categorised execution of IoT and cover the whole levels of data abstraction, that is, from a sensor to server.

CONSENT FOR PUBLICATION

Not applicable.

CONFLICT OF INTEREST

The authors declare no conflict of interest, financial or otherwise.

ACKNOWLEDGEMENTS

Declared none.

REFERENCES

[1] I. Akyildiz, W. Su, Y. Sankarasubramaniam, and E. Cayirci, "A survey on sensor networks", *IEEE Communication Magazine,* vol. 40, no. 8, pp. 102-114, 2002.
[http://dx.doi.org/10.1109/MCOM.2002.1024422]

[2] L. Gao, A. Bourke, and J. Nelson, "Evaluation of accelerometer based multi-sensor versus single-sensor activity recognition systems", *Medical Engineering & Physics,* vol. 36, no. 6, pp. 779-785., 2014.

[3] L. Jiang, D-Y. Liu, and B. Yang, "Smart home research", *Proceedings of 2004 International Conference on Machine Learning and Cybernetics (IEEE Cat. No.04EX826),* vol. 2, p. 659, 2004.663
[http://dx.doi.org/10.1109/ICMLC.2004.1382266]

[4] D. Bandyopadhyay, and J. Sen, "Internet of things: Applications and challenges in technology and standardization", *Wirel. Pers. Commun.,* vol. 58, no. 1, pp. 49-69, 2011.
[http://dx.doi.org/10.1007/s11277-011-0288-5]

[5] D. Cook, J. Augusto, and V. Jakkula, "Ambient Intelligence: tech-nologies, applications, and opportunities", *Pervasive Mobile Comput.,* vol. 5, no. 4, pp. 277-298, 2009.
[http://dx.doi.org/10.1016/j.pmcj.2009.04.001]

[6] A. Makarenko, A. Brooks, T. Kaupp, H.F. Durrant-Whyte, and F. Dellaert, Decentralised data fusion: a graphical model approach. *Proc. of the International Conference on Information Fusion,* 2009, pp. 545-554.

[7] A. De Paola, P. Ferraro, S. Gaglio, G. Lo Re, and S.K. Das, "An Adaptive Bayesian System for Context-Aware Data Fusion in Smart Environments", *IEEE Trans. Mobile Comput.,* vol. 16, no. 6, pp. 1502-1515, 2016.

[8] A. De Paola, and L. Gagliano, "Design of an adaptive Bayesian system for sensor data fusion", In: *Advances onto the Internet of Things.* Springer, 2014, pp. 61-76.
[http://dx.doi.org/10.1007/978-3-319-03992-3_5]

[9] Y. Zhang, and Q. Ji, "Active and dynamic information fusion for multi-sensor systems with dynamic Bayesian networks", *IEEE Trans. Systems, Man, and Cybernetics, Part B: Cybernetics.,* vol. 36, no. 2, p. 467, 2006.472

[10] B. Khaleghi, A. Khamis, F.O. Karray, and S.N. Razavi, "Multi-sensor data fusion: a review of the state-of-the-art", *Inf. Fusion,* vol. 14, no. 1, pp. 28-44, 2013.

[http://dx.doi.org/10.1016/j.inffus.2011.08.001]

[11]   M.A. Hossain, P.K. Atrey, and A. El Saddik, "Learning multi-sensor confidence using a reward-an-
        -punishment mechanism", *IEEE Trans. Instrum. Meas.,* vol. 58, no. 5, pp. 1525-1534, 2009.
        [http://dx.doi.org/10.1109/TIM.2009.2014507]

[12]   Y. Zheng, and P. Zheng, "Multi-sensor image fusion using fuzzy logic for surveillance systems", In:
        Proc. 7th Int'l Conf. on Fuzzy Systems and Knowledge Discovery (FSKD), 2010, pp. 588-592.

[13]   D. Hall, and S. McMullen, *Mathematical techniques in multi-sensor data fusion.* Artech House, 2004.

[14]   A. Padovitz, S.W. Loke, A. Zaslavsky, B. Burg, and C. Bartolini, "An approach to data fusion for
        context awareness", In: *Modeling and Using Context.* Springer, 2005, pp. 353-367.
        [http://dx.doi.org/10.1007/11508373_27]

[15]   A. De Paola, M. La Cascia, G. Lo Re, M. Morana, and M. Ortolani, "User detection through multi-
        sensor fusion in an AmI scenario", In: *Proc. 15th Int'l Conf. on Information Fusion (FUSION),* 2012,
        pp. 2502-2509.

[16]   A. De Paola, S. Gaglio, G. Lo Re, and M. Ortolani, "Multi-sensor fusion through adaptive Bayesian
        networks", In: *AI*IA 2011: Artificial Intelligence Around Man and Beyond* Springer, 2011, pp. 360-
        371.
        [http://dx.doi.org/10.1007/978-3-642-23954-0_33]

[17]   S. Boulkaboul, and D. Djenouri, "DFIOT: Data Fusion for Internet of Things", *J. Netw. Syst. Manage.,*
        vol. 28, no. 4, pp. 1-25, 2020.
        [http://dx.doi.org/10.1007/s10922-020-09519-y]

[18]   H. Kumar, and P. Pimparkar, "Data Fusion for the Internet of Things", *International Journal of
        Scientific and Research Publications,* vol. 8, no. 3, pp. 278-282, 2018.
        [http://dx.doi.org/10.29322/IJSRP.8.3.2018.p7541]

[19]   J. Qi, P. Yang, L. Newcombe, X. Peng, Y. Yang, and Z. Zhao, "An overview of data fusion techniques
        for Internet of Things enabled physical activity recognition and measure", *Inf. Fusion,* vol. 55, pp.
        269-280, 2020.
        [http://dx.doi.org/10.1016/j.inffus.2019.09.002]

[20]   D. Sanchez, M. Tentori, and J. Favela, "Hidden Markov Models for activity recognition in Ambient
        Intelligence environments", *8th Mexican Int'l Conf. on Current Trends in Computer Science, IEEE-
        2007,* pp. 33-40
        [http://dx.doi.org/10.1109/ENC.2007.31]

[21]   L.A. Zadeh, "Information and control", *Fuzzy Sets.,* vol. 8, no. 3, pp. 338-353, 1965.

[22]   A. Gelman, J.B. Carlin, H.S. Stern, and D.B. Rubin, *Bayesian data analysis.* Chapman and Hall/CRC,
        1995.
        [http://dx.doi.org/10.1201/9780429258411]

[23]   J.V. Stone, *Bayes' rule: A tutorial introduction to Bayesian analysis.* Sebtel Press, 2013.

[24]   T. Diethe, N. Twomey, M. Kull, P. Flach, and I. Craddock, "Prob-abilistic sensor fusion for ambient
        assisted living", In: *arXiv preprint arXiv,* 2017.

[25]   A.R.M. Forkan, I. Khalil, Z. Tari, S. Foufou, and A. Bouras, "A context-aware approach for long-term
        behavioural change detection and abnormality prediction in ambient assisted living", *Pattern
        Recognit.,* vol. 48, no. 3, pp. 628-641, 2015.
        [http://dx.doi.org/10.1016/j.patcog.2014.07.007]

[26]   G. Shafer, *A Mathematical Theory of Evidence.* vol. 42. Princeton University Press, 1976.
        [http://dx.doi.org/10.1515/9780691214696]

[27]   R. Paoli, F.J. Fern'andez-Luque, G. Dom'enech, F. Mart'ınez, J. Zapata, and R. Ruiz, "A system for
        ubiquitous fall monitoring at home via a wireless sensor network and a wearable mote", *Expert Syst.
        Appl.,* vol. 39, no. 5, pp. 5566-5575, 2012.

[http://dx.doi.org/10.1016/j.eswa.2011.11.061]

[28]   Y. Charlon, N. Fourty, W. Bourennane, and E. Campo, "Design and evaluation of a device worn for fall detection and localization: Appli-cation for the continuous monitoring of risks incurred by dependents in an alzheimer's care unit", *Expert Syst. Appl.,* vol. 40, no. 18, pp. 7316-7330, 2013. [http://dx.doi.org/10.1016/j.eswa.2013.07.031]

[29]   M. Jude, IBM: Working Towards a Smarter Connected Home. Internet: http://docs.caba.org/documents/IBM-Smart-Cloud-Home-SPIE2012.pdf

[30]   P.G. Ande, and D.V. Rojatkar, "A Survey: Application of IOT", *International Research Journal of Engineering and Technology (IRJET),* vol. 04, no. 10, pp. 347-350, 2017.

[31]   Z. Hu, "The research of several key question of Internet of Things", In: *International Conference on Intelligence Science and Information Engineering (ISIE),* 2011. [http://dx.doi.org/10.1109/ISIE.2011.107]

[32]   Y. Mano, B. S. Faical, L. Nakamura, P. G. Gomes, R. Libralon, G. Meneguete, G. Filho, G. Giancristofaro, B. Pessin, Krishnamachari, and U. Jo, "Exploiting IoT technologies for enhancing Health Smart Homes through patient identification and emotion recognition", *Computer Communications,* vol. 89.90, pp. 178-190, 2015.

[33]   S.V. Zanjal, and G.R. Talmale, "Medicine reminder and monitoring system for secure health using IOT", *Procedia Comput. Sci.,* vol. 78, pp. 471-476, 2016. [http://dx.doi.org/10.1016/j.procs.2016.02.090]

[34]   L. Da Xu, W. He, and S. Li, "Internet of things in industries: A survey", *IEEE Trans. Industr. Inform.,* vol. 10, no. 4, pp. 2233-2243, 2014. [http://dx.doi.org/10.1109/TII.2014.2300753]

[35]   M. Miraz, M. Ali, P. Excell, and R. Picking, "Internet of Nano-Things, Things and Everything: Future Growth Trends", *Future Internet,* vol. 10, no. 8, p. 68, 2018. [http://dx.doi.org/10.3390/fi10080068]

[36]   I.I. Pătru, M. Carabaş, M. Bărbulescu, and L. Gheorghe, "Smart home IoT system", In: *Netw. Educ. Res. RoEduNet Int. Conf* 15ᵗʰ Ed.. RoEduNet, 2016, pp. 365-370. [http://dx.doi.org/10.1109/RoEduNet.2016.7753232]

[37]   J. Kuusisto, and M. Martin, "Insights into services and innovation in the knowledge intensive economy", *Technology Review,* vol. 134, no. 2003, 2003.

[38]   Z. Guo, Z. Zhang, and W. Li, "Establishment of intelligent identification management platform in railway logistics system by means of the Internet of Things", *Procedia Eng.,* vol. 29, pp. 726-730, 2012. [http://dx.doi.org/10.1016/j.proeng.2012.01.031]

[39]   M. Chen, J. Wan, and F. Li, "Machine-to-machine communications: Architectures, standards and applications", *KSII Trans. Internet Inf. Syst.,* vol. 6, no. 2, pp. 480-497, 2012.

[40]   M. Zhang, T. Yu, and G. F. Zhai, "Smart transport system based on the internet of things", *Applied mechanics and materials,* vol. 48, Trans Tech Publ, pp. 1073-1076, 2011. [http://dx.doi.org/10.4028/www.scientific.net/AMM.48-49.1073]

CHAPTER 3

Role of Artificial Intelligence in Medicine and Health Care

Upasana Pandey[1,*] and **Arvinda Kushwaha**[1]

[1] *Department of Computer Sciences & Engineering, (AI) ABES Institute of Technology, Ghaziabad, India*

[2] *Department of Computer Science and Engineering, Meerut Institute of Engineering and Technology, Meerut, India*

Abstract: With the passing decades, Artificial Intelligence (AI) is gaining high popularity in various domains. In this chapter, we aim to present the current scenario of the application of AI in the field of medical science. Firstly, we will introduce the early and basic role of AI in the medical field. We preceded the chapter with a summary of the most current applications of AI in various areas of medicine and health care. In this review, we have discussed the latest developments of applications of AI in biomedicine while predicting the risk of disease. Estimating the success ratio of the therapy also manages or reduces the severity of complications, taking care of ongoing patients, living assistance, biomedical information processing, biomedical research, and medical imagining. We also present a survey on AI techniques, which were used by many authors with different objectives in medical science. Furthermore, we showcase the effects of the usage of AI by highlighting the reduction in the rate of mortality, and fast and accurate diagnostics which help in decreasing errors related to human fatigue and lessening medical costs. Finally, we draw attention to some of the possible weaknesses, apprehensions, and uncertainties in using AI in medical science. We briefly review the efforts being made to improve the healthcare industry by offering various AI-based healthcare products.

Keywords: Artificial Intelligence, Biomedical, Health Care, Machine Learning.

INTRODUCTION

Artificial Intelligence (AI) was introduced in the field of medical sciences in the year 1984. AI was limited to the programs that were being used in the performance analysis, recommending treatment, and suggesting cures. Furthermore, it focuses on observing the performance of these programs with human intelligence [1]. The solution for this said problem was checked by using

---

[*] **Corresponding author Arvind Kushwaha:** Department of Computer Sciences and Engineering, Meerut Institute of Engineering & Technology, India; E-mail: arvindakush@gmail.com

Rijwan Khan, Pawan Sharma, Sugam Sharma and Santosh Kumar (Eds.)

the Turing test. It is stated that these programs are intelligent as a human and they report positive results in more than 50% of cases.

Thereafter, the researchers aim to explore the field of AI in medical sciences. Initially, AI obtained results in the development of devices useful for disease diagnosis, information retrieval, and expertise [2]. Over the past decades, AI has played a role in medicine and healthcare system. Several authors worked in the area of intelligent tools and devices, which became a great aid in the medical field. Nowadays, medical knowledge engineering has been introduced as a new stream of artificial intelligence for research purposes [3]. Due to the large availability of data, AI is also proving its significant role in the supremacy of decision making by using AI based algorithms [4]. Some authors [5] reported that doctors are being helped in classification, segmentation, detection, and other medical practices by integrating deep learning with AI [5].

RECENT APPLICATIONS OF AI IN MEDICINE AND HEALTH CARE

Diagnosis of Disease and Prediction

These days, cardiovascular disease is one of the major healthcare issues where AI is playing an influential role in handling this problem. It is an estimation using an Artificial Neuron Network (ANN) model which is similar to the biological neural network. This model is designed for informal learning and is used in predicting the hazards of congenital heart disease (CHD) in pregnant women. Their observation reported that the model was aiding in the identification of patients who have a greater risk of CHD in their early stages of pregnancy [6]. The ANN was applied in a multicentre comparison study evaluation. Here, the authors aimed at determining a comparative study between the diagnosis precision of an ANN-based diagnosis system and conventional quantization [7].

The application of machine learning is beneficial in improving the accuracy of predicting cardiovascular disease risk in a group of over 3,700,000 disease-free patients. They could benefit from preventive treatment. This study also concluded on patients not requiring any treatment [8]. Jelliffe Jeganathan *et al.* [9] evaluated the analysis of the mitral valve's performance using AI. It was a manual process to diagnose patients with mitral valve disease. After careful observation, they suggested that a good reading could be found without user intervention through self-diagnosis. JW Timothy *et al.* [10] concluded that the prediction of the machine learning model using three-dimensional heart movement. They were able to achieve results without the usual risk factors in patients with newly diagnosed pulmonary hypertension. Aliza Becker *et al.* [11] show that researchers have developed a neural network model to identify reduced human speech patterns at MIT. During the implementation of the model, it did not include the information that the speaker shares with their physician. In line with the previous work, various authors presented their work which detailed the translation of brainwaves into decipherable speech. The contribution of their work benefited those patients who were not able to talk [12].

In Reduction of Complications

AI is not only helpful in disease diagnosis but also in alleviating or reducing complications during disease creation. Dente J C presented a study on machine learning algorithms used to identify predictive profiles of bacteremia [13]. In a European Union-funded MOSAIC project, type 2 diabetes mellitus complications were predicted by employing a machine learning-based predictive model. It was helpful in the study of retinopathy, neuropathy, and nephropathy with the help of the available medical records online [14]. Additionally, Wise *et al.* [15] estimated preoperative factors in patients undergoing bypass grafting for the coronary arteries. They focused on optimizing the identification of patients at risk before surgery using the artificial neural network [16]. Jirsa K. V. *et al.* used AI based model for focal epilepsy patients. AI has also been used in the prediction of stroke [17]. Hu *et al.* applied a machine learning model to identify common problems in electronic health records [18]. Zhen Hu *et al.* [19] also put their efforts to collect data for research.

Taking Care of Patients Under Treatment

AI also plays a significant role in taking care of those patients who are under treatment. In the study, the authors used the computer-aided detection of brain metastasis by radiologists' diagnostic performance. They employed the technique in the assessment of 3D brain magnetic resonance imaging. The authors concluded that this aid is shown in the improvement of their diagnostic performance [20].

Hyunkwang Lee *et al.* [21] used AI to evaluate the ability of patients to face major surgery or complex therapies by studying age and muscle quantification relatedness. Hyunkwang Lee *et al.* [22] also assessed the bone age of patients by using AI. Other investigations also indicated that AI has entanglement in intraoperative pathological diagnosis [23], evaluation of patients suffering from echo cardio graphics [24], and breath samples for determining the status of the patient's health [25].

In Assisting to Improve the Success Ratio of Treatment

AI can play a significant role in reducing the mortality rate. AI learns from the past reports of the patients and can prioritize those who need immediate attention.

Thomas Grote *et al.* lightened upon how Google's new AI based algorithm predicts the risk of heart disease by observing patients' eyes and saving their lives [26]. AI enabled robots also diagnosed 340 brains with 100% accuracy by using MRI technique [27]. Bloch & Budzier illustrated the Google technology, which alerts doctors of serious kidney injury. AI also helps in assisting surgeons in protecting patients from any kind of illness [28].

Herath, H. M. *et al.* proposed a possible solution for predicting cardiovascular diseases using artificial intelligence technology. Multilayer perceptron neural networks, backpropagation (Levenberg Marquardt) training algorithm, and tensing activation function were used to develop the prediction system [29].

Yaron Kinar *et al.* observed that machine learning models were helpful in labelling persons at elevated risk for colorectal cancer [30].

Living Assistance

AI is also helpful in assisting elderly and disabled people. A brief of smart home functions and tools offered by people suffering from loss of autonomy (PLA) was explained. They also provided a wireless sensor network and data mining based intelligent solution model [31].

Yassine Rabhi *et al.* [32] proposed a capable interface model for analyzing facial expressions for monitoring wheelchairs and robotic aided devices without any other support. The RUDO is an "ambient intelligent system" used for helping blind people to be in a team of sighted people. They worked in the specialized fields of informatics and electronics [33].

Lloret, Jaime *et al.* [34] developed a small communication architecture to gather information for ambient assisted living. This may be used to identify the events which give clues for the assistance needed by old age people.

In the article [35], Qisong Wu *et al.* proposed a fall detection system making it possible to reduce the risk of falls in the elderly. AI-based technologies can be activated on mobile devices and personal digital assistants (PDAs). This can be useful for people with long-lasting memory problems. These technologies improve their memory capacity, allowing them to live independently of their daily routines [36].

Biomedical Information Processing

There is another area of medical science that AI can use to find quick and correct answers to user queries for various documents and datasets. The application of

NLP techniques can be used for this purpose in the search for informative answers [37].

In another paper [38], Mourad Sarrouti *et al.* used the machine learning technique to categorize the biomedical question in four classes and reported 90% accuracy. Mourad Sarrouti *et al.* have proposed an intelligent search system for biomedical documents [39].

This system is capable of retrieving sections of documents that are important for answering biomedical questions. Binary answer-based scheme was proposed by Sarrouti M. *et al.* They introduced the Yes/No answer provider. The clue of the proposal was clued by word sentiment analysis [40]. It may work significantly for information extraction from binary answers.

AI in Biomedical Research

In accumulation to all previously discussed domains, AI has also been explored in biomedical research [41]. Nowadays, AI is being used in ranking the academic literature in this field [42, 43]. By using AI, various authors are screening and ranking figures from the bag of literature [44]. Few medical devices are also enabled with consciousness and experimented [45, 46]. Scott Christley *et al.* proposed a computational modelling assistant, which is useful in constructing simulation models from the conceptual model by using their intelligence [47].

AI in Medical Imaging

Medical Imaging is now being reshaped by AI, rapidly evolving into the future. In another article, Yinghuan Shi *et al.* review recent advances in AI-enabled medical imaging [48]. They discussed the background of AI. This continued with the current scenario of AI success in different medical imaging tasks. They concluded that AI would play an important role in changing the medical imaging process.

Victor Cheng *et al.* proposed a model used for the data readiness scale in medical imaging named as Medical Imaging Data Readiness (MIDaR) scale. This technique is designed to provide data with the expected quality to the researchers as well as clinical providers [49].

Yi Xiao & Shiyuan Liu *et al.* explored the recent conditions for the association of medical imaging, clinical demand for AI techniques in medical imaging, and AI technology. They also concluded that AI needs a core algorithm, doctor's association, and sufficient capital in upgrading medical imaging tools [50].

Alan Alexander *et al.* [51] highlighted how the market will be developed for medical imaging. Therefore, tools will be helping them to enhance scan time, accurate diagnosis and reduction in their workload. Andreas S. Panayides *et al.* presented a detailed review of medical image informatics [52].

LATEST AI TECHNIQUES IN MEDICAL SCIENCES

Table **1** represents the summary of a survey on the latest AI techniques used in various applications of medical sciences. These studies represent the significance of machine learning techniques for several usages in medical purposes.

Table 1. Survey of latest AI techniques used in medical sciences.

Objective	Method/ Techniques Used	Datasets used	Pros and Cons	Author' Name	Year
Data mining models and artificial intelligence methods are used to predict early-stage heart disease	Many data mining methods, *e.g.* decision tree, naive bay clustering algorithm, *e.g.*, regression tree techniques, KNN.	It's used data of people who have cholesterol and risk factors like heart disease with chest pain.	At most 90% accuracy was achieved by all the models. Up to mark accuracy was not achieved only because they have not used deep learning, big data analysis using artificial intelligence.	Banu, N. S., & Swamy, S. [53]	2016
Support vector machine (SVM) and artificial neural network method is used to classify and predict heart syndrome risk.	Data mining, Kernel functions, SVM, ANN back propagation.	Stat log database, Cleveland heart database collected from USI repository.	Support vector machine model gives better accuracy than other models in predicting heart disease.	Radhimeenakshi, S. [54]	2016
Application advantages and disadvantages of Artificial intelligence. Its use in the segmentation of medical images, biomedical image processing.	Data mining method, ANN classification, grey scale and colour image analysis, fuzzy logic.	I/P images of different body parts.	It gives speedy. Diagnose and potential solutions to a variety of health problems. Programmed work can be done through this very limited technique.	Shukla, S. *et al.* [55]	2016
It gives a solution to the complex problem of thyroid disease.	MDC(medical data cleaning).	Real world data sets of thyroid disease received from SMBBMU.	A precision of 95.6% was achieved with a 10,000-fold cross-validation using the TDTD approach.	Ahmed, J. *et al.* [56]	2016

(Table 1) cont.....

Objective	Method/ Techniques Used	Datasets used	Pros and Cons	Author' Name	Year
Advantages of using AI in medical predictions.	Probabilistic reasoning, Knowledge based solution.	Blood samples of patients.	It is very simple in the implementation. The graph will become too complex if the task has a lot of data with complex connections.	Albu, A., & Stanciu, L [57]	2015
AI medical investigation Systems capable of diagnosing the underlying causes of a specific headache.	Neuro diary web application.	Neuro diary web application.	The web application has been enhanced in various ways. The web app merely targets one type of headache.	Farrugia, A. *et al.* [59]	2013
System of personal medical records for patients with autism spectrum disorders.	Hidden Markov models, template matching methods, wearable sensors, and machine learning algorithms.	Clinical data from the Department of Child Psychiatry of the Santo Bono Pausilipon Children's Hospital in Naples.	The accuracy obtained was 92%	Vajda, S. [60]	2014
Algorithm for disease diagnosis.	ACO, SVM, AI, information gain.	Datasets of pima Indians diabetes, hepatitis, Wisconsin breast cancer.	Only Ant colony optimizations give 93.88%, 73.32%, and 81.76 in three cases.	He, F. *et al.* [61]	2012
Immune based clustering for medical diagnostic systems	Clustering techniques, an Artificial immune system algorithm.	Iris dataset contains 150 samples and group 5 from the Wisconsin breast cancer record.	DBSCAN and K-means having good clustering capability under aiNET algorithms K-means have high precision.	Abu-Zeid *et al.* [62]	2012
MRI Cases Containing Brain Tumor Recovery Using Bayesian network	Bayesian network model.	Medical cases from Sahloul hospital.	The outcome was obtaining 68%. Tumor recognition is difficult when there is a great likeness between the description of tumors.	Yazid, H. [63]	2010

(Table 1) cont.....

Objective	Method/ Techniques Used	Datasets used	Pros and Cons	Author' Name	Year
Dynamic modelling of pneumatic muscle	ANN, FIS, genetic algorithm, modified genetic algorithm gradient descent method.	Single pneumatic muscle and extensive records.	After dynamic modeling, PMA provides better prediction accuracy. Modifications still required.	Jamwal, P. K. *et al.* [64]	2009
An AI system for PET tumor detection.	Artificial neural network.	Phantom and real positron emission tomography images.	Good performance of ANN in the detection of tumors Even more, precision can be achieved.	Sharif, M. S., & Amira, A. [65]	2009
Intracardiac electrogram model for joining virtual heart and implantable cardiac devices.	IEGM	EGM device and Virtual heart	The model is capable of reproducing clinically observed detection problems, expanding its capabilities. Morphology can still be enhanced by refining the heart model for defibrillator validation.	Ai, W [66]	2017

EFFECTS OF USAGE OF AI TECHNIQUES

Fast and Accurate Diagnostics Reduce the Mortality Rate

The role of AI plays a significant role in medical diagnosis efficiently and accurately. It is essential for treating patients. On time, treatment of patients reduces the mortality rate. Therefore, a correct and timely diagnosis is essential for saving patients [58]. Macdonald proposed robots, such as Husky, can spot skin tumours more correctly and efficiently [67]. Several researchers developed diagnostic robots which work as human doctors with full efficiency. Muhammad Faisal Siddiqui *et al.* [68] presented a study where 340 brains had been diagnosed using MRI with 100% accuracy. Veebot, a blood-drawing robot was proposed, which takes no time to search for the vein for blood drawing. Sunarti S. *et al.* reported 83% accuracy in doing their job, which is approximate correct as a professional nurse [69].

Reduce Errors Related to Human Fatigue

A report presented by the Centres for Disease Control and Prevention has shown that the 3rd leading reason of death in the United States is misdiagnosis and medical errors. AI may give assistance in reducing doctor's errors and reducing the mortality rate [70]. Diprose and Buist concluded that machines are better workers than humans alone [71]. AI enabled tools and models will not lead to any misses, which may be missed by doctors usually. These tools diagnose patients completely. As a result, we may achieve 100% accurate results for diagnosis and treatment. The human makes machines, so there is a greater chance to improve their efficiency by updating them [72]. In another paper, T. Shyrock *et al.* suggested that these machines and models diagnosed 72% with more correctness than the error rate of doctors [73].

Decrease in Medical Cost

By the arisen of AI in medical sciences, this is a big question that we can overcome with the high cost of medical treatment and facilities. In the survey [74], Marcello Ienca *et al.* reported a 25% fall in hospital's stay and 91% in discharge facilities, which showed the significant outcome of using AI techniques in medical concerns. Many articles present ways to cut off the administrative cost, patient care cost, and medicinal care on the owner without any consultation.

AREA OF CONCERNS

In this section, we have focused on studies of weaknesses, apprehensions, and uncertainties in using AI in medical science.

Care of Old Age People

We have many AI-based applications but still have a number of concerns where we need to use more realization for accepting AI into medicine. First ethical concern is taking care of old age people [75]. AI has shown its significance in medicine in two categories. Firstly, for virtual assistance and secondly, for physical assistance. Virtual assistance is implemented by mathematical algorithms, while physical assistance is the use of robots [76]. However, regardless of these implications, it has been suggested that we can rely on the care of elders with the help of robot technology [77], although they need to focus on more research on the same [78].

Replacement of Humans with AI Techniques

Radiology is another area of concern where we need to explore the replacement of medical technicians or physicians. In 2018, Bluemke [79] raised a question about radiologists: "are radiologists working with AI or AI being a replacement for radiologists? Previous research described the potential threat while including AI in medical sciences. However, they also suggested considering these threats as an augment rather than disheartening [80 - 82]. Hakacova *et al.* [83] observed that automated ECG scans are also not significantly better if physicians are incorrect in diagnosing cardiac rhythm disorders in patients. It also reported the apprehension about AI's opportunity to use the propagation of a large amount of patient records, which leads to diagnosing more complex processes [84].

Data Collection and its Security

Electronic medical records and their security are other major issues to be addressed. The collection of patient data and its storage and efficacy is becoming a major concern with the increasing complexity of computer systems [85, 86]. With the advancement of technology and devices, the privacy of patient data has become a more worrying and complex issue [87, 88]. The idea of using patient medical records in research is adding more complexity to it [89].

RECENTLY USED AI-BASED MEDICAL TOOLS

Table **2** presents a summary of AI-based medical tools used for various purposes in medical sciences with their usages and developing organizations.

Table 2. Summary of the AI based medical tools.

Tools	Usage	Developing organization	Year	Refer
IDx-DR software program	It is used to analyze images of the eye taken with a retinal camera for symptoms of diabetes-related vision loss.	IDx, LLC, Coralville, IA, USA.	2018	[90, 91]
20/20NOW	to aid in the diagnosis of retinal diseases.	20/20NOW New York, NY.	2019	[92]
viz.ai lvo stroke system.	tomography scanner is used to vigilant the stroke.	Viz.ai, Inc. Palo Alto, CA, USA.	2016	[93]
Imagen Technologies	analyze two-dimensional X-ray images for signs of distal radius fracture in an adult patient.	Imagen Technologies Hospital & Health Care, New York.	2015	[94]
EchoMD AutoEF s/w	fully automated clip selection and left ventricular ejection fraction calculation.	Bay Labs.	2018	[95]
Butterfly Networks	AI-powered Ultrasound Imaging System for iPhone.	Butterfly Network Inc.	2011	[96]
Subtle PET	which improves the quality of images taken during positron emission?	*Enhao Gong,***Founder***& CEO, Subtle Medical.*	2018	[97]

(Table 2) cont.....

Tools	Usage	Developing organization	Year	Refer
HeartVista's AI-driven	MRI solution to enable faster and more efficient scans that benefit patients, technicians and radiologists.	William Overall and Itamar Kandel, Lost Altos, California.	2012	[98]
Artery's	To complement cardiac MRI, it has additional enhancements to its unique Cardio AI MR.	**Artery's Inc.** Company	2007	[99]
QVCAD	automated breast ultrasound simultaneous reading system.	Bob Wang, Founder & CEO, Los Altos, United States.	2012	[100]
Kardia Pro	Tracks important physiology measures like weight, activity, and blood pressure.	AliveCor, Inc	2017	[101]
AliveCor artificial intelligence technology.	AliveCor and Mayo Clinic Announce Collaboration to Develop Artificial Intelligence Technology to Help Prevent Sudden Cardiac Death.	AliveCor and Mayo Clinic	2019	[102]
iLet Bionic Pancreas System.	a portable, pocket-sized device used to monitor blood sugar in people with diabetes.	Beta **Bionics**	2019	[103]
Luna	Luna Aims to Reduce Your Hot Flash Symptom.	VRHealth	2018	[104]
Amazon Comprehend Medical	Machine learning is used to determine a patient's diagnosis symptoms, medical test results, treatments, and other related medical data to facilitate the review of "unstructured" medical texts, such as doctor notes.	Dr. Taha, A. Kass-Hout and Dr. Matt Wood.	2019	[105]
Aidoc and SaferMD	Aidoc, a leading provider of AI radiology solutions, today announced a joint venture with SaferMD to provide the first comprehensive solution that uses AI to get better clinical performance and reward radiologists with higher scores on the Incentive Based Payment System. The Merit of Medicare (MIPS).	Aidoc and SaferMD Team.	2019	[106]

CONCLUSION

The authors of the chapter presented a detailed literature review on the role of AI in medical sciences. There are various domains of medical sciences where AI is playing very significant role in automation, accurate diagnosis, and treatment, reduction of the mortality rate, virtual assistance to patients in research, and many more. The AI techniques reported awesome findings that assist doctors and technicians in preventing patients at an early age of disease. With the advent of more AI based technologies medical costs has been reduced in European countries. Several organizations are also working on offering AI based tools in the market.

However, there is always another face of developing new trends and technologies. Many concerns need to be addressed in the medical sciences based on AI techniques. Many authors reported flaws in using AI for virtual assistance to elder people, replacement of humans, and an increased bag of patients' information. Therefore, these concern areas are available for more research and findings. We can update the techniques to report more accurate results without major flaws by exploring the possibilities for improvements.

CONSENT OF PUBLICATION

Not applicable.

CONFLICT OF INTEREST

The author declares no conflict of interest, financial or otherwise.

ACKNOWLEDGEMENTS

Declared none.

REFERENCES

[1]   D.L. Hunt, R.B. Haynes, S.E. Hanna, and K. Smith, "Effects of computer-based clinical decision support systems on physician performance and patient outcomes: a systematic review", *JAMA*, vol. 280, no. 15, pp. 1339-1346, 1998.
[http://dx.doi.org/10.1001/jama.280.15.1339] [PMID: 9794315]

[2]   L. Bishnoi, and S.N. Singh, "Artificial intelligence techniques used in medical sciences: a review", In: *8th International Conference on Cloud Computing, Data Science & Engineering (Confluence)* IEEE, 2018.
[http://dx.doi.org/10.1109/CONFLUENCE.2018.8442729]

[3]   C.R. Pereira, D.R. Pereira, S.A.T. Weber, C. Hook, V.H.C. de Albuquerque, and J.P. Papa, "A survey on computer-assisted Parkinson's Disease diagnosis", *Artif. Intell. Med.*, vol. 95, pp. 48-63, 2019.
[http://dx.doi.org/10.1016/j.artmed.2018.08.007] [PMID: 30201325]

[4]   J.W. Kim, K.L. Jones, and E. D'Angelo, "How to prepare prospective psychiatrists in the era of artificial intelligence", *Acad. Psychiatry*, vol. 43, no. 3, pp. 337-339, 2019.
[http://dx.doi.org/10.1007/s40596-019-01025-x] [PMID: 30659443]

[5]   https://www.nvindia.com/en_us/deeplearningai/industries/healthcare

[6]   H. Li, M. Luo, J. Zheng, J. Luo, R. Zeng, N. Feng, Q. Du, and J. Fang, "An artificial neural network prediction model of congenital heart disease based on risk factors: A hospital-based case-control study", *Medicine (Baltimore)*, vol. 96, no. 6, p. e6090, 2017.
[http://dx.doi.org/10.1097/MD.0000000000006090] [PMID: 28178169]

[7]   K. Nakajima, T. Kudo, T. Nakata, K. Kiso, T. Kasai, Y. Taniguchi, S. Matsuo, M. Momose, M. Nakagawa, S. Sarai, S. Hida, H. Tanaka, K. Yokoyama, K. Okuda, and L. Edenbrandt, "Diagnostic accuracy of an artificial neural network compared with statistical quantitation of myocardial perfusion images: a Japanese multicenter study", *Eur. J. Nucl. Med. Mol. Imaging*, vol. 44, no. 13, pp. 2280-

2289, 2017.
[http://dx.doi.org/10.1007/s00259-017-3834-x] [PMID: 28948350]

[8]   F. Stephen Weng, "Can machine-learning improve cardiovascular risk prediction using routine clinical data?", *PloS one,* p. e0174944, 2017.

[9]   J. Jeganathan, "Artificial intelligence in mitral valve analysis", *Annals of cardiac anaesthesia 20.2,* vol. 129, 2017.

[10]   T.J.W. Dawes, A. de Marvao, W. Shi, T. Fletcher, G.M.J. Watson, J. Wharton, C.J. Rhodes, L.S.G.E. Howard, J.S.R. Gibbs, D. Rueckert, S.A. Cook, M.R. Wilkins, and D.P. O'Regan, "Dawes, "Machine learning of three-dimensional right ventricular motion enables outcome prediction in pulmonary hypertension: a cardiac MR imaging study", *Radiology,* vol. 283, no. 2, pp. 381-390, 2017.
[http://dx.doi.org/10.1148/radiol.2016161315] [PMID: 28092203]

[11]   A. Becker, "Artificial intelligence in medicine: What is it doing for us today?", *Health Policy Technol.,* vol. 8, no. 2, pp. 198-205, 2019.
[http://dx.doi.org/10.1016/j.hlpt.2019.03.004]

[12]   D. Zandi, "New ethical challenges of digital technologies, machine learning and artificial intelligence in public health: a call for papers", *Bull. World Health Organ.,* vol. 97, no. 1, pp. 2-2, 2019.
[http://dx.doi.org/10.2471/BLT.18.227686]

[13]   C.J. Dente, M. Bradley, S. Schobel, B. Gaucher, T. Buchman, A.D. Kirk, and E. Elster, "Towards precision medicine: Accurate predictive modeling of infectious complications in combat casualties", *J. Trauma Acute Care Surg.,* vol. 83, no. 4, pp. 609-616, 2017.
[http://dx.doi.org/10.1097/TA.0000000000001596] [PMID: 28538622]

[14]   N. Sinha, J. Dauwels, M. Kaiser, S.S. Cash, M. Brandon Westover, Y. Wang, and P.N. Taylor, "Predicting neurosurgical outcomes in focal epilepsy patients using computational modelling", *Brain,* vol. 140, no. 2, pp. 319-332, 2017.
[http://dx.doi.org/10.1093/brain/aww299] [PMID: 28011454]

[15]   E.S. Wise, D.P. Stonko, Z.A. Glaser, K.L. Garcia, J.J. Huang, J.S. Kim, J.A. Kallos, J.R. Starnes, J.W. Fleming, K.M. Hocking, C.M. Brophy, and S.S. Eagle, "Prediction of prolonged ventilation after coronary artery bypass grafting: data from an artificial neural network", *Heart Surg. Forum,* vol. 20, no. 1, pp. E007-E014, 2017.
[http://dx.doi.org/10.1532/hsf.1566] [PMID: 28263144]

[16]   V.K. Jirsa, T. Proix, D. Perdikis, M.M. Woodman, H. Wang, J. Gonzalez-Martinez, C. Bernard, C. Bénar, M. Guye, P. Chauvel, and F. Bartolomei, "The Virtual Epileptic Patient: Individualized whole-brain models of epilepsy spread", *Neuroimage,* vol. 145, no. Pt B, pp. 377-388, 2017.
[http://dx.doi.org/10.1016/j.neuroimage.2016.04.049] [PMID: 27477535]

[17]   X. Li, "Integrated machine learning approaches for predicting ischemic stroke and thromboembolism in atrial fibrillation", In: *AMIA Annual Symposium Proceedings* American Medical Informatics Association, 2016.

[18]   Olivier Niel, and Paul Bastard, "Artificial intelligence improves estimation of tacrolimus area under the concentration over time curve in renal transplant recipients", *Transpl. Int.,* vol. 31, no. 8, pp. 940-941, 2018.
[http://dx.doi.org/10.1111/tri.13271] [PMID: 29687486]

[19]   Z. Hu, "Accelerating chart review using automated methods on electronic health record data for postoperative complications", In: *AMIA Annual Symposium Proceedings* American Medical Informatics Association, 2016.

[20]   Leonard Sunwoo, "Computer-aided detection of brain metastasis on 3D MR imaging: Observer performance study", *PLoS One,* p. e0178265, 2017.
[http://dx.doi.org/10.1371/journal.pone.0178265]

[21]   H. Lee, F.M. Troschel, S. Tajmir, G. Fuchs, J. Mario, F.J. Fintelmann, and S. Do, "Pixel-level deep

segmentation: artificial intelligence quantifies muscle on computed tomography for body morphometric analysis", *J. Digit. Imaging,* vol. 30, no. 4, pp. 487-498, 2017.
[http://dx.doi.org/10.1007/s10278-017-9988-z] [PMID: 28653123]

[22]   H. Lee, S. Tajmir, J. Lee, M. Zissen, B.A. Yeshiwas, T.K. Alkasab, G. Choy, and S. Do, "Fully automated deep learning system for bone age assessment", *J. Digit. Imaging,* vol. 30, no. 4, pp. 427-441, 2017.
[http://dx.doi.org/10.1007/s10278-017-9955-8] [PMID: 28275919]

[23]   J. Zhang, Y. Song, F. Xia, C. Zhu, Y. Zhang, W. Song, J. Xu, and X. Ma, "Rapid and accurate intraoperative pathological diagnosis by artificial intelligence with deep learning technology", *Med. Hypotheses,* vol. 107, pp. 98-99, 2017.
[http://dx.doi.org/10.1016/j.mehy.2017.08.021] [PMID: 28915974]

[24]   C. Nath MS, and S. R. Jonnalagadda, "A natural language processing tool for large-scale data extraction from echocardiography reports", *PLoS One,* vol. 11.4, p. e0153749, 2016.

[25]   T. Grote, and P. Berens, "On the ethics of algorithmic decision-making in healthcare", *J. Med. Ethics,* vol. 46, no. 3, pp. 205-211, 2020.
[http://dx.doi.org/10.1136/medethics-2019-105586] [PMID: 31748206]

[26]   K-H. Yu, A.L. Beam, and I.S. Kohane, "Artificial intelligence in healthcare", *Nat. Biomed. Eng.,* vol. 2, no. 10, pp. 719-731, 2018.
[http://dx.doi.org/10.1038/s41551-018-0305-z] [PMID: 31015651]

[27]   M.F. Siddiqui, A.W. Reza, and J. Kanesan, An automated and intelligent medical decision support system for brain MRI scans classification. *PloS one,* vol. 10.8, p. e0135875, 2015.

[28]   S. Bloch-Budzier, "NHS using Google technology to treat patients", *BBC News,* p. 22, 2016.

[29]   H.M.K.K.M.B. Herath, G.M.K.B. Karunasena, H.D.N.S. Priyankara, and B.G.D.A. Madhusanka, "High-performance cardiovascular medicine: artificial intelligence for coronary artery disease",
[http://dx.doi.org/10.21203/rs.3.rs-642228/v1]

[30]   Y. Kinar, "Performance analysis of a machine learning flagging system used to identify a group of individuals at a high risk for colorectal cancer", *PLoS One,* vol. 12.2, p. e0171759, 2017.

[31]   K. Dahmani, "An intelligent model of home support for people with loss of autonomy: A novel approach", In: *2016 International Conference on Control, Decision and Information Technologies (CoDIT)* IEEE, 2016.
[http://dx.doi.org/10.1109/CoDIT.2016.7593557]

[32]   Y. Rabhi, M. Mrabet, and F. Fnaiech, "A facial expression controlled wheelchair for people with disabilities", *Comput. Methods Programs Biomed.,* vol. 165, pp. 89-105, 2018.
[http://dx.doi.org/10.1016/j.cmpb.2018.08.013] [PMID: 30337084]

[33]   M. Hudec, and Z. Smutny, "RUDO: A home ambient intelligence system for blind people", *Sensors,* vol. 17.8, p. 1926, 2017.
[http://dx.doi.org/10.3390/s17081926]

[34]   J. Lloret, "A smart communication architecture for ambient assisted living", *IEEE Commun. Mag.,* vol. 53, no. 1, pp. 26-33, 2015.
[http://dx.doi.org/10.1109/MCOM.2015.7010512]

[35]   Q. Wu, "Radar-based fall detection based on Doppler time–frequency signatures for assisted living", *IET Radar Sonar & Navigation,* vol. 9, no. 2, pp. 164-172, 2015.
[http://dx.doi.org/10.1049/iet-rsn.2014.0250]

[36]   D.W.K. Man, S.F. Tam, and C.W.Y. Hui-Chan, "Learning to live independently with expert systems in memory rehabilitation", *NeuroRehabilitation,* vol. 18, no. 1, pp. 21-29, 2003.
[http://dx.doi.org/10.3233/NRE-2003-18104] [PMID: 12719618]

[37]   A. Ben Abacha, and P. Zweigenbaum, "MEANS: A medical question-answering system combining

NLP techniques and semantic Web technologies", *Inf. Process. Manage.,* vol. 51, no. 5, pp. 570-594, 2015.
[http://dx.doi.org/10.1016/j.ipm.2015.04.006]

[38]   M. Sarrouti, and S. Ouatik El Alaoui, "A machine learning-based method for question type classification in biomedical question answering", *Methods Inf. Med.,* vol. 56, no. 3, pp. 209-216, 2017.
[http://dx.doi.org/10.3414/ME16-01-0116] [PMID: 28361158]

[39]   M. Sarrouti, and S.O. El Alaoui, "A generic document retrieval framework based on UMLS similarity for biomedical question answering system", In: *Intelligent Decision Technologies 2016.* Springer: Cham, 2016, pp. 207-216.
[http://dx.doi.org/10.1007/978-3-319-39627-9_18]

[40]   M. Sarrouti, and S. Ouatik El Alaoui, "A passage retrieval method based on probabilistic information retrieval model and UMLS concepts in biomedical question answering", *J. Biomed. Inform.,* vol. 68, pp. 96-103, 2017.
[http://dx.doi.org/10.1016/j.jbi.2017.03.001] [PMID: 28286031]

[41]   G.S. Handelman, H.K. Kok, R.V. Chandra, A.H. Razavi, M.J. Lee, and H. Asadi, "eDoctor: machine learning and the future of medicine", *J. Intern. Med.,* vol. 284, no. 6, pp. 603-619, 2018.
[http://dx.doi.org/10.1111/joim.12822] [PMID: 30102808]

[42]   H. Almeida, M.J. Meurs, L. Kosseim, and A. Tsang, "Data sampling and supervised learning for hiv literature screening", *IEEE Trans. Nanobioscience,* vol. 15, no. 4, pp. 354-361, 2016.
[http://dx.doi.org/10.1109/TNB.2016.2565481] [PMID: 28113721]

[43]   A. Névéol, S.E. Shooshan, S.M. Humphrey, J.G. Mork, and A.R. Aronson, "A recent advance in the automatic indexing of the biomedical literature", *J. Biomed. Inform.,* vol. 42, no. 5, pp. 814-823, 2009.
[http://dx.doi.org/10.1016/j.jbi.2008.12.007] [PMID: 19166973]

[44]   F. Liu, and H. Yu, "Learning to rank figures within a biomedical article", *PloS one,* p. e61567, 2014.
[http://dx.doi.org/10.1371/journal.pone.0061567]

[45]   G. Ruffini, "An algorithmic information theory of consciousness", *Neurosci. Conscious.,* vol. 2017, no. 1, p. nix019, 2017.
[http://dx.doi.org/10.1093/nc/nix019] [PMID: 30042851]

[46]   X.D. Arsiwalla, I. Herreros, and P. Verschure, "On three categories of conscious machines", In: *Conference on Biomimetic and Biohybrid Systems* Springer: Cham, 2016.
[http://dx.doi.org/10.1007/978-3-319-42417-0_35]

[47]   S. Christley, and G. An, "A proposal for augmenting biological model construction with a semi-intelligent computational modeling assistant", *Comput. Math. Organ. Theory,* vol. 18, no. 4, pp. 380-403, 2012.
[http://dx.doi.org/10.1007/s10588-011-9101-y] [PMID: 23990750]

[48]   Y. Shi, and Q. Wang, *The Artificial Intelligence-Enabled Medical Imaging: Today and Its Future.,* pp. 71-75, 2019.

[49]   V. Cheng, and L. Chun-hung, "Combining supervised and semi-supervised classifier for personalized spam filtering", In: *Pacific-Asia Conference on Knowledge Discovery and Data Mining.* Springer: Berlin, Heidelberg, 2007.
[http://dx.doi.org/10.1007/978-3-540-71701-0_45]

[50]   Y. Xiao, and S.Y. Liu, "Collaborations of industry, academia, research and application improve the healthy development of medical imaging artificial intelligence industry in China", *Chin. Med. Sci. J.,* vol. 34, no. 2, pp. 84-88, 2019.
[PMID: 31315748]

[51]   A. Alexander, A. Jiang, C. Ferreira, and D. Zurkiya, "An intelligent future for medical imaging: a market outlook on artificial intelligence for medical imaging", *J. Am. Coll. Radiol.,* vol. 17, no. 1 Pt B, pp. 165-170, 2020.

[http://dx.doi.org/10.1016/j.jacr.2019.07.019] [PMID: 31918875]

[52] A.S. Panayides, Z.C. Antoniou, and A.G. Constantinides, "An overview of mHealth medical video communication systems", In: *Mobile Health* Springer Cham, 2015, pp. 609-633.
[http://dx.doi.org/10.1007/978-3-319-12817-7_26]

[53] N.K. Salma Banu, "Prediction of heart disease at early stage using data mining and big data analytics: A survey", In: *2016 International Conference on Electrical, Electronics, Communication, Computer and Optimization Techniques (ICEECCOT)* IEEE, 2016.

[54] S. Radhimeenakshi, "Classification and prediction of heart disease risk using data mining techniques of Support Vector Machine and Artificial Neural Network", In: *2016 3rd International Conference on Computing for Sustainable Global Development (INDIACom)*, 2016.

[55] S. Shukla, A. Lakhmani, and A.K. Agarwal, "Approaches of artificial intelligence in biomedical image processing: A leading tool between computer vision & biological vision", In: *2016 International Conference on Advances in Computing, Communication, & Automation (ICACCA)(Spring)*, 2016.
[http://dx.doi.org/10.1109/ICACCA.2016.7578900]

[56] J. Ahmed, and M. Abdul Rehman Soomrani, *"TDTD: Thyroid disease type diagnostics."* 2016 *international conference on intelligent systems engineering (ICISE)*. IEEE, 2016.

[57] A. Albu, and L. Stanciu, *"Benefits of using artificial intelligence in medical predictions."* 2015 E-Health and Bioengineering Conference (EHB). IEEE, 2015.

[58] I.K. Agung Enriko, G. Wibisono, and D. Gunawan, "Designing machine-to-machine (M2M) system in health-cure modeling for cardiovascular disease patients: Initial study", *2015 3rd International Conference on Information and Communication Technology (ICoICT)*, 2015.

[59] A. Farrugia, "Medical diagnosis: Are artificial intelligence systems able to diagnose the underlying causes of specific headaches?", *2013 Sixth International Conference on Developments in eSystems Engineering*, 2013
[http://dx.doi.org/10.1109/DeSE.2013.72]

[60] A.G.S.D. Herrera, "Semi–supervised learning for image modality classification", In: *International Workshop on Multimodal Retrieval in the Medical Domain*. Springer: Cham, 2015.
[http://dx.doi.org/10.1007/978-3-319-24471-6_8]

[61] F. He, H. Yang, and L. Fan, "A novel algorithm for disease diagnosis", In: *Proceedings of 2012 2nd International Conference on Computer Science and Network Technology*. IEEE, 2012.
[http://dx.doi.org/10.1109/ICCSNT.2012.6525884]

[62] N. Abu-Zeid, R. Kashif, and O.M. Badawy, "Immune based clustering for medical diagnostic systems", In: *2012 International Conference on Advanced Computer Science Applications and Technologies (ACSAT)*. IEEE, 2012.
[http://dx.doi.org/10.1109/ACSAT.2012.42]

[63] H. Yazid, "MRI cases containing cerebral tumors retrieval using Bayesian networks", In: *In The 10th IEEE International Symposium on Signal Processing and Information Technology*. IEEE, 2010, pp. 7-10.
[http://dx.doi.org/10.1109/ISSPIT.2010.5711742]

[64] P.K. Jamwal, S. Hussain, and Q.X. Sheng, "Dynamic modeling of pneumatic muscles using modified fuzzy inference mechanism", *2009 IEEE International Conference on Robotics and Biomimetics (ROBIO)*, 2009
[http://dx.doi.org/10.1109/ROBIO.2009.5420384]

[65] M.S. Sharif, and A. Abbes, "An intelligent system for PET tumour detection and quantification", In: *16th IEEE International Conference on Image Processing (ICIP)*. IEEE, 2009, pp. 2625-2628.
[http://dx.doi.org/10.1109/ICIP.2009.5414100]

[66] W. Ai, P. Nitish, and R. Partha, "An intracardiac electrogram model to bridge virtual hearts and implantable cardiac devices", In: *39th Annual International Conference of the IEEE Engineering in*

Medicine and Biology Society (EMBC) IEEE, 2017, pp. 1974-1977.
[http://dx.doi.org/10.1109/EMBC.2017.8037237]

[67]   S. Yeasmin, "Benefits of artificial intelligence in medicine", In: *In 2019 2ⁿᵈ International Conference on Computer Applications & Information Security (ICCAIS)* IEEE, 2019, pp. 1-6.
[http://dx.doi.org/10.1109/CAIS.2019.8769557]

[68]   Muhammad Faisal Siddiqui, Ahmed Wasif Reza, and Jeevan Kanesan, "An automated and intelligent medical decision support system for brain MRI scans classification", *PloS one,* p. e0135875, 2015.
[http://dx.doi.org/10.1371/journal.pone.0135875]

[69]   S. Sunarti, F. Fadzlul Rahman, M. Naufal, M. Risky, K. Febriyanto, and R. Masnina, "Artificial intelligence in healthcare: opportunities and risk for future", *Gac. Sanit.,* vol. 35, no. Suppl. 1, pp. S67-S70, 2021.
[http://dx.doi.org/10.1016/j.gaceta.2020.12.019] [PMID: 33832631]

[70]   M. Heidi, "Understanding emotional intelligence and its relationship to clinical reasoning in nursing students: a mixed methods study", *Electronic Theses and Dissertations.,* 2019.

[71]   J. Lorkowski, O. Grzegorowska, and M. Pokorski, "Artificial Intelligence in the Healthcare System: An Overview", *Adv. Exp. Med. Biol.,* vol. 1335, pp. 1-10, 2021.
[http://dx.doi.org/10.1007/5584_2021_620] [PMID: 33768498]

[72]   M. McFarland, Google uses AI to help diagnose breast cancer 2017.

[73]   T. Shyrock, Can computers help doctors reduce diagnostic errors? 2016.

[74]   www.healthcarefinancenews.com/news/how-artificial-intelligence-can-be-used-reduce-costs-and-improve-outcomes-total-joint

[75]   M. Ienca, T. Wangmo, F. Jotterand, R.W. Kressig, and B. Elger, "Ethical design of intelligent assistive technologies for dementia: a descriptive review", *Sci. Eng. Ethics,* vol. 24, no. 4, pp. 1035-1055, 2018.
[http://dx.doi.org/10.1007/s11948-017-9976-1] [PMID: 28940133]

[76]   V. Kaul, S. Enslin, and S.A. Gross, "History of artificial intelligence in medicine", *Gastrointest. Endosc.,* vol. 92, no. 4, pp. 807-812, 2020.
[http://dx.doi.org/10.1016/j.gie.2020.06.040] [PMID: 32565184]

[77]   M. Shishehgar, D. Kerr, and J. Blake, "The effectiveness of various robotic technologies in assisting older adults", *Health Informatics J.,* vol. 25, no. 3, pp. 892-918, 2019.
[http://dx.doi.org/10.1177/1460458217729729] [PMID: 28927331]

[78]   M. Coeckelbergh, "Care robots and the future of ICT-mediated elderly care: a response to doom scenarios", *AI Soc.,* vol. 31, no. 4, pp. 455-462, 2016.
[http://dx.doi.org/10.1007/s00146-015-0626-3]

[79]   D.A. Bluemke, "Radiology in 2018: are you working with AI or being replaced by AI?", *Radiology,* vol. 287, no. 2, pp. 365-366, 2018.
[http://dx.doi.org/10.1148/radiol.2018184007] [PMID: 29668407]

[80]   M. Recht, and R.N. Bryan, "Artificial intelligence: threat or boon to radiologists?", *J. Am. Coll. Radiol.,* vol. 14, no. 11, pp. 1476-1480, 2017.
[http://dx.doi.org/10.1016/j.jacr.2017.07.007] [PMID: 28826960]

[81]   Caroline O'Neill, "Is AI a threat or benefit to health workers?", *CMAJ,* vol. 189, no. 20, p. E732, 2017.
[http://dx.doi.org/10.1503/cmaj.1095428]

[82]   A. Garg, B. Sharma, and R. Khan, "Heart disease prediction using machine learning techniques", *IOP Conference Series: Materials Science and Engineering.,* vol. 1022, 2021.
[http://dx.doi.org/10.1088/1757-899X/1022/1/012046]

[83]   N. Hakacova, E. Trägårdh-Johansson, G.S. Wagner, C. Maynard, and O. Pahlm, "Computer-based rhythm diagnosis and its possible influence on nonexpert electrocardiogram readers", *J. Electrocardiol.,* vol. 45, no. 1, pp. 18-22, 2012.

[http://dx.doi.org/10.1016/j.jelectrocard.2011.05.007] [PMID: 21816409]

[84] M. Komorowski, and L.A. Celi, "Will artificial intelligence contribute to overuse in healthcare?", *Crit. Care Med.,* vol. 45, no. 5, pp. 912-913, 2017.
[http://dx.doi.org/10.1097/CCM.0000000000002351]

[85] C. Petersen, "Through patients' eyes: regulation, technology, privacy, and the future", *Yearbook of medical informatics,* vol. 27, no. 1, pp. 10-15, 2018.
[http://dx.doi.org/10.1055/s-0038-1641193]

[86] I.T. Agaku, A.O. Adisa, O.A. Ayo-Yusuf, and G.N. Connolly, "Concern about security and privacy, and perceived control over collection and use of health information are related to withholding of health information from healthcare providers", *J. Am. Med. Inform. Assoc.,* vol. 21, no. 2, pp. 374-378, 2014.
[http://dx.doi.org/10.1136/amiajnl-2013-002079] [PMID: 23975624]

[87] C. Papoutsi, "Patient and public views about the security and privacy of Electronic Health Records (EHRs) in the UK: results from a mixed methods study", *BMC Medical Informatics and Decision Making.,* vol. 15, no. 1, p. 86, 2015.
[http://dx.doi.org/10.1186/s12911-015-0202-2]

[88] B. Aliza, "Artificial intelligence in medicine: What is it doing for us today?", *Health Policy Technol.,* vol. 8, no. 2, pp. 198-205, 2019.
[http://dx.doi.org/10.1016/j.hlpt.2019.03.004]

[89] P. Coorevits, M. Sundgren, G.O. Klein, A. Bahr, B. Claerhout, C. Daniel, M. Dugas, D. Dupont, A. Schmidt, P. Singleton, G. De Moor, and D. Kalra, "Electronic health records: new opportunities for clinical research", *J. Intern. Med.,* vol. 274, no. 6, pp. 547-560, 2013.
[http://dx.doi.org/10.1111/joim.12119] [PMID: 23952476]

[90] R. Varma, Clinical see all 2018.

[91] D. Michael, "Abràmoff, "Pivotal trial of an autonomous AI-based diagnostic system for detection of diabetic retinopathy in primary care offices", *NPJ Digit. Med.,* vol. 1, no. 1, pp. 1-8, 2018.

[92] J. V. Cordeiro, "Digital Technologies and Data Science as Health Enablers: An Outline of Appealing Promises and Compelling Ethical, Legal, and Social Challenges", *Advancing AI in the NHS,* 2021.
[http://dx.doi.org/10.3389/fmed.2021.647897]

[93] N. Noorbakhsh-Sabet, R. Zand, Y. Zhang, and V. Abedi, "Artificial intelligence transforms the future of health care", *Am. J. Med.,* vol. 132, no. 7, pp. 795-801, 2019.
[http://dx.doi.org/10.1016/j.amjmed.2019.01.017] [PMID: 30710543]

[94] J.R. Debray, J. Chrétien, M. Gueniot, J.P. Hardouin, J. Himbert, P. Pichot, G. Richet, C. Roussel, and A.R. Ryckewaert, "A new concept of preventive medicine using automatic data processing by computer. II. Application to diseases and risks of the digestive apparatus and to cardiovascular diseases and risks", *Ann. Med. Interne (Paris),* vol. 120, no. 10, pp. 589-596, 1969.
[PMID: 4928452]

[95] "A window into the human body for less than $2,0 0 0 enabled by breakthrough Ultrasound-on- a-Chip technology", Available at: k.com/press-releases/first-ultrasound-on-a-chip-

[96] PRNewswire, "Subtle medical receives FDA 510(k) clearance and CE mark approval for SubtlePET TM", Available at: https://www. prnewswire.com/news-releases/subtle-medical-receives-fda-510k-clearance- and- ce- mark- approval- for- subtlepet- 3007604 4 4.html

[97] PRNewswire, "HeartVista announces the first AI-driven, One Click TM Autonomous MRI solution to enable faster and more efficient scans that benefit patients, technicians, and radiologists", Available at: https://www.prnewswire.com/news-releases/heartvista-announces-the-first- ai- driven- one- click –autonomous- mri- solution- to- enable- faster- and- more- efficient- scans- that- benefit- patients-technicians- and- radiologists- 300754565. html

[98] PRNewswire, "Arterys introduces first complete AI- and Cloud-powered so- lution for most challenging medical imaging analysis workflow", Available at: https://www.prnewswire.com/news-

releases/arterys-introduces-first- complete- ai –and- cloud- powered- solution- for- most- challenging-medical- imaging- analysis- workflow- 300735885.html

[99]   PRNewswire, *QVCAD, first AI system for concurrent reading of ABUS exams, featured in research and education sessions at RSNA.*. Available at: https://www.prnewswire.com/news-releases/qvca--first-ai-system-for- concurrent-reading-of-abus-exams-featured-in-research-and-education- sessions-at- rsna- 300754370.html

[100] AliveCor, "AliveCor unveils first AI-enabled platform for doctors to im- prove stroke prevention through early atrial fibrillation detection", Available at: https://www.alivecor.com/press/press _ release/alivecor-unveils-first- ai- enabled- platform- for- doctors/

[101] AliveCor, "AI that sees the invisible: aAliveCor and Mayo Clinic announce collaboration to develop groundbreaking AI technology to help prevent sudden cardiac death", Available at: https://www.alivecor.com/press/press _ release/ai- that- sees- the- invisible/

[102] B. Bionics, "Beta bionics receives IDE approval from the FDA to be- gin a home-use clinical trial testing the new iLetTM bionic pan- creas system", Available at: https://docs.wixstatic.com/ugd/6df851 711995f7e8684c6fb2bec5d1e733c5fe.pdf

[103] PRNewswire, *VRHealth announces new virtual reality AI-therapist that eases hot flashes.*. Available at: https://www.prnewswire.com/news-releases/ vrhealth- announces- new- virtual- reality- ai-therapist- that- eases- hot- flashes- 300764227.html

[104] PRNewswire, *Notal Vision engages Wasatch Photonics, bringing AI-enabled home-based optical coherence tomography ccloser to market.*.https://www.prnewswire.com/news-releases/notal- vision-engages- wasatch- photonics- bringing- ai- enabled- home- based- optical- coherence- tomography-closer- to- market- 300767431.html

[105] T.A. Kass-Hout, and M. Wood, *Introducing medical language processing with Amazon Comprehend Medical.*.https://aws. amazon.com/blogs/machine- learning/introducing- medical- language-processing- with- amazon- comprehend- medical/

[106] PRNewswire, "Aidoc and SaferMD team up to close the loop of AI ra- diology Medicare payments", Available at: https://www.prnewswire.com/ news-releases/aidoc-and-safermd-team-up-to-c-ose-the-loop-of-ai- radiology-medicare-payments-809895876.html

CHAPTER 4

Threat Detection and Reporting System

Devika Bihani[1,*], **Saransh Sharma**[1] and **Harshit Jain**[1]

[1] *Computer Science Engineering, Shri Vaishnav Vidyapeeth Vishwavidyalaya, Indore, India*

Abstract: We live in a world brimming with technology and crime. Even being in large numbers, law enforcers lack the required presence and resources. Although there are a lot of surveillance devices being installed in a general view of the public, most of them require an operator to monitor them. Even if they are smart devices, they lack the ability to cover all aspects of a situation. The proposed solution emphasizes computer vision to develop software that leverages the widely available network of surveilling cameras to detect criminal threats using object detection, violent activities such as CNN, detection of a person in need of medical aid, and sending the same to ground zero. Thus, effectively covering all 3 major aspects of a threat, namely, the crucial time before a crime is conducted, detecting an ongoing act of violence, and finally sending help as soon as possible to the victims in the aftermath. This would serve as an additional eye for law enforcement and will certainly aid in reducing the response time from authorities and mitigate most of the rising threats.

Keywords: CNN, Computer Vision, Violence detection, Weapon detection, YOLO object detection.

INTRODUCTION

Modern technologies are thoroughly assimilated into our daily routine life in the past decade. One of the prominent reasons for this rapid advancement is the consistent breakthrough of innovations in computer science. It is quite clear from the fact that police and law enforcement agencies have been regularly increasing the count of surveillance cameras. This ensures a wider coverage and monitoring of the general population. With a large number of cameras, there comes the great responsibility to monitor them. A conventional approach would be to increase the workforce, but we can assume that this field belongs to computer vision with recent breakthroughs. Recent pioneers in computer vision further promote the feasibility of deploying it and the established network of cameras. Common

* **Corresponding author Devika Bihani:** Computer Science Engineering, Shri Vaishnav Vidyapeeth Vishwavidyalaya, Indore, India; E-mail: devikabihani@gmail.com

Rijwan Khan, Pawan Sharma, Sugam Sharma and Santosh Kumar (Eds.)

threats to the general public are weapon exposure in public places, violent incidents & unreported medical emergencies. This chapter will cover these "threats" in detail. Hence, similar motivations can be derived for detecting other outlier activities like kidnapping, robbery, *etc.*

Motivated by these factors, along with a zeal to build something for society, we came up with a solution that considers the future, past, and present of any calamity. Foremost, detecting a threat is pivotal in averting it, and the first case of our solution is to detect any publicly exposed weapon in which a person might commit a crime. Thus, averting a threat before it converts into a felony. The second case is based on detecting an act of violence in progress and raising an alert. It is not dependent on whether a weapon is being used, as this is targeting violence in the video feed. This case deals with any threat in transit as the event is currently taking place. The last case is specially fabricated to detect any victim who needs medical attention as a part of the aftermath of the mishap. In a lot of cases, it is observed that the victims succumb to their injuries after surviving the tragedy due to the delay in medical treatment provided to them [1 - 3]. In the worst cases, no treatment is provided to them as the onlooker often tends to ignore or hesitate before calling for help for the victim. This way, we propose a system that could target any threat, whether it is life-threatening, on multiple levels, *i.e.*, before its initiation, during it, and providing immediate caution to medical services in the event of an unmitigated threat.

RELATED WORK

There is an established precedent regarding deploying computer vision to identify the basic anatomy of the human body, *i.e.*, movement of the head, arms & legs concerning the torso. Further research in the domain enables pose detection even in a situation where multiple people are involved. These detected poses were in turn, classified as threatening or peaceful depending on different parameters. Understanding the pivotal difference between a person aiming a gun at another and the victim currently in a submissive pose paves a straight path for the authorities to be alerted when threatening actions are taking place. There were 5 instances used in this project, 80% of the algorithm detections for 5 body parts were positive, and 20% that could not be detected had problems because the body parts were not distinguishable due to shadows and arms being very close to the body [4].

The observation occurred during a study at the AGH University of Science and Technology in Krakow, Poland, titled "Automated Detection of Firearms and Knives in CCTV Images". It used computer vision through sliding window mechanisms, background detection, and canny edge detection with already existing surveillance c-+cameras, CCTV cameras provided interesting results. This project worked in the direction of detecting both knives and firearms. The way the Computer-Vision works is that from the frames it has fed, it looks for individuals and once found, it detects the arm of that person to check for the objects of that person. If they are holding any object, it attempts to determine if the objects they have in their hands are knives or firearms by looking into their database of positive and negative results. With a specificity of 94.93% and sensitivity of 81.18% for the knife detection algorithm, the project showed a specificity of 96.69% and 35.98% sensitivity for the firearm detection algorithm in videotapes and CCTV recordings containing lethal objects. The algorithms showed a specificity of 100% for video with harmless objects for firearm detection. This implies that the algorithm will consider all cases detected with 100% firearms whenever detecting any firearms. Not all cases here gave true positives for firearms [5]. From the statistics which were observed during the experiment, it was shown that guns are more detectable objects than knives. These are because of several facts, including the database, which comprised guns and knives or not being of a broader spectrum of situations. For a particular movement in the day time, indoor or outdoor pictures of the weather can be captured. However, the main issue was that they were using images from CCTV recordings and videotapes, which had really low resolution and blurriness because of the poor quality of inexpensive cameras. Due to all these issues in front of the project, they had finally sent an alert to a human who would operate the entire system, and this person would be the responsible one to decide about informing any activity to the cops. To overcome this scenario, one solution is to train algorithms using CCTV videos, and the other would be to take a super-resolution image and process it.

Another parameter that is of great significance is detecting vicious behavior. The usual norm to tackle this problem was to separate descriptors around the fascinating spatiotemporal focus and concentrate measurement highlights inside the movement districts. These advancements are superb and profiling yet have restricted capacity for distinguishing video-based viciousness exercises [6]. The impediments of past advances lead to the proposal of a novel answer for recognizing brutality groupings. Initially, the movement restricts portion according to the dispersion of optical stream fields. Besides the local movements, the proposal to extricate two sorts of low-level highlights to speak to the perception and elements were for fierce practices. The low-level highlights are the Local Histograms (LHOG) of Oriented Gradient descriptors extricated from RGB images. Furthermore, the Local Histogram of Optical Flow descriptor (LHOF) is separated from the optical stream pictures. Thirdly, the extricated highlights are coded utilizing [7] Bag of Words (Bow) model to wipe out repetitive data, and a particular length vector is got for each video cut. Finally, the video-level vectors are ordered by Support Vector Machine (SVM). Test results exhibit that the proposed identification approach is better than the past strategies.

If any violent activity or behavior is observed in any area, it is important to determine the need for a medical emergency in it. Getting proper and early treatment for the injured is essential. Therefore, a vision-based solution can be devised to identify the injured, in which the whole process can be done in two stages, first detecting the person and then classifying the injured.

Both stages will use two different approaches. The first stage will be done using a deep learning-based computer vision method to detect the person. The second stage will be done by using the learning-based Support Vector Machine (SVM) classifier to classify injured people. For the final solution, the researchers suggested combining the YOLOv3 algorithm based on the Convolutional Neural Network (CNN) to identify individuals and a Support Vector Machine (SVM) to classify the injured person [8]. This method gave results with better accuracy than its predecessors. It should be noted that this Medical Emergency Detection can accurately detect any situation with people of different heights, compared to the previous fall detection solutions that fail to differentiate the resting position and actual fall scenarios [9, 10].

PROPOSED METHOD

The proposed solution is tripartite. Video feed received from a surveillance camera is fed to the system. Frames from the video are selected and processed for all 3 use cases, the details of which are further described below. If the results come out positive for the assignment of the threat level on a scale of ten, a snapshot of the same will be stored in the database and sent to the concerned authorities. The report would compromise a snapshot with a timestamp along with the assigned threat level. Threat level assignment depends on the certainty of the weapon detected by the system. We plan to incorporate other factors like uniform and outlier behavior to gauge the threat level and report to the respective authority.

The proposed solution comprises three different modules parallelly in execution, as shown in Fig. (**1**). The entire idea to run these processes in parallel stems from the fact that this system is required to operate in a real-time scenario, 24 hours a day and 7 days a week. Alternative solutions were to consider a system that sequentially processes the data or a singleton model that could supposedly perform all tasks. Sequentially, the processing of video data would hamper real-time detection. It is a possibility that not every machine running this system at local will have sufficient configuration to process all use cases one after another while keeping up with the continuous data flow. Every second is crucial in our scope, and we can't allow any bottlenecks due to an unexpected lag in this system. Therefore, sequential execution was stroke-out.

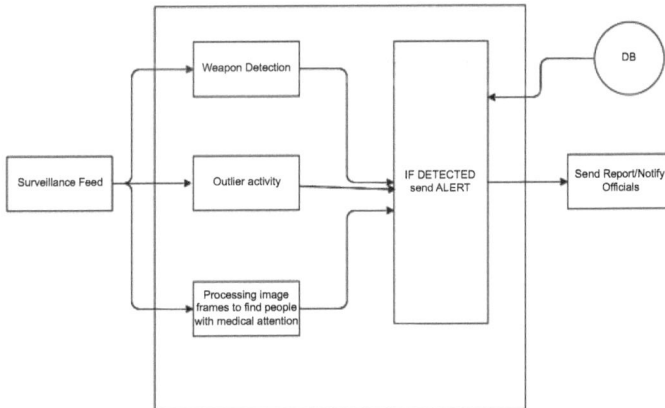

Fig. (1). Proposed system architecture.

Secondly, building a singular model that could generate accurate results quickly across various domains is nothing short of a monumental task in a practical sense. It is theoretically possible and might even generate better results considering ideal conditions, but it would devoid this system of its genuine modularity and flexibility. Now, the main selling point of implementing a parallel processing system is the intersection of ideologies. This system, as mentioned earlier is not limited to the three mentioned use cases. Instead, its ideation was conceived while keeping in mind the prospects and the impact it could generate. Every threat to our society can't be covered in measly three cases. Therefore, the system must be capable of expanding when the system conceives new threats. Parallel execution makes it a simple plug-and-play work in case of expansion of the system according to prospects. This implementation strategy makes it future-ready as well as light-weight so that it becomes simple to implement irrespective of the hardware. The video feed will be processed in real-time, and any anomaly detected by the system will generate an alert while the snapshots are being stored in the database. To dive deeper into the individual aspects of the system, all 3 components are described thoroughly in the following section.

Weapon Detection

We have selected a tiny Yolo model for weapon detection and retrained it on a dataset of handgun images. Yolo, You Only Look Once, is an Object detection system that works at 30 fps in real-time on a Pascal Titan X with an mAP of 57.9% on COCO test dev. YOLOv3 is not only accurate but also works fast, *i.e.*, mAP at .5 IOU YOLOv3 is comparable to Focal Loss, however, about 4x quicker. Tiny YOlo is a smaller version of YOLO to be employed in constrained environments and provides reasonable accuracy of object detection on a variety of datasets.

Weapon detection, as shown in Fig. (**2**), employs two types of datasets firstly, the images from Google, annotated 'using Label image annotation tool'. Secondly, Handgun dataset with the region proposals approaches, which comes with image files and their respective annotations. The challenge faced during the training of the model was that the model was getting stuck at local minima. To resolve this, the adam optimizer comes in handy, it has equipped the model with an adaptive learning rate. The model will detect guns, hence there is just one label - pistol - therefore, the number of filters used is 5*(number of classes+5), 30. Thus, the configuration file for the model consists of 1 class - gun - and 30 filters along with the alternating convolutional and max pool layers.

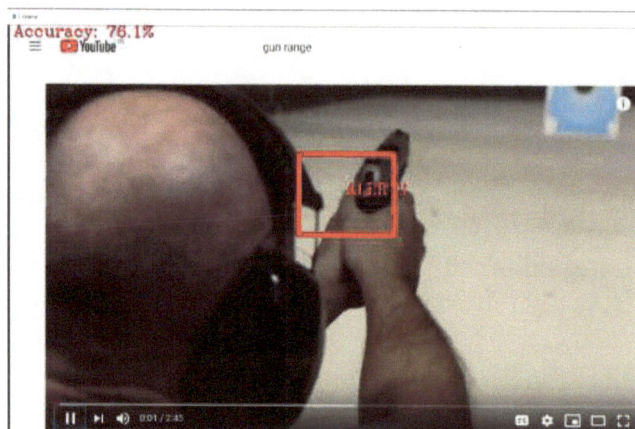

Fig. (2). Weapon Detection.

Violence Detection

Violence detection is one of the keystones of this system. We adopt the method based on a (CNN) Convolutional Neural Network and the (SVM) Support Vector Machine in our solution. This process primarily includes passing the frames through CNN to derive the motion features and understand the violence dynamics. The linear Support Vector Machines (SVMs) are suggested to classify the features, while with the help of the label fusion approach, the performance and accuracy of detection will be improved by synchronizing the appearance and motion information. This method has already been established to yield recent results in previous related research [11, 12]. The results obtained from this proposed system are excellent and can achieve a real-time performance at 30 fps.

To prepare the required model, fight scenes and usual or banal scenes from movies and football games in Fig. (**3**) were employed along with the RWF-2000 dataset -a dataset consisting of video data - consisting of more than 2,000 videos captured by surveillance cameras in a real-world scenario - of violent actions and behaviors in a crowd- to provide more support. These videos were then converted to frames and labeled as violent and nonviolent behaviors to prepare our final dataset, which was used to train the model. This model can currently distinguish between the crowd's usual routine behavior from the abnormal and outstanding one, alerting its officials in case of emergency. Moreover, the brownie point is that with an accuracy of 98.94%, this model can work in surveillance cameras with low video resolution.

Fig. (3). Violent Behaviour Detection.

Medical Emergency Detection

It has been established the general understanding that people collapse when seriously injured. In almost all cases, it has been a common denominator in a majority of the situations. Thus, we decided to detect the falls of a person and if they detect the fall of a person using a model trained on the fall detection dataset as shown in Fig. (4).

Fig. (4). Medical Emergency Detection.

For medical attention detection, **FPDS** - falling person dataset - is taken into account. The FPDS consists of images of a person sitting, walking, sleeping, *i.e.*, doing daily chores along with any unusual activity, like falling at different locations. The dataset consists of Xmin, Ymin, Xmax, and Ymax coordinates that identify people and their labels as 1 and 0, where 1 stands for fall and 0 for not-Fall. Using this csv file, the annotations for each image were created, which were required to train a YOLO model. Since the tiny YOLO with 2 labels - fall and not fall - is used, therefore the number of filters used is 5*(number of classes+5), 35. To the model configuration, While training " consists of 2 classes and 35 filters along with the alternating convolutional and max pool layers.

DATASET & PSEUDOCODE

We have created our own customized model for our project, which is available on the project repository at GitHub and can be accessed from there. The dataset, which was used to train the models, consisted of images of guns, and people who needed medical attention, along with their respective VOC annotation files. The images were obtained from various sources and pre-existing datasets such as RWF-2000 and FPDS and are also scraped from google images, which were then annotated by annotation tools. The dataset also consisted of regular crowd activity along with abnormal activities to facilitate the optical flow or violent crowd flow detection task.

We created three different models for our system to enhance its modularity and make our project reusable and portable. For instance, when an organization's or a person's only need is to use the threat detection system or a medical emergency detection system. They can easily do so by putting the processes running on other threads with different models to rest. Additionally, the different models created can be used distinctly for multiple research or project works.

Brief details on the models which we had trained from our collected database:

1. The .protbuf file is saved to .pb along with its .meta file.

2. The YOLO model for weapon detection was trained on 1000+ images of weapons in various environments and situations.

3. The model for medical need detection consists of over 2000 images.

4. The .mat file can be found for the violent flow detection model, the model is trained on 3000 images.

5. The models are independent of each other to ensure modularity, and it helps us in better training with limited resources

PSEUDOCODE

Input: Live Data Stream

Output: Alert in case of emergency

yoloBased(metafile, protbuf, input)

from darkflow.net.build import **TFNet**

Initialize **tFnet**← Tfnet(meta and protbuf)

for Tfnet.predict(**toFrame(input)**) ←prediction

Store prediction on firebase

if prediction←"Alert"

alertAuthorities()

flowDetect(flowModel, input)

for predict(**toFrame(input)**) ←prediction

Store prediction on firebase

if prediction←"Outlier"

alertAuthorities()

predictFunction()

Switch to case:

case Yolo:

yoloBased(.meta, .pb, input)

case Flow:

flowDetect(.model, input)

CONCLUSION

This system aims to ensure timely detection of a weapon threat, identify any anomalies amongst the crowd, and make sure the medical services are made available to the person in need. This is a computer vision-based project that uses the widespread availability of CCTV cameras. At the same time, this makes the project heavily dependent on CCTV cameras. If they don't provide a complete view of the premises, then the efficiency of the system might decrease.

The system is trained to work in real-time scenarios, therefore, the possibility of false positives and true negatives, however small, exists. Suitable measures have been taken to reduce false alarms and are projected to work in real-time efficiently. If the exposure of weapons to CCTV is very small, then it is a possibility that it might go undetected. This is also an initiative to reduce false alarms so that an alarm is raised only when the threat is certain and imminent.

CURRENT & FUTURE DEVELOPMENTS

Objectively speaking, this project has vast potential if implemented in real scenarios and can be further improved or even customized on the premise of the location being monitored. In real scenarios, it can be further improved or even customized on the premise of the location being monitored.

This project's motto is to identify and mitigate threats to the general public before they turn dangerous while they are under progress and to subdue the aftereffects of a mishap. As such, multiple use cases could be implemented following this philosophy. The general term we use for them is outlier activity detection, *i.e.*, to detect any activity which is out of the ordinary, identify it, and if it turns out to be a threat, then mitigate it by taking appropriate measures. Future developments would mark the addition of more threats into the scope, like kidnapping, mob lynching, riots, *etc.*

Currently, we are working on the detection of the future of any incident. For this, we are planning to collect data samples of people and crowd behavior in their natural and unnatural states, *i.e.*, we are employing flow detection to detect any anomalies or deviations in peoples' behavior to detect any mishap. Moreover, we can use the data model of people's behavior to classify an individual as a culprit, suspicious, or in need of medical attention.

Hence, in short, this work has several possible advantages and would help people and organizations by providing them the security from any mishappenings upon them.

CONSENT FOR PUBLICATION

Not applicable.

CONFLICT OF INTEREST

The authors declare no conflict of interest, financial or otherwise.

ACKNOWLEDGEMENTS

Declared none.

REFERENCES

[1]   K. Bhowmick, and M. Narvekar, "Trajectory Outlier Detection for Traffic Events: A Survey", In: *Intelligent Computing and Information and Communication. Advances in Intelligent Systems and Computing.*, S. Bhalla, V. Bhateja, A. Chandavale, A. Hiwale, S. Satapathy, Eds., vol. 673. Springer: Singapore, 2018.
[http://dx.doi.org/10.1007/978-981-10-7245-1_5]

[2]   A. Bobick, and S. Intille, "Recognizing planned, multi person action", *Comput. Vis. Image Underst.,* vol. 81, no. 3, pp. 414-445, 2001.
[http://dx.doi.org/10.1006/cviu.2000.0896]

[3]   M. Kmiec, and A. Glowacz, "An Approach to Robust Visual Knife Detection", *Mach. Graph. Vis.,* vol. 20, pp. 215-227, 2011.

[4]   J. Dever, L. Niels da Vitoria, and M. Shah, "Automatic visual recognition of armed robbery", *In 2002 International Conference on Pattern Recognition,* vol. 1, IEEE, pp. 451-455, 2002. http://crcv.ucf.edu/papers/robbery.pdf

[5]   M. Grega, A. Matiolański, P. Guzik, and M. Leszczuk, "Automated detection of firearms and knives in a CCTV image", *Sensors (Basel),* vol. 16, no. 1, p. 47, 2016.
[http://dx.doi.org/10.3390/s16010047] [PMID: 26729128]

[6]   P. Zhou, Q. Ding, H. Luo, and X. Hou, "Violence detection in surveillance video using low-level features", *PLoS One,* vol. 13, no. 10, p. e0203668, 2018.
[http://dx.doi.org/10.1371/journal.pone.0203668] [PMID: 30281588]

[7]   L. Fei-Fei, and P. Perona, "A Bayesian hierarchical model for learning natural scene categories", *2005 IEEE Computer Society Conference on Computer Vision and Pattern Recognition (CVPR'05),* vol. 2, pp. 524-531, 2005.
[http://dx.doi.org/10.1109/CVPR.2005.16]

[8]   S. Maldonado-Bascón, C. Iglesias-Iglesias, P. Martín-Martín, and S. Lafuente-Arroyo, "Fallen People Detection Capabilities Using Assistive Robot", *Electronics,* vol. 8, no. 9, pp. 915-21, 2019.

[http://dx.doi.org/10.3390/electronics8090915]

[9]   L.H. Chen, H.W. Hsu, L.Y. Wang, and C.W. Su, "Violence detection in movies", In: *Computer Graphics, Imaging and Visualization (CGIV)*, 2011, pp. 119-124.
[http://dx.doi.org/10.1109/CGIV.2011.14]

[10]   T. Zhang, W. Zhang, L. Qi, and L. Zhang, "Falling detection of lonely elderly people based on NAO humanoid robot", *Proceedings of the 2016 IEEE International Conference on Information and Automation (ICIA)*, IEEE: Piscataway, NJ, USA, pp. 31-36, 2016.
[http://dx.doi.org/10.1109/ICInfA.2016.7831793]

[11]   Q. Xia, P. Zhang, J. Wang, M. Tian, and C. Fei, "Real Time Violence Detection Based on Deep Spatio-Temporal Features", *Chinese Conference on Biometric Recognition,* Springer, Cham, pp. 157-165, 2018.

[12]   T., Thtrieu/darkflow, https://github.com/thtrieu/darkflow

CHAPTER 5

Offbeat Load Balancing Machine Learning based Algorithm for Job Scheduling

Anand Singh Rajawat[1,*], Kanishk Barhanpurkar[2] and Romil Rawat[2]

[1] *Department of CS Engineering, Shri Vaishnav Vidyapeeth Vishwavidyalaya, Indore, India*

[2] *Department of CS Engineering, Sambhram Institute of Technology, Bengaluru, Karnataka, India*

Abstract: In cloud computing environments, parallel processing is required for large-scale computing tasks. Two different tasks are taken, and these tasks are independent of each other. These tasks are independently applied to Virtual Machines (VM). We proposed Offbeat Load Balancing (LB) Machine Learning algorithm using a task scheduling algorithm in Cloud Computing (CC) environments to reduce execution time. In this paper, the proposed algorithm is based on the concept of Random Forest Classifier and Genetic Algorithm and K-Means clustering algorithm for optimized load. The proposed algorithm shows that the average execution time of 3.5104 seconds (20 jobs, 5 Machines) and 15.85 seconds (20 jobs, 10 machines) is based on a study of load balancing algorithms that needs less execution time than other algorithms.

Keywords: Improved Genetic Algorithm, K-Means Algorithm, Machine Learning, Optimization, Random Forest Classifier, Task Scheduling.

INTRODUCTION

Cloud storage services are scarce, so it is not possible for cloud vendors to meet all user demands within a short timeframe. Cloud services must be shared in an equal way such that no job is waiting in queue for the resource, and all resources need to be fully used. It is also a big problem for cloud providers to provide customers with QoS satisfaction.

Standard methods for the allocation of jobs are not sufficient since they lack the versatility of the environment and the scalability of the available resources. A significant benefit of cloud computing is that it offers hardware heterogeneity, predicting the workload to fulfill the objectives of the Cloud Customer Service Level Agreement. The basic aim of resource utilization in the cloud world is to

* **Corresponding author Anand Singh Rajawat:** Department of CS Engineering, Shri Vaishnav Vidyapeeth Vishwavidyalaya, Indore, India; E-mail: kanishkbarhanpurkar@yahoo.com

Rijwan Khan, Pawan Sharma, Sugam Sharma and Santosh Kumar (Eds.)

maximize the income of the cloud supplier and reduce the costs of the cloud consumer.

Cloud computing helps a wide range of customers to use cloud resources free of geographical restrictions. Users send their roles or activities to the cloud system and order cloud services. Scheduling this vast mumber of tasks is a problem for the cloud world due to the need for the shortest possible time of execution along with equal Load Sharing between jobs [1]. The need for a secure and flexible scheme with relatively low overhead is also a core prerequisite for job execution. Another problem with scheduling is Data Locality and Task Relocation (TR) from one node to another at any time. Load balancing is also a crucial parameter for optimum resource sharing to be considered in cloud computing that results in higher QoS and cost benefits. The extremely competitive cloud computing world often poses problems and needs to be constantly tackled as servers become accessible and unavailable while consumer demand varies suddenly. LB is one of the most challenging problems we face right now [2]. LB can be defined as the uniform distribution of workloads at all nodes to avoid a condition where some nodes are overloaded whereas other nodes are overloaded or idle. LB system importantly disturbs the presentation of the system. It is supposed that agents have modern computer programs that work automatically for consumers once too much work is done [3]. Voguish most cases, multiple agents are frequently needed before there are more apps to meet the user's needs resourcefully. Resource management & task scheduling (TS) are the main issues that need to be addressed in CC. Therefore, cloud providers need to define services & implement scheduling policies that allow VMs to deploy & deploy VMs [4]. There are 2 categories of TS in CC; Static TS, dynamic TS, and static scheduling allows the advancement of data & pipelines needed for various performance phases [5]. Static scheduling imposes some runtime overhead. In the case of dynamic scheduling, job mechanisms/task information is not known in advance. Therefore, the performance phase of the task may not be identified & the distribution of tasks to flies while solicitation is consecutive. Several machine learning algorithms were used for job scheduling in a cloud computing environment. The classifying algorithms used with VM scheduler are capable of scheduling each task in a more efficient manner [6]. In IoT-based frameworks, machine learning algorithms play an important role in the scheduling process. It distributes the load in which different tasks are distributed and the load-balancing process will occur [7]. Classification algorithms help in separating the classes from each other within the machine learning domain. Random Classifier algorithm is a machine algorithm based on a classification technique, which is a set of decision trees [8].

The framework of the machine learning algorithms, plays an important role in the scheduling process. It distributes the load in which different tasks are distributed, and the load balancing process will occur [7]. In the machine learning domain, classification algorithms were used to separate different classes which are completely separated from each other. A random Classifier algorithm is a machine algorithm based on the classification technique, which is a set of decision trees [8].

In this paper, the proposed algorithm offers a method for vigorously achieving process-based most favorable load balancing with low computational power. The major contributions to this article are as follows:

1. Incorporate the idea of process-based load balancing in the cloud computing world in contrast to the immediate load balancing techniques in the current literature. The advantages are multiple: to minimize excessive computational overhead and improve implementation reliability when providing service output to customers using a machine learning algorithm.
2. Incorporate the generating algorithm, random forest, and K-means clustering algorithm on the optimum deployment of activities to determine the probabilities of optimal physical hosts.
3. We proposed an Offbeat Load Balancing Machine Learning based Algorithm for Job Scheduling.

RELATED WORK

The static algorithms only use some static information that cannot accurately represent complex load shifts in the host cluster and have low adaptive capabilities. Today, most open-source IaaS platforms have used static algorithms for resource scheduling. Sreelakshmi, S. *et al.* [9] proposed a multi-objective particle cluster optimization for function determination, target time, time frame & communication cost. It has been shown that the proposed method helped to reduce the time & communication cost of the makespan to complete the task on time [10].

This chapter presents a method based on a Parallel Genetic Algorithm (GA) for preparation tasks done in a cloud computing environment. The main goal of the research in this paper is to use all available resources efficiently and reduce the expenditure of resources in cloud computing environments. This can be achieved by refining the LB rate and selecting the best resources to complete the tasks in a short span of time. When our proposed method is implemented, it is replicated through MATLAB software. Two methods are compared, the hybrid agent colony-honey technique and round-robin (RR) scheduling based on LB technique. Y. Samadi *et al.* [11] proposed an algorithm to realize a balanced load in VM by reducing specific applications' makeup. In this application, they increased the initial end time under user-specified financial constraints. Padmavathi M. *et al.* [12] used the services of remote computers & CC servers. Load balancing can be used to balance the load between different systems in a data center using scheduling techniques. They studied and analyzed the current techniques, using an original dynamic & elastic algorithm for performing Load Balancing & Colony Optimization LB between existing systems in data centers. Relative analysis shows that the proposed LB-ACO gives better results than NSGA-II algorithm, providing better LB & less makeup. Simulation has been performed by the CloudSim toolkit [13]. Fang Y. *et al.* [14] proposed VM real-state augmentation agent colony algo (VM-ACO) to resolve the difficult task scheduling in cloud environments. The algorithm takes time to complete the workload balancing. Experiments on CloudSim stage suggest that VM-ACO algorithm executes with a better task latency, task fulfillment time, resource status & polling-based anti-colony algorithm & better scheduling in cloud environments [15]. W. Sun *et al.* [16] took care of the errand planning issue in distributed computing, intermittent ACO based booking algo (PACO) is proposed in this paper. K. Li *et al.* [17] used LB Ant Colony optimization (LBACO) algorithm for the same work. The fundamental commitment of our work is to load the whole framework loads while attempting to limit the cosmetics of a particular work set. Thus, a new booking technique was recreated utilizing CloudSim toolbox bundle. Experimental outcomes improve the proposed LBACO algo FCFS (first cum first service) & basic ACO. A number of researchers used K-means algorithm for load balancing in a cloud computing environment [18]. Below, Table **1** briefly classifies the types of machine learning algorithms with a number of studies carried out in the respective following years.

Table 1. Analysis of various load balancing experiments based on multiple machine learning techniques.

S.No.	Study	Year	Number of Studies	Machine Learning Algorithms
1.	Sui X. *et al.* [19]	2019	2	Genetic Algorithm
2.	Bies R.R *et al.* [20]	2005	47	Hybrid Machine Algorithms
3.	Guo K. *et al.* [21]	2020	2	Genetic Algorithm
4.	Hassanzadeh H. *et al.* [22]	2014	4	Ensemble Learning Algorithms
5.	Toma, R.N. *et al.* [23]	2020	7	Classification Algorithms
6.	Zhou, Y. *et al.* [24]	2020	0	Classification Algorithms

PROPOSED WORK

In a cloud computing environment, the system requires parallel processing for distributing large-scale computing tasks. We include a large task in sub-tasks that are independent of each other and then assign m to VM nodes to perform exactly as shown in Fig. (**1**), & participants to the independent sub-task set D= {d1, d2,..,dn}(di: task i). assign to determine. System usages optimal plan to handle tasks allocated to various source nodes, & we usage R = {r1, r2, ..., r3} (ri: virtual node i) standard. The proposed approach represents the execution speed, and the task length instruction of every resource node signified. It may also allocate every separate job for running in a single virtual node. Thus, each resource node's execution time matrix is presented by *t*. The initial load balancing server delivers the requests stably so that the current calculating resources are not indolent to recover the system. The initial load balancing server delivers the requests stable so that the current calculating resources are not indolent to recover system use.

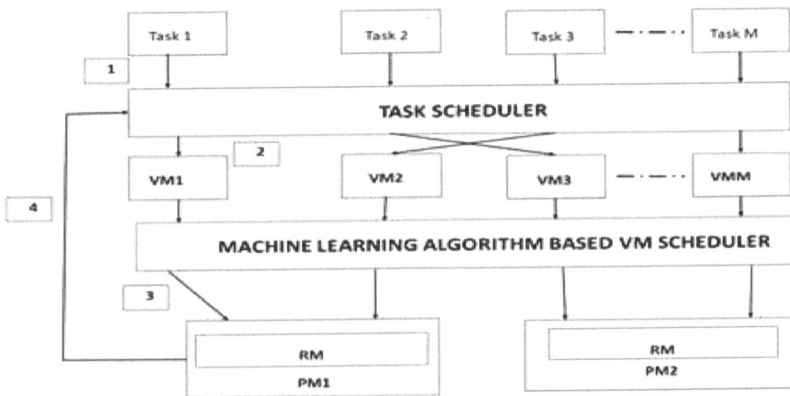

Fig. (1). Flow diagram of Task & VM scheduling in cloud computing.

GA, K-Means clustering (KMC), and RF have strong global search capability to solve such difficulties, nonetheless also defects, e.g., premature & weak local examination capability. Instead, GA K-Means clustering and RF does not have resilient local search ability & premature problems. Thus, the grouping of GA, K-Means clustering, and RF can three overawed drawbacks & implement their advantages & improve their efficiency. This algorithm is also known as an improved genetic algorithm using GA, K-Means clustering, and RF by Offbeat Load Balancing Machine Learning Algorithm for Job Scheduling in Cloud Computing Environment.

HYBRID APPROACH

This algorithm seeks a resource allocation sequence dependent on task criteria and arrivals. As the number of resources and machines is large, we have to find a successful work chain to increase the usage of capital so that it is also high. This paper has also implemented a hybrid algorithm to locate this work sequence in less time. This work is complex in nature as the market for computer workers changes, and the hybrid algorithm (HA (GA, KMC, and RF)) also seeks a better approach.

PRODUCE POPULATION (PP)

In this step of the proposed algorithm, a random combination of the entire work series was created. Hybrid algorithm (HA (GA, KMC, and RF)) has been used in a pattern, which incorporates the optimisation and instructor learning method of the KMC and RF. This is why population production was conducted by the hybrid algorithm (HA (GA, KMC, and RF)) in this step, in which each chromosome is a single sequence of workers. We specified the Number of chromosomes as Q and represented the Number of populations as an N,

PP = Indiscriminate the value of Number of chromosomes and Number of populations as an N.

FITNESS FUNCTION (FF)

This function was conducted to determine any chromosome where each chromosome with the least time is called the better solution. This function is an optimal time for the turnaround time of the job. This can be understood by an example. If 'n' workers work in a batch and the fitness function is turnaround time, then the fitness function is the last task completed by the batch. The amount of time taken (Vinod *et al.*, 2020) by all machines to perform and a job in the batch is the total time taken by (HA (GA, KMC, and RF)).

FF=Compute the turnaround time on the basis of fitness function

NATIVE PREEMINENT (NP)

Input: Produce Population (PP), a specified number of jobs Scheduling (JS)

Output: (HA (GA and RF)), Process running in the basic manner

Step 1: Applying the conditional statement (Check the nearest or local process)

Step 2: CMS <=PP [Number of populations named N]

Step 3: (HA (GA and RF)) Compute the Turnaround time on the basis of Fitness function Fitness (CMS, job Scheduling)

Step 4: Close conditional

Step 5: NP<=Compute the minimum value ((HA (GA and RF)))

The lowest local value serves as the highest global value. This LB and GB is for the (HA (GA and RF)) algorithm, all values are the same for the first iteration.

CROSSWAY

This phase modifies chromosomes to find a new population at work. The generation of these new chromosomes depends on the right chromosome values. As per the hybrid algorithm (HA (GA, KMC, and RF)), the best fitness attribute of a chromosome is adjusted by other solutions. Transverse operations performed as per Z and Y values can be found in the algorithm step above. Thus, the Number of positions Z in chromosome was the best chromosome value to produce a new chromosome.

CMS (Number of populations as an N) <= CROSSWAY (CMS (Number of populations as an N), CMS (Getting the best value after competition), Z).

UPDATE GLOBAL PREEMINENT

At the completion of each iteration, the optimal global value was compared to the latest best local value. Therefore, when the local best value chromosome value is higher than the global best solution means that the chromosome (HA (GA, KMC, and RF)) value is less than the global best value when updated.

RANDOM FOREST TRAINING

As per the sequence of workers, the final set of work sequences for resource use was obtained from the hybrid algorithm (HA (GA, KMC, and RF)). Paper has now learned this sequence collection for input, job, and resource specifications. As a result, input for the (HA (GA, KMC, and RF)) algorithm is pre-processed data [25] and the work sequence derived from a hybrid algorithm (HA (GA, KMC, and RF)). Here the work evolves T number of trees in the forest, as each tree seeks a job location in the execution as per the time of execution needed for the capital.

PROPOSED TRAINING ALGORITHM

Input: Training Dataset

Output: Predicted Class

Training of (HA (GA, KMC and RF)).

Input: Number of free resource for allocation

Output: After the hybrid operation generated, the proper resource allocation policy

Step 1: Number of process for allocation <= perform the preprocessing task

Step 2: CMS = Indiscriminate value of the Number of chromosomes and Number of populations as an N

Step 3: Checked condition (same resource not allocated within the two different process)

Step 4: Compute the fitness of each resource

Step 5: Modified and assign the proper resource for allocation

Step 6: perform the test operation for checking allocation policy

Step 7: Modified and add the proper solution according to internal and external process allocation

Step 8: Terminating condition

Step 9 assigns the all-selected process for decision (Random forest algorithm and k-means clustering)

Above the algorithm, the proposed work stage was defined, where decision trees were created for each job and were projected according to the job resource requirement matrix execution location.

PROCEDURE

In this work, we have applied the concept of Random forest (RF), k-means clustering with genetic algorithm to load balancing optimization problem. First, task loading & computing resources capability is measured. In each physical machine, the dispersion of resource utilization ratio of computing resources occurs while loading large relative balances. Implement Random forest (RF), k-means clustering. This involves launching randomly generated populations & executing individual coding. We start with loading every VM & computing capacity on every PM. Calculate the common value of variance in resource residence as FF. The basic fitness of different individuals & the possibility of each person being selected will be resolved. The individuals selecting the activity will be based on pairs selected by the tournament to transfer certain genes of the two characters and procedure different chromosomes. The two-point transverse functionality optimizes the global search optimization process to eliminate the local optimal solution & specified the optimal solution for the local range. When the mutation function achieves local search optimization, it is gradually switched to an optimum resolution. Here, the single-bit mutation function was performed in a random state. After coding the chromosome, the last problem is for every VM with load. It analyses the task using any user's virtual machine. Therefore, decoding has to be done.

PROPOSED ALGORITHM

Step 1: Start

Step 2: Applying a random number (Random forest (RF), k-means clustering) of tasks allocated to the system in which every task contains loading & computing capacity as in Fig. (**2**).

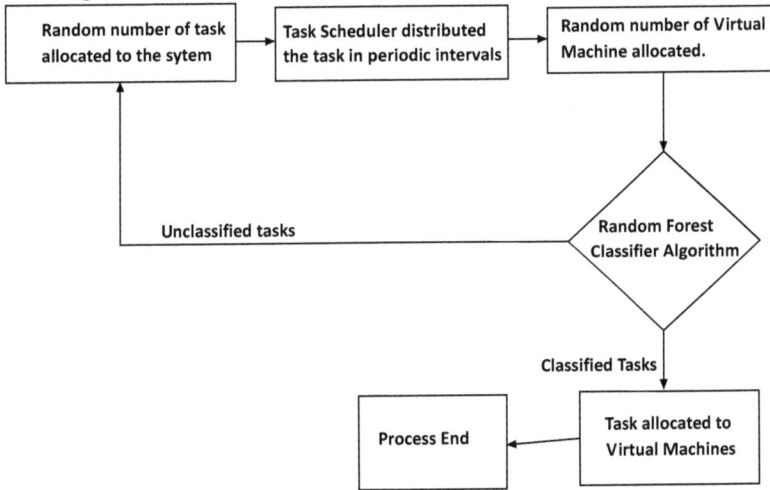

Fig. (2). Algorithm flowchart for random classifier-based algorithm.

Step 3: Task schedulers (TS) distributes the task in regular time interval (TI) and the complete system depends on TI for its distribution.

Step 4: Calculation of net tasks allocated (Random forest (RF), k-means

clustering) (NTA) $= \dfrac{Number\ of\ tasks\ allocated\ to\ scheduler\ (K)}{Total\ Time\ Duration\ (t)}$

Step 5: If NTA> Threshold Value (V_k), then it will wait for other iterations.

Else, it will move to Step 5.

Step 6: Random Number (Random forest (RF), k-means clustering) of virtual machines allotted to perform given tasks.

Step 7: (Random forest (RF), k-means clustering) used for classification.

If task labelled= classified task

Then accept.

Else

Task labelled= unclassified task.

Return to Step 2

Step 8: End

IMPROVED GENETIC ALGORITHM WITH HYBRID ALGORITHM (HA (GA, KMC AND RF))

Load balancing is completed at the first level of work. The work request is consistently dispersed to different physical servers conferring on the required assets, so CC server tasks are executed while maintaining high efficiency. Load balancing using virtual machine distributed physical servers is accomplished at another level. Once the task is received, the server installs a virtual machine that runs each task independently. When a server is overloaded, the virtual machine is moved to the physical machine.

LOAD BALANCING UNDER CLOUD COMPUTING ENVIRONMENT

Assignment booking centred processing assumes a significant job in asset adjusting burden adjusting, and many burden-adjusting methodologies are powerful in assessing asset adjusting. The model built up in this paper depends on figuring the asset equalization of errand booking. To begin with, task stacking and registering assets are estimated. Stacking and figuring will outline the capacity of the asset to create advanced scientific models. The asset proportion of processing assets in each physical machine will be conveyed to figuring assets with the goal that the stacking equalization is not large and moderately adjusted. Assignment stacking estimations are dictated by prescient time and outstanding burden, yet the registering limit of the physical machine is considered, for example, CPU type, recurrence center number, and CPU size.

It calculates the computing source occupancy rate of fleshly machine J

$$OR_j = \frac{L_i}{C_j} \qquad\qquad (1)$$

Here, Lj is the weight of the virtual machine, & cj is the computing power of *j*. Average computing calculation of computing source residence rate for altogether physical machines

$$AOR = \frac{\sum_{i=1}^{n} OR_i}{n} \tag{2}$$

Computing Equations of Differentiation of Computing Resource Business Rate

$$VOR = \frac{\sum_{i=1}^{n}(OR_i - AOR)^2}{n} \tag{3}$$

Here, n represents the number of physical machines. If the VOR is low, the load balancing effect is excellent. Consequently, the objective function of the LB model is min $\{VOR\}$.

RELEVANT OPERATIONS OF GA

1. **Encoding.** GA is being developed to better solve the populace of candidate solutions (named characters) for the optimization problem. With a set of attributes, each individual can alter & alter its own chromosomes or genotype. Traditionally, the solution was represented in binary as strings of 0 & 1 s. The Q_i operator task is mapped to V, $_{mj}$ VM.
2. **Fitness Function (FF).** FF is an exceptional kind of target work utilized to gauge the nature of the spoke to the arrangement. In this investigation, the wellness capacity is characterized as

$$f\ (i) = 1/VOR \tag{4}$$

3. **Selection.** In every successive generation, the Number of the present population is designated for the different populations to grow. Individual solutions are chosen to conclude a fitness-based procedure, wherever fitness resolutions (calculated as a function of fitness) are generally more prospective. Transverse is the process of taking more than one parent & making one of them a child. Transverse is utilized to change the software design of chromosomes or genes of one generation to another. A two-point transverse is utilized in this chapter.
4. **Mutation.** Mutation is utilized to preserve GA of one person to another generation. Mutations in GAS are intended to develop & introduce diversity. Mutation also should prevent populations of individuals from becoming identical to each other to slow down the local minimum or prevent growth.

Simple & efficient mutation functions, *i.e.*, single-bit mutations, are used.

SIMULATION RESULT ANALYSIS

CloudSim is the most effective device that can be utilized to perform demonstration of cloud conditions. There are a number of fundamental segments in Cloudsim engineering which are useful to set up the essential distributed computing condition. This condition is utilized to gauge the adequacy of the assignment booking algorithm. These segments are Data-centre, Data-centre Broker, Virtual Machine, and Cloudlet. The data centre is in charge of giving equipment-level administration to cloud clients. The VM Data-centre Broker makes and dispenses with the requirements of the task. This hides the organization of VM as operator. VM tasks, as in Table **2** are processed according to the policy issued by Cloudlet Scheduler. Cloudlet is a job that works in a virtual machine.

Table 2. Simulation Parameters.

Parameter	Value
No. of server machines	2000
Machine CPU/MIPS	(2500/3000)
Server memory/GB	(4,8)
B&width/Mbps	(50, 100)
No. of VMs	3200
Dem& of VMs	4200
Bandwidth of virtual machines/GB	10-15
Task size/MI	(10000,50000)
No. of tasks	(0,100)

This experimentation groups 2000 physical service nodes & r& arbitrarily produces CPU presentation of every physical server in [2500, 3000] (unit MIPS). Temporarily the presented task length is usually to [10000, 50000] (unit MI), & is used randomly to form each task length. At the same time, suppose that all presented tasks come at a similar time, that is, the time of work is similar. Task deadlines will be randomly produced in [0,100] (units).

Table **3** depicts the number of cloudlets (*i.e.*, 20 cloudlets), that are successful on various virtual machines. It also displays the started time & finished time. Therefore, the total execution time for each cloudlet has been displayed. Similarly, this will be performed for 4, 8, 3, 9, 2, 5, 7, 6, 1, 0, 15, 17, 10, 19, 12, 14, 18, 16, 13, 11 cloudlets. This is the comparison between the improved genetic algorithm (HA (GA, KMC, and RF)) to optimize load balance and the improved genetic algorithm.

Table 3. Load balancing comparison of hybrid algorithms (HA (GA, KMC, and RF)) at 20 cloudlets.

Cloudlet_ID	Status	DataCenter_ID	VM_ID	Finish_Time
4	Success	2	7	4.41
8	Success	2	1	4.50
3	Success	2	4	8.5
9	Success	2	5	8.60
2	Success	2	66	11.32
5	Success	2	46	12.69
7	Success	2	47	14.20
6	Success	2	32	14.44
1	Success	2	43	15.34
0	Success	2	78	17.54
15	Success	2	23	18.54
17	Success	2	20	19.32
10	Success	2	21	20.32
19	Success	2	45	22.21
12	Success	2	32	22.50
14	Success	2	56	22.82
18	Success	2	34	23.10
16	Success	2	55	23.30
13	Success	2	30	23.43
11	Success	2	29	24.30

The user accepts task completion time, task completion time, and operating of task. The completion time of the user indicates the completion time of the task. The intensity of 3 algorithms in CC resource LB is shown in Fig. (**3**), showing the completion time for the last virtual machine. It represents the comparison of the existing improved genetic algorithm for load balancing with the improved genetic algorithm with RF for load balancing at various traffic volumes in cloudlets per second.

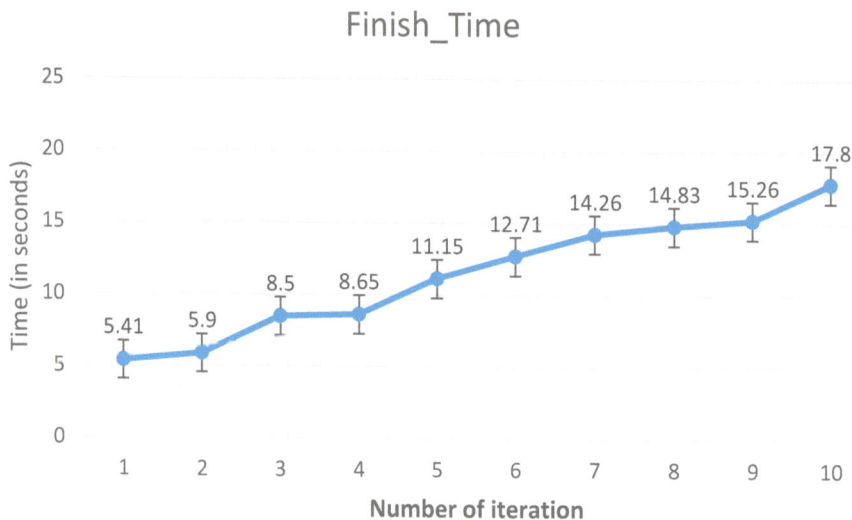

Fig. (3). Time-Span of the hybrid algorithm (HA (GA and RF)).

RESULT ANALYSIS

Table **4** shows that the proposed paradigm of hybrid learning and random forest algorithm cuts the time span of the various work schedules. This reduction of work was achieved by developing the hybrid algorithm (HA (GA, KMC, and RF)) through the transverse operation of instructor learning.

Table 4. (HA (GA, KMC, and RF)) based comparison of load balancing algorithms.

-	Job Sequences	
Algorithms	n= 20 Jobs, 5 machines	n= 20 Jobs, 10 machines
RF	1427	1821
GA	1532	1623
(HA (GA, KMC and RF))	1366	1533

Table **5** found that the suggested model of the hybrid learning and particle swarm optimization algorithm decreases the cumulative flow time of the various job schedules. This reduction of work was achieved by developing the hybrid algorithm (HA (GA, KMC, and RF)) algorithm through the transverse operation of instructor learning.

Table 5. Total flow time based on a study of load balancing algorithms.

-	Job Sequences	
Algorithms	n= 20 Jobs, 5 machines	n= 20 Jobs, 10 machines
RF	15327	17654
GA	25678	29087
(HA (GA, KMC and RF))	13876	17890

Table **6** shows that the suggested paradigm of hybrid learning and random forest algorithm learning and algorithm decreases (HA (GA, KMC, and RF)) the algorithm time of multiple work schedules. This reduction of work was achieved by developing the (HA (GA, KMC, and RF)) algorithm through the transverse operation of instructor learning.

Table 6. (HA (GA, KMC, and RF)). Algorithm average time comparison.

-	Job Sequences	
Algorithms	n= 20 Jobs, 5 machines	n= 20 Jobs, 10 machines
RF	17.6578	9.6787
GA	27.5467	7.9876
HA (GA and RF)	14.8765	6.7689

Table 7. (HA (GA, KMC and RF)) algorithm Average Flow Time comparison.

-	Job Sequences	
Algorithms	n= 20 Jobs, 5 machine	n= 20 Jobs, 10 machine
RF	2.8976	18.654
GA	50.876	60.9087
(HA (GA, KMC and RF))	4.8765	10.897

Table 8. (HA (GA, KMC, and RF)). Algorithm Average Time-based comparison.

-	Job Sequences	
Algorithms	n= 20 Jobs, 5 machine	n= 20 Jobs, 10 machine
RF	19.88	8.8976
GA	36.5643	50.12
(HA (GA, KMC and RF))	7.4563	4.7689

Tables **4** - **8** show that the suggested model decreases the cumulative flow time of various work schedules. This reduction of work was achieved by developing the hybrid algorithm (HA (GA, KMC, and RF)) algorithm through the intersect operation of the instructor.

Conclusion and Future Work

In this chapter, we discuss the load balancing algorithms based on machine learning in a cloud environment. Tournament selection strategy & (HA (GA, KMC, and RF)) have been presented to establish a fitness function model based on traditional genetic algorithms & to advance a better genetic algorithm-based resource loading optimization model. Formerly, we choose CloudSim as the ultimate replication stage to pretend data center virtual resources & users' tasks in the cloud environment. Operator's task completion period & LB are compared with (HA (GA, KMC, and RF)) to optimize load balancing using a better genetic algorithm than a better genetic algorithm. Experimental results suggest that our scheme is better & can be considered a current LB algorithm in cloud location. This takes less execution time than the previous method & is also useful for better resource allocation. Therefore, this study has suggested a hybrid algorithm (HA (GA, KMC, and RF)) model that can classify the collection of task sequences from the input job sequence for different system specifications. Although Random Forest and k-means clustering knows the task execution sequence as per the work resource criteria, further identification of the job sequence has been performed more specifically. Thus, the arrangement of methods increased the operating performance of load balancing.

FUTURE SCOPE

Experiment results reveal that the suggested model decreased the input work matrix by 3.18 percent compared to the hybrid algorithms (HA (GA, KMC, and RF)) and by 5.03 percent compared to another. Further development can be rendered in future studies by invoking deep learning for resource allocation.

CONSENT OF PUBLICATION

Not applicable.

CONFLICT OF INTEREST

The author declares no conflict of interest, financial or otherwise.

ACKNOWLEDGEMENTS

Declared none.

REFERENCES

[1]   E. Ibrahim, N.A. El-Bahnasawy, and F.A. Omara, "Task Scheduling Algo in Cloud Computing Environment Based on Cloud Pricing Models", *World Symposium on Computer Applications & Research (WSCAR)*, IEEE, pp. 65-71, 2016.
[http://dx.doi.org/10.1109/WSCAR.2016.20]

[2]   J-T. Tsai, J-C. Fang, and J-H. Chou, "Optimized task scheduling and resource allocation on cloud computing environment using improved differential evolution algorithm", *Comput. Oper. Res.*, vol. 40, no. 12, pp. 3045-3055, 2013.
[http://dx.doi.org/10.1016/j.cor.2013.06.012]

[3]   M. Li, J. Zhang, and J. Wan, "Distributed machine learning load balancing strategy in cloud computing services", *Wirel. Netw.*, vol. 26, pp. 5517-5533, 2020.
[http://dx.doi.org/10.1007/s11276-019-02042-2]

[4]   N.K. Nair, K.S. Navin, and C.S.S. Chandra, "A survey on load balancing problem & implementation of replicated agent-based load balancing technique", *2015 Global Conference on Communication Technologies (GCCT)*, pp. 897-901, 2015.
[http://dx.doi.org/10.1109/GCCT.2015.7342791]

[5]   M.A.R. Dantas, and A.R. Pinto, "A load balancing approach based on a genetic machine learning algorithm", *19th International Symposium on High Performance Computing Systems and Applications (HPCS'05)*, 2005, pp. 124-130 Guelph, ON, Canada.
[http://dx.doi.org/10.1109/HPCS.2005.8]

[6]   C.A. Gomez, A. Shami, and X. Wang, "Machine Learning Aided Scheme for Load Balancing in Dense IoT Networks", *Sensors (Basel)*, vol. 18, no. 11, p. 3779, 2018.
[http://dx.doi.org/10.3390/s18113779] [PMID: 30400631]

[7]   A. Bala, and I. Chana, "Prediction-based proactive load balancing approach through VM migration", *Eng. Comput.*, vol. 32, pp. 581-592, 2016.
[http://dx.doi.org/10.1007/s00366-016-0434-5]

[8]   R. Díaz-Uriarte, and S. Alvarez de Andrés, "Gene selection and classification of microarray data using random forest", *BMC Bioinformatics*, vol. 7, p. 3, 2006.
[http://dx.doi.org/10.1186/1471-2105-7-3] [PMID: 16398926]

[9]   S. Sreelakshmi, and M. Sindhu, "Multi-Objective PSO Based Task Scheduling - A Load Balancing Approach in Cloud", In: *2019 1st International Conference on Innovations in Information & Communication Technology (ICIICT)*Chennai, India, 2019, pp. 1-5.
[http://dx.doi.org/10.1109/ICIICT1.2019.8741463]

[10]   M. Ashouraei, S.N. Khezr, R. Benlamri, and N.J. Navimipour, "A New SLA-Aware Load Balancing Method in the Cloud Using an Improved Parallel Task Scheduling Algo", *2018 IEEE 6th International Conference on Future Internet of Things & Cloud (FiCloud)*, Barcelona, pp. 71-76, 2018.

[11]   Y. Samadi, M. Zbakh, and C. Tadonki, "E-HEFT: Enhancement Heterogeneous Earliest Finish Time algo for Task Scheduling based on Load Balancing in Cloud Computing", In: *2018 International Conference on High Performance Computing & Simulation (HPCS)* Orleans, 2018, pp. 601-609.
[http://dx.doi.org/10.1109/HPCS.2018.00100]

[12]   M. Padmavathi, and S.M. Basha, "Dynamic & elasticity ACO load balancing algo for cloud computing", In: *2017 International Conference on Intelligent Computing & Control Systems (ICICCS)* Madurai, 2017, pp. 77-81.

[13]   "Load Balancing Based Task Scheduling with ACO in Cloud Computing", In: *2017 International Conference on Computer & Applications (ICCA)*, Doha, 2017, pp. 174-179.

[14]   Y. Fang, and X. Li, "Task Scheduling Strategy for Cloud Computing Based on the Improvement of Ant Colony Algo", In: *2017 International Conference on Computer Technology, Electronics & Communication (ICCTEC)*Dalian, China, 2017, pp. 571-574.

[http://dx.doi.org/10.1109/ICCTEC.2017.00129]

[15]   S. Aslanzadeh, and Z. Chaczko, "Load balancing optimization in cloud computing: Applying Endocrine-particale swarm optimization", In: *2015 IEEE International Conference on Electro/Information Technology (EIT)*, Dekalb, IL, 2015, pp. 165-169.
[http://dx.doi.org/10.1109/EIT.2015.7293424]

[16]   W. Sun, N. Zhang, H. Wang, W. Yin, and T. Qiu, "PACO: A Period ACO Based Scheduling Algo in Cloud Computing", In: *2013 International Conference on Cloud Computing & Big Data,* Fuzhou, 2013, pp. 482-486.
[http://dx.doi.org/10.1109/CLOUDCOM-ASIA.2013.85]

[17]   K. Li, G. Xu, G. Zhao, Y. Dong, and D. Wang, "Cloud Task Scheduling Based on Load Balancing Ant Colony Optimization", In: *2011 Sixth Annual Chinagrid Conference,* Liaoning, 2011, pp. 3-9.
[http://dx.doi.org/10.1109/ChinaGrid.2011.17]

[18]   J. Chen, K. Li, Z. Tang, K. Bilal, S. Yu, C. Weng, and K. Li, "A Parallel Random Forest Algorithm for Big Data in a Spark Cloud Computing Environment", *IEEE Trans. Parallel Distrib. Syst.,* vol. 28, no. 4, pp. 919-933, 2017.
[http://dx.doi.org/10.1109/TPDS.2016.2603511]

[19]   X. Sui, D. Liu, and L. Li, "Virtual machine scheduling strategy based on machine learning algorithms for load balancing", *J Wireless Com Network,* vol. 160, p. 2019, 2019.
[http://dx.doi.org/10.1186/s13638-019-1454-9]

[20]   V. Patidar, S.S. Shrivastava, and S.K. Gupta, "Random Forest Dynamic Load Balancing Using Hybrid Genetic Algorithm", *Int. J. Grid Distrib. Comput.,* vol. 13, no. 1, pp. 2865-2879, 2020.

[21]   K. Guo, M. Yang, and H. Zhu, "Application research of improved genetic algorithm based on machine learning in production scheduling", *Neural Comput. Appl.,* vol. 32, pp. 1857-1868, 2020.
[http://dx.doi.org/10.1007/s00521-019-04571-5]

[22]   H. Hassanzadeh, T. Groza, A. Nguyen, and J. Hunter, "Load Balancing for Imbalanced Data Sets: Classifying Scientific Artefacts for Evidence Based Medicine", In: *PRICAI 2014: Trends in Artificial Intelligence.,* Pham D.N, Park SB, Eds., vol. 8862. Springer, Cham, 2014.
[http://dx.doi.org/10.1007/978-3-319-13560-1_84]

[23]   R.N. Toma, A.E. Prosvirin, and J.M. Kim, "Bearing Fault Diagnosis of Induction Motors Using a Genetic Algorithm and Machine Learning Classifiers", *Sensors (Basel),* vol. 20, no. 7, p. 1884, 2020.
[http://dx.doi.org/10.3390/s20071884] [PMID: 32231167]

[24]   Y. Zhou, N. Zhou, L. Gong, and M. Jiang, ""Prediction of photovoltaic power output based on similar day analysis", genetic algorithm and extreme learning machine", *Energy,* vol. 204, p. 117894, 2020.
[http://dx.doi.org/10.1016/j.energy.2020.117894]

CHAPTER 6

A Pattern Optimization for Novel Class in Multi-Class Miner for Stream Data Classification

Harsh Pratap Singh[1,*], **Vinay Singh**[2], **Divakar Singh**[3] and **Rashmi Singh**[4]

[1] *CSE, SOE, SSSUTMS, Sehore, India*

[2] *CSE, SISTEC Gandhinagar, Bhopal, India*

[3] *CSE, BUIT, Bhopal, India*

[4] *MIS Head Trident Group, Hosangabad, India*

Abstract: Stream data classification involves a predicament of new class generation through pattern evaluation. The evaluation process of the pattern raised new ways of data classification. The evolving decoration discrepancies dispensed the session for rivulet data arrangement. Now, the twisted pattern fashions innovative classes for cataloging progression. For this method of regulation, multi-class sapper method is used. A catastrophic spread of new decorating appraisal methods for multiclass mine workers is used nowadays. We cast off the pattern optimization performance using a transmissible algorithm aiming at the group of patterns and their heightened process for instructing multiclass. The enhanced pattern stables the new class while enhancing the successful multiclass miners. For the empirical appraisal, we used health care data such as cancer and some other deride for the evolutionary progression of the pattern optimization process.

Keywords: Feature evaluation, Genetic algorithm, Pattern, Stream data classification.

INTRODUCTION

Stream data classification is a basic personality in stream data organization. The component examination technique of stream information instigates a problem for the course of action, for example, boundless length [1]. Hence, it is not potential to store the information and use it for preparation. The boundless term, idea development, and idea float are the principal challenges in information streaming [2]. The endless durational issue isolates the stream into equivalent estimated pieces so that each lump is put away in memory and handled on the web. Each

---

* **Corresponding author Harsh Pratap Singh:** CSE, SOE, SSSUTMS, Sehore, India; E-mail: drharshprataps@gmail.com

Rijwan Khan, Pawan Sharma, Sugam Sharma and Santosh Kumar (Eds.)

lump is used for preparing association models when each example in the piece is renamed. Idea float occurs when the view of time changes bigger than normal time. Idea development happens when new classes are embroiled in the information. The ensemble arrangement framework is utilized to recognize the episode of the idea, float, and immense estimation, where every classifier is set up with a novel class indicator. In this method, an agreeable set of mockups is utilized to organize the unlabeled information, notwithstanding identifying novel classes [3]. Each model in the get-together is assessed and it was then estimated that old, obsolete models are not vital. The information stream is isolated by getting shared by indistinguishable sizes called pieces, and the assortment characterizes the information point encompassed by the lumps. Each outer stream is checked with an anomaly module. If there is a production of an exception, it is additionally put away from the boundary. However, on the chance that an exception is not made in vagueness, it is named a predominant period utilizing an assortment strategy. Ensemble procedures need to streamline tasks to some degree to change the current impression of their single model partners and handle the idea. An information stream multiclass digger is utilized further to identify the novel class front line. Multiclass excavator is a gathering of OLINDDA and FAE approaches. This gathering works with a dynamic example course sees novel classes. OLINDDA is utilized to detect the novel class using FAE arrangement of the information lumps. MCM identifies exception plans and is furthermore utilized in perceiving novel class occurrences. MCM is the quickest technique in all datasets [4]. MCM is generally 25% quicker than the Mine Class. For the updating of the assortment cycle of the new property process, the step design framework was utilized by intrinsic calculations. Put away example practice is an improvement of a characteristic example that blended during the examination of another class. To store design creation, a specific point genetic capacity is used. The genetic capacity pedals are put away as an example for the evaluation of highlights [3], where the paper respites are structured as surveys. In Sector-II, the confer-related work is for stream classification discussing Sector III for proposing a technique. Sector IV offers a comparative result of the methods followed by a conclusion in Sector V.

RELATED WORK FOR STREAM CLASSIFICATION

In this area, the discourse strategy is pointed to partner downpour information for limiting and eliminating reprobates like limitless length information, float impression assessment, and example assessment. Each one of these techniques gathers such issues. Yan-Nei Law and Carlo Zaniolo [5] assign a strategy for stream information order by adjusting the lining groupings. This happens as the procedure achieves uncommon execution by devouring more modest arranged ventures, where examination mistake areas are sure to terminate with each consistent size. Mohammad M. *et al.* [4] articulates an act of stream information association by novel meeting acknowledgment. In Concept-Drifting Data Streams Under Time Limitations as novel class acknowledgment delinquent revamps moving in the sign of idea float after the vital information spread improvement in streams. Qing Chen *et al.* [3], in this strategy, articulate an interaction of stream information arrangement by Concept-Evolution worry of unique classes advancing in the stream. This inside Concept-Drifting Data Stream as Concept-advancement happens as a meaning of new classes undeveloped in the stream. This interaction discusses the idea of advancement in computation up to the close to the face of limitless length, moreover idea float. Valerio *et al.* [6] creator expected a technique for stream information characterization by Kernel-Based keen Cooperative Learning as kernel practice allowed the portrayal of setting up information during information calculations, though they are computationally troublesome. In this cycle, Li Su Xi *et al.* [7] depicts an act of stream information order through associative arrangement (AC). These affiliated groupings depend on relationship rules uncovering colossal embraces over various other characterization procedures on still datasets. Earth Woolam *et al.* [8], in this procedure, portrays a strategy for stream information arrangement by creating stream information with restricted names. The reason is convenient as it assumes a little division of occasions in the stream to be marked. Mohammad M. Masud, Qing Chen, Jing Gao, Latifur Khan, Jiawei Han, and Bhavanim Thuraisingham [3] are a portion of the creators who depicted the technique for stream information arrangement by DXMiner. It addresses the four most basic conflicts with order information streams unequivocally with the boundless span, idea float, idea advancement, and example development. Information streams are implicit and long, used for single-pass steady with versatile hierarchical strategies. Idea float happens in an information stream, albeit the essential hypothesis changes over time. Most introduced information stream order procedures address singular endless length and idea float issues. [Charu C. Aggarwal, Jiawei Han, Jianyong Wang, Philip S. Yu] [9]. This model reproduces the genuine requirements ingeniously since it gets stricken to categorize examination streams in exact time in the pointless of an expanding direction and exploration stream.

Xiangjun Li *et al.* [10] expected a requesting and novel class appreciation calculation dependent on the cohesiveness and takeoff record of Mahalanobis separation. The preliminary results show that the calculations capably mitigated the effect of idea float on characterization and novel class uncovering.

K. Vasantha *et al.* [11] extended a novel approach of the Concept Drift Detector and Resampling Ensemble (CDRE), assessing calculation for dazzling culpable of discernment float in multi-class. Mis-arrangement falls irregularly because of harshness, proportion, and information conveyance. It carried out definite investigations based on dissimilar degrees of disparity proportion and information dispersal. There is a decrease in precision when multiclass issues struggle with the origination float as well. When likened to an ordinary multiclass disparity delinquents, the class lopsidedness delinquent with insight float is noticed. The Concept Drift Detector and Resampling Ensemble (CDRE) calculation was performed to bargain the origination float's multi-class troubles. CDRE calculation shows altered results in recognition accuracy and F-measure with a normal 85% as related to calculation denied of enhancement.

PROPOSED ALGORITHM FOR PATTERN CLASSIFICATION IN MCM

In this area, we converse the change of multi-class minor algorithm with genetic algorithm. Genetic algorithm is a heuristic function; the idea of the genetic calculation is single unbiased for enhancement of the accepted issues. In a multi-class digger, genetic calculations are utilized for producing fixed examples for the signature characters of a novel class. Keeping examples of a genetic calculation offers the element assortment advancement while discovering the elements diverse in stream information measure, reviewing a put-away examples in grouping. The strategy of multi-class minor continues with the diagram crossing framework on the side of bunching and order. In the strategy of MCM, the diagram points to the number of examples [4] of point combinations carried out by genetic calculation. The cycle of improved MCM with put-away example is portrayed here:

Input: N_list: List of novel class events

Output: N_type: predicted class label of novel instances

1: G = (V, E) ←empty //initialize graph

2: NP list ← K-means (N list, Kv)

3: Input NP, list x, the clustering number cn, inhabitant scale XN, crossover probability cP, mutation probability mP, Pattern probability vP, stop condition cS;

4: Code the chromosome in real numbers and initialize population A(i), i= 0 at random;

5: Determine the fitness of each individual in the existing instant;

6: MCM amass creates accrue patterns for classification, which designate the unearth unrelated attribute clusters. Subsequently, the fitness function of the algorithm is determined by f(x).

7: $F(x) = \{(\alpha + 2\beta) - \alpha i, \ \alpha i < \beta + 2\alpha$

1. $0, \ \alpha i \geq \alpha i + 2\beta$

2. $I = 1, 2, \dots\dots\dots\dots\dots\dots, N$

8: Evaluate the termination conditions. If the execution environment is fulfilled, trail by turn to step 9, or else, turn to step 10;

9: Decide to uncover and determine the optimal clustering and blueprint matrixes. And set the optimal clustering designed for classification.

10: Do the parallel intersect and alteration procedure on population A(i), then we can search out population B(i), C(i), respectively;

11: Carry out the genetic variety of the moment unruffled of population A(i), B(i), C(i) and population D(i) is got;

12: Proceeds the MCM optimization on population D(i) and engender the subsequent generation A(i+1). Formerly turn to step

13: for h $\in$ A(i+1) do

14: h.nn $\leftarrow$ Nearest-neighbor (A(i+1)- {h})

15: h.sc $\leftarrow$ Compute-SC (h, h.nn)

16: V$\leftarrow$V $\cup$ {h}

17: V$\leftarrow$V $\cup$ {h.nn}

18: if h.sc <thsc then

19: E$\leftarrow$E $\cup$ {(h,h.nn)}

20: Endif

21: end for

22: count $\leftarrow$ Con-Components (G) for each pair of components (g1, g2) $\in$ G do

23: $\mu 1 \leftarrow$mean-dist (g1), $\mu 2 \leftarrow$mean-dist (g2)

24: if $\frac{\mu_1 + \mu_2}{2*centroid\_dist(g1,g2)} > 1$ then g1$\leftarrow$Merge (g1, g2)

25: end for

// Now allocate the class labels

26: N_type ← empty

27: for x∈Nlist do

28: h ← Pattern-recallOf (x)

29: N_type ← N_type ∪ {(x, h.componentno)}

30: end for

Fig. (1) shows the process block diagram of multi-class pattern miner that is proposed here.

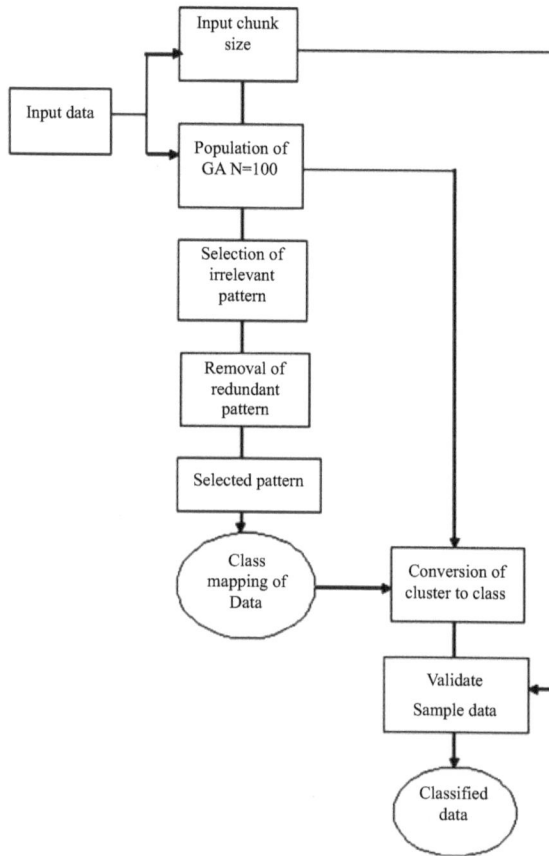

Fig. (1). The process block diagram of multi-class pattern miner.

RESULT ANALYSIS

To assess the presentation of MCM and MCM-Pattern, we simulated our algorithm in MATLAB 7.8.0 and, for the test of the outcome, using the UCI machine mutuality data set. Here, we used three data sets: cancer, breast cancer, and skin disease data set. For measuring the performance, the following parameter is Fnew, Mnew and the error rate of classification is used.

Fig. (**2**) shows the executing time for classification for MCM and MCM-Pattern. (It increases the loss of feature attributes for the dissimilar patterns in the case of the MCM technique).

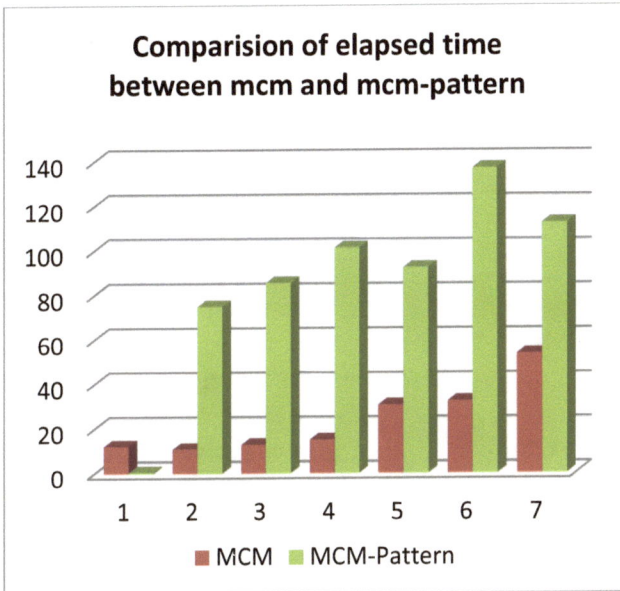

Fig. (2). Classification for MCM.

Fig. (**3**) shows that the comparative feature evaluation process for novel class detection is based on MCM and MCM-Pattern processes. (The result shows that pattern-based techniques for feature evaluation evolved more relevant features instead of MCM).

Comparision of FNew time between mcm and mcm-pattern

■ MCM   ■ MCM-Pattern

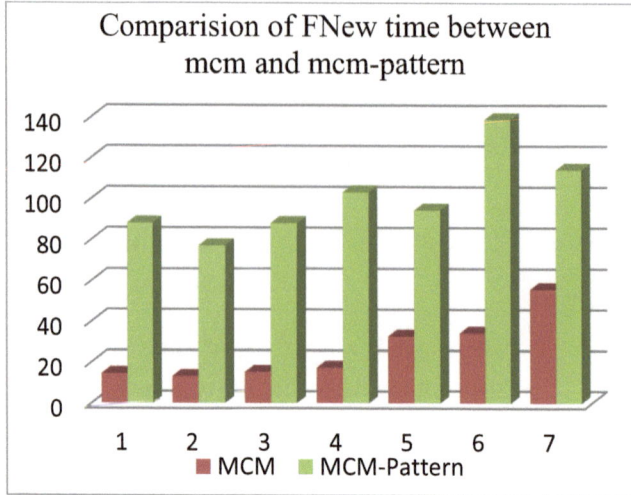

Fig. (3). Comparative Feature Based on MCM.

Fig. (**4**) shows a comparative feature evaluation process for novel class detection based on MCM and MCM-Pattern processes. The result shows that pattern-based techniques for feature evaluation evolved more relevant features instead of MCM.

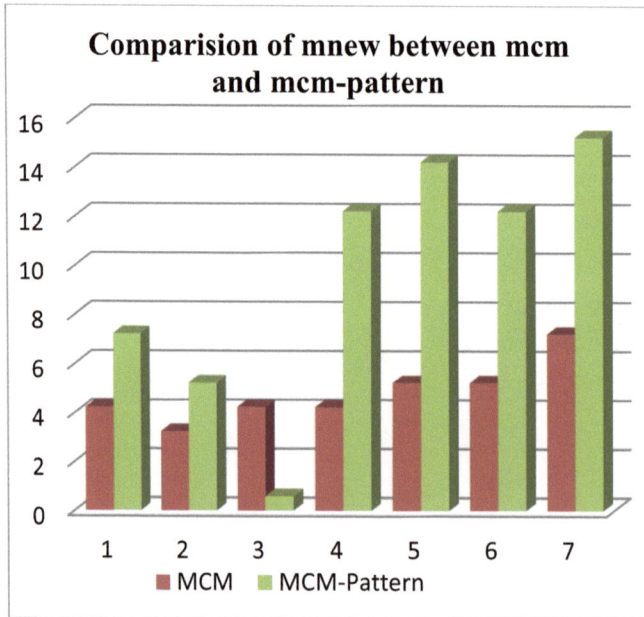

Comparision of mnew between mcm and mcm-pattern

■ MCM   ■ MCM-Pattern

Fig. (4). Comparative feature detection based on MCM.

CONCLUSION

In this research, the pattern evolution process is applied to multi-class miners. The pattern evaluation process is functional with a genetic algorithm in the clustering method for classification. The pattern processing intensifications evaluate Fnew and Mnew features on behalf of the stream data organization. The empirical evaluation of the improved algorithm is the recovery of the MCM algorithm in compression. The error rate of the improved algorithm decreases in the density of the MCM algorithm and finally enhances the rate of Fnew and Mnew for the evolution of the result.

CONSENT FOR PUBLICATION

Not applicable.

CONFLICT OF INTEREST

The authors declare no conflict of interest, financial or otherwise.

ACKNOWLEDGEMENTS

Declared none.

REFERENCES

[1]   U. Bhowan, "Evolving diverse ensembles using genetic programming for classification with unbalanced data", *IEEE Trans. Evol. Comput.,* vol. 17, no. 3, pp. 368-386, 2012.
[http://dx.doi.org/10.1109/TEVC.2012.2199119]

[2]   M. Masud, "Addressing concept-evolution in concept-drifting data streams", *IEEE Transaction,* 2010.
[http://dx.doi.org/10.1109/ICDM.2010.160]

[3]   Q. Chen, ""Classification and Novel Class Detection of Data Streams in a Dynamic Pattern Space", in ISMIS", *LNAI,* vol. 5722, p. 552, 2009.

[4]   M. Masud, "Classification and novel class detection in concept-drifting data streams under time constraints", *IEEE Trans. Knowl. Data Eng.,* vol. 23, no. 6, pp. 859-874, 2010.
[http://dx.doi.org/10.1109/TKDE.2010.61]

[5]   Y-N. Law, and C. Zaniolo, "An adaptive nearest neighbor classification algorithm for data streams", In: *European Conference on Principles of Data Mining and Knowledge Discovery.* Springer: Berlin, Heidelberg, 2005.
[http://dx.doi.org/10.1007/11564126_15]

[6]   G. Valerio, and A. Sperduti, "Kernel-Based Selective Ensemble Learning for Streams of Trees", In: *Proceedings of the Twenty-Second International Joint Conference on Artificial Intelligence.,* 2010.

[7]   Li Su, Liu Hong-yan, and Song Zhen-Hui, "A new classification algorithm for data stream", *IJ Modern Education and Computer Science,* vol. 4, pp. 32-39, 2011.

[8]   C. Woolam, M.M. Mohammad, and K. Latifur, "Lacking Labels in the Stream: Classifying Evolving Stream Data with Few Labels", In: *International Symposium on Methodologies for Intelligent Systems* Springer: Berlin, Heidelberg, 2009, pp. 552-562.

[9]   C.C. Aggarwal, ""A Framework for On-Demand Classification of Evolving Data Streams" in ECML PKDD, Part II", *LNAI,* vol. 6322, pp. 337-352, 2010.

[10]   X. Li, "A classification and novel class detection algorithm for concept drift Data stream-based on the cohesiveness and separation index of mahalanobis distance", *Journal of Electrical and Computer Engineering,* 2020.
        [http://dx.doi.org/10.1155/2020/4027423]

[11]   K. Vasantha Kokilam, "Learning of Concept Drift and Multi-Class Imbalanced Dataset using Resampling Ensemble Methods", *Int. J. Recent Technol. Eng,* vol. 1332, no. 1340, 2019.

CHAPTER 7

Artificial Intelligence in Healthcare: on the Verge of Major Shift with Opportunities and Challenges

Nahid Sami[1,*] and **Asfia Aziz**[1]

[1] School of Engineering Science and Technology, Jamia Hamdard, New Delhi, India

Abstract: In the last few decades, artificial intelligence (AI) has shown rapid growth in medicine with the evolution of computer vision, robotics, natural language processing, and deep neural networks. The technology has also been applied to healthcare with an inexact thought that AI will replace the workforce. AI works as a helping hand for human clinicians because a machine can never replace a human brain. Present healthcare systems can implement AI technology for diagnosing patients and their treatments, drug invention, prediction of disease outbreaks, real-time monitoring of critical patients, radiology, and many more. The latest achievements by Google for the diagnosis of cancer, and diabetic retinopathy by JAMA using deep learning algorithms and surgical robots show substantial shifts in medicine. A simple assessment of electronic health records (EHR) provides more opportunities for the medical experts during the invention and application of improving medicines. The coming future of health care depends on the advancement of AI. However, with ease comes difficulty, such as the privacy of data and causality problems which should be considered when deploying such strategies.

Keywords: Artificial Intelligence (AI), Deep Learning (DL), Medicine epidemiology, Natural Language Processing (NLP), Neural Network, Support Vector Machine (SVM).

INTRODUCTION

Artificial Intelligence (AI) has a tremendous capacity to perform in science and technology. It has already over-ruled almost every sector of society, whether it is social, economic, or industrial. It helps to communicate ideas to society with a large range of algorithms for making life easier. The science behind AI provides a large amount of data in the electronic form of the algorithm to achieve a certain conclusion. AI can make better use of the data to improve the quality of care people need. The beginning of the 21st century has marked its rapid growth in the field of healthcare and medicine [1]. It has created a large confusion among

* **Corresponding author Asfia Aziz:** School of Engineering Science and Technology, Jamia Hamdard, New Delhi, India; E-mail: asfiaaziz@jamiahamdard.ac.in

Rijwan Khan, Pawan Sharma, Sugam Sharma and Santosh Kumar (Eds.)

people that it may replace physicians in the future, but this is not true because a machine will never overcome a doctor's brain, and in the end, a patient can always need a human touch. Instead, it will make the work easier, like diagnosis, treatment, or keeping a real-time record of critical patients. Medical health records are a massive collection of data in healthcare organizations. Searching for important hidden information within these data is a tedious job that can be done in seconds by using AI technology. Eventually, AI will make our work fast with accuracy, further helping in decision-making [2].

AI algorithm has the potential to improve pathology to enhance the service required by the patient. There are algorithms that can detect cancer and improve the performance with accuracy. Such algorithms work faster than human pathologists and make their tedious, time-consuming tasks easier, saving an enormous amount of time that can be utilized later by doctors to focus on more high-level intellectual tasks. AI technology can learn from a large amount of healthcare data and further implement it for future use. Its self-learning capability from feedback makes it more accurate with time. It can assist physicians in providing ideal care for patients and further reducing therapeutic and diagnosis errors. AI has proved its patronizing execution in many fields like translation and recognition of speech, classification of images and objects, detection, decision-making in sport and law [3]. Due to the results shown by AI technology, radiologists have been advised to use it while performing diagnoses over medical images.

Fig. (**1**) shows different areas which have been empowered by AI technology. There are various algorithms like Natural Language Processing (NLP), the concept of Neural networks, machine learning (ML) techniques, *etc.*, using the models for building and working accordingly. The vast section of medical data management has become easier and available in a real-time environment with security. Treatment plans can be easily designed to reduce the waiting time of patients. Drug creation has also been highly affected to make it available earlier than ever before. Medication can be easily managed as it depends less upon human interaction and more upon smarter machines. The benefits of AI cannot be ignored as it affects the pharmaceutical industry, clinicians, as well as patients. In the next few decades, it will improve the sector greatly for the betterment of society.

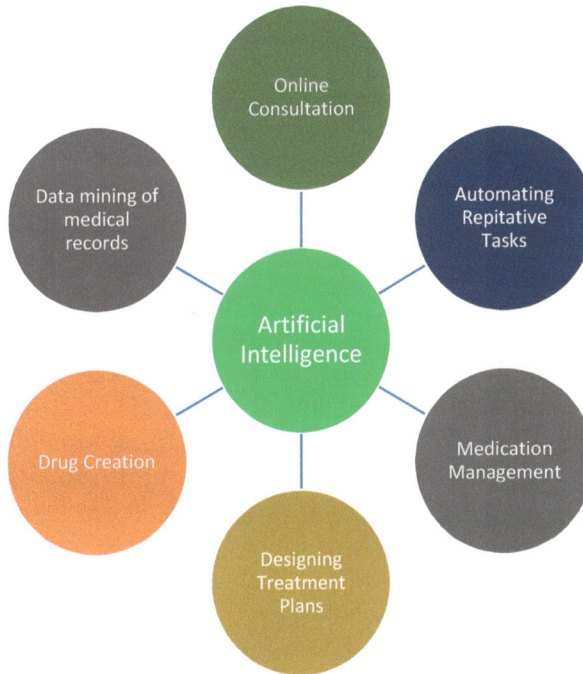

Fig. (1). Impact of Artificial Intelligence in Healthcare.

Why AI in Healthcare

In recent years, there has been an integration of technology in all realms of life, and healthcare has been no exception. Technology has infiltrated virtually all aspects of healthcare, starting from patient data records to diagnosing, biomedical investigation, research, pharmacotherapy, and even assisted living at home for the elderly and differently-abled. According to Frost &Sullivan, AI systems are projected to be a $ 6 billion industry by 2021, and McKinsey predicted healthcare to be one of the top five industries using AI. With such forecasting, AI is definitely a game-changer, poised to be the transformational force of the future.

AI, a concept of the 1950s, aims to teach machines to think like humans, here machines think like human minds in learning and analysis but much faster and with greater accuracy and thus work in problem-solving. This kind of intelligence is also referred to as machine learning [4]. AI has a software as well as hardware components. The software part deals with algorithms having a conceptual framework for executing AI algorithms in a sequence functioning like the neurons of the brain, hence called the neural network. These NNs have been devised to do supervised, unsupervised, and reinforced learning with increased computational power, even deep learning. The hardware component provides a computational platform in a multithread or multicore configuration using GPUs along with customisable accelerator and hardware platforms such as field-programmable gate arrays (FPGAs) and application-specific integrated circuits (ASICs) such that a customised application can run more efficiently [5].

Artificial Intelligence and high-performance computing is redesigning healthcare, bringing in a new era of precision medicine. The health care industry is quickly taking advantage of AI/ML and deep learning. Medical applications are used in medicine to accelerate and improve patient recoveries. Automation, cloud technology, and screw line are more important than ever before. Machine Learning diagnoses conditions through medical imaging, cloud sources medical data and suggests treatment and drug development. This matters when diagnosis and treatment depend on quickly and actively interpreting MRI, CT scans and X-rays to identify tumours, fractures, and medical conditions. With the advances in deep learning driven by the invention of powerful GPU accelerators, the medical industry is heading towards even more sophisticated approaches such as certified medicine, wearable medical devices, and automated robotic surgery, with researchers and start-ups already beginning to improve accuracy in medical imaging and cardiac analysis.

The benefits of AI in medicine have been discussed [6] with the help of big data in combination with advanced computing techniques for the diagnosis and treatment of cardiac disease. Its ability to learn features from large healthcare data and then practical implementation makes it a sophisticated algorithm with better accuracy due to self-correcting features feedback. In addition, errors related to diagnosis and therapeutic were removed to a greater extent [7].

Fig. (2) shows the various services that a patient will enjoy while applying AI techniques in medicine. It will be convenient for the patient to make appointments as data are stored online and faster too. Moreover, the payment process has become more convenient and saves a lot of time standing in a queue waiting for their turn. Updating clinical data will be less tedious as it is not restricted to the manual and can be done digitally. The physicians will be able to look after a greater number of patients in less time duration because of the available data.

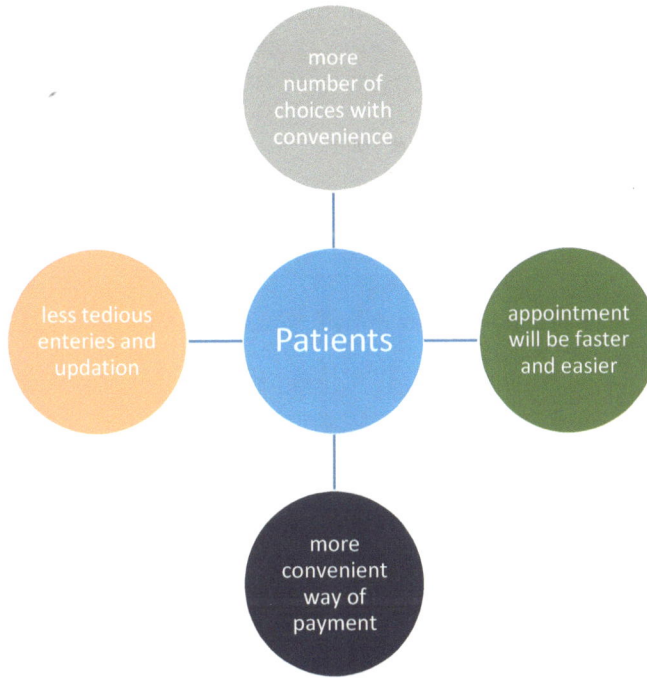

Fig. (2). Showing the self-service benefits of patients.

The traditional model built using AI technique for clinical purposes will help in the diagnosis, prognosis, and further treatment. The interpretation of medical images using AI tools serves an important role in diagnosing diseases. Medical health records help in prognosis by predicting the mortality rate. The AI model plays a major role in predicting treatment effects on individual patients.

AI TECHNIQUES IN HEALTHCARE

Machine Learning

Machine learning being a subset of AI provides many tools to tackle medicinal issues. ML is more accurate, scalable, and actionable regarding predictive and perspective real-time decision making. It is considered more accurate than the physician regarding storing previous information and deciding on the basis of the earlier and present condition of the patient. It is scalable because no one can recall everything about everyone. ML predicts the attributes of the patient automatically by storing and managing a large amount of healthcare data.

In Fig. (3) a machine learning model is built for medicinal purposes. Firstly, the historical healthcare data is collected and fed into the appropriate machine learning algorithm to learn the features and build a relationship based on the data attributes. After this step, the required machine learning model is ready to work. A new data is provided to the model, and it makes a prediction based on the attributes of the data provided.

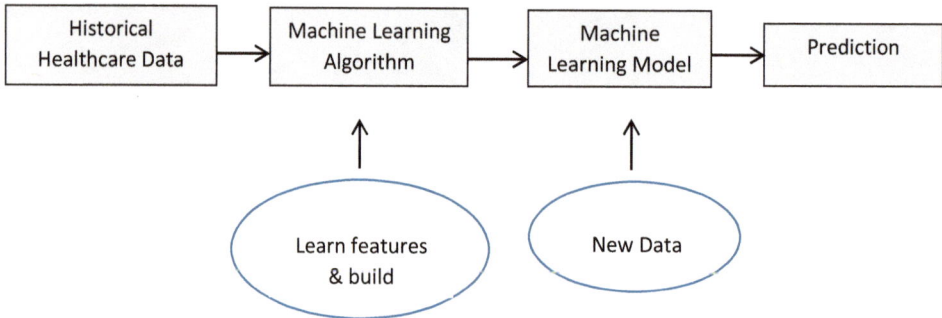

Fig. (3). Building a machine learning model.

Support Vector Machine

SVM is a supervised learning method that recognizes the data and categorizes it accordingly with the help of a trained model using machine learning. The major application areas of Support Vector Machine (SVM) are face detection, classification of images, text and hypertext categorization, and bioinformatics. The advantages of using SVM are high dimensional input space, sparse document vectors, and regularization parameters.

The prediction works by splitting the trained data based on their features and creating a decision boundary. When a new unlabelled data is fed to the model, as shown in Fig. (4), it predicts based on plotting new data on either side of the decision boundary and gives the result accordingly. SVM plays an important role in medical research due to its convex optimization tool. For the diagnosis of cancer, SVM has been extensively used in diseases like psychiatry and neurology [8]. The imaging biomarkers are identified [9] using SVM. The early identification of diseases like Alzheimer's can be identified with the help of SVM in combination with other statistical tools [10]. The figure below describes the workflow of SVM using the supervised learning method.

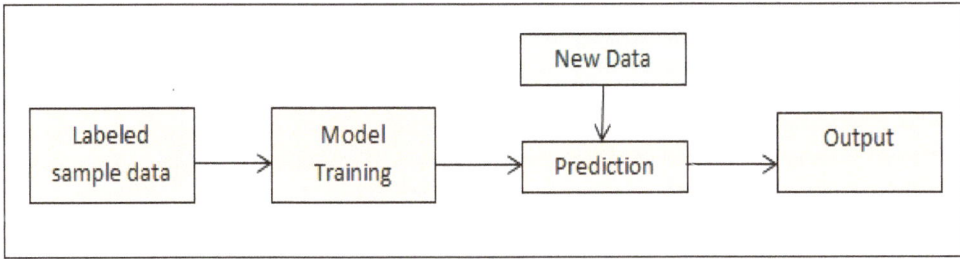

Fig. (4). Work flow of support vector machine.

Neural Network

Fig. (**5**) shows the working of the neural network in which the association between the input and output variables can be calculated based on different hidden layers which work on the basis of predefined functions. The aim of the model displayed in Fig. (**5**) is to calculate the weights with the help of input and output data to reduce the average error between prediction and outcome. This can be executed using optimization algorithms, like gradient descent and a quadratic approximation. This method is used for cancer diagnosis [11], where the output obtained is the tumour category with the help of genes as input. The diagnosis of stroke using a neural network is explained in another study [12]. The prediction of breast cancer using a neural network is made [13], in which the outputs indicate the tumour when the input is given in image form using texture information. The probabilistic neural network approach is used [14] for the diagnosis of Parkinson's disease.

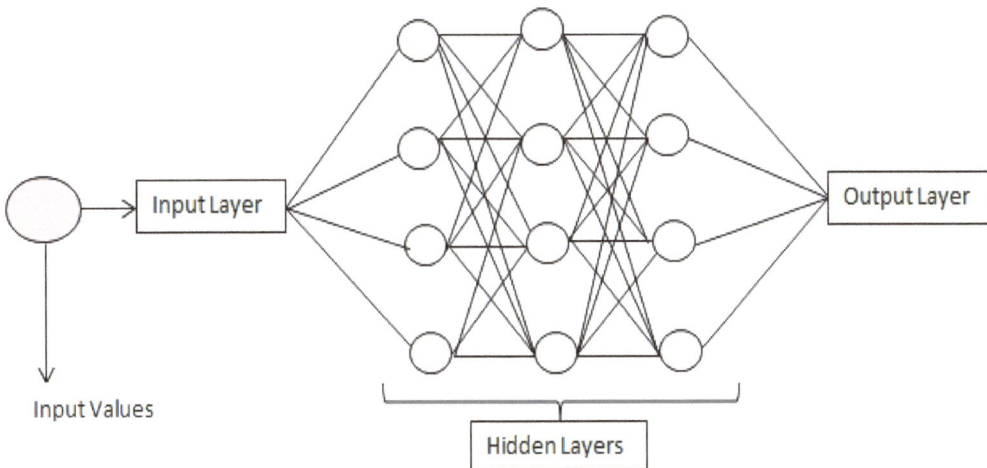

Fig. (5). Neural network architecture.

Deep Learning

The deep learning technique works more appropriately with practice in diagnosis similar to a physician based on the patient's reaction towards a treatment or new symptoms developed. The technology learns by assigning the decision right or wrong. EHR data is used to make the algorithm learn. Once a deep learning technology is built and trained, it runs continuously to improve accuracy. Researchers are using deep learning to compare patients with the broader population predicting heart conditions and cancerous genetic mutations before they even occur with significant treatment options.

The Deep Learning Algorithm has also been developed to detect diabetic retinopathy in retinal fundus photographs, and the work has been published in JAMA [15]. It plays a major role in medical image analysis using massive training in artificial neural networks (MTANN) and convolutional neural network (CNN). Medical image analysis is possible with the application of the deep learning algorithm explained in the review paper [16].

Natural Language Processing

The clinical data that are incomprehensible and unstructured for the computer program, like laboratory reports, discharge summaries, operative notes, and physical examinations are in descriptive text. For such text, natural language processing is used to gather useful information and helps in decision making [17]. Text processing and classification are the two major components of NLP. Using the historical database, the NLP Fig.s out some disease-relevant attributes from the clinical data; this is called text processing. Then subsets of attributes are chosen by observing their impact on the classification of different conditions. To perform decision making, the validated attributes are used over the structured data, and the results showed an accuracy of more than 90% [18].

The laboratory-based unpropitious effect can be automatically monitored using NLP [19]. NLP is also used for the diagnosis of disease, for example, NLP pipeline is applied over the clinical notes to identify variables associated with 14 cerebral aneurysm diseases [20]. Physicians can be alerted for anti-infected therapy by using the antibiotic-assisted system, which is aided by reading the report of chest X-ray using NLP [21]. Such a system built on NLP can automatically help detect acute pneumonia.

Opportunity and its Impact

The need for healthcare to be preventive, predictive, and participatory is paramount, and AI is a powerful tool for that objective. Broadly, the opportunities that AI has created in healthcare are adjuncts for diagnosis, prognosis, therapy, and research.

Diagnosis

The key area where AI offers an advantage in disease management is early diagnosis of any disease process, which will not just improve the prognosis but also decrease treatment costs for the patient and, at the same time, improve the efficiency of the healthcare providing platforms. Diabetic retinopathy is a complication of diabetes that leads to loss of vision. Nikon along with Google, has developed an early diagnostic support system using an ultra-widefield retinal imaging device, collecting data of accumulated images from all over the world and utilising it to train neural networks to acquire diagnostic experience for early detection thereby improving the outcome by preventing blindness. This would not have been possible for a physician to do so at the individual level. Years of medical training being compressed into a neural network that delivers results instantly, this feature has large implications in healthcare delivery.

Use of AI in the early detection and classification of cancers has changed management protocols for patients and care providers. The advantage of AI is that it picks up changes that are so fine that they may be missed even by a trained physician, leading to early and more specific therapy resulting in a better outcome. Researchers are developing AI protocols for screening the general population to identify those at an increased risk of developing cancer at a later stage in life. The use of AI with data collated worldwide has led to increased sensitivity and specificity for these tests, decreasing the number of false positives.

AI and machine learning are particularly helpful in areas where data is already digitized, for instance, radiology and many others where this large amount of data used in algorithms lead to a conclusive diagnosis in a fraction of a second, and this can be replicated inexpensively all over the world giving everyone access to the latest and the best in healthcare.

Therapy

Cancer is a major challenge in terms of early diagnosis and treatment. AI gives us a window of opportunity to take it head-on, not just in early diagnosis but also for use in therapy, research, and rehabilitation. Cancer cells have genomic variability, so they may react differently to drugs at different stages resulting in failure of established drug regimens [22]. Data is used in an automated process that can rapidly identify active compounds, antibodies, or genes, and the results serve as templates for drug design. Many such decision trees are built, leading to the better predictive value of the activity of anticancer drugs on cancer cell DNA [23].

Researchers have developed drug sensitivity models based on a machine learning model called elastic net regression, thereby customizing drug regimens for patients taking into account drug resistance, something which would have been time-consuming if not impossible for a human mind.

AI has a role to play in radiotherapy also by helping in mapping out target areas using three-dimensional image reconstruction. Even response to treatment can be predicted by combining deep learning technology with radionics. Deep learning technology makes the treatment of cancers and other diseases more intelligent [24].

Drug Development and Research

The use of AI in drug development uses available documented information from various sources such as high-throughput compound fragment screening and computational modelling information. This inductive-deductive cycle eventually leads to optimised hit and lead compounds. Specific parts of the cycle are automated to decrease the random nature of results and the errors resulting in increased efficiency of drug development [25].

Rehabilitation of Elderly

According to a UN report, 15% of the world population, or close to a billion people, live with disabilities, and most of these are in the developing world. AI allows us to make life easier for these people with disabilities (PWD). The scope of support here is immense. The use of AI-enabled assistive robots can help such people perform their daily tasks independently. Vision assist devices give the ability to participate in spoken communication to paralysed stroke and cerebral palsy patients.

Using the implanted eye tracking system, the users are able to communicate with their eyes and write words using a keyboard on a screen and translate these words into spoken communication. For patients with low vision AI-aided devices allow them to recognise friends and their facial expressions as well as read documents, bar codes, and currency. With wearable devices available now, there is a great reduction in disability for such patients with neurological disorders.

The Future

The future of healthcare and AI are deeply interconnected. With the passage of time, its role in medical diagnostics, drug discovery, and clinical trials will only increase, thereby improving patient outcomes. Robot-assisted surgery and automated image diagnosis will become increasingly common in the coming times. With virtual nursing assistants, administrative workflow assistance, and connected machines, the work flow will be seamless.

Challenges and Limitations

Although AI has large potential in healthcare with growing technical space, the opportunities are endless due to certain limitations, and challenges that do exist. With the introduction of any new technology, there are some teething issues; the hesitancy to initial adoption needs to be actively overcome by the stakeholders who need to not just invest but also highlight successful case studies.

Digitization of Clinical Data

For researchers, it is difficult to find quality data and the AI projects need to be executed upon reliable and relevant clinical data. The data available is distributed over various organizations as patients often change their preference of hospitality. Many developing countries have poor data record systems and seem challenging regarding the digitization of health records. The digitization of sorted clinical data is a tedious process and requires large computing power for implementation but will surely bring more accuracy and efficiency to medicine in the coming future.

Privacy and Security

Data privacy concerns are genuine as patient data is extremely sensitive and confidential. There are always questions about who owns the data, and whether hospitals can sell or share data. In healthcare, the data can be unstructured and difficult to interpret at times; therefore, in case of misinterpretation, liability fixation may be an issue. Developing regulations for a technology that is cloud-based and evolving poses an obvious challenge. Data breaches by hackers may also be a concern.

Role of Stakeholder

Stakeholders in the adoption of technology should be flexible and amenable to change; there may be pushback from clinicians. The decision-makers (for instance, regulatory agencies, governments, and hospital administration), knowledge experts (for example, ML researchers, clinical experts, and health information experts), and users (like physicians, patients, lab technicians, *etc.*) should be ready to cooperate with the technical changes.

Facing the Causality

Causality is an important issue when deploying such technology in healthcare as it may lead to health risks. The black box implementation of such models works without including any causality link due to the lack of fundamental theory. What if the doctor prescribed incorrect treatment to the patient? The model should be implemented to handle such situations.

Black Box Issue

When implemented in healthcare, AI models require interpretability, as the modern learning process is deployed as a black box and considered complex. For a censorious application like medicine, there is a demand for a highly understandable and accurate ML model. Black box problems will always exist, no matter what.

If key challenges can be overcome, healthcare is definitely poised for a quantum jump. As Bill Gates had said in 1996, "We always overestimate the changes that will occur in the next two years and underestimate the changes that will occur in the next ten".

CONCLUSION

Traditional healthcare services can be transformed by using artificial intelligence technology. This paper clearly explains why and how AI will play a major role in healthcare. Moreover, different techniques used for implementation and showed great results have been described. With ease comes difficulty, and so is with the opportunities. There are challenges which cannot be ignored. The current research is going on deploying AI algorithms where the vulnerabilities should also need to be considered. AI application in the healthcare field will greatly affect society on a large scale.

CONSENT OF PUBLICATION

Not applicable.

CONFLICT OF INTEREST

The author declares no conflict of interest, financial or otherwise.

ACKNOWLEDGEMENTS

Declared none.

REFERENCES

[1]   M.W. Peterson, R. Jane, K. Clarence, and M. Jess, "Medical students' use of information resources: Is the digital age dawning?", *Acad. Med.,* vol. 79, no. 1, pp. 89-95, 2004.
        [http://dx.doi.org/10.1038/s41591-018-0322-1] [PMID: 30617338]

[2]   V.H. Buch, I. Ahmed, and M. Maruthappu, "Artificial intelligence in medicine: current trends and future possibilities", *Br. J. Gen. Pract.,* vol. 68, no. 668, pp. 143-144, 2018.
[http://dx.doi.org/10.3399/bjgp18X695213] [PMID: 29472224]

[3]   L. Xing, E.A. Krupinski, and J. Cai, "Artificial intelligence will soon change the landscape of medical physics research and practice", *Med. Phys.,* vol. 45, no. 5, pp. 1791-1793, 2018.
[http://dx.doi.org/10.1002/mp.12831] [PMID: 29476545]

[4]   G. Huang, *"Trends in extreme learning machines: A review,"* in *Neural Network.* Elsiver, 2015, pp. 32-48.

[5]   E. Nurvitadhi, S. David, S. Jaewoong, M. Asit, V. Ganesh, and M. Debbie, "Accelerating Binarized Neural Networks: Comparison of FPGA, CPU, GPU, and ASIC", *International Conference on Field-Programmable Technology (FPT).,* IEEE, pp. 77-84, 2016.

[6]   S.E. Dilsizian, and E.L. Siegel, "Artificial intelligence in medicine and cardiac imaging: harnessing big data and advanced computing to provide personalized medical diagnosis and treatment", *Curr. Cardiol. Rep.,* vol. 16, no. 1, p. 441, 2014.
[http://dx.doi.org/10.1007/s11886-013-0441-8] [PMID: 24338557]

[7]   V.L. Patel, E.H. Shortliffe, M. Stefanelli, P. Szolovits, M.R. Berthold, R. Bellazzi, and A. Abu-Hanna, "The coming of age of artificial intelligence in medicine", *Artif. Intell. Med.,* vol. 46, no. 1, pp. 5-17, 2009.
[http://dx.doi.org/10.1016/j.artmed.2008.07.017] [PMID: 18790621]

[8]   N.H. Sweilam, A.A. Tharwat, N.K. Abdel Moniem, and N.K.A. Moniem, "Support vector machine for diagnosis Cancer disease: a comparative study", *Egyptian Informatics Journal,* vol. 11, no. 2, pp. 81-92, 2010.
[http://dx.doi.org/10.1016/j.eij.2010.10.005]

[9]   G. Orrù, W. Pettersson-Yeo, A.F. Marquand, G. Sartori, and A. Mechelli, "Using Support Vector Machine to identify imaging biomarkers of neurological and psychiatric disease: a critical review", *Neurosci. Biobehav. Rev.,* vol. 36, no. 4, pp. 1140-1152, 2012.
[http://dx.doi.org/10.1016/j.neubiorev.2012.01.004] [PMID: 22305994]

[10]   L. Khedher, J. Ramírez, J.M. Górriz, A. Brahim, and F. Segovia, "Early diagnosis of Alzheimer?s disease based on partial least squares, principal component analysis and support vector machine using segmented MRI images", *Neurocomputing,* vol. 151, pp. 139-150, 2015.
[http://dx.doi.org/10.1016/j.neucom.2014.09.072]

[11]   J. Khan, J.S. Wei, M. Ringnér, L.H. Saal, M. Ladanyi, F. Westermann, F. Berthold, M. Schwab, C.R. Antonescu, C. Peterson, and P.S. Meltzer, "Classification and diagnostic prediction of cancers using gene expression profiling and artificial neural networks", *Nat. Med.,* vol. 7, no. 6, pp. 673-679, 2001.
[http://dx.doi.org/10.1038/89044] [PMID: 11385503]

[12]   L. Mirtskhulava, J. Wong, S. Al-Majeed, and G. Pearce, "Artificial Neural Network Model in Stroke diagnosis. Modeling and simulation (UKSim)", *2015 17th UKSim-AMSS International Conference on: IEEE,* 2015.

[13]   J. Dheeba, N. Albert Singh, and S. Tamil Selvi, "Computer-aided detection of breast cancer on mammograms: a swarm intelligence optimized wavelet neural network approach", *J. Biomed. Inform.,* vol. 49, pp. 45-52, 2014.
[http://dx.doi.org/10.1016/j.jbi.2014.01.010] [PMID: 24509074]

[14]   T.J. Hirschauer, H. Adeli, and J.A. Buford, "Computer-Aided Diagnosis of Parkinson's Disease Using Enhanced Probabilistic Neural Network", *J. Med. Syst.,* vol. 39, no. 11, p. 179, 2015.
[http://dx.doi.org/10.1007/s10916-015-0353-9] [PMID: 26420585]

[15]   V. Gulshan, L. Peng, M. Coram, M.C. Stumpe, D. Wu, A. Narayanaswamy, S. Venugopalan, K. Widner, T. Madams, J. Cuadros, R. Kim, R. Raman, P.C. Nelson, J.L. Mega, and D.R. Webster, "Development and Validation of a Deep Learning Algorithm for Detection of Diabetic Retinopathy in

Retinal Fundus Photographs", *JAMA,* vol. 316, no. 22, pp. 2402-2410, 2016.
[http://dx.doi.org/10.1001/jama.2016.17216] [PMID: 27898976]

[16]   G. Litjens, T. Kooi, B.E. Bejnordi, A.A.A. Setio, F. Ciompi, M. Ghafoorian, J.A.W.M. van der Laak, B. van Ginneken, and C.I. Sánchez, "A survey on deep learning in medical image analysis", *Med. Image Anal.,* vol. 42, pp. 60-88, 2017.
[http://dx.doi.org/10.1016/j.media.2017.07.005] [PMID: 28778026]

[17]   P. Kantor, *Foundations of statistical natural language processing.* MIT Press, 1999, pp. 91-92.

[18]   N. Afzal, S. Sohn, S. Abram, C.G. Scott, R. Chaudhry, H. Liu, I.J. Kullo, and A.M. Arruda-Olson, "Mining peripheral arterial disease cases from narrative clinical notes using natural language processing", *J. Vasc. Surg.,* vol. 65, no. 6, pp. 1753-1761, 2017.
[http://dx.doi.org/10.1016/j.jvs.2016.11.031] [PMID: 28189359]

[19]   T.P. Miller, Y. Li, K.D. Getz, J. Dudley, E. Burrows, J. Pennington, A. Ibrahimova, B.T. Fisher, R. Bagatell, A.E. Seif, R. Grundmeier, and R. Aplenc, "Using electronic medical record data to report laboratory adverse events", *Br. J. Haematol.,* vol. 177, no. 2, pp. 283-286, 2017.
[http://dx.doi.org/10.1111/bjh.14538] [PMID: 28146330]

[20]   V.M. Castro, D. Dligach, S. Finan, S. Yu, A. Can, M. Abd-El-Barr, V. Gainer, N.A. Shadick, S. Murphy, T. Cai, G. Savova, S.T. Weiss, and R. Du, "Large-scale identification of patients with cerebral aneurysms using natural language processing", *Neurology,* vol. 88, no. 2, pp. 164-168, 2017.
[http://dx.doi.org/10.1212/WNL.0000000000003490] [PMID: 27927935]

[21]   M. Fiszman, W.W. Chapman, D. Aronsky, R.S. Evans, and P.J. Haug, "Automatic detection of acute bacterial pneumonia from chest X-ray reports", *J. Am. Med. Inform. Assoc.,* vol. 7, no. 6, pp. 593-604, 2000.
[http://dx.doi.org/10.1136/jamia.2000.0070593] [PMID: 11062233]

[22]   G. Liang, W. Fan, H. Luo, and X. Zhu, "The emerging roles of artificial intelligence in cancer drug development and precision therapy", *Biomed. Pharmacother.,* vol. 128, p. 110255, 2020.
[http://dx.doi.org/10.1016/j.biopha.2020.110255] [PMID: 32446113]

[23]   A.P. Lind, and P.C. Anderson, "Predicting drug activity against cancer cells by random forest models based on minimal genomic information and chemical properties", *PLoS One,* vol. 14, no. 7, p. e0219774, 2019.
[http://dx.doi.org/10.1371/journal.pone.0219774] [PMID: 31295321]

[24]   Y. Wang, Z. Wang, J. Xu, J. Li, S. Li, M. Zhang, and D. Yang, "Systematic identification of non-coding pharmacogenomics landscape in cancer", *Nat. Commun.,* vol. 9, no. 1, pp. 1-15, 2018.
[http://dx.doi.org/10.1038/s41467-018-05495-9] [PMID: 29317637]

[25]   K-K. Mak, and M.R. Pichika, "Artificial intelligence in drug development: present status and future prospects", *Drug Discov. Today,* vol. 24, no. 3, pp. 773-780, 2019.
[http://dx.doi.org/10.1016/j.drudis.2018.11.014] [PMID: 30472429]

CHAPTER 8

A Review on Automatic Plant Species Recognition System by Leaf Image Using Machine Learning in Indian Ecological System

Sugandha Chakraverti[1], Ashish Kumar Chakraverti[2,*], Jyoti Kumar[3], Piyush Bhushan Singh[4] and Rakesh Ranjan[5]

[1] *Department of Computer Science and Engineering, Greater Noida Institute of Technology, Gr. Noida, UP, India*

[2] *Department of Computer Science and Engineering, School of Engineering and Technology, Sharda University, Gr. Noida, India*

[3] *Department of Design, Indian Institute of Technology, Delhi, India*

[4] *Department of Information Technology, Pranveer Singh Institute of Technology, Kanpur UP, India*

[5] *Department of Information Technology, Pranveer Singh Institute of Technology, Kanpur UP, India*

Abstract: India is the land of agriculture with many varieties of plant species. These species have different uses in the medical, food, and harvesting industries. Despite having such a large collection of plants and agricultural assets, most of the Indian population is not aware of the goodness and properties of these precious plants except the usual ones. In this chapter, discussion and possibilities in this area are given and explored for the awareness of Indian people regarding the Indian plants. In this area, artificial intelligence and machine learning will likely develop an automated detecting machine that can classify and describe the plants by their images of leaves, bark, flowers, and stems. Looking forward in this direction, this chapter discusses an AI and ML based technique to recognize vegetation by the image of its leaves. In this approach, SIFT and ORB-based technique removes leaf image features and then tests the data set to match with a trained data set. The system is trained with 32 plant leaves. Henceforth, this system can recognize these plants by the image of their leaves. The uniqueness of this system is its data set. In the data set, the image of the leaf is prepared so that both sides of a leaf can be used to recognize the plant. This increase distinguishes the image irrespective of its color and shape. The system is still in an evolving phase that has the target of including all rare and useful plant information in this dataset. This system is very useful to preserve the information of all users, rare plants and those plants that are about to be extinct.

* **Corresponding author Ashish Kumar Chakraverti:** Department of Computer Science and Engineering, School of Engineering and Technology, Sharda University, Gr. Noida, India; E-mail: ashish.me08@gmail.com

Keywords: Agriculture, Image Feature extraction, KNN Classifier, KNN/BF Matcher, Machine learning, ORB, Plants, SIFT.

INTRODUCTION

We all are surrounded by plants. Plants are the lifeline of this planet. Let's consider the Indian scenario about the plant varieties and the availability of those varieties. It is large because India has a diverse climate, so almost every type of plant is found here in India. It is quite challenging to identify trees, but their availability in protecting agricultural sectors, industries, medicine, environment, and pale ecology is reliable. These assistances are trifling these days due to global warming, which is caused due to environmental damages and rapid urban expansion. Humans forget to assess vegetation destroying flora and fauna in bulk. This results in the quick extinction of enormous plant species every upcoming year. Protecting vegetation and its species isn't a movement but a necessity. The acknowledgment of the plant can be the first step towards protecting them and crosschecking their nativity. However, many species still prove to be a mystery to humankind. The development of a traditional system is efficient in recognizing and storing information of all the species. Researchers are working towards classifying plant parts such as its skin, leaves, flowers, fruits, seeds, and many more. Besides being the most important organ of a plant, the leaf is considered the most convenient reason for advancing several methods to recognize any plant species [1]. It is impractical to pick up positive results once the shapes of leaves are in substantial variability [2]. Despite these difficulties, plant recognition by leaves is a very popular and convenient method, so researchers and academicians are trying to find new ways to recognize plants by leaf images.

In this area, image processing, artificial intelligence, machine learning, and deep learning are applied to develop an accurate and automatic solution/system. To develop these systems, many features of the leaves are considered to identify the plants. These features include color, texture, and shape. Recognizing the tree in advance of its full development is beneficial to farmers in so many aspects, like whether this tree or plant is beneficial for agriculture and the economy. This also alerts the farmer to create a favourable conditions for trees and plants for better growth of plants. The advancement in machine learning (ML), along with model lapsing and classification, recognition of objects, and computer vision, steadily protects crops during intense potential cases while helping to decide agricultural management. These assistances include fungicide spraying systems, specific periodic issues which vary according to the environment, good harvesting period, production and estimation of fruits, and flowers according to each area unit, *etc.* [3]. Automation in agriculture technology and the area is in full swing and many things are being developed, but not properly in recognition of the plant species.

The leaf of a plant isn't the only medium to identify the species of a plant. Even a plant's skin, flowers, seeds, branches, and fruit can contribute equally to the identification process. However, the vigorous attributes of a leaf are still a topic of discussion in scientific studies such as computers, algorithms, botany, image processing, and machine learning. The identification of plant species is more than just a study. Thus, it can rapidly help and influence several botanists and environmentalists across the world to protect species diversity [4]. Plant taxonomical theories suggest that the leaves and flowers of plants are capable enough to distinguish a plant's nativity. The 2-dimensional structure of a leaf and the 3-dimensional structure in flowers widely help automated identification of plants to provide accurate results. However, the problem with the flower is its presence only in certain plants and its availability in specific seasons. Whereas, if compared to leaves, their existence can persist during the entire life span of a plant or a tree. Besides this, their shape, consistency, scale, rotation, movement, reflection, and limited dependability dynamically prepare to contribute to the inter-class discrimination and intra-class discrepancies of a leaf [5]. Plants leaf images are easily available entities to recognize the plants, as well as these methods, may be handy for all. In this scenario, image procession and computer vision essentially process and classify the leaf images. Image processing in the field of computer science in which images are processed digitally as a stored medium. Computer vision is the field of study of the perception of visuals by computers, making them human vision alike. Using AI and machine learning techniques, this task is impossible to complete. The k-nearest-neighbor approach can be perhaps the easiest of every technique to predict the test class example. A clear drawback of the k-NN method has the time complexity of creating the predictions.

Moreover, neural networks may be tolerant to noise inputs. However, in neural networks, it is very tricky to appreciate the structure of methods. SVM found a competitive as well as the best accessible machine learning techniques in the classification of high-dimensional information sets. The computational of SVM complexity can reduce the quadratic optimization difficulty, and it is very easy to manage the difficulty of the decision rule with the error of frequency. The disadvantage of SVM is that it is hard to decide the optimal parameter when the training information cannot be linearly separable.

Furthermore, SVM is very complex to comprehend and execute [6]. These days, plant taxonomy follows classical measures to considerably help create a conventional automated system for recognizing plants. The major aid is to increase production frequency and streak to operate industries where the products of plants are commonly used.

Majority of research on leaf shape-based distinction has been completed. The research says that the blank sides of leaf's images are separated for implementing simplicity. Another study shows that the attributes of leaves are extracted for diagnosing the leaf briefly. The geometrical features of a leaf include the rectangularity of a leaf, sphericity, form factor, aspect ratio, convexity, and many more. Morphological features are usually helpful for implementing simplicity and deriving prominent results for distinguishing the leaves of a plant. Their secondary methods, such as Hough Transform and Fourier Descriptors, differentiate themselves in the level of accuracy. The presentation of leaves through the Fourier Descriptor method seems prominent in its detailing compared to the Hough Transform method. The two algorithms which Ehsanirad used were, namely Gray-Level Co-occurrence Matrix (GLCM) and Principal Component Analysis (PCA) for the extraction of the leaf's textures, following an orthogonal instruction setting upon 12 features. These 12 leaf texturing features converted to 5 elements important for the algorithms used for recognizing a leaf deployed on FLAVIA dataset. Plants can be, however, classified by exerting three proposed methods, namely: PNN (Probalistic Neural Network) method, Fourier moment method for resolving issues in several categories, and lastly, the SVM-BDT method (Support Vector Machine with Binary Decision Tree, that is known to be far better than the other two techniques. Apart from recognizing a leaf through its textured features, the features in shape contribute to the recognizing process steadily. The process gets carried out through a hyper sphere classifier. The spatial data extracted from a leaf's weight distinction is captured on a vertical axis along with variable positioning. This technique is called RMI (Regional Moments of Inertia) [7].

IMAGE PROCESSING

Image processing is a strategic performance or operation on images to extract an intensified image or any valuable data from the input. It is the typical processing of the signal that results in images or their attributes. Advancements in technology and major scientific fields use these image processing methods as their core utility centers for prominent research [8].

Image processing gradually follows major three steps:

- Importing an image using image acquisition tools;.
- Strict inspection and operation of that image.
- Image analysis results in an image report alteration.

Image analysts use analogue and digital image processing methods while explicating images. Through analogue methods, imagists print out photographs, whereas using digital techniques, the entire data passes through preprocessing methods, amplification, exhibition, and finally through extraction methods *via* computer.

Appropriate digital methods digitize the image function f (x,y) both in dimensions and proportions. Analogue video signals are passed through frame grabbers or digitizers, transforming continuous data into digitalization for creating digitalized images. The two steps to perform it are:

- Sampling.
- Quantization.

In a digitized image, the sampling rate helps dictate spatial or dimensional resolutions, whereas quantization tries to dictate grey levels in the image. The immensity of the sampled image indicates its digital value in the process. Quantization is the transformation of the continuous value and digital equivalency of an image function. Human consciousness requires a high level of quantization that details the image with its fine shading. The major problem of an image occurs when there is a false contour in the image. The brightness level that was initially quantized isn't generally enough to restore the issue.

The distortion of an image from one-pixel grid to the other grid consequences in image interpolation, whereas the distortion of an image and its correction result in remapping. Necessities for resizing images prevail during the increment or decrement of pixel number. The increase in aggregate pixels while sprinting an image exhibits more prominent detailing that refers to zooming.

Interpolation functions use valid information to approximate the evaluation at unidentified points. Their two distinguished directions try to execute the intensity of pixels compared to the pixels in the surrounding. Their algorithms are differentiated into two varied categories, the first being the adaptive one and the latter being non-adaptive. Adaptive algorithms are relative to interpolating. Their dependency changes according to the change in interpolation. Non-adaptive algorithms include the nearest neighbor, sinc, lanczos, bicubic, bilinear, *etc.*, as they are parallel to every pixel. Qimage, PhotoZoom Pro, and Genuine Fractals are some of the adaptive algorithms, which also happen to be certain proprietary algorithms.

Both optical and digital zooming are the common features of a digital camera. While a common nondigital camera executes optical zooming smoothly, the increment in the light magnification helps the camera to easily move the lens for zooming. In the case of digital cameras, an image gets interpolated due to the degrading of its quality. The difference in detailing between optical and digital zoom decides the photo clarity and quality. Since it is more in the case of optical zoom, no matter how aggregated the pixels are, the detailing in digital zoom is still unmatchable.

The result of clear frequency signals is due to the signals of digital sampling, their sound, and their digital photographs. Whenever there is any kind of sampling that is less compared to the presence of double higher frequencies in the signal, there is an occurrence of aliasing. To avoid any form of frequency signals in the original sound, the filtration of frequency signals above the sampling rate is a must. This is why an equipment recording digital sound is usually accommodated with low-passing filters to eliminate any existing signal that proved to be above half of the sampling frequency.

Sinusoids in total are the inputs of a sampler or a linear system, and the total number of sampled sinusoids are known to be the outputs of that system. This theory proclaims Nyquist frequency while there is an unavailability of any frequency in the input. This unavailability is convenient for further preparing the existing samples' sinusoidal components. This theory, thus, is known as Nyquist-Shannon sampling theory.

The minimization of the artifacts of the diagonal edges, that of an alias by representing an image with peak resolution and smoothening edges, defines anti-aliasing. Its work overlaps adjacent pixels with those of ideal edges briefly.

Human interpretation standards require images prepared with image enhancing mechanisms with a deep subjective quality. These subjects in the quality of an image evaluate contrast to be its primary factor. It is prepared from two surfaces that are adjacent to each other reflecting luminance in visual proportions. In other words, contrast is defined as the difference within visual properties active to distinguish an object from the rest. These contrasts can be differentiated easily through colors and the brightness level of an object when compared to other objects. The sensitivity of our visual system is more towards any contrast than any absolute luminance. Algorithms such as contrast-enhancing methods are constructed to utilize properly in image processing units.

Any excessive and uniform concentrations of the contrast of an image tend to lose the data of those specific areas. To avoid such issues, the only successful method is optimizing the contrast upon any image. This helps exhibit all important data required to distinguish an input image [8].

The preprocessing step aims to initially methodize an image's scale and direction or orientation from featuring computation. By orienting or directing the image at an arbitrary angle and size, the first image denoted below (I) stands for a raw image, as shown in Fig. (1). It is initially transformed into a binary form (bw). The angle is abstracted from the image in which there is a horizontal orientation in the major axis of the leaf w.r.t rotation. This aligns its major axis horizontally (rb) to make a rotation uniform angle. Even though it is a horizontal leaf, there are varied translating factors with reference to the origin. The diminishing background of the leaf makes possible measures to fit the rectangular boundary (db) to transform features into translational variants. The dimension of a leaf is assimilated to convert the images into a scale variation. However, due to the variation of an aspect ratio along with leaves, these leaf shapes tend to affect their distinguishing performance following even its distortion during shape modeling. Segments are minimized when leaf images depend upon the value of their aspect ratio (R). The observation of true values in a dataset signifies almost seven different segmentations that can easily scale an image without any form of distortion. The detailing of the aspect ratio corresponding to its segment number and dimensions is provided in Table **1** [9].

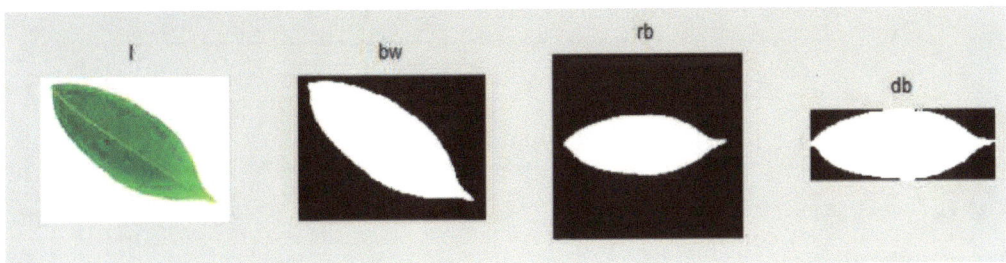

Fig. (1). Leaf image pre-processing steps (I).

Table 1. Comparison of 5 leaf image datasets.

-	plantCLEF 2015 [3]	Leafsnap [1]	Flavia [10]	MlaynKew [5]	Moip
Number of images	113205	30866	1907	2816	2739
Image size	Various	About 700x525	1600x1200	256x256	300x400 or 300x533
Number of species	1000	185	33	44	63
Background	Nature	White	White	Black	Nature, bark, sky, white
Segmentation ground truth	X	O	X	O	X
Image acquisition constraint	None	Strong	Strong	Strong	Weak

A Typical Image-Based Plant Identification System (SATTI Et Al., 2013)

The system shown in Fig. (**2**) requires the distinction of a plant which is typically an image base. Necessary steps are explained consecutively in sub-sections.

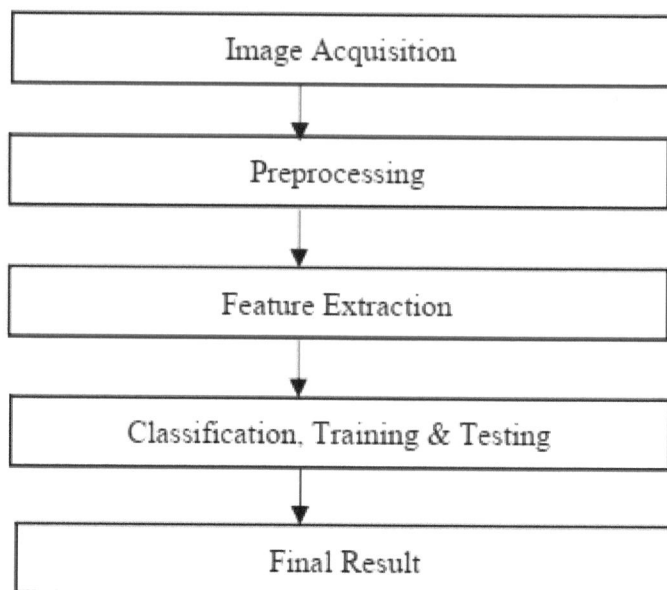

```
┌─────────────────────────────────────┐
│          Image Acquisition          │
└─────────────────────────────────────┘
                  │
                  ▼
┌─────────────────────────────────────┐
│            Preprocessing            │
└─────────────────────────────────────┘
                  │
                  ▼
┌─────────────────────────────────────┐
│          Feature Extraction         │
└─────────────────────────────────────┘
                  │
                  ▼
┌─────────────────────────────────────┐
│   Classification, Training & Testing │
└─────────────────────────────────────┘
                  │
                  ▼
┌─────────────────────────────────────┐
│             Final Result            │
└─────────────────────────────────────┘
```

Fig. (2). Flow diagram of the proposed scheme.

Image Acquisition

Scanners or digital cameras can easily capture a leaf image of any shape or size. However, the image background must be necessarily monochromatic without any petioles.

Pre-processing

Image pre-processing system is a rudimentary process in which a leaf image is an input to rectify any distortions and minimize noise. These steps are carried out for extracting any important data before analyzing the data of an image. The illustration in Fig. (**3**) depicts techniques for enhancing the images of any leaf. They include conversions such as grayscale, smothering, filtering, detection of edges, binarization, and many more successful methods to study the leaves carefully.

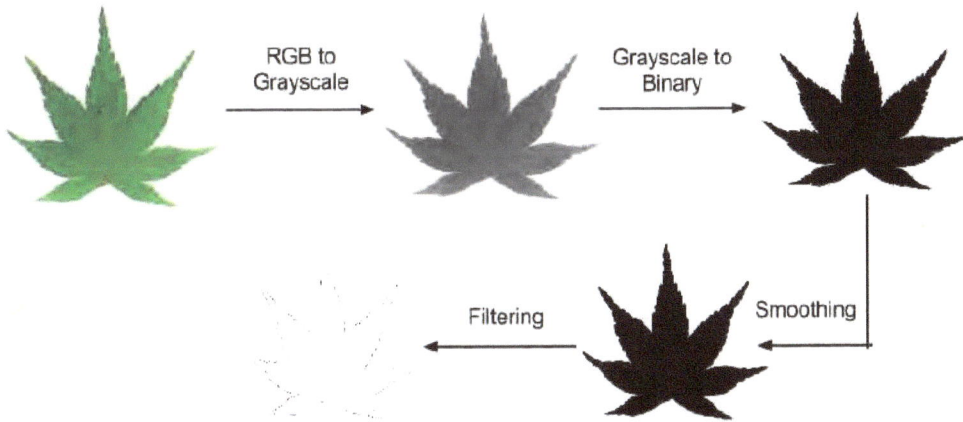

Fig. (3). Pre-processing steps were performed on an Acer Palmatum leaf image.

Feature Extraction

This feature extracts the shape of the leaf along with its color. It is, however difficult to extract the necessary output due to the invariable similarity between them, comparable to different plants.

Color Features

Retrieval of image searching method focuses on the color generating features by calculating the vector of its average means. The separation of red, green, and blue colors forms a proposed algorithm that calculates each plane, row mean, and column means in an average. These three planes primarily combine to structure a feature vector to store in a featuring database after getting generated from a particular image.

Shape Features

Here, the shape features are solely based on morphological and tooth features:

A). Geometric Features

Commonly used 5 geometric features (DMFs), illustrated in Fig. (4), derived from the following 5 basic features:

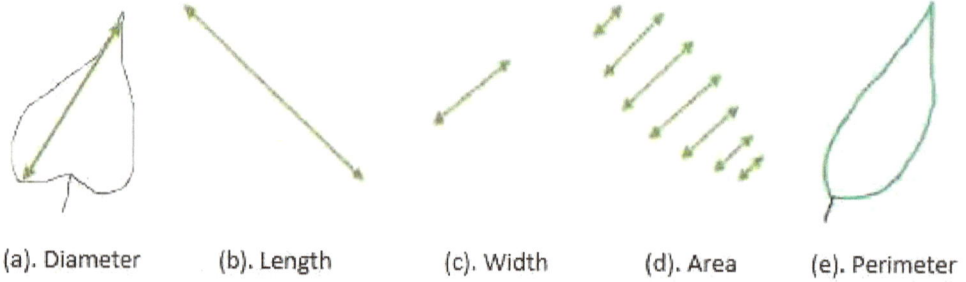

(a). Diameter   (b). Length   (c). Width   (d). Area   (e). Perimeter

Fig. (4). The five basic morphological features.

(1). Diameter: The longest distance on a closed contoured leaf between any two points is known here as a diameter.

(2). Physiological Length: A long line connects the two terminal points on the main vein of a leaf. This long length is called physiological length.

(3). Physiological Width: The longest segmented line perpendicular to the two endpoints of a leaf is called the physiological width.

(4). Leaf Area: The number of pixels of binary value 1 on a smoothed leaf image is the leaf area.

(5). Leaf Perimeter: The number of pixels enclosed by the contouring side of the leaf is the perimeter of a leaf.

B). Morphological Features

Based on the above 5 basic geometric features, we can define the following 12 digital morphological features:

(1). Smooth Factor: The ratio between the rectangular averaging filter smoothed on the surface of a leaf by 5x5 and by 2x2.

(2). Aspect Ratio: the physiological ratio between length to width,.

i.e., L/W.

(3). Form Factor: A differentiation between a leaf and a circle is calculated by the.

formula$4\pi A/P2$.

(4). Rectangularity: The similarity of a leaf to a rectangle is calculated as L,.

i.e., L=W/A.

(5). Narrow Factor: The narrowness in leaf is calculated as D/L.
(6). Perimeter Ratio of Diameter: The perimetrical ratio of a leaf with that of the diameter.

i.e., P/D.

(7). Perimeter Ratio of a leaf: The ratio of a leaf's perimeter is defined in addition to the leaf's physiological length and width,.

i.e., P=(L+W).

(8). 5 Features of a Leaf vein:

Leaf vein is the perfunctory composition of a leaf that helps in the classification and characterization of a leaf. Although various species of plants have different patterns of veins, they contribute themselves in distinguishing a leaf that seems to be of a similar size and shape. The morphological opening operation on a grayscale image is a standardized method for extracting leaf veins and its features. The resultant image is minimized from the leaf contour whenever using a flat disk-shaped structure with a radius of around 1,2,3,4. The 5 vein features following: A1/A, A2/A, A3/A, A4/A, A4/A1 calculate whenever there is a resemblance of the output with that of the vein structure in a leaf. Here, Ar refers to the remaining leaf extracted while structuring the element of radius r, and the leaf area A.

C). Tooth Features

The notched, indented pixel and toothed surrounding the edges of a leaf is known as a tooth. The representation of a tooth point in a leaf is shown in Figs. (**5a** and **5b**) shows the toothed leaf.

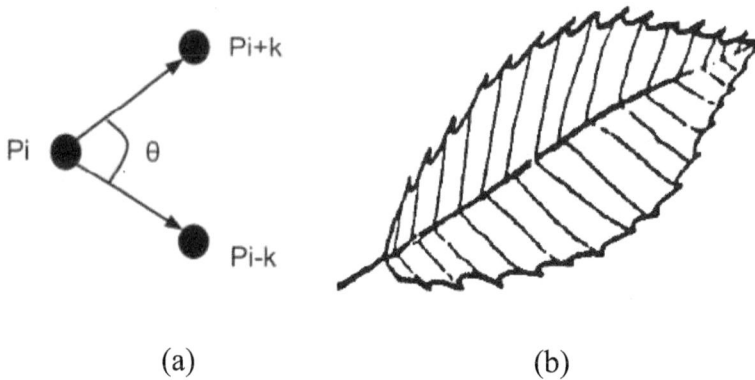

Fig. (5). (a). A tooth point (b). Toothed leaf.

The point on the leaf margin, Pi is subtended to examine the angle θ with its neighbors, *i.e.*, Pi-k and Pi+k (k being the threshold) to determine whether the leaf is a tooth point or not. Pi is determined to the tooth when the angle θ is within a particular range, else not.

INDIAN PLANTS IMAGE DATA SETS

Plants and the environment equally contribute nourishments to the atmosphere. Even though their relationship to each other is a theory of complexity, they are considered significant for regulating carbon emissions and periodical climatic changes. Humans are responsible for destroying vegetation without any hesitation. This has resulted in a massive loss of variable species and vulnerable changes in the climate. The recovery can only be retained if proper space and time are provided. Massive studies and research have been done and are still in progress to recover vegetation. Several contributions have been made towards studying plant leaves, which resulted in identifying and diagnosing processes of diseases, *etc.* in a plant. The plants selected for this purpose are Mango, Lemon, Pomegranate, PongamiaPinnata, Basil, Arjun, Guava, AlstoniaScholaris, Bael, Jamun, Chinar, and Jatropha. The diagnosing processes detected the healthiness of diseases in these plants, separating them into different modules for further research and study.

The classifications of leaf images detected to be either healthy or diseased have been labeled extending from P0 to P11. In the next step, the complete data sets among 22 subjective categories have been divided from 0000 to 0022. The classes ranging from 0000 to 0011 were marked as healthy, whereas the classes of 0012 to 0022 were labeled as diseased ones. Around 4503 images have been collected, of which 2278 are healthy, and 2225 are not. All images of the leaves were typically accumulated at Shri Mata Vaishno Devi University, Katra, from March to May in the year 2019. The entire acquisition process was carried out in an occupied environment with a complete wi-fi facility enabled across the compound. Nikon D5300 camera was used throughout the event to capture all images practically on the spot. This camera is known to have inbuilt performance timing so that JPEG images can be shot at (seconds/frame, max resolution) = 0.58 and for RAW+JPEG = 0.63. The images in JPEG format were captured without any flash under 18-55mm lens with sRGB color representation, 24-bit depth, 2 resolution units, and 1000-ISO. In conclusion, researchers and academicians may find this study helpful for developing identification, classification methods of plants, monitoring their growth, diagnosing diseases *etc.*, and many more. The main objective behind this study is to understand the plants in a more prominent way while managing their suitability [10].

This is the recent data set of plant leaves created by any researcher in Indian territory. Instead, so many data sets of plant leaves and other parts are available, but all of them are for non-native plants and created outside India.

Table **1** summarizes 5 datasets, including the fore mentioned 2 datasets and Flavia MalayaKewmoip dataset. Fig. (**6**) shows a sample from five datasets [11].

Fig. (6). Sample images from five datasets.

In this chapter, a novel dataset of plant's leave is introduced that is influenced by Chauhan S. S. *et al.* [10]. In this data set, leaves are captured by both sides to create uniqueness and support efficient classification during recognition. This is shown in Fig. (**7**). It consists of approximately 14 plant leaves, and every plant set has 8-10 snaps. This data set is in the development phase and continuously updating.

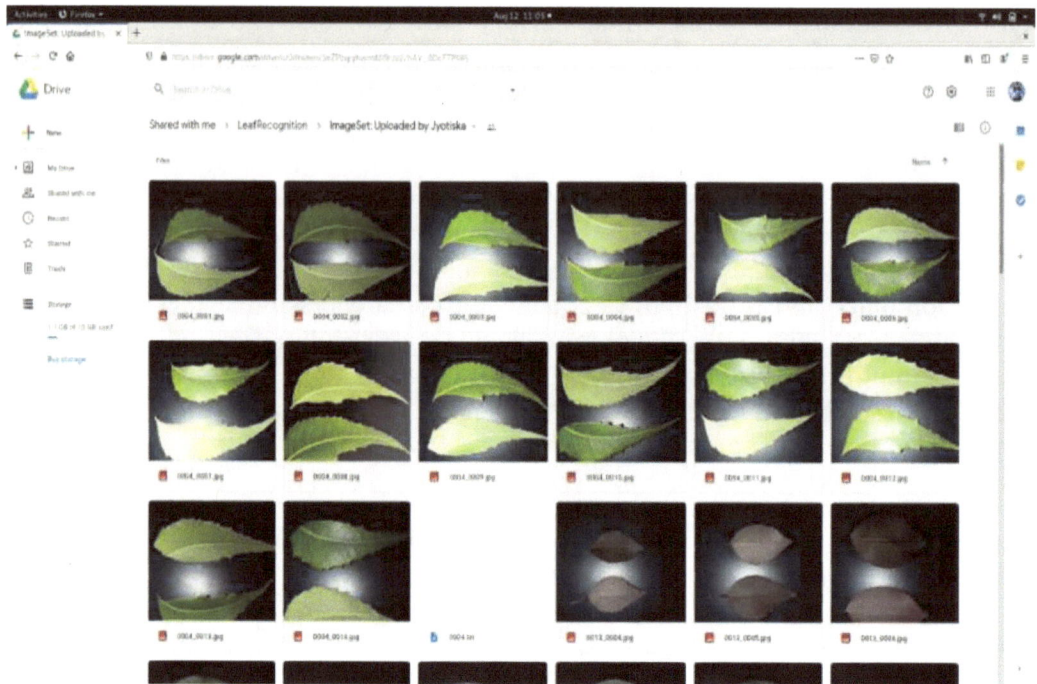

Fig. (7). Novel data set of Indian plant leaves having both side snaps.

MACHINE LEARNING TECHNIQUES FOR LEAF RECOGNITION

Today, machine learning is frequently used in classification and recognition problems; in this section, some popular machine learning techniques are being discussed.

The automated plant detection techniques with the help of computer vision proved to be a great help to the protectors of the environment, land managers and foresters. Jou-Ken Hsiao *et al.* [12] proposed the detection technique of a leaf image be conducted automatically only through sparse representation. A brief study has been conducted on sparse representations to represent each descriptor by less number of dictionary atoms in a linear combination.

The calculation upon each test leaf image correlates between an image and a leaf species to identify a successful leaf image. This is how an efficient leaf can be recognized on the public leaf dataset. This is entirely based on proposing a framework that is more compressed and richer within the leaf image compared to the clustering propositions of a classical method. In addition to this, the method utilized in our study seems to adapt to new species without even refreshing the classifications. They suitably and equivalently are integrated with any extracted descriptors of any leaf image.

Besides extracting features, the pre-processing of an image is also required to classify the image as per the future. In [13] an improved pre-processing method based on the dynamic block technique is discussed, that is used fully to extract the features of an image effectively. With the increasing applications of digital imaging, differing kinds of software programming tools are introduced for processing images and photographs [14].

Recent agricultural studies manifested the minimization of the dependency of farmers on agricultural products to protect their crops is due to the successful utilization of image processing techniques, helpful variedly in recognizing and classifying plant diseases. The proposition of Jaya Optimization Algorithm (JOA) to recognize and classify the paddy leaf diseases is executed by utilizing Optimized Deep Neural Network (DNN) [15]. Images are procured directly from the paddy fields for detecting diseases like bacterial light, brown spot, blast, and sheath rotting. RGB images are reverted to HSV ones to remove the background from the pre-processing. The binary images are obtained based on saturation and hues by splitting off the diseased and the non-diseased part. These diseased portions are later segmented using the clustering method. The precise stability of the following approach is pushed to generate a feedback loop during the post-processing step.

Crops and weeds are productively categorized using ANN as a develop model, since it is potentially enough for quick recollection and categorization. Kodak digital camera was operated to capture 8-bit BMP images, converting them into indexed based ones on RGB color systems. The pixel values ranging in black and white from 0 to 255 are presented in integers. These assigned color indexes served as input to ANN. One output in the first classifier and two in the second one are used in the image process. Output value discriminates between the crop and weed. Classifications were done according to Type 1-A, 1-B, 2-A, 2-B, they are generally compared with each other in the hidden layers of ANN for various PE's. The number of PE's was kept at 3% of the input PE's. Success rate was between 60-80% and can be improved with a higher number of PE's in hidden layers [16].

Computer vision aids pre-processing the image systems in detaching noise from the image, scale disconnection, and rotation invariant feature set from the image, and recovering the matches of similar species in the labeled images with the help of weighted KNN search on a data set. This application is a remedy to photograph a leaf placed on a white-colored background and finally submit it as an input query image. This helps the application analyze leaf features and real-time plant species [17].

A framework was proposed by Jou-Ken Hsiao *et al.* [18] to recognize a novel image of a leaf using sparse representation. This conducted a comparative thesis for putting BoW-based framework into practice for major comparisons. Accurate recognition was achieved by learning sparse representations of each species from the images of leaves. However, several features came using sparse coding theory while the framework executed better recollecting performance. They include:

i. The proposed framework for adapting new leaf species without refreshing the classifications for its high appropriation; leaf image feature alignment and assimilation.

ii. The proposed framework is more compact and richer in leaf image recognition, yet it can find itself vigorous and may be inaccurate while extracting features from the leaf images. Advancement in image features will be integrated with the help of our framework, which in return will be extended *via* sparse coding. The proposed system could be implemented for achieving mobile visual research through a mobile application. The extension of applications will be exploited for recognizing images and videos.

DEVELOPMENTS OF AUTOMATIC SYSTEMS/MOBILE APPS FOR LEAF RECOGNITION

Many Automatic systems/mobile apps for leaf recognition are available, but very few are for Indian plants. Here, the introduction of such systems/apps is being stated [19].

Plantifier

Plantifier is a free community-based plant image acknowledging application that authorizesanyone to upload photos of unknown plants. The users of the MyGarden.org community behind this free tool will strive to recognize the plant image uploading and delivering answers in less time.

Garden

Garden Answers is a groundbreaking plant recognizing application known to identify almost around 20,000 accurate plant information. The plant that looks unknown and suspicious to you can now be easily identified with the Garden Answers Plant Identification app. Its not just for fun but also prevents your children or pets from getting harmed. Followed by just two easy steps: Snaping and Submitting! The answer is instant, with details beyond unimaginable accuracy. No only this, the details also include its nativity and horticultural experts. Easy keyword research for the infestation in your plants also has a concerning availability. Garden Answers App was launched in April, 2013, which is believed to be one of the earliest plant recognizing applications. Due to its early launches, the downloading rate ranks on the list. The regular updates and improvement of the app make it one of the most user-friendly applications in terms of garden theories.

PlantNet

Pl@ntNet is a handy botanist application that resolves to identify any plant with a capture. The capturing is collected and properly examined by plant experts across the globe. The motto of this application is to understand the modification and progression of plant biodiversity and a movement to preserve it. The application is known to identify flowering plants, ferns, vines, grasses, a large number of cultivated plants, wild plants, *etc.* Interestingly, the research also involves the plants beside sidewalks which are wild, unnoticed, and unaware. Even the thorns, buds, or hair of the stem can help experts across the globe to analyze it accurately and discover its species. The app is not restricted to small photographs or capturing. Even a photograph of the entire tree or a plant will definitely work.

iNaturalist

Many people believe the iNaturalist application to be the most accurate one compared to others. This may be the reason why it is considered to be one of the most recommended nature applications. With a large community of around 400,000 scientists, environmentalists, and naturalists, the research quality data by them is intact to its valid information. It is not just limited to photographs; the application authorizes anyone to record and share over the global community. It is an initiative collaborated by the California Academy of Sciences and The National Geographic Society.

KEY ATTRIBUTES

- Revelation of data about the unknown species around you.
- One can capture directly submit a photograph, and even record his studies about the unknown plants to share them with the global community.
- Counselling and cooperative identifications about the plants you discovered.
- Discussions to help others clarify their doubts.
- One can follow projects that involve several small-scale communities and scientists who are expertized and passionate about plant species.

FlowerChecker

FlowerChecker is a modernized application available to international markets that consists of a team of experts holding decades of experience in the botanical field. This reliable application is known to variedly identify mosses, lichen as well as fungi. Although this application is not as advanced as a computer base, the human involvement behind this application is the source to provide absolutely accurate results. It is a handy community for nature lovers who are just charged a minimum fee to maintain the quality of the application service. The team responds in less than 48 hours of uploading and possibly marks 90% of its accuracy level.

Agrobase

While other applications are user-friendly to any nature lover, Agrobase is typically known to have been built for farmers, agronomists, Crop Advisors, Growers, Trainee, as well as Agricultural students. It is used for easy identification of weeds, diseases, and even insects systematized by the agro-expert community. Apart from the inspections, the problems of farmers include the type of product to be used for the crops, economical quality pesticides, fungicides, and herbicides. The devices have helped a lot of farmers to stop from spending too much or unnecessarily on expensive crop products. This reliable and farmer-friendly application is designed to provide practical aids on site. Several countries have poorly educated farmers. Hence, this application is also an agro-based educational platform for farmers where the experts explain in their regional languages. The source helps agronomists, farmers, *etc.*, to find the product by its active material, name, category, or culture. Other than this, livestock farmers can accurately perceive manufacturers of crop products. Some of them include BAYER, BASF, SYNGENTA, *etc.* Calculators, Calibrators, Calibration, Sprayer tank mix, fertilizer application, *etc.*, which can be used as pesticides properly and safely.

LEAF RECOGNITION APP

This is one of the apps which is in the development phase to recognize the Indian plants by their leaves. This mobile as well as the web app is aimed at dynamically uploading images for leaf recognition, to seek a user-friendly application. We used flask to create servers, web development ideas, and android app techniques to create the application. Depending on the user approach, we developed a simple basic application that is easy to handle and use. To know the leaf type and description of a particular leaf, we just need to upload the image and display the output.

The project mainly focuses on the leaf detection mechanism by which we know the various types of unknown leaves and display the description of the particular selected leaf uploaded into the folder using a mobile application. The mobile application is developed using React Native and Flask at the backend server side. Other technologies used are Nodejs along with HTML, CSS, and JavaScript. The leaf image needs to be uploaded using a smartphone in the mobile app developed during this internship, and we can get the description of the image using the Adhoc Algorithm running for leaf detection.

Methodology

The app was designed in the traditional client-server model. One backend program was developed in Python, which was deployed on a remote server. The backend program was meant to run 24/7. If the user asks for service from the backend, it will deliver its service at any time. The client part was a mobile phone app, which would be installed on the user's devices for direct user interaction and better user experience. Initially, we designed a web application for front-end UI purposes. Then, we converted the web application into a native mobile application using the web-view feature of react-native. The Web-view simply calls the backend server, where our backend program is stored to run the web application. In the future, a purely hybrid or native app, written in react-native can be developed for a greater user experience purpose instead of using a web view. The main code segment for this UI was written in app.js files.

The backend program was written in Python. Here, we are using the flask framework of Python to handle the client-server communication model. HTML and CSS are used to design the appearance of the web application. On receiving a call from the client-side, the homepage is shown. This asks for a photograph of a leaf from the user. The user selects a photograph from their device using a multipart form data element and sends it to the backend Python program by generating a POST request. A JavaScript function is used in the front-end to ensure that the selected file is in .jpg or.jpeg format only. The image is sent to the Python program and a response is sent back to the front-end homepage. The response contains the information on the founding matches of the selected image. Moreover, if a match is found, it displays the description of that plant as received from the backend in the response. The codes for the front-end home page are shown below. The codes for the stylesheet (.css) are not included here.

After receiving the POST request, the backend program can store the image in a directory in the server itself. Then, it checks if the uploaded image matches with any of the previously uploaded datasets of images of leaves. If a match is found, it sends back the description of that plant and the matched image as a response to the UI. If no matches are found, a message is sent back to the client that the uploaded image does not match any of the images in the database. An open-c--based SHIFT algorithm is used for the matching purpose.

Integration of the Front-End with the Backend

After sending the image to the backend by the client, it is examined with the adhoc_algo, which is a SHIFT-based image matching algorithm designed for this purpose. If a match is found, the details of that plant along with the matched image are sent back to the front-end as a response. Whenever a response is received, the front-end program displays it on the screen as components. Figs. **(8-10)** shows the web view, mobile view, and GUI of the software product developed for leaf recognition application.

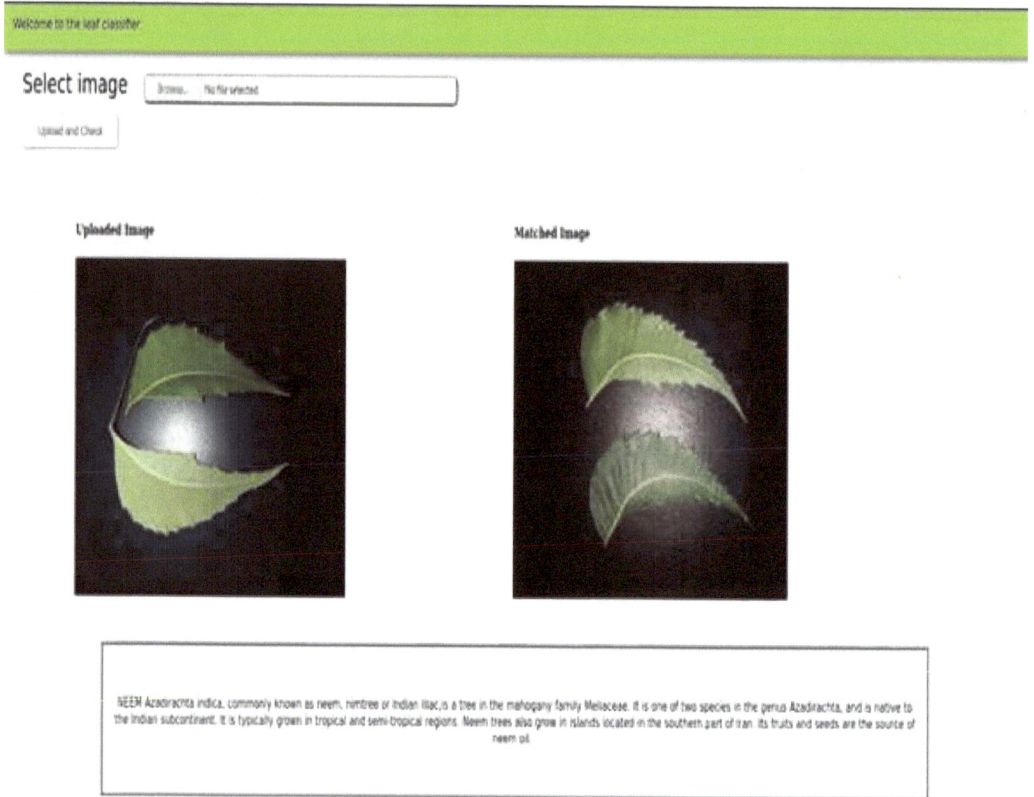

Fig. (8). Web-view of the output.

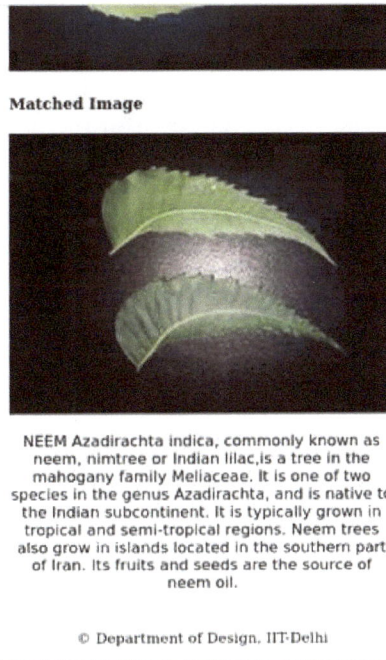

Matched Image

NEEM Azadirachta indica, commonly known as
neem, nimtree or Indian lilac,is a tree in the
mahogany family Meliaceae. It is one of two
species in the genus Azadirachta, and is native to
the Indian subcontinent. It is typically grown in
tropical and semi-tropical regions. Neem trees
also grow in islands located in the southern part
of Iran. Its fruits and seeds are the source of
neem oil.

© Department of Design. IIT-Delhi

Fig. (9). Mobile view of the output.

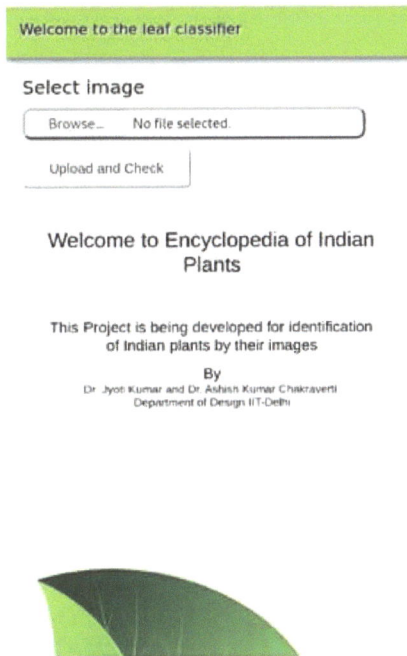

Welcome to the leaf classifier

Select image

Browse...   No file selected.

Upload and Check

Welcome to Encyclopedia of Indian
Plants

This Project is being developed for identification
of Indian plants by their images

By
Dr. Jyoti Kumar and Dr. Ashish Kumar Chakraverti
Department of Design IIT-Delhi

Fig. (10). The basic UI of the app.

Description

The final product is a single view mobile application where we can get leaf information of a particular leaf with its description. When started, the app opens with an interface where the user can choose an image from the folder and then check by uploading the desired image with an output of the image description.

This application is very easy to use. Once it opens, we just need to upload the image by choosing from the clicking on the upload button, and we get the description of the image in the desired format.

CONCLUSION

In this chapter, discussion and possibilities in this area are given and explored for the awareness of Indian people regarding the Indian plants. Artificial intelligence and machine learning substantially develop an automated plant detection system and describe the plants by their images of leaves, barks, flowers and stems. In this direction, this chapter discusses an AI and ML-based technique to recognize the plants through pictures of the leaves. In this approach, a SIFT and ORB based technique helps to remove characteristics of the leaf image, and based on these features image of the test data set is matched with the trained data set. The system is trained with 32 plant leaves so this system can recognize these plants by the image of their leaves only. The uniqueness of this system is its data set. In the data set, the image of the leaf is prepared so that both sides of the leaf can be used to recognize the plant. This increases the uniqueness of the image irrespective of colors and shape. The system is still evolving and has the target of including all rare and useful plant information in the dataset. It will also be very useful for the preservation of the information of all useful and rare as well as near to extinct plants and available to all.

CONSENT FOR PUBLICATION

Not applicable.

CONFLICT OF INTEREST

The authors declare no conflict of interest, financial or otherwise.

ACKNOWLEDGEMENT

The author/s acknowledge the Summer Fellowship Research programme (SFRP-2020) of CEP, IIT Delhi, which enabled Dr. Ashish Kumar Chakraverti to pursue research in IIT Delhi and develop this project under the guidance of Dr. Jyoti Kumar, Associate Professor, Department of Design, IIT Delhi.

REFERENCES

[1] S. Zhang, W. Huang, Yu-an Huang, and C. Zhang, "Plant Species Recognition Methods using Leaf Image: Overview", *Neur ucom.201ocomputing.*, vol. 2020, no. xx, pp. 1-48, 2019. [http://dx.doi.org/10.1016/j.neucom.2019.09.113]

[2] S. Bertrand, R. Ben Ameur, and G. Cerutti, "Bark and leaf fusion systems to improve automatic tree species recognition", In: *Ecological Informatics*, 2018, pp. 1-51. [http://dx.doi.org/10.1016/j.ecoinf.2018.05.007]

[3] C.F. Gaitán, "Machine learning applications for agricultural impacts under extreme events", In: *Climate extremes and their implications for impact and risk assessment.* Elsevier, 2020, pp. 119-138.

[4] S. Zhang, C. Zhang, and W. Huang, "Integrating leaf and flower by local discriminant CCA for plant species recognition", *Comput. Electron. Agric.*, vol. 155, no. xx, pp. 150-156, 2018. [http://dx.doi.org/10.1016/j.compag.2018.10.018]

[5] S. Das Choudhury, J-G. Yu, and A. Samal, "Leaf recognition using contour unwrapping and apex alignment with tuned random subspace method", In: *Biosystems Engineering* vol. 170. , 2018, pp. 72-84. [http://dx.doi.org/10.1016/j.biosystemseng.2018.04.001]

[6] S.G. Suman, and B.K. Deshpandey, "A Survey on Plant Leaf Identification in the Field of Agriculture", *International Journal of Innovative Research in Computer and Communication Engineering,* vol. 5, no. 3, pp. 6325-6330, 2017.

[7] C. Uluturk, and A. Ugur, "Recognition of leaves based on morphological features derived from two half-regions", *2012 International Symposium on Innovations in Intelligent Systems and Applications,* vol. vol. xx, 2012pp. 1-4 Trabzon [http://dx.doi.org/10.1109/INISTA.2012.6247030]

[8] Anbarjafari G. 2014, https://sisu.ut.ee/image processing/avaleht

[9] J. Chaki, R. Parekh, and S. Bhattacharya, "Recognition of whole and deformed plant leaves using statistical shape features and neuro-fuzzy classifier", *IEEE 2 nd International Conference on Recent Trends in Information Systems (ReTIS).,* vol. xx, no. xx, pp. 189-194, 2015. [http://dx.doi.org/10.1109/ReTIS.2015.7232876]

[10] S.C. Siddharth, K. Ajay, and P.G. Uday, 2020, https://data.mendeley.com/datasets/hb74ynkjcn/4

[11] E. Kang, and I-S. Oh, "Weak constraint leaf image recognition based on convolutional neural network", *International Conference on Electronics, Information, and Communication (ICEIC),* vol. xx, p. xx, 2018. [http://dx.doi.org/10.23919/ELINFOCOM.2018.8330637]

[12] K. Jou-Ken, K. Li-Wei, C. Ching-Long, and L. Chih-Yang, "Comparative Study of Leaf Image Recognition with a Novel Learning-based Approach", *Science and Information Conference.,* vol. xx, no. xx, pp. 1-5, 2014. [http://dx.doi.org/10.1109/SAI.2014.6918216]

[13] A.K. Chakraverti, and V. Dhir, "A hybrid approach to find cloned objects in copy move forged images", *Int. J. Forensic Software Engineering,* vol. 1, no. 1, pp. 3-20, 2019. [http://dx.doi.org/10.1504/IJFSE.2019.104705]

[14] A.K. Chakraverti, and V. Dhir, "A Review on Image Forgery & its Detection Procedure", *International Journal of Advanced Research in Computer Science,* vol. 8, no. 4, pp. 440-443, 2017.

[15] S. Ramesh, and D. Vydeki, "Recognition and classification of paddy leaf diseases using Optimized Deep Neural network with Jaya algorithm", *Inf. Process. Agric.,* vol. xx, no. xx, p. xx, 2020. [http://dx.doi.org/10.1016/j.inpa.2019.09.002]

[16] A. Vibhute, and S.K. Bodhe, "Applications of Image Processing in Agriculture: A Survey", *Int. J. Comput. Appl.,* vol. 52, no. 2, pp. 34-40, 2012.

[17]   A. Sahay, and M. Chen, "Leaf Analysis for Plant Recognition", *7th IEEE International Conference on Software Engineering and Service Science (ICSESS).,* vol. xx, no. xx, pp. 914-917, 2016. [http://dx.doi.org/10.1109/ICSESS.2016.7883214]

[18]   H. Jou-Ken, L-W. Li-Wei, C-L. Chang, C-Y. Hsu, and C-Y. Chen, "Learning sparse representation for leaf image recognition", *2014 IEEE International Conference on Consumer Electronics - Taiwan (ICCE-TW) Authors,* pp. 209-210, 2014. [http://dx.doi.org/10.1109/ICCE-TW.2014.6904061]

[19]   R. Kumar, 2019, www.arkasoftwares.com

CHAPTER 9

Recognizing Rice Leaves Disorders by Applying Deep Learning

Taranjeet Singh[1,*], Krishna Kumar[2], S. S. Bedi[2] and Harshit Bhadwaj[3]

[1] *Department of Computer Science and Engineering, IFTM University, Moradabad, India*

[2] *Department of Computer Science and Engineering, MJPRU, Bareilly, India*

[3] *Department of Computer Science and Engineering, MIET, Greater Noida, India*

Abstract: Rice is one of the staple crops in the world, as it is a rich source of protein, minerals, fibre, and vitamins. It is cultivated almost in every part of the world, but its productivity decreases due to several diseases. If these diseases are identified at the initial stages, then preventive measures can be taken, but their symptoms are quite similar for human eyes to recognize them correctly. Therefore, there is an immense need to apply automated techniques for recognizing rice diseases. Various Artificial Intelligence (AI) based prototypes have been surveyed in this chapter. These techniques were proposed by researchers for diagnosing rice disease. Here, our main goal is to present ideas on how Pretrained Neural Networks can be used in the recognition of rice diseases. Therefore, a brief description of AI techniques and their comparison is also outlined.

Keywords: Convolution Neural Networks, Deep Learning, Disease classification, Image Classification, Machine Learning, Pretrained models, Rice diseases, Transfer Learning.

INTRODUCTION

The introduction section includes the background and aims of the research in a comprehensive manner. Rice is cultivated in every part of the world and plays a vital role as it is a rich source of protein, minerals, fibres, and vitamins. The biological name of Rice is (Oryza sativa), commonly known as Paddy [1]. Consumption of Rice is highest in Asian Countries, among which China, India, Bangladesh, Indonesia, Thailand, and Vietnam are its leading producers [2]. High yield and high-quality rice are essential, but quality and yield both degrade due to the attack of several diseases, pests, and weeds. Plant disease can occur in several

---
[*] **Corresponding author Taranjeet Singh**: Department of Computer Science and Engineering, IFTM University, Moradabad, India; E-mail: taranjeetsingh.cse@gmail.com

parts (leaves, fruit, stem, root, *etc.*) of plants, but while surveying the literature, it is found that in most of the literature present, the researchers [3-11] have used leaves because the majority of diseases occur in plant's leaves in comparison to other parts of a plant.

In earlier times, farmers used their own experience, referred to guidebooks, or contacted experts for recognizing disorders in their crops, but now a days, with the enhancement of technology, it has become possible to detect and classify diseases without the help of books or experts. Although several Artificial Intelligence (AI) techniques are found in the literature to identify and classify types of disease in plants, the current scenario is mostly shifted towards Deep Learning to simplify the process. In the current era, several deep learning models have been proposed by researchers all over the world; among them, CNN (Convolution Neural Network) is widely being used for the process. CNN has been used in image recognition, video classification, human action recognition, traffic sign recognition [12], feature extraction [13], face recognition, character recognition, generic object recognition, pose estimation [8], *etc.* The working of CNN is inspired by the biological vision and the nervous system, where unsupervised deep learning is employed for classifying and recognizing the object with very high accuracy [3]. CNN models can either be trained from scratch or can be pre-trained by using their existing architectures. Training the network from scratch may require a large number of images (thousands to millions), which will be a time taking process, but the existing architecture of CNN requires only a few images (hundreds to thousands), and they can be modified with the help of transfer learning for solving similar problems [14]. Bera *et al.* [1] discussed several diseases of rice crops and presented several approaches for identifying these diseases using data mining and image processing techniques. The authors presented an extensive literature survey on decision support systems in the agricultural domain and concluded that several disease identification systems are already present, but there is a need for improving the accuracy of such systems. Lu *et al.* [12] proposed a novel technique for identifying 10 common rice plant diseases using CNN andtenfold cross validation techniques, different resolution, images, orientation, *etc.* The authors concluded that the proposed system gives accurate results and requires very little computation effort; future work will enhance models for estimating severity and classifying more diseases from banana leaves. Phadikar S. *et al.* [4] aim to recognize multiple rice diseases by using diseased regions of rice plants to extract features. The author proposed a Fermi-based method for segmenting diseased pixels from the background pixels. Consequently, using the extracted features, a rule-based classifier was developed to classify several rice diseases.

Rezende *et al.* [15] used image processing to enhance multiple diseases of multiple plant species, which belong to the XDB plant dataset (VGG16 and VGG 19); the architectures of the CNN model were used for classifying diseases, and the results were compared with other existing models. Finally, the authors concluded that VGG16 architecture performance was better than VGG19. Suresha *et al.* [5] used a KNN classifier along with global thresholding for identifying Rice Blast and Rice Brown spot diseases. The overall accuracy of the proposed model was 76.59%, and in the future, the author aims to identify bacterial and viral diseases in rice crops. Baranwal *et al.* [6] used CNN to automatically detect apple leaf disease. First, the Plant Village dataset was used, later, techniques of image compression, image filtering, and image generation were applied, and finally, GoogleLeNet architecture was used for training the proposed model. Alfarisy *et al.* [16] used the CaffeNet model for detecting diseases and pests of paddy crops. Firstly, 4,511 images were collected, and the dataset was formed; these images were later augmented and fed into the CaffeNet model for processing. Overall accuracy achieved for this model was 87%. Singh *et al.* [8] explored several loss functions and optimizers for optimal schemes for detecting several diseases in the plant's leaves. CNN was used in the proposed model, later compared with Random Forest with high-performing CNN. For improving accuracy, a combination of loss functions and optimizers was provided. Singh *et al.* [9] aim to develop effective methods for determining diseases of mango leaves. This paper used Multilayer Convolutional Neural Network (MCNN) for classifying Anthracnose disease in Mango tree leaves. MCNN was trained and could achieve 97.13% accuracy, much higher than the existing models. Venkataramanan *et al.* [10] used deep learning approaches for identifying and classifying various plant diseases using leaves. Using the YOLOv3, detector, features of the input image are extracted, and then ResNet18 models are trained using transfer learning for identifying the disease type. Mohan *et al.* [11] proposed a system that could detect and classify several diseases of paddy plants. For disease detection, AdaBoost classifier, and Haar-like features, the extractor was used, and an accuracy of 83.33% was achieved. For recognizing disease, SIFT (Scale Invariant Feature Transform), Support Vector Machine (SVM), and K-Nearest Neighbor (KNN) were used, whereby using KNN, 93.33% accuracy was achieved, and by using SVM, an accuracy of 91.10% was obtained. Singh *et al.* [17] presented a survey for plant disease detection, and the general structure of plant disease identification systems was discussed. The next section summarizes some of the diseases occurring in paddy. The remaining chapter is subdivided as Section 2 outlines some of the diseases occurring in rice plants, Deep Learning, its comparison with Machine Learning, and its models are summarized in Section 3. In Section 4, several pre-trained networks are discussed and finally, several layouts about how these PNNs can be used in classifying rice diseases.

PADDY DISEASES

Disease in paddy crops occurs in several parts of the plant, such as roots, grains, stems, leaves, and sheaths. Although there are multiple diseases that affect paddy crops, a few of the diseases are discussed below [1, 4].

- **Blast-** It is a fungal disease with white to circular gray spots having dark colour boundaries at the initial stage, but at the later stage, the spots become elliptical in shape with reddish to brown borders.
- **Brown Spot-** It is also a fungal disease with a circular to oval shape. Symptoms are generally light brown in colour, and they mostly have a reddish to brown colour at the margins.
- **Tungro-** It is caused by a virus due to which the diseased plant gets undersized and of pale green colour leaves. There is excessive tillering, due to which leaves become weak and drop off. Streaks in the leaves are parallel to each other.
- **Rot-** Infected leaves have types of irregular spots. Centres of these spots are of light brown in colour, and the boundaries are of dark brown colour.
- **Bacterial Blight-** This disease is caused by bacteria, it develops water-soaked spots starting from the tip of leaves to its base. The colour of this disease is generally yellow to light brown.

DEEP LEARNING (DL)

DL is a subset of Machine Learning (ML), which is a further subset of AI. Machine Learning is an algorithm-based approach where learning is done from observational data, and the machine is not programmed explicitly. ML has revolutionized several domains within the last few years. ANN (Artificial Neural Networks) is a subfield of ML, and this subfield has introduced us to DL. The introduction of DL has resulted in a more accurate classification of images. AI was introduced in the 1950s, ML in the 1980s, and DL in 2015. AI system can process thousands of Floating-Point Instructions per second (FLOPS), ML is much faster as it can process millions of FLOPS, but DL broke all records by processing quadrillions of FLOPS [18]. The most prominent factor contributing to boosting DL is the empowerment of GPU computing. Transition is done from CPU based training to GPU based training, which leads to acceleration in the entire process of training [19]. Due to DL, the research community can develop intelligent and complex algorithms which have displayed higher performance in all aspects. The deep word in deep learning is derived from deep models for learning. In ML, features are extracted manually, but in DL, with the use of CNN, feature extraction and recognition tasks are performed by the model itself. When we talk about the dataset size, the ML model requires only a small amount of dataset, but DL requires a large amount, but the accuracy of DL model is much higher than that of ML. In DL, we can use an existing model, which has been trained for some tasks, and this technique is described in the subsection. DL algorithms have several layers of nonlinear units between layers, known as Artificial Neurons (AN) or neurons. The piling of these neurons in an incremental hierarchical manner allows feature learning and pattern recognition with the aid of efficient learning algorithms.

DL approaches can be categorized as follows: supervised, semi-supervised, and unsupervised. In supervised learning, labelled data is used, while for unsupervised DL, the context incorporates sets of input and the corresponding output. A criterion that evaluates the algorithm's performance is the degree time called loss or cost function. Optimizing function minimizes the loss function with respect to the input data. Semi-supervised learning models only use semi-labelled datasets where a small amount of labelled data and a large amount of unlabelled data are present. Generative Adversarial Networks (GAN) are an example of semisupervised learning models. In unsupervised learning techniques, no labelled data is present. There are two learning techniques in DL: a. Transfer Learning b. Active Learning [19].

• **Transfer Learning (TL):** It is a category of learning which allows us to use the knowledge obtained while solving any of the tasks and then retraining it to any other related task, *i.e.*, a model trained on one recognition task (for example, potato leaf identification) having the ability to assist another recognition (tomato leaf identification) task. TL is a technique of machine learning where the first step is to adopt existing transfer learning techniques for plant disease classification, the authors used several Convolution Neural Network (CNN) examples, GoogleNet, AlexNet, VGGN, *etc.*, which are already trained on the ImageNet dataset. With the assistance of TL, they could beat the existing LifeCLEF by 15% accuracy [19].

• **Active Learning (AL):** It is an incremental learning technique that selects the best and optimal samples to train. For training, a model with deep neural network labelled data is required. The AL approach model continuously communicates with the user's annotator by using labels from images, as all images present in the dataset are of very high importance [19]. In the next section, several deep learning architectures are discussed briefly.

Pretrained Neural Network (PNN)

A pre-trained network is a network that has already learned features from real environment images, and we can use this network to learn some other tasks. Mostly pre-trained networks are trained on the ImageNet database, where millions of images can be recognized into thousands of object categories [15]. Training a network from scratch is a little difficult task compared to using pretrained networks and transfer learning. These pre-trained networks can be used for classification, feature extraction, and transfer learning. Some of the pre-trained networks are described below [15, 20, 21]: -

• **AlexNet:** It has around 61 million parameters and consists of 5 convolution layers,3 pooling layers, and 2 fully connected layers. The size of AlexNet is 227 MB with an input image size of 227*227.

• **GoogLeNet:** This architecture has 7 million parameters and consists of two convolution layers, two pooling layers, and nine inception layers. Each of these inception layers has six convolution layers and one pooling layer. The overall size of this architecture is 27 MB, with the input image size of 224*224. This architecture is more complex than the other remaining architectures.

• **VGG:** There are two versions of this network, *i.e.*, vgg16 and vgg19. The size of the input image is similar (224*224) for both networks. The number of input parameters for vgg16 is 138 million, and for vgg19, it is 144 million parameters. The size of vgg16 and vgg19 is 515MB and 535 MB, respectively.

• **Inception V3:** This network has 23.9 million parameters with an input image size of 299*299. Overall network size is 89 MB. Another variant of Inception V3 is inceptionresnetv2, where the network size is extended to 209MB, and the number of parameters has increased to 55.9 million.

• **ResNet18:** The size of ResNet18 is 44MB with 224*224 as input image size. It has 11.7 million parameters. Other two variants of ResNet18 are RestNet50 and ResNet101, which have 25.6 and 44.6 million parameters, respectively. The size of its variants includes 44MB and 96 MB, but the input image size is the same (224*224) for all variants.

Using three research articles as a reference, a brief description of how PNNs are being used for classifying rice crop diseases. The section explores the work of three papers where PNNs have been applied. All three proposed models have used AlexNet in the process and have obtained very high performance. AlexNet model was used by Srivastava *et al.* [22] as a feature extractor. Image dataset of Rice was collected from IGA (Indira Ghandhi Agricultural) University, Chattisgarh, India.

Digital and mobile cameras were used for acquiring images later, and the background of each image was converted to black for better extraction of features, reducing computation cost and complexity. Image dataset consisted of 612 image samples (Rice Blast-88, Bacterial Leaf Blight-240, Sheath Blight-100, and

Healthy-191) and four classes. The input size of the network is 227*227*3, so the input images were resized . Partitioning was performed on the dataset for training-testing purposes and it was partitioned into three categories i) 80% training and 20% testing ii) 70% training and 30% testing iii) 60% training and 40% testing. After extracting image features using AlexNet model, SVM (Support Vector Machine) was used as a classifier. By choosing the partition category randomly, the experiment was conducted ten times, and the classification accuracies obtained were in the range of 89.45% to 91.37%. The highest accuracy was obtained by the first (80% training and 20% testing) partition. Although the number of image samples in the dataset was very few, it becomes necessary to test the model on the lager dataset to improve its performance. Fig. (1) displays the layout of the model proposed by Srivastava *et al.* [22].

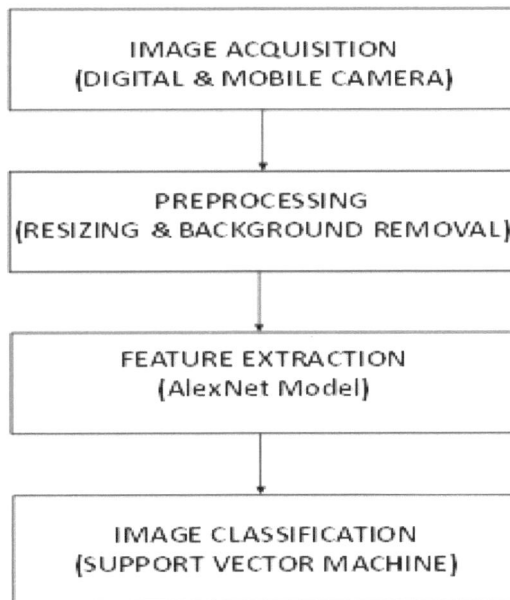

Fig. (1). Disease detection using Transfer Learning [22].

Bharathi [23] proposed a method using AlexNet model of Convolution Neural Network for the classification of sixteen diseases, weeds, and pests of paddy crop. Firstly, images were captured using a digital camera and were stored in ImageNet dataset; then in preprocessing step, the background noise was removed, for image enhancement, RGB image was transformed into gray scale images for detecting pests, weed, and diseases clearly.

In image segmentation, blob detection was performed to obtain the interest region and separate it from the background following the application of threshold operation. The next step was to extract features where object orientation features used in Gabor feature extractor, colour features using Histogram Oriented Gradient (HOG), texture, and shape features using Gaussian Mixture Model, were obtained. Finally, AlexNet model was used for classifying the input images. Fig. (**2**) displays the model proposed by Bharthi [23].

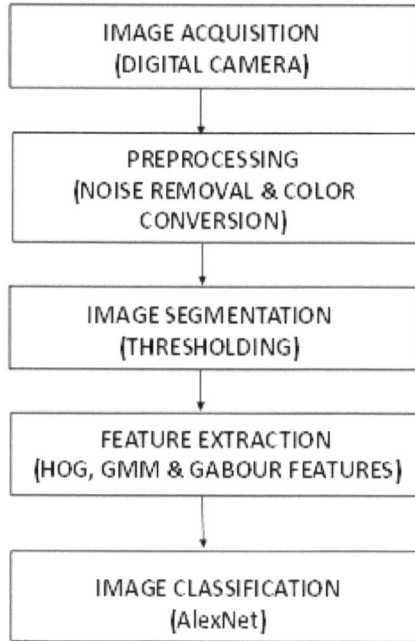

```
┌─────────────────────────────────┐
│      IMAGE ACQUISITION           │
│      (DIGITAL CAMERA)            │
└─────────────────────────────────┘
                │
                ▼
┌─────────────────────────────────┐
│        PREPROCESSING             │
│   (NOISE REMOVAL & COLOR         │
│        CONVERSION)               │
└─────────────────────────────────┘
                │
                ▼
┌─────────────────────────────────┐
│      IMAGE SEGMENTATION          │
│       (THRESHOLDING)             │
└─────────────────────────────────┘
                │
                ▼
┌─────────────────────────────────┐
│      FEATURE EXTRACTION          │
│  (HOG, GMM & GABOUR FEATURES)    │
└─────────────────────────────────┘
                │
                ▼
┌─────────────────────────────────┐
│      IMAGE CLASSIFICATION        │
│          (AlexNet)               │
└─────────────────────────────────┘
```

Fig. (2). Identifying paddy pests, weeds, and diseases using AlexNet [23].

Rao *et al.* [24] presented a framework for classifying rice diseases, namely, Leaf Smut, Brown Spot, and Bacterial Leaf Blight. A picture of rice plant could be uploaded by the user through the user interface, and then it passes through AlexNet model for accurate extraction of features and classification. The training accuracy achieved by the model was 91.34%, and the testing accuracy achieved was 84%. Fig. (**3**) displays the layout of the model proposed by Rao *et al.* [24].

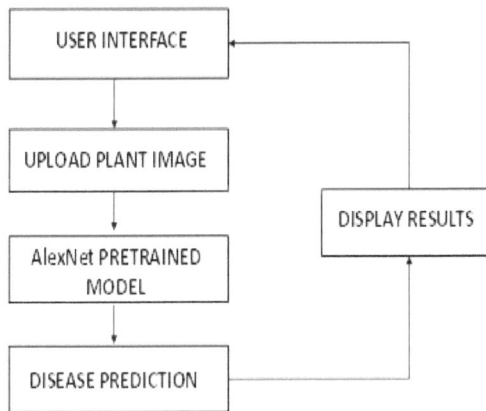

Fig. (3). Rice disease prediction using Deep Learning [24].

CONCLUDING REMARKS

Here we have discussed various Artificial Intelligence (ML and DL) based techniques proposed by several researchers, discussing several diseases of rice crop, including the introduction of various models of deep learning. The main goal was to present an idea of how Pre-trained Neural Networks can be used in recognition of rice diseases. High yield and high-quality rice are essential, but quality and yield both degrade due to the attack of several diseases, pests, and weeds. Therefore, it becomes vital to recognize diseases at early stages and diagnose them with very little effect on the environment. As we have seen that deep learning approaches can easily identify and classify diseases. There are several pre-trained networks available that can be used with very little computation power. These pre-trained networks save our time compared to designing the network from scratch. Future work would be exploring more about these networks and implementing them in the plant disease detection domain.

CONSENT OF PUBLICATION

Not applicable.

CONFLICT OF INTEREST

The author declares no conflict of interest, financial or otherwise.

ACKNOWLEDGEMENTS

Declared none.

REFERENCES

[1]   T. Bera, A. Das, J. Sil, and A.K. Das, "A survey on rice plant disease identification using image processing and data mining techniques", In: *Emerging Technologies in Data Mining and Information Security.* Springer: Singapore, 2019, pp. 365-376.
[http://dx.doi.org/10.1007/978-981-13-1501-5_31]

[2]   http://www.knowledgebank.irri.org/

[3]   J. Amara, B. Bouaziz, and A. Algergawy, "A deep learning-based approach for banana leaf diseases classification", *Datenbanksysteme für Business, Technologie und Web (BTW 2017)- Workshopband.,* 2017.

[4]   S. Phadikar, J. Sil, and A.K. Das, "Rice diseases classification using feature selection and rule generation techniques", *Comput. Electron. Agric.,* vol. 90, pp. 76-85, 2013.
[http://dx.doi.org/10.1016/j.compag.2012.11.001]

[5]   M. Suresha, K.N. Shreekanth, and B.V. Thirumalesh, "Recognition of diseases in paddy leaves using knn classifier", In: *2017 2nd International Conference for Convergence in Technology (I2CT)* IEEE, 2017, pp. 663-666.
[http://dx.doi.org/10.1109/I2CT.2017.8226213]

[6]   S. Baranwal, S. Khandelwal, and A. Arora, "Deep learning convolutional neural network for apple leaves disease detection", In: *Proceedings of International Conference on Sustainable Computing in Science Technology and Management (SUSCOM)* Amity University Rajasthan Jaipur India, 2019.
[http://dx.doi.org/10.2139/ssrn.3351641]

[7]   H.S. Abdullahi, R. Sheriff, and M. Fatima, "Convolution neural network in precision agriculture for plant image recognition and classification", In: *Seventh International Conference on Innovative Computing Technology (INTECH).* vol. 10. IEEE, 2017.

[8]   P.P. Singh, R. Kaushik, H. Singh, N. Kumar, and P.S. Rana, *"Convolutional Neural Networks Based Plant Leaf Diseases Detection Scheme", IEEE Globecom Workshops (GC Wkshps).* IEEE, 2019, pp. 1-7.

[9]   U.P. Singh, S.S. Chouhan, S. Jain, and S. Jain, "Multilayer convolution neural network for the classification of mango leaves infected by anthracnose disease", *IEEE Access,* vol. 7, pp. 43721-43729, 2019.
[http://dx.doi.org/10.1109/ACCESS.2019.2907383]

[10]   A. Venkataramanan, P.H. Deepak Kumar, and P. Agarwal, "Plant disease detection and classification using deep neural networks", *Int. J. Comput. Sci. Eng,* vol. 11, no. 9, pp. 40-46, 2019.

[11]   K.J. Mohan, M. Balasubramanian, and S. Palanivel, "Detection and recognition of diseases from paddy plant leaf images", *Int. J. Comput. Appl.,* vol. 144, no. 12, 2016.

[12]   Y. Lu, S. Yi, N. Zeng, Y. Liu, and Y. Zhang, "Identification of rice diseases using deep convolutional neural networks", *Neurocomputing,* vol. 267, pp. 378-384, 2017.
[http://dx.doi.org/10.1016/j.neucom.2017.06.023]

[13]   M. Jogin, *3rd IEEE International Conference on Recent trends in Electronics, Information & Communication Technology (RTEICT)* IEEE, 2018, pp. 2319-2323.

[14]   https://in.mathworks.com/help/deeplearning/ref/resnet50.html?s_tid=srchtitle

[15]   V.C. Rezende, M. Costa, A. Santos, CL. Roberto, and de. Oliveira, "Image processing with convolutional neural networks for classification of plant diseases", *8th Brazilian Conference on Intelligent Systems (BRACIS).,* IEEE, pp. 705-710, 2019.

[16]   A.A. Alfarisy, Q. Chen, and M. Guo, "Deep learning-based classification for paddy pests & diseases recognition", In: *Proceedings of 2018 International Conference on Mathematics and Artificial Intelligence,* 2018, pp. 21-25.
[http://dx.doi.org/10.1145/3208788.3208795]

[17] S. Taranjeet, and K.C. Krishna, "A review on pdis (plant disease identification systems)", *International Journal of Engineering Research & Technology (IJERT) ENCADEMS,* vol. 8, no. 10, 2020.

[18] https://www.mathworks.com

[19] A.L. Chandra, S.V. Desai, W. Guo, and V.N. Balasubramanian, "Computer vision with deep learning for plant phenotyping in agriculture: A survey", *arXiv preprint arXiv,* vol. 11391, no. 2020, 2006.

[20] H-C. Shin, H.R. Roth, M. Gao, L. Lu, Z. Xu, I. Nogues, J. Yao, D. Mollura, and R.M. Summers, "Deep convolutional neural networks for computer-aided detection: CNN architectures, dataset characteristics and transfer learning", *IEEE Trans. Med. Imaging,* vol. 35, no. 5, pp. 1285-1298, 2016. [http://dx.doi.org/10.1109/TMI.2016.2528162] [PMID: 26886976]

[21] S. Hershey, and S. Chaudhuri, *Daniel PW Ellis, Jort F. Gemmeke, Aren Jansen, R. Channing Moore, Manoj Plakal et al. "CNN architectures for large-scale audio classification." IEEE international conference on acoustics, speech, and signal processing (icassp).* IEEE, 2017, pp. 131-135.

[22] V. K. Shrivastava, M. K. Pradhan, S. Minz, and M. P. Thakur, "Rice plant disease classification using transfer learning of deep convolution neural network", *Rice Plant Disease Classification Using Transfer Learning of Deep Convolution Neural Network.,* 2019. [http://dx.doi.org/10.5194/isprs-archives-XLII-3-W6-631-2019]

[23] R.J. Bharathi, "Paddy Plant Disease Identification and Classification of Image Using AlexNet Model", *The International Journal of Analytical and Experimental Modal Analysis.,* vol. 7, no. 3, pp. 1094-1098, 2020.

[24] D.S. Rao, N. Kavya, K.L. Naveen, V. Yasaswi, and N. Pranay Kumar, "Detection and classification of rice leaf diseases using deep learning", *Int J Adv Sci Tech,* vol. 29, no. 03, pp. 5868-5874, 2020.

Artificial Intelligence and Natural Algorithms, 2022, 153-174

CHAPTER 10

Shallow Cloud Classification using Deep Learning and Image Segmentation

Amreen Ahmad[1,*], Chanchal Kumar[1], Ajay Kumar Yadav[1] and Agnik Guha[1]

[1] *Department of Computer Engineering, Faculty of Engineering and Technology, Jamia Millia Islamia, New Delhi-25, India*

Abstract: Shallow clouds play a significant role in the earth's radiation balance, but they're still poorly represented in climatic models. Our project analyzes the cloud images taken from satellites and attempts to build a deep learning model to classify cloud patterns. This will help us to identify the cloud formations and help improve the earth's climate understanding. We will use various deep learning and image segmentation techniques like UNet to produce a model which can classify the shallow layers of clouds into various labels (fish, flower, gravel, and sugar). Various data augmentation techniques are implemented to improve the proposed model. Additionally, transfer learning is implemented by using ResNet backbones to improve the performance of the segmentation model. This will help gain insights into the matter of shallow cloud effects on the earth's climate, there by helping in the development of next-gen climate models without having to go through the tedious task of classifying the clouds present in the images first.

Keywords: Deep Learning, Image Segmentation, RAdam, Shallow Clouds, UNet.

INTRODUCTION

What are Shallow Clouds?

Weak convective currents create shallow cloud layers due to the dry, stable air, preventing continued vertical development. Shallow clouds over land are usually only several kilometers wide and rarely produce rain. They are generally many and quite effective at resisting the sun and maintaining the evaporation of water from the land. They can occur quite locally; they can also be widespread, covering the mesoscale.

---

[*] **Corresponding author Amreen Ahmad:** Department of Computer Engineering, Faculty of Engineering and Technology, Jamia Millia Islamia, New Delhi-25, India; E-mail: amreen.ahmad10@gmail.com

Rijwan Khan, Pawan Sharma, Sugam Sharma and Santosh Kumar (Eds.)

Why is it Important to Study Shallow Clouds?

Shallow clouds have a significant role in the world's temperature balance, yet they are most represented in climate predicting models. It is important that Earth system models accurately take the effect of these shallow clouds considerably on the trading of water particles and vitality between the surface and the atmosphere.

Cloud mistakes can have wide arriving impacts on the exactness and nature of results on climate figures. This study explains the need to precisely consider the impact of shallow mists in barometrical models that can be used to imitate climate and atmosphere. It will go about as a manual for enhancements for the portrayal of shallow convection in Earth framework models.

Motivation for an Automated System for Cloud Classification

It is simple for a researcher to take a look at a picture and recognize the highlights of intrigue. The premise of recognizing designs is distinguishing comparatively organized highlights over various pictures. AI strategies can imitate this human capacity to recognize designs; however, they require adequate training data information. The application and appraisal of such strategies turn into a dull undertaking.

Shallow clouds have a significant role in the world's temperature balance, yet they are most certainly represented in climate predicting models. Most of the studies conducted were on 'whether clouds are present or not', and the classification of clouds based on their type (Cirrus Cumulus, Stratus Nimbus). Limited research work has been done in Mesoscale cloud identification [1]. Gauging shadiness precisely stays one of the significant difficulties in numerous pieces of the world.

This undertaking will assist researchers with a better insight into how mists will shape our future atmosphere without experiencing the dreary work of distinguishing designs. Specifically, the center is extremely shallow during cumulus convection in the exchange wind region. This task will control the advancement of cutting-edge models, which could decrease the vulnerabilities in atmosphere projection.

Benefits

It can reduce the workload of those people who will try to identify cloud patterns in satellite images. They can directly study its effect on weather. It will guide researchers in developing a more accurate weather prediction model. It will help the aviation sector, which has strict cloud-related safety guidelines.

RELATED WORK

There has been very little research regarding the development of a robust model for detection as well as segmentation of shallow layer clouds. Patterns of shallow clouds at the mesoscale (20 to 2,000 km) level in the downstream observed from space were subjectively defined and learned by trained scientists. Four patterns in the mesoscale organization were recognized, which could be labelled in a reproducible manner. These cloud patterns were introduced by 811902:19367082 [2], which was based on mesoscale cloud patterns present in the trade winds, and they were labelled as Sugar, Gravel, Fish, and Flowers.

In 2019, researchers from Max-Planck Institute of Meteorology conducted research on a crowd-sourcing activity to detect and label cloud structures from satellite images [1]. Through crowd-sourcing, they hoped to label many more images than was possible in the previous study. They hypothesized that this research would help in exploring how deep learning methods could be applied to extend the analysis and learn more about the patterns.

Researchers [3] briefly discuss previous efforts for applying deep learning models. They presented two models as proof of concept and comparison. They mention the use of a Retina net with Resnet50 backbone for object detection. Images were downscaled from 1400 by 2100 pixels to 700 by 1050 pixels to fit batches of 4. UNet model with Resnet50 backbone was used for segmentation. Images were downscaled to 466pixels by 700 pixels with a batch size of 6. The models were primarily used to compare with human labelling performance using the mean accuracy of correctly labeled pixels.

Our problem is to segment the images into various cloud patterns. Image segmentation, a part of computer vision, can be done using Fully Convolutional Networks. This idea was well presented in 2014 by Jonathan Long [4] in his research. Biomedical imaging introduced a powerful model for image segmentation, *i.e.*, U-NET, in 2015 by Olaf Ronneberger. This model is now used in various other fields. Fabian Isensee [5], in 2020, conducted research on biomedical image segmentation, introducing us to 3D biomedical segmentation models using UNet. Here, segmentation of organs is performed. It also introduces the idea of using a combined loss function (bce and dice loss) for training the model. The idea for using RAdam as the optimizer is taken from the research conducted by Liyuan Liu [6] in 2019. It introduces the idea of a warmup to reduce the variance that might be caused in the initial stages of training. The name Rectified Adam corresponds to the rectified version of the standard Adam optimizer.

PROPOSED METHODOLOGY

Data Preprocessing

Data Processing is an important step that helps to transform the raw data into a useful and efficient format. Here, we will try to understand the dataset and search for any null value or garbage value. Expand the train data frame to include image ID and labels and perform one-hot encoding for labels.

Data Analysis

Analysis of the dataset should be done before training. It helps to gather more information about the data provided. Here, we see the distribution of the data among the labels and whether the labels have any correlation between them. Visualizing a sample image along with its mask helps to understand the structure of masking the cloud patterns. For this, the given dataset is visualized.

Model Used

UNet

U-Net is a convolutional neural system that was produced by the Biomedical Picture division at the Computer Science Department of the University of Freiburg, Germany. The system depends on a completely convolutional system, and its engineering was changed and reached out to work on preparing pictures and yield progressively exact segmentations. U-Net was made by Olaf Ronneberger, Philipp Fischer, Thomas Brox in 2015 with the paper "U-Net: Convolutional Networks for Biomedical Image Segmentation". It's an improvement and advancement of FCN: Evan Shelhamer, Jonathan Long, Trevor Darrell (2014). "Completely convolutional systems for semantic division".

Idea Behind UNet

While converting an image into a vector, we already learned the feature mapping of the image, so why not use the same mapping to convert it again to the image.

Architecture UNet

This architecture is divided into three sections:

  I. Contraction
 II. BottleNeck
III. Expansion

The contraction segment is made of numerous contraction blocks. Each block takes information and is applied to two 3X3 convolution layers followed by a 2X2 max pooling. The number of parts or highlight maps after each block duplicates to the goal that engineering can become familiar with the mind-boggling structures successfully.

The bottom most layer intercedes between the compression layer and the expansion layer. It utilizes two 3X3 CNN layers followed by a 2X2 convolution layer. The core of this design lies in the expansion area. Like the contraction layer, it comprises a few extension blocks. Each block passes the input to two 3X3 CNN layers followed by a 2X2 sampling layer. Additionally, after each block number, feature maps are utilized by the convolutional layer to get half look-after balance.

Be that as it may, each time, the input is additionally added by the feature maps of the corresponding contraction layer. This activity would guarantee that the features that are found while contracting the picture will be utilized to reproduce it. The quantity of expansion blocks is the same as the quantity of contraction blocks. From that point forward, the resultant mapping goes through another 3X3 CNN layer with the number of feature maps equivalent to the number of segments wanted.

UNet on ResNet34 Backbone: Residual Network

ResNet is a convolutional Neural Network (CNN) architecture made up of an arrangement of leftover blocks with skip connections separating ResNets from different CNNs.

Residual Blocks

Convolutional networks [1] can be substantially deeper, more accurate, and more efficient to train if they contain shorter connections between layers closer to the input and closer to the output.

Architecture

An exceptionally successful answer is to include cross connections between layers of the system, permitting large segments from being skipped if needed. This makes a misfortune surface resembling the picture on the right. This is much simpler for the model to be trained with optimal loads to lessen the loss. The basic architecture of UNet is shown in Fig. (**1**).

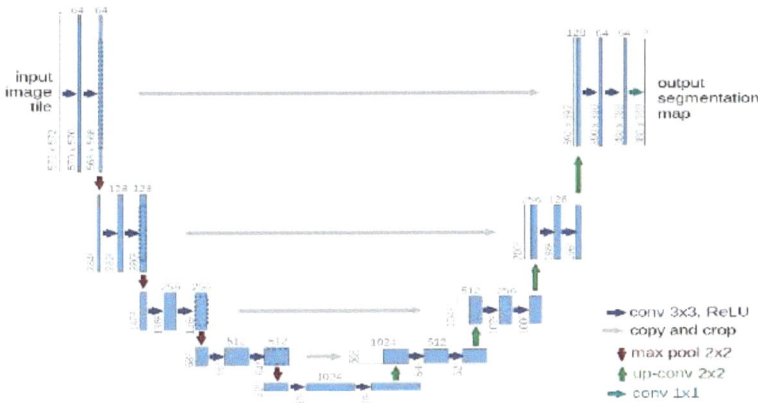

Fig. (1). Basic architecture of a UNet.

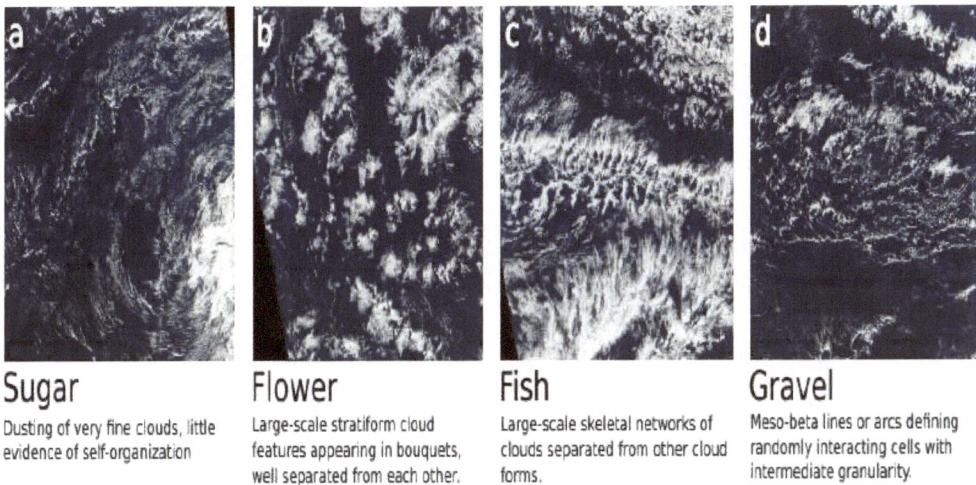

Sugar
Dusting of very fine clouds, little evidence of self-organization

Flower
Large-scale stratiform cloud features appearing in bouquets, well separated from each other.

Fish
Large-scale skeletal networks of clouds separated from other cloud forms.

Gravel
Meso-beta lines or arcs defining randomly interacting cells with intermediate granularity.

Fig. (2). Canonical examples of four cloud organizations.

Cross Entropy

This loss analyzes every pixel individually, comparing the class predictions (depth-wise pixel vector) to our one-hot encoded target vector. Since the cross-entropy misfortune assesses the class forecasts for every pixel vector independently and afterward midpoints over all pixels, this can be an issue if your different classes have uneven portrayal in the picture. It is because training can be ruled by the most predominant classes. There are two:

   i. Weighted Cross entropy
 ii. Balanced cross entropy

Dice Loss

Another popular loss function for image segmentation tasks is based on the Dice coefficient [7], which is essentially a measure of overlap between two samples. This measure ranges from 0 to 1, where 1 denotes the perfect and complete overlap. The Dice coefficient developed for binary data can be calculated as:

$$\text{Dice} = 2\,|A \cap B| \,/\, (|A|+|B|) \tag{1}$$

Intended approach

$$\text{loss} = \sum_{c \in \{Sugar, Flower, Fish, Gravel\}} BCE_c(y_t, y_p) + \left(1 - DSC(y_t, y_p)\right) \tag{2}$$

Where c is the cloud formation class, y_t (is the ground truth, y_p is the model's prediction, and BCE is the binary cross entropy loss for class c.

RAdam Optima

RAdam (Rectified Adam) [7] is a new variation of the classic adam optimizer that provides an automated, dynamic adjustment to the adaptive learning rate based on their detailed study of the effects of variance and momentum during training.

Evaluation Metric

Dice Coefficient can be explained as twice the Overlapping Area of two images divided by the total number of pixels in both images. The Dice for two images can be calculated as:

$$\text{Dice} = 2\,|A \cap B| \,/\, (|A|+|B|) \tag{3}$$

DATA SET

The dataset used includes satellite images of clouds [6]. The colored (RGB) satellite images are downloaded from the NASA Worldview. The images contain cloud formations, with label names, Fish, Flower, Gravel, and Sugar. The resolution of these satellite images is 1400 by 2100 pixels. The satellite images are taken from three chosen Earth regions. These earth regions span over 21 degrees longitude and 14 degrees latitude. Two polar-orbiting satellites, namely,

TERRA and AQUA pass a specific region once a day while being used to collect the images. Some of the images were joined together by two orbits. The portion of the resultant satellite image, marked black, depicts the areas that are not covered by the two orbits. To obtain more images and samples with a greater diversity of clouds, we subsequently added images from two further regions in the Pacific, which were chosen based on their climatological similarity to the original study region upwind of Barbados presented in Fig. (**3**). The labels were created in a crowd-sourcing activity at the Max-Planck-Institute for Meteorology in Hamburg, Germany, and the Laboratoire de Météorologie Dynamique in Paris, France, by a team of 68 scientists and domain experts.

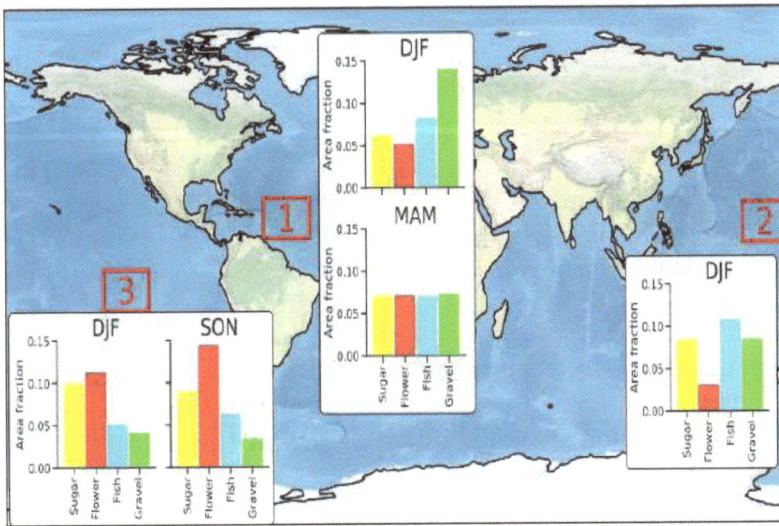

Fig. (3). Worldwide view of three selected regions for labeling clouds in the zooniverse platform.

Each picture in the dataset was labeled by around three distinct scientists. The union of the bounding boxes which were marked by all labelers, constitutes the ground truth.

The csv file presented in Fig. (**4**) consists of two features, image label and Encoded Pixel fields.

Image_Label	EncodedPixels
0031ae9.jpg_Fish	3510 690 4910 690 6310 690 7710 690 9110 690 1...
0031ae9.jpg_Flower	2047 703 3447 703 4847 703 6247 703 7647 703 9...
0031ae9.jpg_Gravel	NaN
0031ae9.jpg_Sugar	658170 388 659570 388 660970 388 662370 388 66...
0035239.jpg_Fish	NaN

Fig. (4). CSV file.

The image name and the cloud label can be found in the Image Label field (a unique index for the dataset). For the same image id, there are four records, one for every label. The Encoded Pixel field uses RLE (run length encoding) to mention all pixels, which come under a label for a particular image. This encoding specifies pixels in each class and reduces the label sizes. For example, '3 8'denotes the starting pixel is 3 and a running total of 8 pixels (3,4,...,10). The cloud formation in the images is classified under four labels, Fish, Flower, gravel, and Sugar.

Fish cloud patterns have elongated skeletal structures. This pattern can span up to 1,000 km, mostly longitudinally. These features appear similar to clouds. They are particularly well-structured cloud forms taken from all ocean basins, near but typically downwind regions where stratocumulus maximizes.

Flowers are areas with isotropic cloud structures, each ranging from 50 to 200 km in diameter, with similarly wide cloud-free regions in between. This pattern overlaps to some degree with the canonical closed-cell MCC. Flowers, however, are often less densely packed than typically closed cells, having narrow cloud-free regions at the edges. They are identified well outside the regions where stratocumulus is found.

Gravel describes fields of granular features, which are marked by arcs or rings. This pattern has a coarser structure than the sugar-cloud type pattern. The cloud patches can very well reach higher altitudes and eventually hit the trade-wind inversion. They show small proof of strati form cloud patterns. These features are organized on smaller scales, often with clouds along the arcs that might be associated with gust fronts and cold pools.

Sugar-cloud type pattern can be described by the widespread areas of very fine cumulus clouds. These cloud fields do not seem to very reflective. They do not contain spaces of cloud-free regions. They may sometimes look like larger scale flows, which gives them some structure. However, regarding the above situation, very little proof has been found.

Around 6000 satellite images are labeled, which are present on GitHub. Each image contained at least one of the four cloud patterns. Although it was less frequent, the images could contain all four cloud formations. The dataset is well balanced. The dataset of images was created using the crowd-sourcing Zooniverse platform. All data is available at https://github.com m/raspstephan/sugar-flowe--fish-or-gravel.

EXPERIMENTAL ANALYSIS

Exploratory Data Analysis

Fig. (2) presents the different cloud patterns identified by ISSI team. The csv file given in Fig. (4) consists of two features, Image_Label and Encoded Pixel fields. From Fig. (2), we conclude that:

For each image in the dataset, there are 4 records for the corresponding cloud labels. Image_Label is a concatenation of the image id and a cloud label. If a certain type of cloud is present in the image, the Encoded Pixel column is non-null and contains an encoded mask for the corresponding cloud type.

From Fig. (5), almost half of the records given in the dataset are empty (NaN). The dataset is well balanced. The four different cloud formation classes are equal in the dataset.

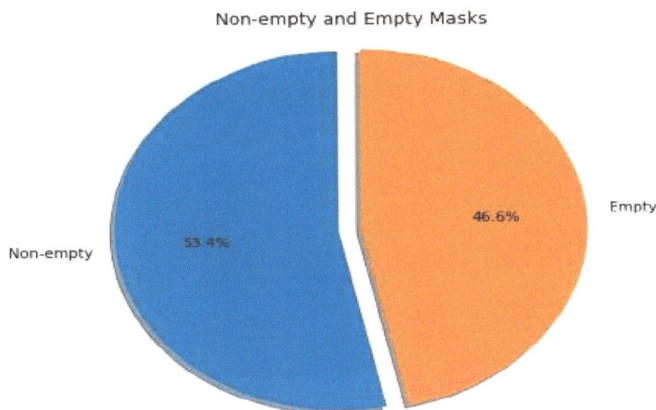

Fig. (5). Non-Empty and Empty Masks.

Figs. (**6** and **7**) present the percentage of different clouds. A number of images per label were found – 2781 fish clouds, 2365 flower clouds, 2939 gravel clouds, 3751 sugar clouds as shown in Fig. (**8**). We mostly have 2 types of cloud formation in one image. Three types of cloud forming together are also frequent. It is very rare to see images with all four cloud labels. Explore the number of labels per image CORRELATION between different types of CLOUD labels. Fig. (**9**) represents the correlation between different types of CLOUD labels. The correlation values visible inside the heat map are close to 0. Therefore, no solid relationship can be observed between the types of clouds. Any kind of combination of cloud formation can happen within the atmosphere.

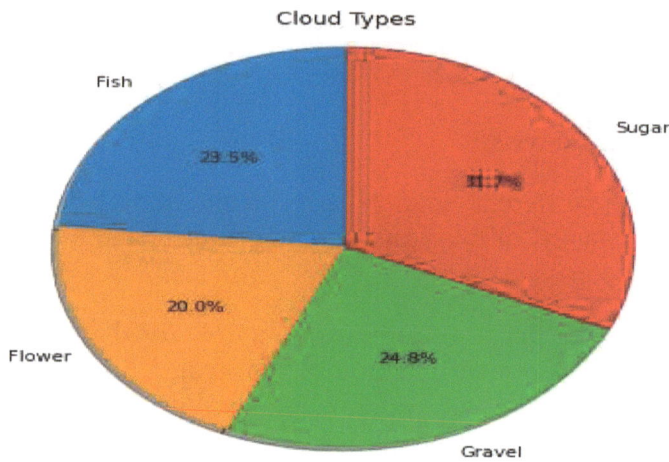

Fig. (6). Pie chart of cloud patterns.

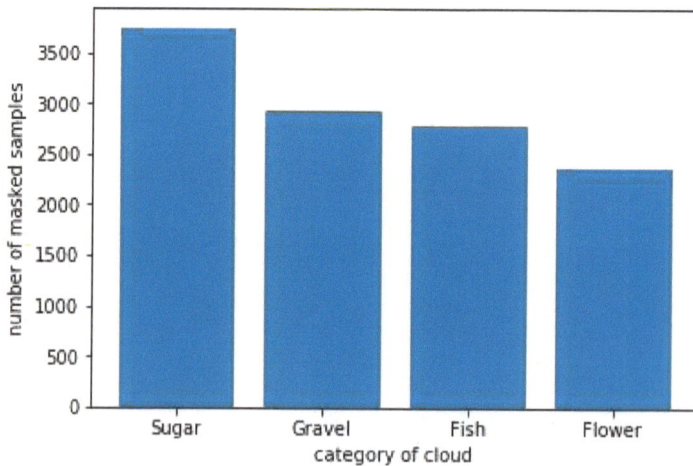

Fig. (7). Histogram of cloud patterns.

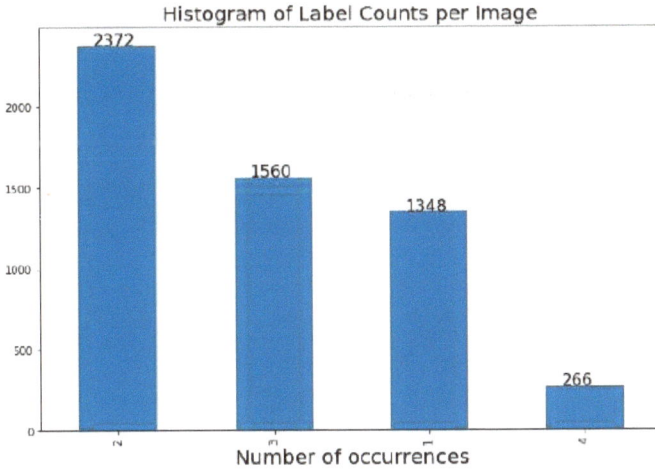

Fig. (8). Histogram of Label Counts per image.

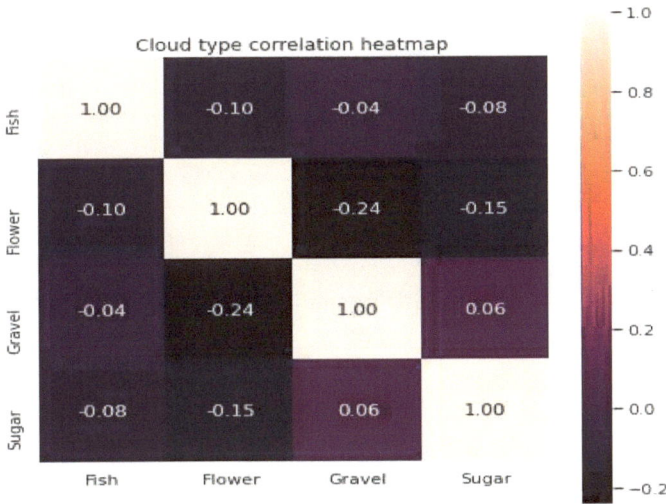

Fig. (9). Correlation Heatmap of cloud patterns.

From Fig. **(9)**, we can conclude that there is no strong correlation present between the cloud patterns (all correlation coefficients are very small).

Data Augmentation

During the training, various data augmentation is performed to prevent over-fitting by adding random rotations, flipping, and shifting to the input images and augmenting the ground truth mask accordingly. The result of the data augmentation performed is presented in Figs. **(10-14)**.

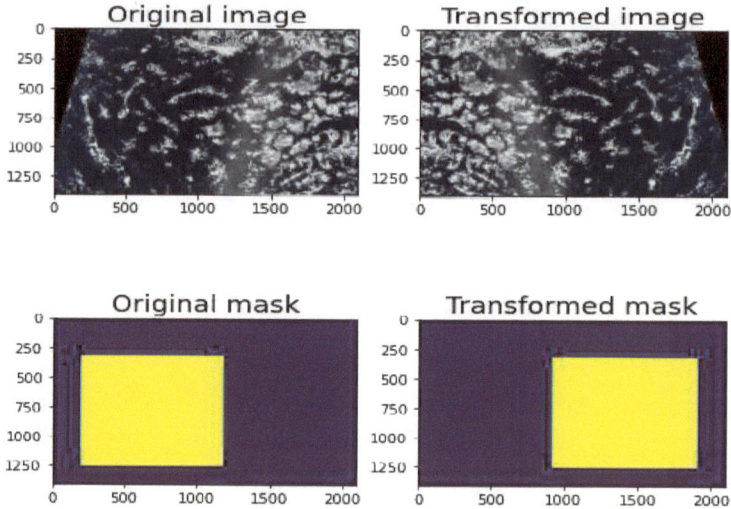

Fig. (10). Horizontal Flip.

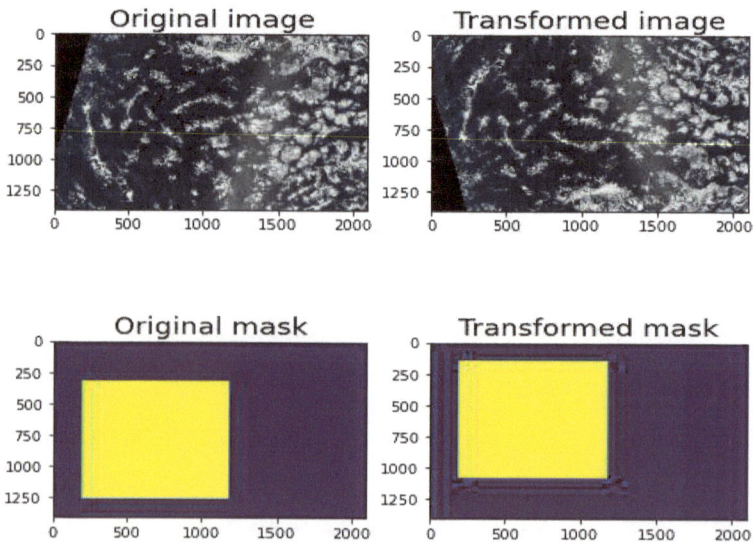

Fig. (11). Vertical Flip.

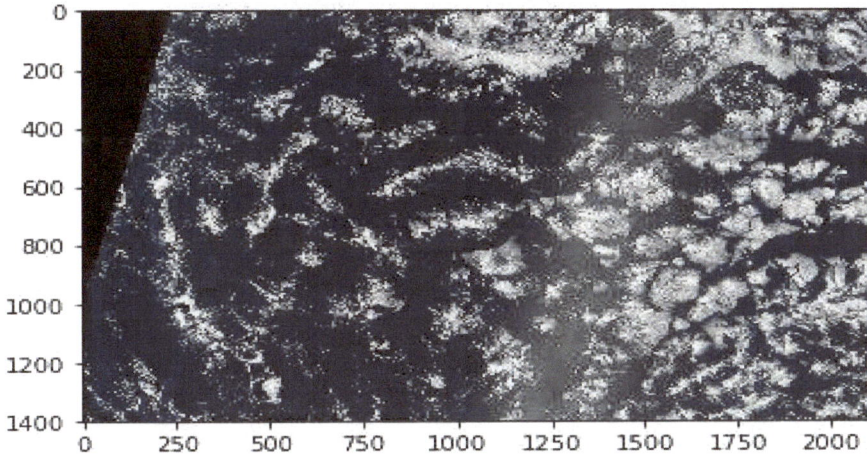

Fig. (12). Original image.

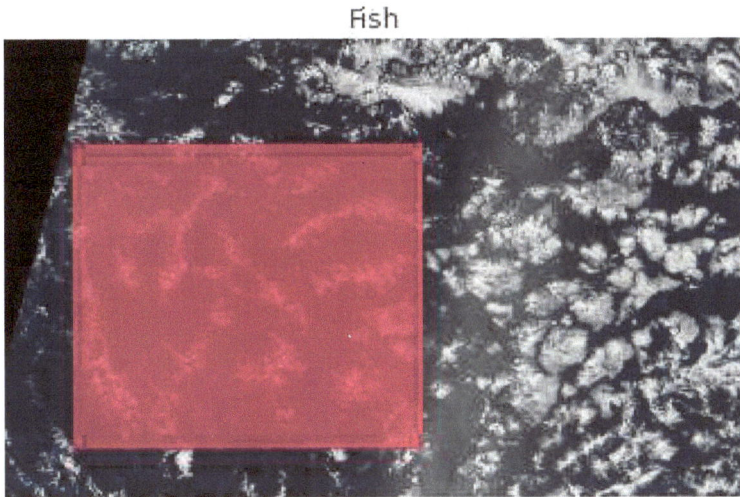

Fig. (13). Fish Mask.

Fig. (14). Flower Mask.

Visualization of Mask

The mask does not show the exact cloud boundary but roughly the area with the same kind of patterns. We can observe that there might be more than one type of cloud pattern.

Training

To save time on computation and fit more number of images to the GPU, training, and prediction are performed on smaller images, downscaled to 320x480 pixels, and batch sizes vary depending on the GPU.

The vanilla UNet consists of 600,756 trainable parameters. The UNet on ResNet34 backbone consists of 24,456,589 parameters out of which 24,439,239 are trainable parameters. These parameters are the weights and biases which the model learns during the training process. Learning the weights and biases helps the model better segment the various cloud patterns in the images.

The vanilla UNet model trained with RAdam optimizer is used as the baseline. All other models also use RAdam as the optimizer. Observed training convergence and performance were best with α=0.001, β_1=0.9, β_2=0.999, default hyper parameters of the optimizer. Initially, the baseline model was trained up to 50 epochs to search for overfitting issues. The models are trained for up to 30 epochs to get the final result (depending on the best result).

The benchmark model was prepared by differing the number of feature maps present in the convolutional layers during both up sampling and down sampling. Increasing the number of feature maps in the conv layer means an increase in the trainable parameters. We observed an increase in the training time of the baseline model, which was a result of more parameters. Dice score showed improvement. On training the benchmark model with different batch sizes, very small differences were observed. Therefore, the maximum batch size was selected for faster training.

RESULTS

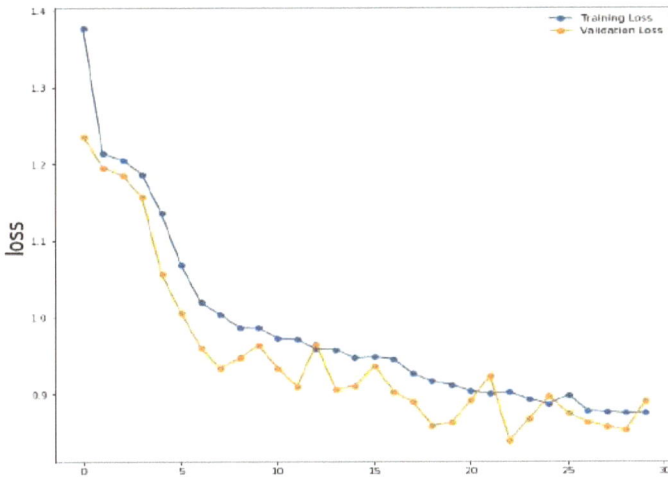

Fig. (15). Loss Graph of Vanilla UNet.

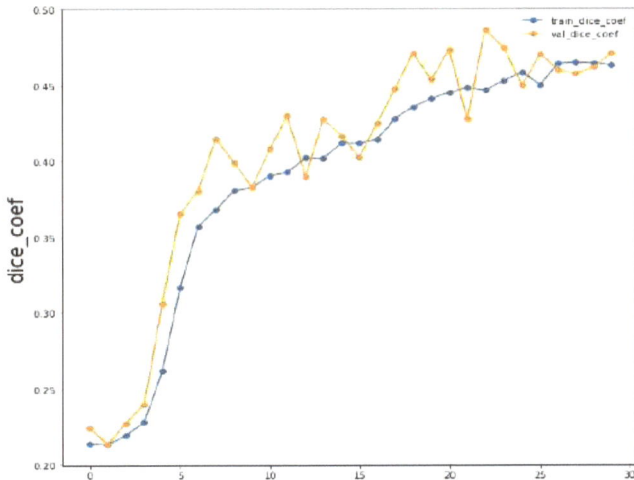

Fig. (16). Dice Score of Vanilla UNet

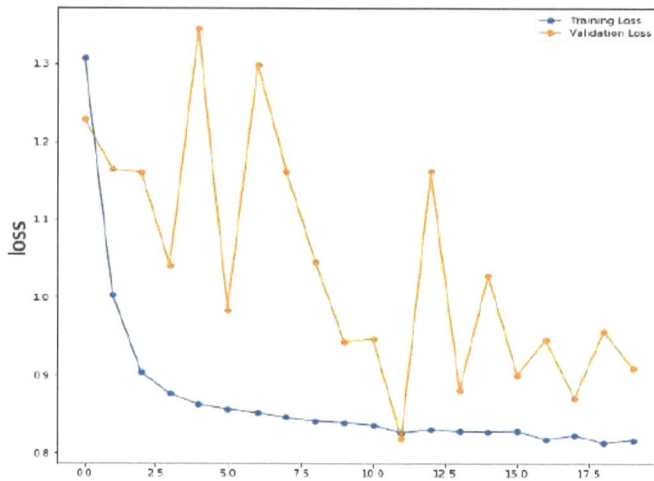

Fig. (17). Loss Graph of UNet on ResNet34 Backbone.

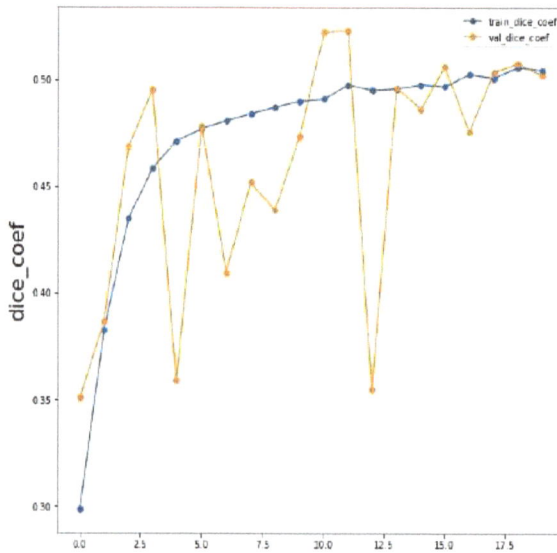

Fig. (18). Dice Score of UNet on ResNet34 Backbone.

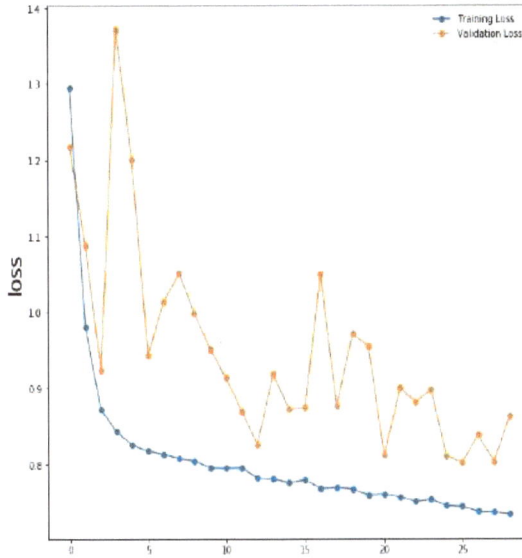

Fig. (19). Loss Graph for improved Unit with ResNet34.

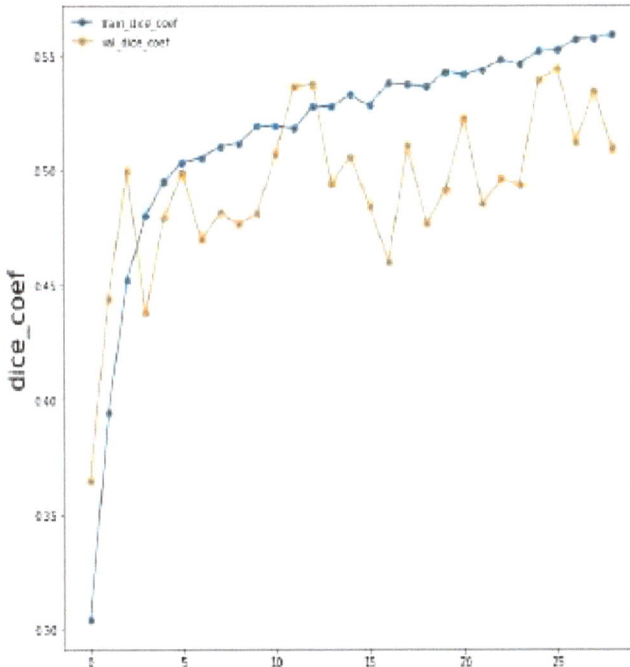

Fig. (20). Dice Score.

Table **1** presents the results of the proposed approach. As is evident from Table **1**, by increasing the number of epochs from 20 to 30 and adding data augmentation, we can see a slight improvement in the performance of our model. The results of the proposed approach are presented diagrammatically in Figs. (**15-20**).

Table 1. Final Result.

Model	Train Loss	Val Loss	Train DICE	Val Dice	Test DICE
UNet	0.8757	0.8902	0.4629	0.4707	0.484
UNet Resnet34	0.8166	0.9085	0.5046	0.5022	0.539
UNetResNet34 (Improved)	0.7343	0.8634	0.5588	0.5093	0.577

PREDICTED SEGMENTS

- ### *Vanilla UNet*

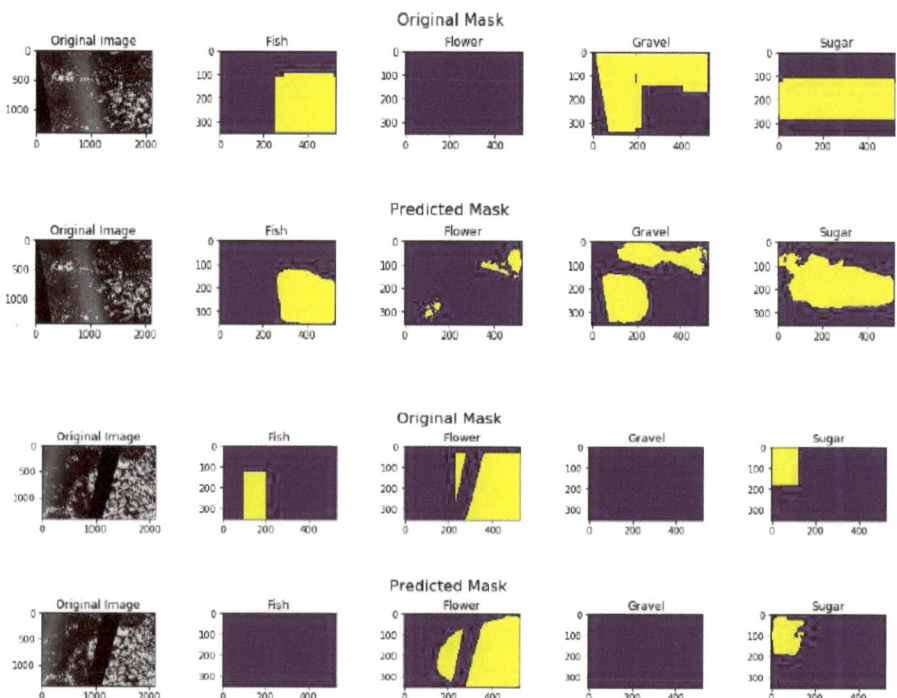

Fig. (21). Vanilla U-Net predictions.

- ### <u>*UNet on ResNet34*</u>

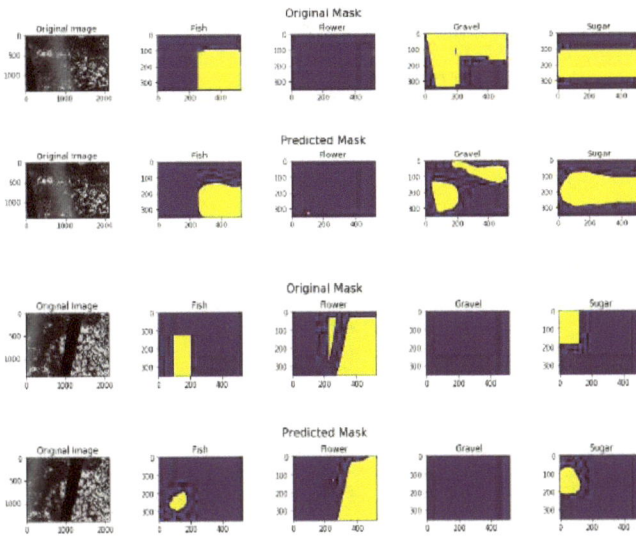

Fig. (22). U-Net ResNet34 predictions.

- ### <u>*UNet on ReNet34 improved*</u>

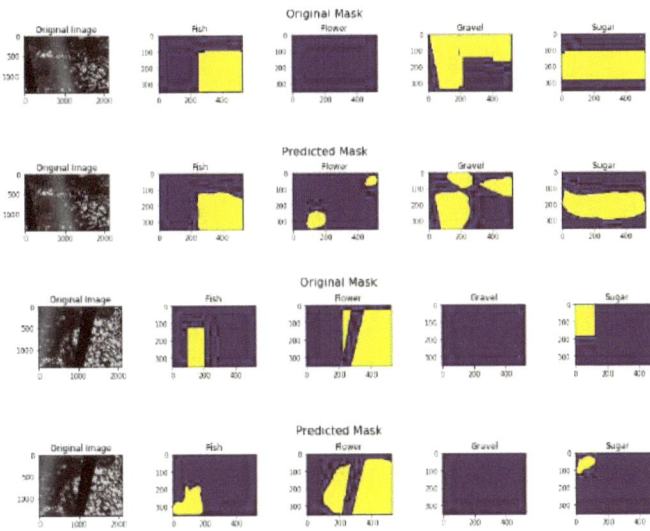

Fig. (23). U-Net ResNet34 predictions, improved version.

We can clearly verify from the prediction masks given in Figs. (**21-23**) that the models with backbones outperform the baseline model. From the predicted masks, we can conclude that the improved model is able to anticipate more of the segmented portion of the cloud patterns. Our baseline model failed to identify many such segmented portions. The dice score of 0.577 is obtained by our best model, which ran for 29 epochs.

CONCLUSION

Classification of shallow clouds means recognizing the type of cloud design that is present in the satellite picture and the area covered by the cloud pattern. Various image segmentation models like UNet help to get the masked images of cloud patterns in the satellite image. Models with backbone show better performance in getting the predicted masks. Moreover, data augmentations help to boost the model performance by artificially creating training images and help to generalize the model.

The models learned to segment the formation areas of the various cloud patterns rather than create fairly large bounding boxes used for our labels. This is a considerable assumption for the generally low dice scores, which are close to 0.5. It is also intuitive because the models will generally structure with empty areas.

The dataset is fairly small. Expanding the preparation dataset can help in improving the model performance. Thresholding can also be performed to remove the small segmented cloud patterns which may have been falsely predicted by the model.

CONSENT FOR PUBLICATION

Not applicable.

CONFLICT OF INTEREST

The authors declare no conflict of interest, financial or otherwise.

ACKNOWLEDGEMENTS

Declared none.

REFERENCES

[1]   S. Rasp, H. Schulz, S. Bony, and B. Stevens, "Combining crowd-sourcing and deep learning to understand meso-scale organization of shallow convection", *ArXiv, abs/1906.01906,* 2019.

[2]   C.C. Liu, Y.C. Zhang, P.Y. Chen, C.C. Lai, Y.H. Chen, J.H. Cheng, and M.H. Ko, "Clouds classification from sentinel-2 imagery with deep residual learning and semantic image segmentation", *Remote Sens.,* vol. 11, no. 2, 2019.

[http://dx.doi.org/10.3390/rs11020119]

[3]   B. Stevens, S. Bony, H. Brogniez, and L. Hentgen, "C., Kiemle, C. Hohenegger, & J. Vial, "Sugar, gravel, fish and flowers: Mesoscale cloud patterns in the trade winds", *Q. J. R. Meteorol. Soc.,* vol. 146, no. 726, pp. 141-152, 2020.
[http://dx.doi.org/10.1002/qj.3662]

[4]   O. Ronneberger, P. Fischer, and T. Brox, "U-net: Convolutional networks for biomedical image segmentation", In: *International Conference on Medical image computing and computer-assisted intervention* Springer: Cham, 2015, pp. 234-241.
[http://dx.doi.org/10.1007/978-3-319-24574-4_28]

[5]   J. Long, E. Shelhamer, and T. Darrell, "Fully convolutional networks for semantic segmentation", In: *Proceedings of the IEEE conference on computer vision and pattern recognition*, 2015, pp. 3431-3440.

[6]   L. Liu, H. Jiang, P. He, W. Chen, X. Liu, J. Gao, and J Han, "On the variance of the adaptive learning rate and beyond", *arXiv preprint arXiv:1908.03265,* 2019.

[7]   F. Isensee, P.F. Jäger, S.A. Kohl, J. Petersen, and K.H Maier-Hein, "Automated design of deep learning methods for biomedical image segmentation", *arXiv preprint arXiv:1904.08128,* 2019.

CHAPTER 11

Artificial Intelligence Based Lung Disease Classification By Using Evolutionary Deep Learning Paradigm

Archana P. Kale[1,*], **Ankita R. Angre**[1], **Ankita R. Angre**[1] and **Dhanashree V. Paranjape**[1]

[1] *Department of Computer Engineering, Modern Education Society's College of Engineering, SPPU Pune, India*

Abstract: Pattern classification is also called pattern reorganization. The classification of pattern is one of the critical problems in Artificial Intelligence. COVID-19 is the most viral lung disease that has put the whole world in such a difficult situation that it has become necessary to develop a machine-learning algorithm to classify lung disease. This research paper is ready to propose Artificial Intelligence Intelligence-based Lung Disease Classification by using an Evolutionary Deep Learning Paradigm to solve the said problem. It delineates an integrated bioinformatics approach in which different aspects of information from a continuum of structured and unstructured data sources are put together to form user-friendly platforms for physicians and researchers. The main objective of the proposed system is to find the probability, diagnosis, and treatment of the COVID-19 disease. Artificial Neural Network-based tool for challenges is associated with COVID-19. There is some specification of our platform as it includes various forms of input data containing medical as well as clinical data. This helps in improving the performance of the system. Experimental results are calculated and statistically analyzed. For benchmarking, the performance of the proposed approach is compared and statistically analyzed.

Keywords: Artificial Intelligence, COVID-19, Deep Learning, Lung diseases, Pattern classification problem.

INTRODUCTION

In December 2019, coronavirus originated from Wuhan and soon spread globally, causing above 150,000 deaths and 2 million confirmed cases until April 18 throughout the globe. It is a Contagious Respiratory and vascular disease that occurs when one gets infected with this virus. It causes difficulty in breathing as it

* **Corresponding author Archana P. Kale:** Department of Computer Engineering, Modern Education Society's College of Engineering, SPPU Pune, India; E-mail: angreankita4@gmail.com

Rijwan Khan, Pawan Sharma, Sugam Sharma and Santosh Kumar (Eds.)

gives rise to viral pneumonia in a patient. The incubation period varies from person to person but mainly lies in between one to fourteen days. Right now, there is no therapeutic treatment or vaccine available for it.

Due to its faster and easy transmissibility and seriousness, "COVID-19" is declared as a pandemic by WHO. The constant increase in cases alarmed an impact on the health care department. The serious patients were required to be treated with the help of mechanical ventilators to stabilize their condition.

As a result, it has become vital to diagnose COVID-19 as early as possible, to reduce the pressure on the healthcare system. Immediate isolation was required for the suspected patients to decrease the chance of them coming in contact with the healthy population.

Usually, pneumonia is diagonalizable by using a person's chest x-ray image. X-rays play an important role in diagnosing pneumonia as they are cheaper and faster, and patients get minimal exposure to radiation than CT scans. This facility is easily available in all healthcare systems, making them a primary source for evaluating a patient for pneumonia caused by COVID-19.

Mainly data like X-rays are interpreted by a medical expert. However, it is restricted due to the extensive variation that exists across different interpreters, the complexity of the image, and its subjectivity.

COVID-19 diagnosis can be made with the help of the patient's chest x-ray images. Radiological expertise is the one who interprets this data to make the results completely dependent on them. The large number of patients in this enormous situation turned the work quite hard and increased the frequency of errors. A substituted system or application for diagnosing disease or examining x-ray images is believed to reduce the load on health workers as well as on the system.

Due to the major development in deep learning and its successful implementation in different real-world applications, it has become a key method for ongoing problems in the healthcare section. Its natural potentiality expects to provide a promising accurate result for the problem.

RELATED WORK

Here, an architecture based on CNN has been presented in [1] to identify different lung diseases. A dataset of 110,000 X-ray images is trained in [2] by using CNN model for the identification of more than 13 diseases.

Rajaraman S. K. *et al.* [3] used the genetic deep learning convolution neural network (GDCNN) technique in their research. They trained the data from scratch and after extracting the required features, it is classified into Covid-19 images and normal images. 5000CXR images of the dataset were used. It is proved that this technique gives us better results with an accuracy of 98.84%, sensitivity of 100%, and specificity of 97.8% with the precision of 93% in the detection of covid-19 infections in comparison to other transfer learning techniques.

Ramchandani A. *et al.* [4] tried to detect using the transfer learning method, in which they used a residual network using two architectures ResNet-34 and ResNet-50. They also used Opencv and Python programming language with pytorch framework for preprocessing and augmentation of data. Results were as follows where ResNet-34 gives an accuracy of 66.67% and the error rate of 33.33%, while ResNet-50 gives an accuracy of 72.38% and an error rate of 27.62%.

Anthimopoulo M. *et al.* [5] used an iterative pruned deep learning model with the combination of chest X-ray images for the prediction of COVID-19. They tried to improve the performance using the RSNA CXR dataset using pretrained CNNs and customized it according to requirements. They also used modality-specific knowledge transfer techniques. As a result, the best performing model gave an accuracy of 99.01%.

Ramchandani A. *et al.* [4] used a dataset of 6249 chest X-ray images from the GitHub repository and used pre-trained models such as ResNet-50, MobileNet, Xception, Inception V3, etc. These architectures were further compared based on their performance, in which MobileNet was the best with a maximum score of F1 and specificity of 995.

In AlexNet, a pre-trained CNN is used to arrange the images by making small adjustments to achieve the desired output with their lung CT data. CNN is also used for the prediction of pneumonia [2, 6].

A new algorithm named as PathNet algorithm is proposed by Anthimopoulo M. *et al.* [5]. COVID-19-Net is used for detecting pneumonia caused by corona virus using CXR images in [1]. Similarly, Coronet-named CNN model is used for spotting COVID-19 in [7]. A deeper model was stated by categorizing images [6].

A small dataset consisting of just 50 images was compared using seven different pre-existing deep learning neural network architectures [2, 8]. Arranging chest x-rays in different categories is resolved by the researchers [4, 6, 9] by proposing a new CNN architecture.

R.G. Babukarthik *et al.* [9], distinguished influenza pneumonia and novel coronavirus pneumonia using CT images and a deep learning model. Inception ResNetV2, ResNet50, and Inception V3 are three unique deep learning neural networks used to detect COVID-19 with the help of CXR images [10], in which inception- V3 achieved 87% of accuracy and ResNet50 98%.

The dataset consists of 157 CT scan images used to detect COVID-19 infections with the help of different deep learning models [11]. Modified RBM was used for feature extraction and classification of lung tissue [12]. Prediction of COVID-19 is achieved by using a 3D learning model.

METHODOLOGY

Collection of Datasets

The primary aim of the application is to detect the probability of COVID-19 pneumonia infection and other pneumonia-related lung diseases. These applications will help to reduce the pressure on medical management as well as the healthcare system. Therefore, we will proceed according to our following agenda:

Therefore, the first step of the application is to collect data from Kaggle A12 Semantic Scholar, COVID-19 explorer. Our dataset contains more than 216 COVID-19 chest X-ray images. It contains 1000 pulse normal patient chest images and pneumonia images.

Deep Learning Algorithm

Deep learning has special techniques which function like neurons of the human body called an artificial neural networks in which each layer has multiple neurons.

CNN is a very powerful algorithm that is widely used for image classification and object detection. CNN algorithms will train on large databases such as ImageNet. ImageNet need not to train on the first few layers. Upper layers are used to match the current problems known as Transfer Learning, discussed in the next paragraph.

In this model, we are going to use pre-trained CNN models on the ImageNet database, which reduces the need to train the data from scratch.

A pre-trained model is useful when there is a time boundary. It is impossible to build the model from scratch; hence, the reason pre-trained model came into existence. ImageNet is one of the widest, large, real-world databases with the help of the weight of pre-trained models obtained by transferring it to the specific CNN model with the use of the transfer learning technique. Basic diagram of CNN is shown in Fig. (**1**).

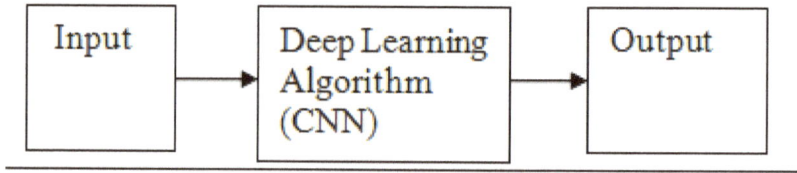

Fig. (1). Basic flow of model.

Transfer Learning

Transfer learning is a type of machine learning technique capable of creating a new artificial intelligence model by an existing neural network. Therefore, by using it as a base for the new model.

The raw image of our deep learning algorithm is given in Fig. (**2**).

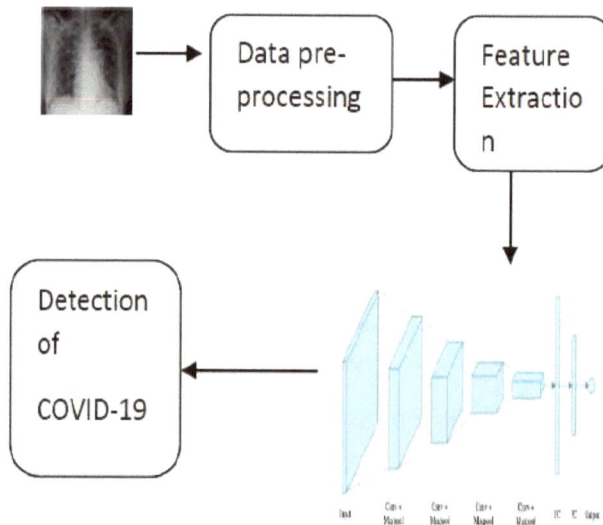

Fig. (2). Raw image of deep learning algorithm.

Image Preprocessing and Features

Image preprocessing is given in Fig. (**3**), and feature extraction techniques are needed for any image-based application. The image preprocessing technique aims to remove the background of the image with a lot of noise. In our application, the raw size of the image is 1012*974. First step of image preprocessing is to prune images with a cropping background, and the newly generated is 140 × 240 pixels. In addition, the median filter is applied. After removing the noisy images, a dataset with images with three labels, COVID-19, PNEUMONIA, and NORMAL, with given images in each label was extracted.

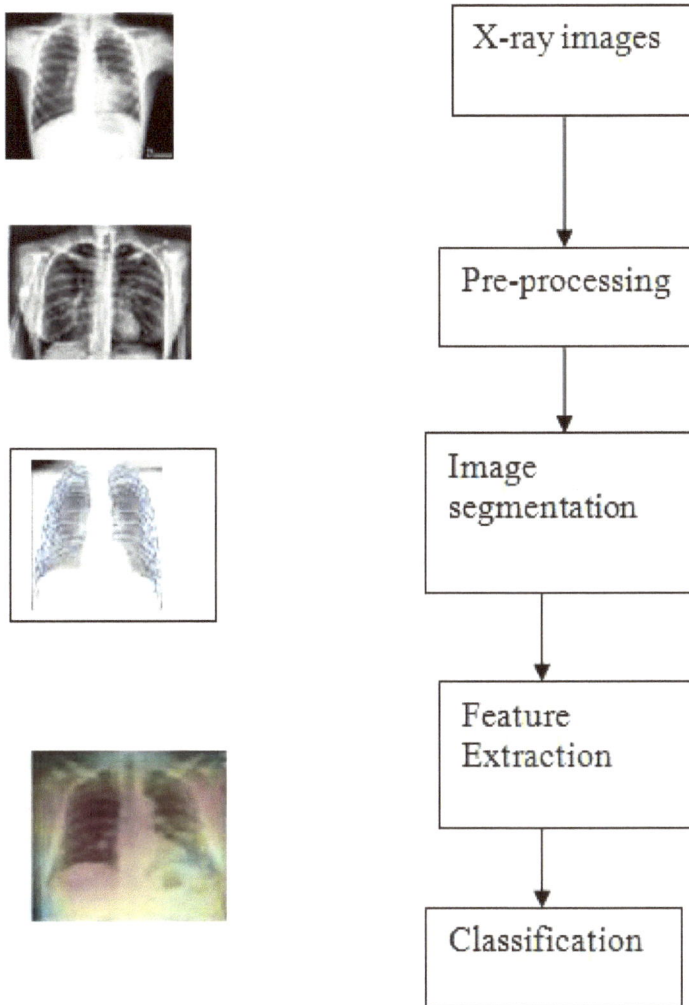

Fig. (3). Image pre-processing.

Training of CNN Model

We will be using Keras framework with TensorFlow. Keras provides pre-trained weights from the ImageNet database using these pre-trained models. ImageNet database on which our model is based may not be similar to images, but it can help make the task more efficient. It also helps to reduce the requirement of large volume dates for training.

We are using Adam algorithm optimization, which is the next version of stochastic gradient descent. Since Adam is getting increasingly popular these days, there is a border adopted for the deep learning application. Furthermore, with the help of ReLu activation function, it is the most commonly used as the activation function for the output of CNN neurons.

As the current dataset is too large, we will require high computational power to train our CNN model. The accuracy of our model will depend on our optimization algorithm, which will be used. The performance of the models which we will be using will be measured on parameters like accuracy, specificity, precision, and recall/sensitivity. It is a great advantage for us that today many datasets are available. With this available dataset further, we will be implementing a system that will be used for detecting COVID-19 and differentiating between Bacterial Pneumonia and COVID-19 pneumonia.

CONCLUSION

COVID-19 disease has greatly impacted daily life all over the world. To resolve this issue, it is necessary to detect the disease as early as possible. Deep learning plays an important role in the medical domain and all other domains. Therefore, we are going to use some deep learning techniques to detect the Covid19 patients.

In this paper, we are going to use some CNN models to detect the disease. We will be using pre-trained models in the ImageNet database to reduce our work to train the CNN model from scratch. Using the transfer learning technique, the weight of the pre-trained models will be transferred to a specific CNN model. On the basis of Chest X-rays of the suspected patients, the training of the model predicts the COVID-19 disease while differentiating between bacterial pneumonia and other types of pneumonia.

To identify COVID 19, a large number of chest X-ray images were trained using the CNN model. In convolutional neural network (CNN), there are different types of models such as ResNet, MobileNet, VGG-16, VGG-19, inception, exception, etc., for checking CNN model performance better to predict the COVID 19 disease.

As the available dataset is too large, we will be requiring high computational power to train our CNN model. As high computational power will be required to train the CNN model, it is better to use kaggle GPU or Jupyter Notebook GPU for fast processing. The accuracy of our model depends on our optimization algorithm useful during the performance of the models, This will assist in measuring parameters like accuracy, specificity, precision, and recall/sensitivity. It is a great advantage for us that today a large number of datasets is available. With this available dataset further, the implementation of the system will be used for detecting COVID-19 and differentiating between bacterial and COVID-19 pneumonia.

CONSENT FOR PUBLICATION

Not applicable.

CONFLICT OF INTEREST

The authors declare no conflict of interest, financial or otherwise.

ACKNOWLEDGEMENTS

All individuals listed as authors must have contributed substantially to the design, performance, analysis, or reporting of the work and are required to indicate their specific contribution. Anyone (individual/company/institution) who has substantially contributed to the study for important intellectual content or was involved in the article's drafting the manuscript or revising must also be acknowledged.

REFERENCES

[1]   S. Rajaraman, J. Siegelman, P.O. Alderson, L.S. Folio, L.R. Folio, and S.K. Antani, "Iteratively Pruned Deep Learning Ensembles for COVID-19 Detection in Chest X-rays", *IEEE Access,* vol. 8, pp. 115041-115050, 2020.
[http://dx.doi.org/10.1109/ACCESS.2020.3003810] [PMID: 32742893]

[2]   R.G. Babukarthik, V.A.K. Adiga, G. Sambasivam, D. Chandramohan, and J. Amudhavel, "Prediction of COVID-19 Using Genetic Deep Learning Convolutional Neural Network (GDCNN)", *IEEE Access,* vol. 8, pp. 177647-177666, 2020.
[http://dx.doi.org/10.1109/ACCESS.2020.3025164] [PMID: 34786292]

[3]   M. Anthimopoulos, S. Christodoulidis, L. Ebner, A. Christe, and S. Mougiakakou, "Lung Pattern Classification for Interstitial Lung Diseases Using a Deep Convolutional Neural Network", *IEEE Trans. Med. Imaging,* vol. 35, no. 5, pp. 1207-1216, 2016.
[http://dx.doi.org/10.1109/TMI.2016.2535865] [PMID: 26955021]

[4]   A. Ramchandani, C. Fan, and A. Mostafavi, "DeepCOVIDNet: An Interpretable Deep Learning Model for Predictive Surveillance of COVID-19 Using Heterogeneous Features and Their Interactions", *IEEE Access,* vol. 8, pp. 159915-159930, 2020.
[http://dx.doi.org/10.1109/ACCESS.2020.3019989] [PMID: 34786287]

[5]   E.M. El-Kenawy, A. Ibrahim, S. Mirjalili, M.M. Eid, and S.E. Hussein, "Novel Feature Selection and Voting Classifier Algorithms for COVID-19 Classification in CT Images", *IEEE Access,* vol. 8, pp. 179317-179335, 2020.
[http://dx.doi.org/10.1109/ACCESS.2020.3028012] [PMID: 34976558]

[6]   K. He, X. Zhang, S. Ren, and J. Sun, "Deep Residual Learning for Image Recognition", *2016 IEEE*

Conference on Computer Vision and Pattern Recognition (CVPR), 2016pp. 770-778 Las Vegas, NV
[http://dx.doi.org/10.1109/CVPR.2016.90]

[7]   M.B. Jamshidi, A. Lalbakhsh, J. Talla, Z. Peroutka, F. Hadjilooei, P. Lalbakhsh, M. Jamshidi, L. Spada, M. Mirmozafari, M. Dehghani, A. Sabet, S. Roshani, S. Roshani, N. Bayat-Makou, B. Mohamadzade, Z. Malek, A. Jamshidi, S. Kiani, H. Hashemi-Dezaki, and W. Mohyuddin, "Artificial Intelligence and COVID-19: Deep Learning Approaches for Diagnosis and Treatment", *IEEE Access,* vol. 8, pp. 109581-109595, 2020.
[http://dx.doi.org/10.1109/ACCESS.2020.3001973] [PMID: 34192103]

[8]   Y. Lecun, L. Bottou, Y. Bengio, and P. Haffner, "Gradient-based learning applied to document recognition", *Proc. IEEE,* vol. 86, no. 11, pp. 2278-2324, 1998.
[http://dx.doi.org/10.1109/5.726791]

[9]   T. Zebin, and S. Rezvy, "COVID-19 detection and disease progression visualization: Deep learning on chest X-rays for classification and coarse localization", *Appl. Intell.,* 2020.
[http://dx.doi.org/10.1007/s10489-020-01867-1] [PMID: 34764549]

[10]   A.M.U.D. Khanday, S.T. Rabani, and Q.R. Khan, "Machine learning based approaches for detecting COVID-19 using clinical text data", *Intj. inf. tecnol.,* vol. 12, pp. 731-739, 2020.
[http://dx.doi.org/10.1007/s41870-020-00495-9]

[11]   J. Ma, Y. Song, X. Tian, Y. Hua, R. Zhang, and J. Wu, "Survey on deep learning for pulmonary medical imaging", *Front. Med.,* vol. 14, no. 4, pp. 450-469, 2020.
[http://dx.doi.org/10.1007/s11684-019-0726-4] [PMID: 31840200]

[12]   S. Huang, F. Lee, R. Miao, Q. Si, C. Lu, and Q. Chen, "A deep convolutional neural network architecture for interstitial lung disease pattern classification", *Med. Biol. Eng. Comput.,* vol. 58, no. 4, pp. 725-737, 2020.
[http://dx.doi.org/10.1007/s11517-019-02111-w] [PMID: 31965407]

CHAPTER 12

Hybrid Deep Learning Model for Sleep Disorders Detection

Anand Singh Rajawat[1,*], **Kanishk Barhanpurkar**[1] and **Romil Rawat**[2]

[1] *Deptartment of CS Engineering, Shri Vaishnav Vidyapeeth Vishwavidyalaya, Indore, India*

[2] *Deptartment of CS Engineering, Sambhram Institute of Technology, Bengaluru, Karnataka, India*

Abstract: The polysomnography test (sleep study) is used to diagnose several sleeping disorders. Sleep study is used to detect sleep disorders such as Insomnia, REM Sleep Behavior, Insomnia, Restless Leg Movement Syndrome, and Sleep Apnea. It measures different parameters such as heart rate, level of oxygen in your blood, body position, brain waves (EEG), breathing rate, eye movement, and electrical activities of muscles. In the world, 700 million people suffer from sleeping disorders. A wide range of sensors was attached to the body of the patient to measure the value of different parameters. However, in 2020, due to the exponential spread of COVID-19 coronavirus disease, the sleep study centers were closed, and it was very difficult to perform sleep studies on patients. Therefore, we developed a hybrid model based on deep learning techniques like Convolutional Neural Network (CNN) and Deep Belief Network (DBN) architectures. Numerous cameras were mounted in rooms at certain angles, which provide live surveillance data and record a patient's movements after a short periodic interval of time. This research paper concludes that non-contact-based hybrid models are highly accurate in detecting sleep disorders based on polysomnography tests.

Keywords: Brain Waves, Convolutional Neural Network (CNN), Covid-19, Deep Belief Network, Physiological electrical signals, Sleep disorders.

INTRODUCTION

Sleep disorders are one of the most common problems in modern civilization, and one-third of the people in the entire world will be suffering from at least one sleep disorder in 2028.

There are several sleeping disorders that depend on various physiological factors. Insomnia, Rapid Eye Movement Disorder (REM), Sleep Apnea, and Restless Leg Syndrome are common sleep disorders that lead to disturbance in sleep. Sleep.

* **Corresponding author Anand Singh Rajawat**: Deptartment of CS Engineering, Shri Vaishnav Vidyapeeth Vishwavidyalaya, Indore, India; E-mail: kanishkbar4321@gmail.com

Rijwan Khan, Pawan Sharma, Sugam Sharma and Santosh Kumar (Eds.)

Apnea is a chronic disorder in which irregularity in the process of breathing is observed, and the pattern is very uncommon [1]. The three types of sleep apnea are Obstructive Sleep Apnea (OSA), Central Sleep Apnea (CSA), and Complex Sleep Apnea Syndrome (CSAS). Obstructive Sleep Apnea (OSA) occurs usually [2].

When the patient's throat muscles contract and expand irregularly, it reduces the flow of air during the inhaling and exhaling process [3]. Sleep Apnea also leads to other severe diseases such as cancer and type 2 diabetes. Similarly, Restless Leg Syndrome (RLS) is the involuntary movement of leg muscles when a person is lying down [4]. This disorder causes unnecessary movement in patients' legs, due to which it is very difficult for the patient to sleep. Insomnia is the most common sleep disorder, which decreases the tendency of the person to sleep [5]. Insomnia is related to many diseases such as severe depression, and anxiety, and is caused due to poor sleeping behavior.

Rapid Eye Movement (REM) disorder occurs when the patient is asleep and physically acts intensely and correspondingly moves limbs violently [6]. Thus, sleep orders play a vital role in the lack of sleep and increase the chances of chronic diseases.

The detection of sleep orders occurs through a polysomnography test (Sleep study), which generally occurs in Sleep Clinics. These clinics are very famous in Western countries and are gradually increasing in Asian countries [7]. The polysomnography test involves many parameters like heart rate (HR), oxygen saturation (SaO_2), breathing rate (BR), eye movement, movement of brain waves (EEG), electrical activities of muscles, and body position. After the assessment of the above-mentioned parameters, the experts diagnose whether a person is suffering from a sleeping disorder or not [8]. In the polysomnography test, sleep disorders can be detected when abrupt changes are certainly observed in the reading of this parameter. A large number of biosensors and actuators were used to record impulsive movements in sleep studies [9].

Deep learning techniques are capable of detecting sleep disorders because many of them contain several types of abnormal physiological movements [10]. In sleep apnea, the irregular movement of the thoracic muscles leads to disturbance of air flow in the breathing process. Moreover, the Restless Leg syndrome is when the spontaneous movement of leg muscles occurs. Additionally, 7REM disease occurs due to spontaneous movement of the eyeballs. Therefore, using the feature as an abnormal physiological movement, we developed a fusion model based on the Convolutional Neural Network (CNN) and Deep Belief Network (DBN), which is capable of detecting sleep order.

We divided the entire research paper into three categories- Section 1, and Section 2. Section 1 contains Introduction and Related Work. This section contains a comparison of work done by previous research studies done to detect various sleep disorders. In Section 2, we have described the proposed work and the description of deep learning architectures. Section 3 contains the result analysis, conclusion, future work, and references.

RELATED WORK

Dey D. *et al.* [11], developed a deep learning-based Convolutional Neural Network (CNN), which is used to detect sleep apnea disease. Machine Learning models were also used to detect sleep apnea, in which features were used as pulse oximetry and airflow. These models are also used to test the patients at home itself. The main aim of this research paper is to detect sleep apnea with a minimum number of parameters [12]. Yulita, I. N. *et al.* [13], developed a sophisticated system for detecting a disturbance in airflow using the Deep Belief Network. NREM-based classifier was used to detect insomnia based on 57 features extracted from the 2 channel EEG mode (Sachin M *et al.*, 2017). It obtained an overall accuracy of 92%. Cooray, N. *et al.* [14], proposed a system based on the study of 53 REM patients in which REM is detected with the help of a deep learning model. Furthermore, the Restless Leg Syndrome can be diagnosed with the help of the hybrid model of deep belief networks [15, 16]. Deep learning models are very highly accurate in detecting several sleep disorders. However, these models detect only one type of disorder. They are not useful in sleep studies because of their tendency to work for just one type of syndrome. The research gap can be trounced by developing a fusion deep learning model for detecting a large number of sleeping disorders based on the spontaneous readings provided by the sensors. Table **1** shows the comparative study.

Table 1. Comparative study of the different deep learning methods used for the detection of sleep disorders.

S.No.	Study	Year	No. of studies	Sleep Disorder	Feature Selection	Deep Learning Technique
1.	Cen, L. *et al.* [17].	2018	3	Sleep Apnea	ECG Signals	Convolutional Neural Network
2.	Prasad B. *et al.* [18].	2020	0	Sleep Apnea	Blood Pressure Measurement	Convolutional Neural Network
3.	Jarchi, D. *et al.* [19].	2020	0	Sleep Apnea	Biological Signals (ECG, EEG)	Deep Neural Network
4.	Korkalainen H. *et al.* [20].	2019	1	Obstructive Sleep Apnea	ECG Signals	Deep Neural Network

(Table 1) cont.....

S.No.	Study	Year	No. of studies	Sleep Disorder	Feature Selection	Deep Learning Technique
5.	Wallis P. *et al.* [21].	2020	0	Rapid Eye Movement Disorder	Polysomnography Signals	-
6.	Sridhar N. *et al.* [22].	2020	0	Rapid Eye Movement Disorder	Eye-balls muscular electric signals	Artificial Neural Network
7.	Eckert M. J. *et al.* [23].	2020	1	Rapid Eye Movement Disorder	ECG Signals	Convolutional Neural Network
8.	Carvelli L. *et al.* [24].	2020	2	Leg Movement Syndrome	Muscular Electric Signals	Convolutional Neural Network
9.	Yang B. *et al.* [25].	2020	2	Insomnia	EEG Signals	Deep Belief Network
10.	Islam M.M. *et al.* [26].	2020	1	Insomnia	EEG Signals	Artificial Neural Network

PROPOSED WORK

In this chapter, a deep learning model has been proposed that can detect a wide range of sleep disorders. The entire system is based on two renowned deep learning architectures which are Convolutional Neural Network (CNN) and Deep Belief Network (DBN).

CONVOLUTIONAL NEURAL NETWORK

Convolutional Neural Network is widely used for various research purposes in the domain of Artificial Intelligence. The CNN architecture is known for its robustness, high accuracy, and classification properties. It is used in natural language processing, feature engineering, and detection of several chronic diseases and recommendation systems [19]. In our proposed system, the main task of CNN is to separate the physiological signals and channelize these signals for further process. ECG Signals, Heart Rate, Breathe Rate, and other physiological signals were channelized and then divided into regular intervals of time.

$$J(W, b) \triangleq \frac{-1}{N} \prod_1^{N=l} y1 + y2 + y3 - - - - - yn \log yk \qquad (1)$$

Here, b denotes the biases of the network layer, and W represents the weight associated with the neural network layer. N is the number of classes assigned during the development of the neural network.

DEEP BELIEF NETWORK

In deep learning, deep neural networks have a single construction because they possess a relatively large number of compound components between the layers. The main reason for the development of DBN is that the hidden layer provides a range of high computability, which can be used in pattern recognition and other applications. The induced DBN architecture was used to segregate the unique features of sleep disorders. Thus, segregation and extraction of features were done by the series of layers of a deep belief network.

SYSTEM ARCHITECTURE

The model in Fig. (**1**) will first initialize the polysomnography signals according to the frequency of signals, within the system. According to the parameters, the learning rate, batch size, and iteration mode will be automatically defined. The system moves to the CNN iteration part, where the entire dataset gets channelized into frames. These frames were divided into uniform intervals of time, making the computation an easy one. CNN looks for the training phases, which transfer to the series of Deep Belief Networks. The DBN performs several iterations on the foundation of limits convergence and produces an output for physiological parameters. Every iteration produces one out, which acts as input to the FCNN testing layer. And after the computation of the FCNN testing, the overall accuracy is generated for the entire dataset.

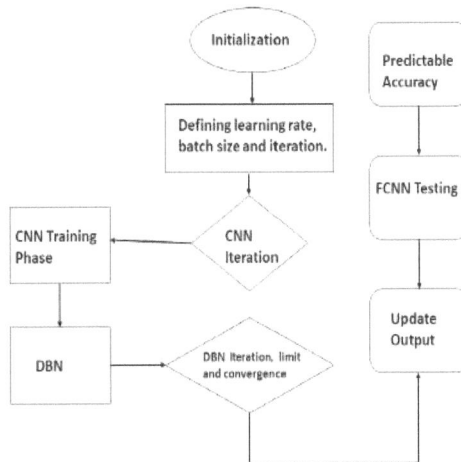

Fig. (1). System architecture of CNN+DBN layer model process.

The different parameters of polysomnography test are input in the form of electrical signals through a 32-layered CNN architecture which is mentioned in

Fig. (**2**). The series architecture provides robust computability due to which the probability of data loss is very less. After performing the iteration for each layer of CNN, the intermediate output enters into the series of DBN networks (16 layers). The intermediate data acts as an input for the series of DBN networks. After performing several iterations, it moves to SoftMax classifier and thus obtains its final output.

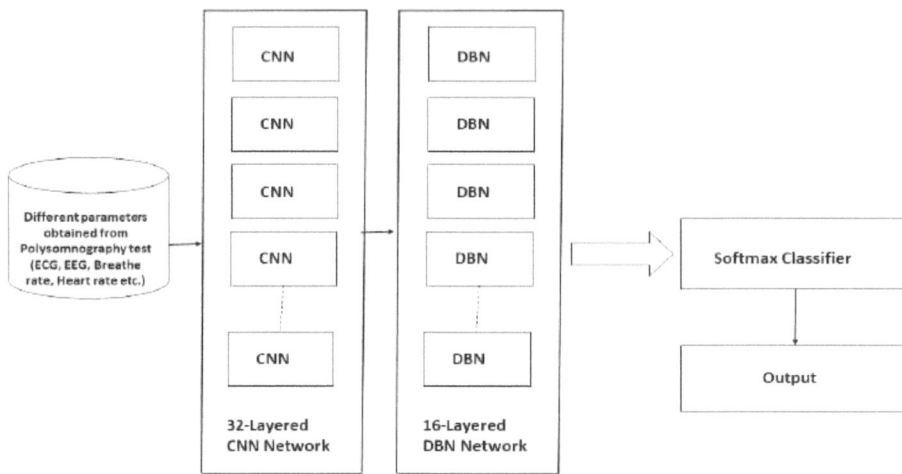

Fig. (2). Dataflow diagram of the proposed system.

DATA-SET

The dataset consisted of a polysomnographic recording of 54 people aged in the range of 44-56. The group is already diagnosed with sleep disorders (Sleep Apnea, Rapid Eye Movement, Leg Movement Syndrome, Insomnia). We divided the whole group equally into 2 categories (Group A and Group B) by performing the polysomnography test once again on Group B. We developed our training set with the help of Group A with previous polysomnographic records. Moreover, we developed the test set from the patients belonging to Group B. The main attributes (physiological electrical signals) that we obtained from Groups A and B are as follows in Table **2**.

Table 2. Description of physiological attributes found in the dataset.

S. No.	Attributes	Description
1.	ECG	Records the electrical impulses through the heart muscles in the chest area.

(Table 2) cont.....

S. No.	Attributes	Description
2.	EMG	Used for finding electrical action produced by movements of skeletal muscles.
3.	EEG	Used for finding the electrical activity of the brain.
4.	Breath rate	Measures changes in thoracic circumference during respiration.
5.	Heart Rate	Measure the heart rate of the patient.
6.	Body Position	Mounted Camera to record body position.
7.	Oximeter	Measure the oxygen carried in the human body.
8.	EOG	Measures the corneo-retinal standing potential.
9.	Leg Movement Sensor	Measures the muscular movement of legs.
10.	Snore Microphone	Detection of high frequencies of snoring.

Algorithm

1. Start.
2. Defining the learning rate and channelizing the physiological signals (electrical) at regular intervals of time.
3. Convolutional Neural Network Training Phase.
4. Deep Belief Network layer phase.
5. Convolutional Neural Network Test Phase.
6. Detection of disease distortion is observed.

Let the probability of happening a sleep disorder be denoted as P_D.

Level of distortion can be given as $D_{(disease)}$.

If $P_D = D_{(sleep\ apnea)}$, Distortion is observed in Snore Microphone, Breathe Rate, and EMG.

ElseIf $P_D = D_{(REM)}$, Distortion is observed in ECG, EOG, and Heart rate.

Else If $P_D = D_{(RLM)}$, Distortion is observed in Leg Movement Sensor, ECG.

Else $P_D = D_{(Insomnia)}$, Distortion observed in EOG, ECG, and Body Position.

Step 7: Diseases detected.

Step 8: Stop.

RESULT ANALYSIS

This section investigates the sleep disorder detection techniques and challenges the proposed model associated with its development. We have divided the results into subgroups according to the dataset (Group A and Group B). The train set is developed in Group A, and the test set is developed in Group B. Accuracy of the model varies for different sleep disorders depending on the number of patients involved in the research study. Hence, we are comparing the results for different patients obtained as follows in Fig. (**3**) and Table **3**.

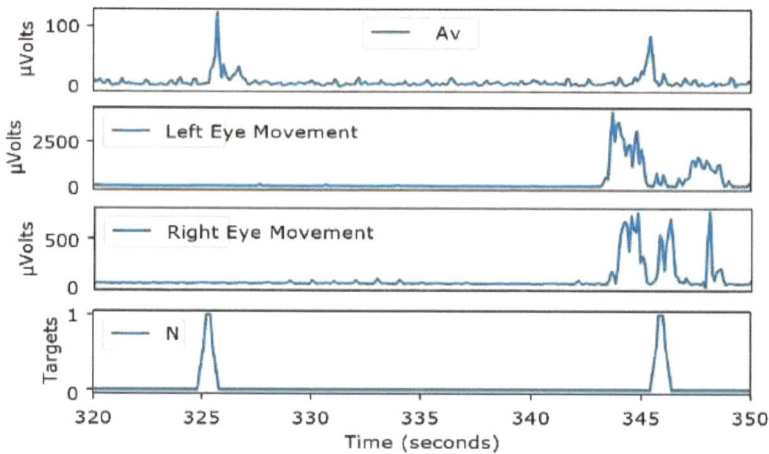

Fig. (3). Physiological Assessment of EOG Signals (Av: Average, Left Eye Movement, Right Eye Movement and N: Normal phase).

Table 3. Comparison of the results obtained for sleep apnea disorder.

Sleep Disorder	Number of Patients in Group A	Number of Patients in Group B
Sleep Apnea	13	8
Rapid Eye Movement (REM)	5	4
Insomnia	7	12
Restless Leg Syndrome	2	3

In addition, we have compared the results of previous deep learning methods used in the detection of disease with our proposed model for every disorder. This comparison is graphed in Fig. (**4**), which is done on the basis of Predicting Time (ms) and Accuracy (in percentage). The predicting time is the net time to execute a model on the test case (Group B). In our proposed model, we obtained an accuracy of 91.29%, 95.77%, 84.66%, and 91.08% for Sleep Apnea, Rapid Eye

Movement (REM), Insomnia, and Restless Leg Movement Syndrome (RLM), respectively. All are shown in Figs. (**5-12**) and Tables **4-7**, respectively.

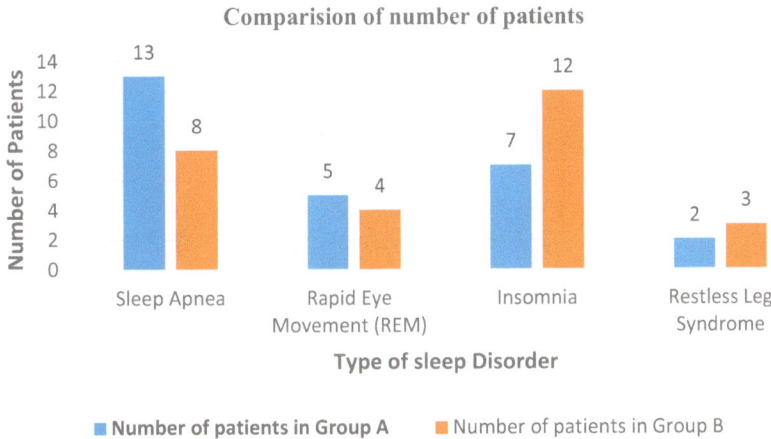

Fig. (**4**). Comparison of the number of patients with various disorders in Group A and Group B.

Table 4. Comparison of the results obtained for Sleep Apnea disorder.

Study	Disease	Predicting time (ms)	Accuracy
Pathinarupothi R.K. *et al.*, 2017 [27]	Obstructive Sleep Apnea	11.75	89.31%
Balunesombatkul N. *et al.*, 2018 [28]	Sleep Apnea	9.09	85.03%
Proposed Model (CNN+LSTM)	Sleep Apnea	7.83	91.29%

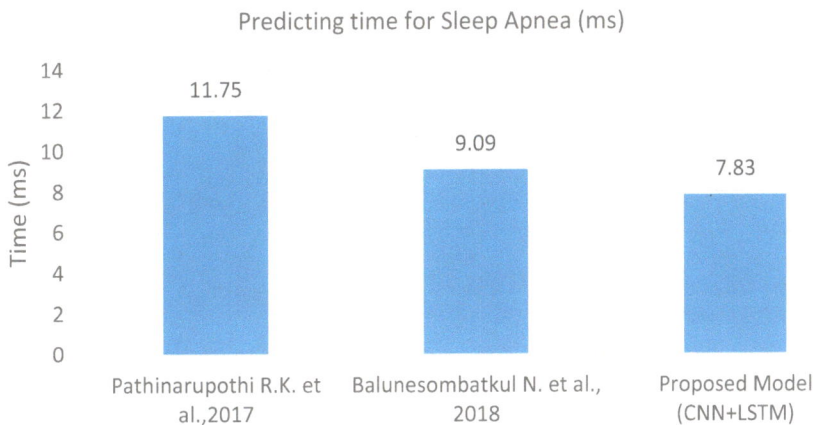

Fig. (**5**). Comparison of predicting time for various methods. (Sleep Apnea).

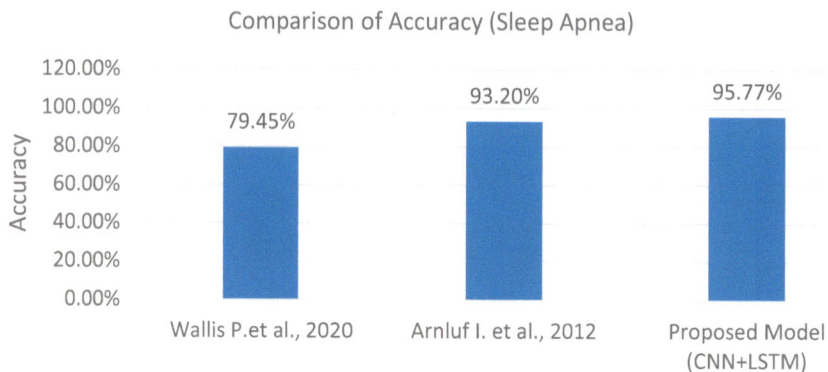

Fig. (6). Comparison of accuracy for various methods. (Sleep Apnea).

Table 5. Comparison of the results obtained for Rapid Eye Movement (REM) disorder.

Study	Disease	Predicting time (ms)	Accuracy
Wallis P.*et al.*, 2020 [21]	Rapid Eye Movement (REM)	7.07	79.45%
Arnluf I. *et al.*, 2012	Rapid Eye Movement (REM)	5.64	93.2%
Proposed Model (CNN+LSTM)	Rapid Eye Movement (REM)	12.11	95.77%

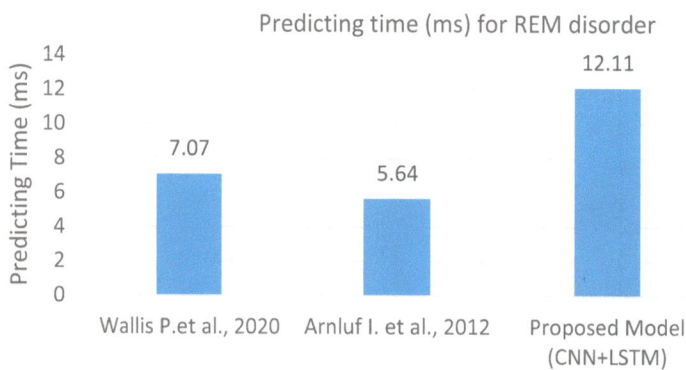

Fig. (7). Comparison of predicting time for various methods. (REM disorder).

Comparison of Accuracy (REM Disorder)

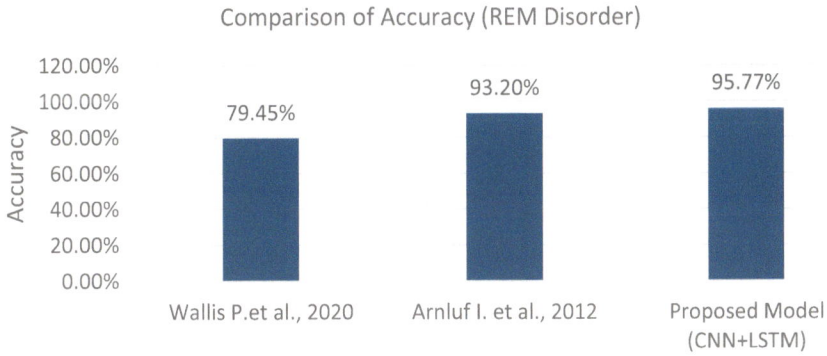

Fig. (8). Comparison of accuracy for various methods. (REM disorder).

Predicting time (ms) for Insomnia

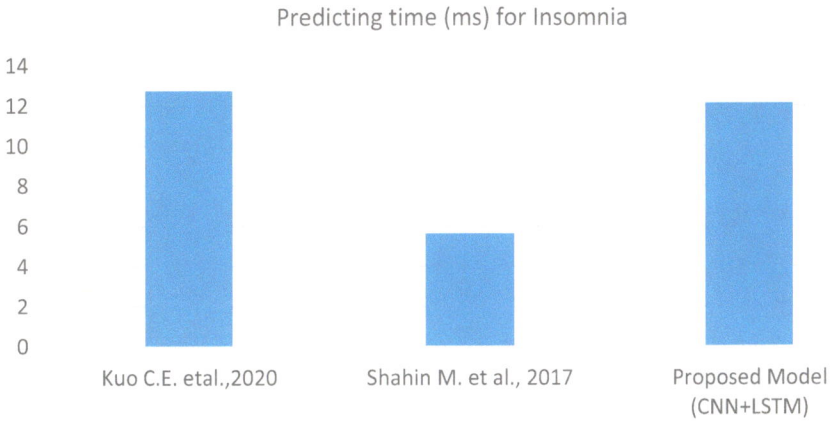

Fig. (9). Comparison of predicting time for various methods. (Insomnia).

Comparision of Accuracy (Insomnia)

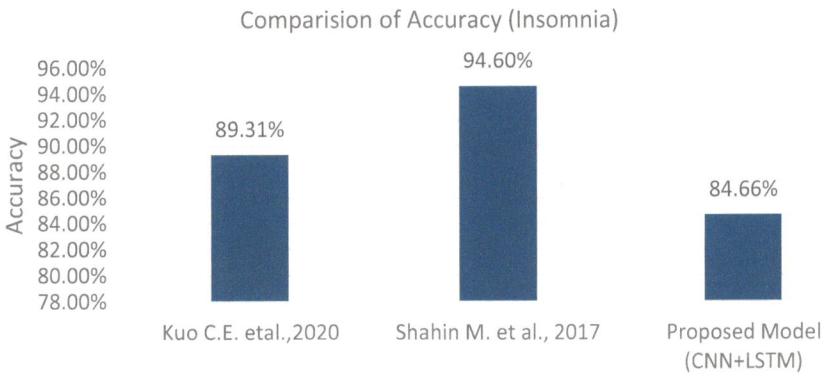

Fig. (10). Comparison of accuracy for various methods. (Insomnia).

Table 6. Comparison of the results obtained for insomnia disorder.

Study	Disease	Predicting time (ms)	Accuracy
Kuo C.E. etal.,2020 [29]	Insomnia	12.74	89.31%
Shahin M. et al., 2017 [30]	Insomnia	5.64	94.6%
Proposed Model (CNN+LSTM)	Insomnia	12.11	84.66%

Table 7. Comparison of the results obtained for Restless Leg Syndrome disorder.

Study	Disease	Predicting Time (ms)	Accuracy
Zhou P. *et al.*,2020 [16]	Restless Leg Syndrome	19.29	77.47%
Shahin M. *et al.*, 2017 [13]	Restless Leg Syndrome	14.48	83.92%
Proposed Model (CNN+LSTM)	Restless Leg Syndrome	11.41	91.08%

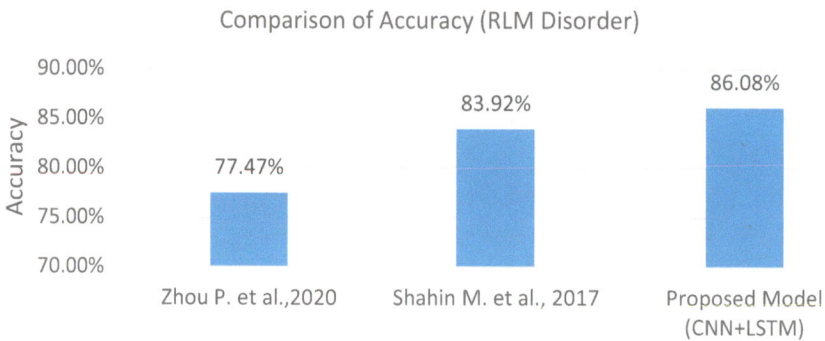

Fig. (11). Comparison of predicting time of various methods. (RLM disorder).

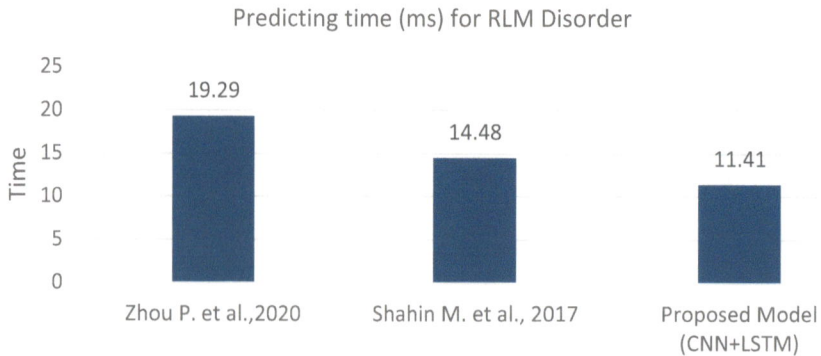

Fig. (12). Comparison of accuracy of various methods (RLM disorder).

CONCLUDING REMARKS

The focus of the research paper is to develop a robust fusion deep learning model which is competent in detecting sleep disorders. In this paper, we observed that our proposed model based on Convolutional Neural Network and Deep Belief Network provides high accuracy in the detection of the four most common sleep disorders (Sleep Apnea, Rapid Eye Movement (REM) Disorder, Insomnia, and Rapid Leg Movement Syndrome). It also provides several benefits over other sleep disordering architectures. Firstly, our proposed system works for a wide range of disorders, whereas the other architectures detect specific sleeping disorders. Secondly, the accuracy of the proposed system is better than other architectures, which depend on the single neural network architecture. Lastly, we consider a greater number of parameters which are in our proposed model. Thus, we conclude that our proposed system is highly accurate in detecting sleep orders.

FUTURE SCOPE

We developed a deep learning architecture completely dependent on the feature selection of physiological signals extracted from the polysomnographic test. In the future, we will further work on noncontact methods of detecting sleep disorders. Non-contact detection methods are methods in which medical experts develop a system to diagnose the disease without physical contact with the patients. Therefore, due to the exponential growth of COVID-19 disease, such a system will be in high demand. And for dataset development, we will use mounted cameras to record the sleep sessions of patients.

CONSENT OF PUBLICATION

Not applicable.

CONFLICT OF INTEREST

The author declares no conflict of interest, financial or otherwise.

ACKNOWLEDGEMENTS

Declared none.

REFERENCES

[1]   I. Arnulf, "REM sleep behavior disorder: motor manifestations and pathophysiology", *Mov. Disord.,* vol. 27, no. 6, pp. 677-689, 2012.
[http://dx.doi.org/10.1002/mds.24957] [PMID: 22447623]

[2]   M. Marin-Oto, E.E. Vicente, and J.M. Marin, "Long term management of obstructive sleep apnea and its comorbidities", *Multidiscip. Respir. Med.,* vol. 14, p. 21, 2019.
[http://dx.doi.org/10.1186/s40248-019-0186-3] [PMID: 31312448]

[3]   X. Lv, and J. Li, "A Multi-level Features Fusion Network for Detecting Obstructive Sleep Apnea Hypopnea Syndrome", In: *Algorithms and Architectures for Parallel Processing. ICA3PP 2020.*, M. Qiu, Ed., vol. 12454. Lecture Notes in Computer Science, 2020.
[http://dx.doi.org/10.1007/978-3-030-60248-2_34]

[4]   S. Guo, J. Huang, H. Jiang, C. Han, J. Li, X. Xu, G. Zhang, Z. Lin, N. Xiong, and T. Wang, "Restless Legs Syndrome: From Pathophysiology to Clinical Diagnosis and Management", *Front. Aging Neurosci.,* vol. 9, p. 171, 2017.
[http://dx.doi.org/10.3389/fnagi.2017.00171] [PMID: 28626420]

[5]   J. Fernandez-Mendoza, and A.N. Vgontzas, "Insomnia and its impact on physical and mental health", *Curr. Psychiatry Rep.,* vol. 15, no. 12, p. 418, 2013.
[http://dx.doi.org/10.1007/s11920-013-0418-8] [PMID: 24189774]

[6]   Y. Zhang, R. Ren, L. Yang, L.D. Sanford, and X. Tang, "Polysomnographically measured sleep changes in idiopathic REM sleep behavior disorder: A systematic review and meta-analysis", *Sleep Med. Rev.,* vol. 54, 2020.101362
[http://dx.doi.org/10.1016/j.smrv.2020.101362] [PMID: 32739826]

[7]   N. Scalzitti, S. Hansen, S. Maturo, J. Lospinoso, and P. O'Connor, "Comparison of home sleep apnea testing versus laboratory polysomnography for the diagnosis of obstructive sleep apnea in children", *Int. J. Pediatr. Otorhinolaryngol.,* vol. 100, pp. 44-51, 2017.
[http://dx.doi.org/10.1016/j.ijporl.2017.06.013] [PMID: 28802385]

[8]   D.C. Lim, D.R. Mazzotti, K. Sutherland, J.W. Mindel, J. Kim, P.A. Cistulli, U.J. Magalang, A.I. Pack, P. de Chazal, and T. Penzel, "Reinventing polysomnography in the age of precision medicine", *Sleep Med. Rev.,* vol. 52, 2020.101313
[http://dx.doi.org/10.1016/j.smrv.2020.101313] [PMID: 32289733]

[9]   H. Azimi, M. Bouchard, R. Goubran, and F. Knoefel, "Unobtrusive Screening of Central Sleep Apnea From Pressure Sensors Measurements: A Patient-Specific Longitudinal Study", *IEEE Trans. Instrum. Meas.,* vol. 69, no. 6, pp. 3282-3296, 2020.
[http://dx.doi.org/10.1109/TIM.2020.2981111]

[10]   S.S. Mostafa, F. Mendonça, A.G. Ravelo-García, and F. Morgado-Dias, "A Systematic Review of Detecting Sleep Apnea Using Deep Learning", *Sensors (Basel),* vol. 19, no. 22, p. 4934, 2019.
[http://dx.doi.org/10.3390/s19224934] [PMID: 31726771]

[11]   D. Dey, S. Chaudhuri, and S. Munshi, "Obstructive sleep apnoea detection using convolutional neural network based deep learning framework", *Biomed. Eng. Lett.,* vol. 8, no. 1, pp. 95-100, 2017.
[http://dx.doi.org/10.1007/s13534-017-0055-y] [PMID: 30603194]

[12]   D. Álvarez, A. Cerezo-Hernández, A. Crespo, G.C. Gutiérrez-Tobal, F. Vaquerizo-Villar, V. Barroso-García, F. Moreno, C.A. Arroyo, T. Ruiz, R. Hornero, and F. Del Campo, "A machine learning-based test for adult sleep apnoea screening at home using oximetry and airflow", *Sci. Rep.,* vol. 10, no. 1, p. 5332, 2020.
[http://dx.doi.org/10.1038/s41598-020-62223-4] [PMID: 32210294]

[13]   I.N. Yulita, S. Purwani, R. Rosadi, and R.M. Awangga, "A quantization of deep belief networks for long short-term memory in sleep stage detection", In: *International Conference on Advanced Informatics, Concepts, Theory, and Applications (ICAICTA)* Denpasar, 2017, pp. 1-5.
[http://dx.doi.org/10.1109/ICAICTA.2017.8090999]

[14]   N. Cooray, F. Andreotti, C. Lo, M. Symmonds, M.T.M. Hu, and M. De Vos, "Detection of REM sleep behaviour disorder by automated polysomnography analysis", *Clin. Neurophysiol.,* vol. 130, no. 4, pp. 505-514, 2019.
[http://dx.doi.org/10.1016/j.clinph.2019.01.011] [PMID: 30772763]

[15]   H. Byeon, "Exploring the Predictors of Rapid Eye Movement Sleep Behavior Disorder for Parkinson's Disease Patients Using Classifier Ensemble", *Healthcare (Basel),* vol. 8, no. 2, p. 121, 2020.
[http://dx.doi.org/10.3390/healthcare8020121] [PMID: 32369941]

[16] P. Zhou, L. Huang, Q. Zhao, W. Xiao, and S. Li, "[A Domestic Diagnosis System for Early Restless Legs Syndrome Based on Deep Learning]", *Zhongguo Yi Liao Qi Xie Za Zhi,* vol. 43, no. 2, pp. 79-82, 2019.
[PMID: 30977599]

[17] L. Cen, Z.L. Yu, T. Kluge, and W. Ser, "Automatic System for Obstructive Sleep Apnea Events Detection Using Convolutional Neural Network", In: *40th Annual International Conference of the IEEE Engineering in Medicine and Biology Society (EMBC)*, 2018.
[http://dx.doi.org/10.1109/EMBC.2018.8513363]

[18] B. Prasad, C. Agarwal, E. Schonfeld, D. Schonfeld, and B. Mokhlesi, "Deep learning applied to polysomnography to predict blood pressure in obstructive sleep apnea and obesity hypoventilation: a proof-of-concept study", *J. Clin. Sleep Med.,* vol. 16, no. 10, pp. 1797-1803, 2020.
[http://dx.doi.org/10.5664/jcsm.8608] [PMID: 32484157]

[19] D. Jarchi, J. Andreu-Perez, M. Kiani, O. Vysata, J. Kuchynka, A. Prochazka, and S. Sanei, "Recognition of Patient Groups with Sleep Related Disorders using Bio-signal Processing and Deep Learning", *Sensors (Basel),* vol. 20, no. 9, p. 2594, 2020.
[http://dx.doi.org/10.3390/s20092594] [PMID: 32370185]

[20] H. Korkalainen, J. Aakko, S. Nikkonen, S. Kainulainen, A. Leino, B. Duce, I.O. Afara, S. Myllymaa, J. Toyras, and T. Leppanen, "Accurate Deep Learning-Based Sleep Staging in a Clinical Population With Suspected Obstructive Sleep Apnea", *IEEE J. Biomed. Health Inform.,* vol. 24, no. 7, pp. 2073-2081, 2020.
[PMID: 31869808]

[21] P. Wallis, D. Yaeger, A. Kain, X. Song, and M. Lim, "Automatic Event Detection of REM Sleep Without Atonia From Polysomnography Signals Using Deep Neural Networks", In: *ICASSP 2020 - 2020 IEEE International Conference on Acoustics, Speech and Signal Processing (ICASSP)*, 2020.

[22] N. Sridhar, A. Shoeb, P. Stephens, A. Kharbouch, D.B. Shimol, J. Burkart, and L. Myers, "Deep learning for automated sleep staging using instantaneous heart rate", *NPJ Digit. Med.,* vol. 3, no. 1, 2020.
[http://dx.doi.org/10.1038/s41746-020-0291-x]

[23] M. J. Eckert, B. L. McNaughton, and M. Tatsuno, "Neural ensemble reactivation in rapid eye movement and slow-wave sleep coordinate with muscle activity to promote rapid motor skill learning Phil", *Trans. R. Soc.*
[http://dx.doi.org/10.1098/rstb.2019.0655]

[24] L. Carvelli, A. N. Olesen, A. Brink-Kjær, E. B. Leary, P. E. Peppard, E. Mignot, and P. Jennum, "Design of a deep learning model for automatic scoring of periodic and non-periodic leg movements during sleep validated against multiple human experts", *Sleep Medicine,* p. 12.032, 2019.
[http://dx.doi.org/10.1016/j.sleep.2019.12.032]

[25] B. Yang, and H. Liu, "Automatic identification of insomnia based on single-channel EEG labelled with sleep stage annotations", *IEEE Access,* pp. 1-1, 2020.
[http://dx.doi.org/10.1109/ACCESS.2020.2999915]

[26] M.M. Islam, A.K.M. Abujar, and S.A. Hossain, "Prediction of chronic Insomnia using Machine Learning Techniques", *11th International Conference on Computing, Communication and Networking Technologies (ICCCNT),* Kharagpur, India, pp. 1-7, 2020.
[http://dx.doi.org/10.1109/ICCCNT49239.2020.9225570]

[27] R.K. Pathinarupothi, P.J. Dhara, E.S. Rangan, E.A. Gopalakrishnan, R. Vinaykumar, and K.P. Soman, "Single Sensor Techniques for Sleep Apnea Diagnosis Using Deep Learning", In: *IEEE International Conference on Healthcare Informatics (ICHI).*, 2017.

[28] N. Banluesombatkul, T. Rakthanmanon, and T. Wilaiprasitporn, "Single Channel ECG for Obstructive Sleep Apnea Severity Detection Using a Deep Learning Approach", *TENCON,* 2018. IEEE Region 10 Conference.

[http://dx.doi.org/10.1109/TENCON.2018.8650429]

[29]   C-E. Kuo, and G-T. Chen, "A Short-Time Insomnia Detection System Based on Sleep EOG with RCMSE Analysis", *IEEE Access,* pp. 1-1, 2020.
[http://dx.doi.org/10.1109/ACCESS.2020.2986397]

[30]   M. Shahin, B. Ahmed, S.T-B. Hamida, F.L. Mulaffer, M. Glos, and T. Penzel, "Deep Learning and Insomnia: Assisting Clinicians With Their Diagnosis", *IEEE J. Biomed. Health Inform.,* vol. 21, no. 6, pp. 1546-1553, 2017.
[http://dx.doi.org/10.1109/JBHI.2017.2650199] [PMID: 28092583]

CHAPTER 13

Identification of Covid-19 Positive Cases Using Deep Learning Model and CT Scan Images

I. Kumar[1,*], S.P Singh[1], Shivam[1], N. Mohd[2] and J. Rawat[3]

[1] *Graphic Era Hill University, Dehradun, India*

[2] *Graphic Era Deemed to be University, Dehradun, India*

[3] *DIT University, Dehradun, India*

Abstract: Today, the coronavirus has widely affected the entire world. In late 2019, a virus with the pandemic potential was reported in the city of Wuhan, situated on the mainland of China. In no time, the virus had spread all over the world, multiplying from person to person. Undoubtedly, COVID-19 has become an important research topic, and many research works are coming forward daily. Thus, COVID-19 patient's detection has become the most personified research for the researchers. CT scanning has been an important and widely used approach for detecting COVID-19 patients. In this work, the identification of COVID-19 patients is performed using two different deep neural network methods. For the image accession, the dataset having 746 samples was used. The entire dataset has been bifurcated into two different classes, *i.e.*, COVID-19 and non-COVID-19. COVID-19 class contains samples of the COVID-19 positive cases, whereas the non-COVID-19 class contains the sample of COVID-19 negative cases. In total, 506 images are used for training purposes, whereas 240 images are used for validation. The identification is performed using MobileNet-V2 and Modified LeNet5 convolutional neural network (CNN) models having a fixed number of convolutional and fully connected layers. The term modified is added before the LeNet architecture because an extra convolutional layer was created for the experiment. As per the details and requirements, the architecture for Modified LeNet was designed, whereas, for the MobileNet-V2, it is imported from predefined libraries and is used further as per the author's need. After the successful completion of the experiment, it has been found that the accuracy of MobileNet-V2 and Modified LeNet5 came out to 85.86%, and 84.38%, respectively.

Keywords: COVID 19, CT Screening, Deep learning models, LeNet5, MobileNet-V2.

* **Corresponding author I. Kumar**: Graphic Era Hill University, Dehradun, India; E-mail: drkumar5898@gmail.com

INTRODUCTION

In 2019, a virus named Corona with pandemic potential was reported in the Wuhan city of China during the tail end of the year 2019 [1] and was given the name "The Novel COVID-19". This virus rapidly spread in all countries in no time [2 - 5], and no one could have even imagined that a virus named Corona would affect millions of people. One of the most important factors that turned out to be a barrier to getting the pandemic under control is a smaller number of medical resources and a shortage in the number of tests [6]. When observed under an electronic microscope, it was found that the virus inhabited the solar corona characteristics, which is how coronavirus's nomenclature occurred [7]. The World Health Organization (WHO), on February 11, 2020, came forward stating this virus was a pandemic outbreak, naming it COVID-19 [8], and further stating that the virus had first occurred in China, making its way to different countries. USA, Brazil, and India have been the most affected countries where the number of cases of this pandemic COVID-19 multiplied rapidly daily. Screening of large numbers, availability of quarantine centers, and better treatment are essential factors to control the spread of this pandemic disease [9].

Today, the entire world is trying its level best to win over this pandemic outbreak completely by putting in all possible efforts day and night. Although for the diagnosis, RT-PCR is the standard method that is taken into consideration. However, it is still found to be more time-consuming to confirm the COVID-19 patients as a high number of false negative reports are resulting [10]. The most familiar symptoms of COVID-19 are fever, cough, breathing or respiratory problems, mild symptoms of pneumonia, etc [11]. To overcome the issue of a high number of negative false reports, CT scans are an effective methodology to detect the disease [12]. Thus, for the confirmation of the COVID-19 patient, especially in the case of children and women, CT scan is the highly suggested and preferred approach [13]. Although CT imaging is an effective approach, there are still a few disadvantages that need to be kept in mind. High dose for the patient and high scanning costs are the major disadvantages of CT imaging [14]. Through this research, the authors mainly focus on detecting COVID-19 patients using the CT scanning method and further comparing with different deep learning models.

Some related works that have been bought forward for this problem are discussed in studies [15 - 19]. The study [15] brought forward a different approach for screening coronavirus disease. The observation or screening of COVID-19 patients was done using the CT screening concept in this work. First, they studied the comparison of different multiple CNN models to classify CT samples into different classes that consisted of COVID-19 patients, influenza, pneumonia, or with no infection. The further comparative study was on 2D and 3D deep learning models that were already developed before achieving an accuracy of 95% for the reference of COVID and Non-COVID-19 patients. Another work related to this problem has been accomplished in "Imaging and clinical features of patients with 2019 novel coronavirus SARS-CoV-2" [16] with the help of different deep learning techniques. They created a model that helped them differentiate the COVID-19 patients from healthy cases and IAVP using CT scanning at the early stage. Sums of total 618 CT samples were taken for the work. With the help of 3D deep learning techniques, the segmentation of a particular infectious region from the CT scan image of a particular candidate was done. Later, these separated images were categorized into three different categories to understand the type of infection. Using the Noisy function, the type of infection along with the positive score is measured for the CT scan cases individually, producing almost 87% (86.7%) accuracy when taking all CT scan cases together.

A similar type of problem has been carried out in a study [17]. In this work, different deep learning models like ResNet50, ResNetV2, and InceptionV3 were used for the screening of COVID 19 patients and the methodology used was radiographs related to Chest X-rays. For these different models that were used, the ROC Analysis, and indecision matrices were given, and with the help of 5 fold-cross-validation, it was analyzed. To automatically recognize the coronavirus using CT imaging concept, an approach was developed in the study [18]. In this study, a new model was proposed by them in which they used Chest X-ray images for the observation of COVID 19 automatically. They had created 17 different convolutional layers and each layer was instigated with different means of filtering. DarkNet miniature was used in the detection system of a synchronal object as a classifier. The accuracy achieved by the model was 98.08%, which shows how well the model worked. Considering the CT imaging technique, to achieve coronavirus diseases detection, an approach was developed by A Jaiswal *et al.* [19]. In this approach, they used different models like DenseNet201, VGG-16, ResNet152V2, *etc.*, that were already trained to recognize the COVID-19 patients. Based on DTL, DenseNet201 model was proposed to determine if a person is suspected to be found as a COVID-19 patient or not. The proposed model was used so that it could extract the features on its own when performed on the ImageNet dataset. A CNN structure was also used.

Although COVID-19 has extensively affected the entire world and is currently the most discussed topic among people throughout the world. However, after studying previously published works, it has been induced that the detection of coronavirus is an interesting and trending topic. Moreover, it has been noticed that most of the studies were based on CT imaging techniques as it results in the most minimal false reports with better accuracy. Therefore, the authors are trying to propose the COVID-19 identification using a deep neural network method that is fully automated. Through this research, the author's main focus is on detecting COVID-19 disease infection with deep Neural Network Methodology and CT scan images.

MATERIALS AND METHODOLOGY

Dataset Preparation

For the completion of this work, CT images are taken from the following source https://github.com/UCSD-AI4H/COVID-CT samples of COVID-19 and Non-COVID-19 cases [20]. The dataset is divided into two different classes that are COVID-19 and non-COVID-19. The number of samples for COVID-19 and non-COVID-19 cases is 349 and 397, respectively. For COVID-19 class, 229 images are taken for the training purpose, whereas 120 images are taken for validation purposes. In the non-COVID-19 class, the number of samples taken for the training purpose is 277, whereas 120 images are taken for the validation purpose. These images are brightened up to make all necessary regions visible and clearer to achieve better results. The complete detail of the preparation of the dataset and its bifurcation is given in Table **1**.

Table 1. Brief details of dataset preparation and its bifurcation.

Considered Class	Data Bifurcation		Total Samples
	Training Set	Validation Set	
Non-COVID-19	*277*	*120*	*397*
COVID-19	*229*	*120*	*349*
Total	*506*	*240*	*746*

Proposed Work

The complete flow diagram of the experiment that has been carried out for the work "Identification of COVID-19 Positive Cases using Deep Learning Model and CT Scan Images" has been displayed in Fig. (**1**). The workflow diagram of this experiment mainly comprises of image preprocessing section, dataset bifurcation section, deep learning model training and validation section, and decision of the system section. The brief description of each section is given in the upcoming sections of the manuscript.

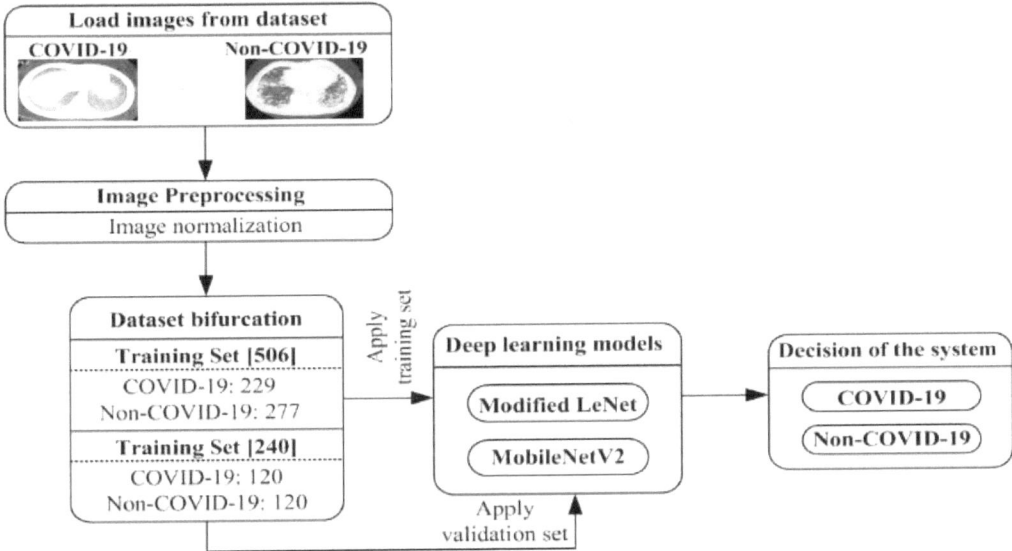

Fig. (1). Experimental workflow diagram of the work carried out for Identification of COVID-19 Positive Cases using Deep Learning Model and CT Scan Images.

Preprocessing Section

In the experiment that has been carried out for the work, it is found that image preprocessing is an essential part. Image normalization is performed in the experiment to validate that every image pixel value lies in the same range and overall processing of the system, producing more effect on the outcome. The output pixel value for the input pixel is defined according to Eq. 1.

$$Y_i = \frac{X_i - \text{least}(X)}{\text{maximal}(X) - \text{least}(X)} \tag{1}$$

Where, the range of intensity varies between 0 to 255.

Dataset Bifurcation Section

In this section, the dataset has been bifurcated into two sets. They are the training set and the validation set in the ratio of 68:32. Talking about the training set and validation set, the training set comprises 506 samples in total, out of which 229 samples belong to the COVID-19 class whereas 277 samples belong to the non-COVID-19 class. The validation set comprises 240 samples, out of which 120 belonged to the COVID-19 class, whereas the rest 120 samples belonged to the Non-COVID-19 class. The brief details of dataset preparation and its bifurcation are given in Table **1**. Training and validation set is passed to the next section of the experimental workflow chart.

Deep Learning Models

In this work, two different deep learning-based neural network models, *i.e.*, Modified LeNet-V5 and MobileNet-V2, were used for the identification of the COVID-19 patients. Kindly refer to the LeNet section to understand why the modified term is used for LeNet model.

The image size chosen for this work is 224 × 224 × 3 and is delegated to the layer responsible for input. After this process, it is further shared between the hidden layers of the constructed CNN. The formula to which we could produce the dimension of the turnout attribute map generated has been discussed in Eq. 2.

$$w_2 = (\frac{w_1 - f + 2p}{s} + 1), \ h_2 = (\frac{h_1 - f + 2p}{s} + 1) \tag{2}$$

Where from the above equation, w_1 x h_1 x d_1 referred to as the input image size whereas w_1 is the width, h_1 resembles the height of the image, and d_1 denotes the total amount of color channels in the image. Well talking about the rest of the entities, f denotes the filter size, whereas p is the total number of padding, and by s, the stride value is represented. The description of both models is given below:

LeNet-5

Modified LeNet5 is an architecture with more than one layer, mainly focusing on categorizing character numbers or numeric digits that are handwritten [21]. The model with multiple layers (LeNet-5) was proposed by LeCun in 2015. The architecture mainly comprises a layer responsible for input and output (separately), two convolutional, two entirely connected, and two pooling layers, respectively. Over a period of time, it has been found that LeNet has been the most widely used approach for the recognition of characters or numeric digits. In this work, the authors have renamed the structure to Modified LeNet-5 architecture as one convolutional layer has been created on its own for the experiment. The architecture of the Modified LeNet model is displayed in Fig. (**2**).

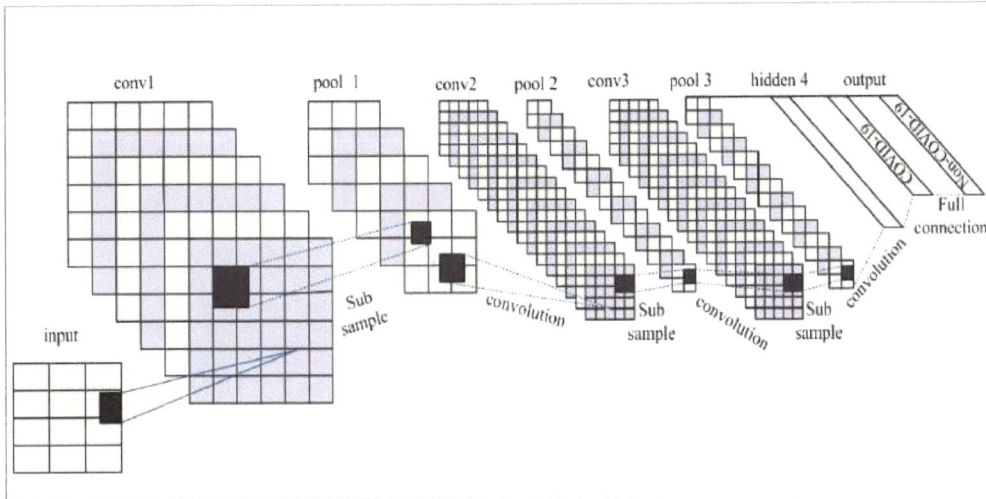

Fig. (2). The Modified LeNet Architecture

The filter sizes that have been taken into action to perform the convolutional operation successfully without any fault on the particular given set of samples are 32, 48, 69 and the matrix size is [3 × 3], [3 × 3], and [3 × 3]. Padding is settled to be valid for the different convolutional layers, that is, conv1, conv2, and conv3 (layer that is created by the authors own) respectively, of the layers that are hidden. Looking at the weight of the filters, the first convolutional filter is [3, 3, 2, 32], whereas the weight for the second convolutional filter is [5, 5, 32, 48], and for the third convolutional filter is of size [3, 3, 48, 69].

MobileNet-V2

An architecture that mainly focuses on the categorization of mobile versions and images is the architecture referred to as MobileNet and was proposed by Andrew G and his team [22]. Depth-wise convolution in which the input is filtered, and point-wise convolution without creating new features. This results in the generation of new features according to the two core cables inside the MobileNet Architecture [23]. The nonlinear activation function used in this experiment is sigmoid and ReLU. MobileNet model and its architecture are shown in Fig. (3).

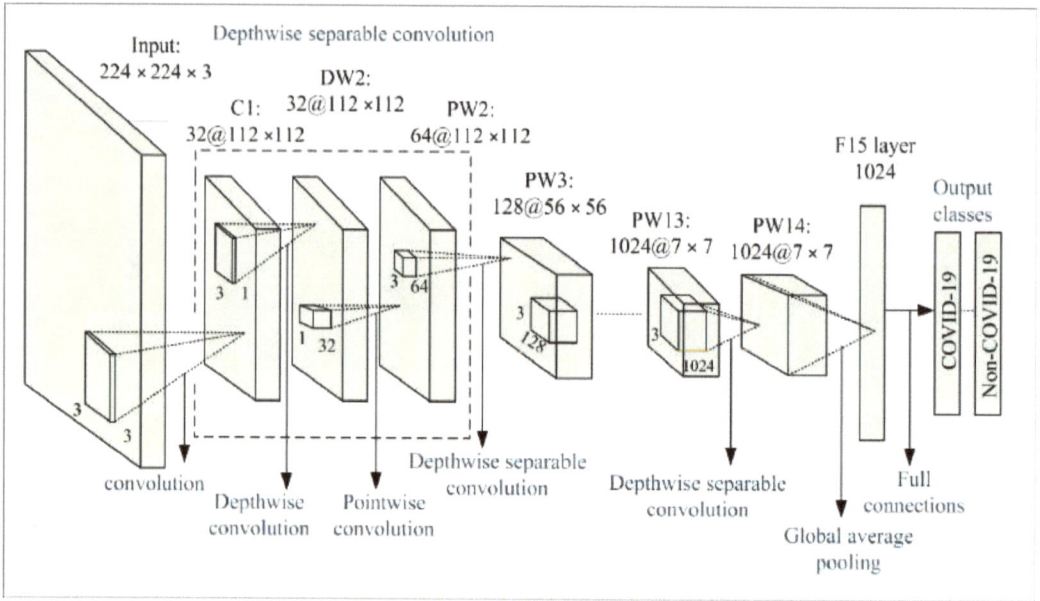

Fig. (3). The MobileNet architecture

Non-Linear Activation Function

Sigmoid: It is an activated function with no negative derivative term defined for all real inputted values with only one inflection point. The sigmoid function *g(x)* is also called a logistic function and is defined by the following formula given in Eq. 3.

$$g(x) = \frac{1}{1 + e^{-z}} \tag{3}$$

The practical formula used for the implementation of the sigmoid function is described in Eq. 4.

$$g = 1.0./ (1.0 + \exp(-z)) \tag{4}$$

ReLU: Over the period, the rectified linear unit or ReLU became very popular when it was required to be in the CNN model [24]. A function method that breaks the linearity and increases nonlinearity is what the function of ReLU generally focuses on. One important factor that needs to be kept in mind is that the images are highly nonlinear. The formula for ReLU is defined as in Eq. 5.

$$f(x) = \max(X, 0)$$

(5)

$$\text{Where, } X = \sum_{i=1}^{m} W_i X_i$$

EXPERIMENT AND RESULTS

Experimental Setup

The complete experimentation has been performed with HP Pavilion Notebook. The specification of the system is given as Intel® Core™ i5-7200U CPU@ 2.50 GHz, 16 Gigabyte RAM, 2 Gigabyte Intel HD Graphic 620, and 4 GB NVIDIA GeForce 940MX, 2TB HDD. All images are stored in this system, and Spyder 4.1.4 (Python 3.7) environment is used for performing the experiments.

RESULTS

Extensive experiments have been carried out in this work using Modified LeNet and MobileNet-V2 deep neural network methods. The obtained results for the experiment carried out for Covid-19 identification using the deep neural network method for 60 epochs and 0.5 dropouts are reported in Table **2**.

Table 2. Obtained results of the experiment were carried out for rice plant disease identification using the deep neural network method.

Model Name	Training Phase			Validation Phase		
	No. of sample	Accuracy (%)	Loss	No. of sample	Accuracy (%)	Loss
Modified LeNet	506	84.38	0.38574	240	65.62	0.67157
Mobile Net-V2	506	85.86	0.36270	240	62.94	0.73911

Fig. (**4**) is used to show the learning curve for the training phase and validation phase. It contains training accuracy, training loss, validation accuracy, and validation loss.

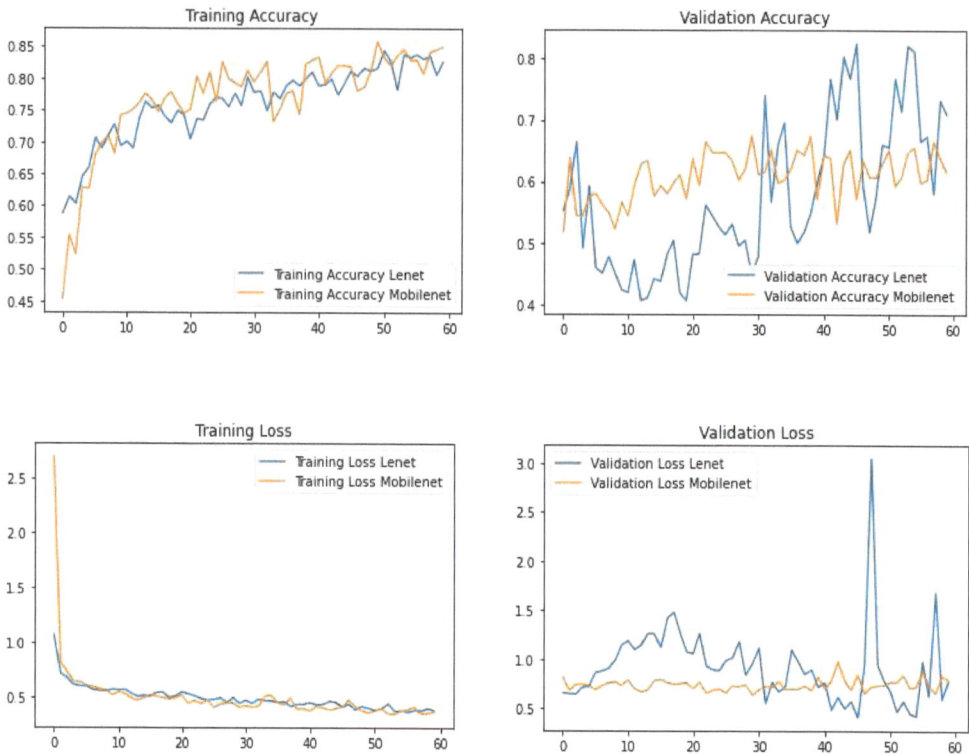

Fig. (4). learning curve for training phase and validation phase.

CONCLUSION

In this work, different CNN models like Modified LeNet, and MobileNetV2 are used mainly to observe how these two different models work when performed on the same dataset. For the completion of this experiment, total 60 numbers of epoch's were used, and the authors concluded that the overall performance of the Modified LeNet model was better compared to the MobileNet. However, it is seen that the training accuracy of MobileNet was better than the Modified LeNet model. We also concluded that the brightening of the sample plays an important role in enhancing the performance of the model for better results. By the end of the completion of this experiment, the MobileNet model produced a training accuracy of 85.86%, whereas 62.94 validation accuracy was achieved. With the help of the Modified LeNet model, the training phase accuracy and validation accuracy came out as 84.38% and 65.62%, respectively. A similar kind of work can be extended to other imaging modalities to get better accuracy, which is helpful in the clinical practice of detecting COVID-19 positive cases and proper diagnosis.

CONSENT OF PUBLICATION

Not applicable.

CONFLICT OF INTEREST

The author declares no conflict of interest, financial or otherwise.

ACKNOWLEDGEMENTS

Declared none.

REFERENCES

[1]   E.E. Hemdan, M.A. Shouman, and M.E. Karar, "Covidx-net: A framework of deep learning classifiers to diagnose covid-19 in x-ray images", *arXiv preprint arXiv,* vol. 11055, 2020.

[2]   N. Zhu, D. Zhang, W. Wang, X. Li, B. Yang, J. Song, X. Zhao, B. Huang, W. Shi, R. Lu, P. Niu, F. Zhan, X. Ma, D. Wang, W. Xu, G. Wu, G.F. Gao, and W. Tan, "A novel coronavirus from patients with pneumonia in China, 2019", *N. Engl. J. Med.,* vol. 382, no. 8, pp. 727-733, 2020.
[http://dx.doi.org/10.1056/NEJMoa2001017] [PMID: 31978945]

[3]   Q. Li, X. Guan, P. Wu, X. Wang, L. Zhou, Y. Tong, R. Ren, K.S.M. Leung, E.H.Y. Lau, J.Y. Wong, X. Xing, N. Xiang, Y. Wu, C. Li, Q. Chen, D. Li, T. Liu, J. Zhao, M. Liu, W. Tu, C. Chen, L. Jin, R. Yang, Q. Wang, S. Zhou, R. Wang, H. Liu, Y. Luo, Y. Liu, G. Shao, H. Li, Z. Tao, Y. Yang, Z. Deng, B. Liu, Z. Ma, Y. Zhang, G. Shi, T.T.Y. Lam, J.T. Wu, G.F. Gao, B.J. Cowling, B. Yang, G.M. Leung, and Z. Feng, "Early transmission dynamics in Wuhan, China, of novel coronavirus–infected pneumonia", *N. Engl. J. Med.,* vol. 382, no. 13, pp. 1199-1207, 2020.
[http://dx.doi.org/10.1056/NEJMoa2001316] [PMID: 31995857]

[4]   J. Cohen, and D. Normile, "New SARS-like virus in China triggers alarm", *Science,* vol. 367, no. 6475, pp. 234-235, 2020.
[http://dx.doi.org/10.1126/science.367.6475.234] [PMID: 31949058]

[5]   T. Lupia, S. Scabini, S. Mornese Pinna, G. Di Perri, F.G. De Rosa, and S. Corcione, "2019 novel coronavirus (2019-nCoV) outbreak: A new challenge", *J. Glob. Antimicrob. Resist.,* vol. 21, pp. 22-27, 2020.
[http://dx.doi.org/10.1016/j.jgar.2020.02.021] [PMID: 32156648]

[6]   J. Zhao, Y. Zhang, X. He, and P Xie, "COVID-CT-Dataset: a CT scan dataset about COVID-19", *arXiv preprint arXiv:2003.13865. 2020 Mar 30.*

[7]   Y. Chen, Q. Liu, and D. Guo, "Emerging coronaviruses: Genome structure, replication, and pathogenesis", *J. Med. Virol.,* vol. 92, no. 4, pp. 418-423, 2020.
[http://dx.doi.org/10.1002/jmv.25681] [PMID: 31967327]

[8]   C. Sohrabi, Z. Alsafi, N. O'Neill, M. Khan, A. Kerwan, A. Al-Jabir, C. Iosifidis, and R. Agha, "World Health Organization declares global emergency: A review of the 2019 novel coronavirus (COVID-19)", *Int. J. Surg.,* vol. 76, pp. 71-76, 2020.
[http://dx.doi.org/10.1016/j.ijsu.2020.02.034]

[9]   S. Wang, B. Kang, J. Ma, X. Zeng, M. Xiao, J. Guo, M. Cai, J. Yang, Y. Li, X. Meng, and B. Xu, "A deep learning algorithm using CT images to screen for Corona Virus Disease (COVID-19)", *MedRxiv,* 2020.
[http://dx.doi.org/10.1101/2020.02.14.20023028]

[10]   P. Huang, T. Liu, L. Huang, H. Liu, M. Lei, W. Xu, X. Hu, J. Chen, and B. Liu, "Use of chest CT in combination with negative RT-PCR assay for the 2019 novel coronavirus but high clinical suspicion",

Radiology, vol. 295, no. 1, pp. 22-23, 2020.
[http://dx.doi.org/10.1148/radiol.2020200330] [PMID: 32049600]

[11]   C. Huang, Y. Wang, X. Li, L. Ren, J. Zhao, Y. Hu, L. Zhang, G. Fan, J. Xu, X. Gu, Z. Cheng, T. Yu, J. Xia, Y. Wei, W. Wu, X. Xie, W. Yin, H. Li, M. Liu, Y. Xiao, H. Gao, L. Guo, J. Xie, G. Wang, R. Jiang, Z. Gao, Q. Jin, J. Wang, and B. Cao, "Clinical features of patients infected with 2019 novel coronavirus in Wuhan, China", *Lancet,* vol. 395, no. 10223, pp. 497-506, 2020.
[http://dx.doi.org/10.1016/S0140-6736(20)30183-5] [PMID: 31986264]

[12]   M. Chen, X. Shi, Y. Zhang, D. Wu, and M. Guizani, "Deep features learning for medical image analysis with convolutional autoencoder neural network", *IEEE Trans. Big Data.,* 2017.

[13]   H. Liu, F. Liu, J. Li, T. Zhang, D. Wang, and W. Lan, "Clinical and CT imaging features of the COVID-19 pneumonia: Focus on pregnant women and children", *J. Infect.,* vol. 80, no. 5, pp. e7-e13, 2020.
[http://dx.doi.org/10.1016/j.jinf.2020.03.007] [PMID: 32171865]

[14]   L.J.M. Kroft, L. van der Velden, I.H. Girón, J.J.H. Roelofs, A. de Roos, and J. Geleijns, "Added value of ultra–low-dose computed tomography, dose Equivalent to chest x-ray radiography, for diagnosing chest pathology", *J. Thorac. Imaging,* vol. 34, no. 3, pp. 179-186, 2019.
[http://dx.doi.org/10.1097/RTI.0000000000000404] [PMID: 30870305]

[15]   C. Butt, J. Gill, D. Chun, and B.A. Babu, "Deep learning system to screen coronavirus disease 2019 pneumonia", *Appl. Intell.,* p. 1, 2020.
[http://dx.doi.org/10.1007/s10489-020-01714-3]

[16]   X. Xu, C. Yu, J. Qu, L. Zhang, S. Jiang, D. Huang, B. Chen, Z. Zhang, W. Guan, Z. Ling, R. Jiang, T. Hu, Y. Ding, L. Lin, Q. Gan, L. Luo, X. Tang, and J. Liu, "Imaging and clinical features of patients with 2019 novel coronavirus SARS-CoV-2", *Eur. J. Nucl. Med. Mol. Imaging,* vol. 47, no. 5, pp. 1275-1280, 2020.
[http://dx.doi.org/10.1007/s00259-020-04735-9] [PMID: 32107577]

[17]   A. Narin, C. Kaya, and Z Pamuk, "Automatic detection of coronavirus disease (covid-19) using x-ray images and deep convolutional neural networks", *arXiv preprint arXiv: 2003.10849,* 2020.

[18]   T. Ozturk, M. Talo, E.A. Yildirim, U.B. Baloglu, O. Yildirim, and U. Rajendra Acharya, "Automated detection of COVID-19 cases using deep neural networks with X-ray images", *Comput. Biol. Med.,* vol. 121, p. 103792, 2020.
[http://dx.doi.org/10.1016/j.compbiomed.2020.103792] [PMID: 32568675]

[19]   A. Jaiswal, N. Gianchandani, D. Singh, V. Kumar, and M. Kaur, "Classification of the COVID-19 infected patients using DenseNet201 based deep transfer learning", *J. Biomol. Struct. Dyn.,* pp. 1-8, 2020.
[PMID: 32619398]

[20]   X. Yang, X. He, J. Zhao, Y. Zhang, S. Zhang, and P. Xie, "Covid-CT-dataset: A CT scan dataset about covid-19", *ArXiv e-prints,* pp. arXiv-2003, 2020.

[21]   T. Guo, J. Dong, H. Li, and Y. Gao, "Simple convolutional neural network on image classification", In: *2017 IEEE 2nd International Conference on Big Data Analysis (ICBDA)* IEEE, 2017, pp. 721-724.
[http://dx.doi.org/10.1109/ICBDA.2017.8078730]

[22]   A. Howard, M. Sandler, G. Chu, L.C. Chen, B. Chen, M. Tan, W. Wang, Y. Zhu, R. Pang, V. Vasudevan, and Q.V. Le, "Searching for mobilenetv3", *Proceedings of the IEEE International Conference on Computer Vision,* pp. 1314-1324, 2019.

[23]   W. Sae-Lim, W. Wettayaprasit, and P. Aiyarak, "Convolutional Neural Networks Using MobileNet for Skin Lesion Classification", In: *2019 16th International Joint Conference on Computer Science and Software Engineering (JCSSE)* IEEE, 2019, pp. 242-247.
[http://dx.doi.org/10.1109/JCSSE.2019.8864155]

[24]   C. Bhatt, I. Kumar, V. Vijayakumar, K.U. Singh, and A. Kumar, "The state of the art of deep learning models in medical science and their challenges", *Multimedia Syst.,* pp. 1-5, 2020.

CHAPTER 14

Application of Nature Inspired Algorithms to Test Data Generation/Selection/Minimization using Mutation Testing

Nishtha Jatana[1,*] and **Bharti Suri**[1]

[1] *Research Scholar, USICT and Assistant Professor, MSIT, USICT, New Delhi, India*

Abstract: This chapter builds the foundation of software testing techniques by classifying the various testing approaches and testing coverage criteria. It gradually advances in the concepts and process of Mutation Testing and its application areas. Mutation testing has been applied at both the source code level and specification level of the software under test. Mutation testing, when applied to the source code, is named as Program Mutation. Similarly, when applied to the specifications, it is named as Specification Mutation. The relevant Mutation Testing tools available for different programming languages for both program and Specification Mutations are hereby listed. Owing to the high cost incurred in applying Mutation Testing to industrial needs, the on-going endeavors of the researchers in the area are elaborated here. Applying nature-inspired algorithms along with Mutation Testing for data generation/selection/minimization is an upcoming area of research. Search based Mutation Testing (SBMT) applies evolutionary techniques like Genetic Algorithms or other metaheuristic approaches for automating the tasks associated with mutation testing, which otherwise requires a lot of human effort, thus, making it a practical approach. This chapter concludes by giving the seminal recent advancements in the area.

Keywords: Generation/Selection/Minimization of test data, Metaheuristics, Mutation Testing, Nature–Inspired Algorithms.

INTRODUCTION

"To err is human" [1]. Software codes are written by humans, and humans make mistakes. Therefore, a system that is built must be validated and tested. Software testing is an activity that verifies and validates the functioning of the software. It entails 50% of the total software development effort, time, and cost [2]. Inade-
.

* **Corresponding author Nishtha Jatana:** Research Scholar, USICT and Assistant Professor, MSIT, USICT, New Delhi, India; E-mail: nishthajatana@msit.in

Rijwan Khan, Pawan Sharma, Sugam Sharma and Santosh Kumar (Eds.)
All rights reserved-© 2022 Bentham Science Publishers

quate testing leads to the wastage of millions of dollars wastage, especially in large projects [3]. The following subsections explain the basics of software testing:

Basics of Software Testing

Testing software requires a methodical procedure of executing software using different inputs, intending to authenticate its functioning and reveal faults wherever encountered. These faults are also known as bugs or defects. These faults may lead to system failure. A fault can occur due to a requirement misinterpreted or due to logical errors or coding errors. Test data is a collection of input values that reveals some behavior of the software being tested. A program "input" is a means of communication with it. In the case of a function, the parameters act as an input. In the case of an Android application, the inputs correspond to the events on the UI (user interface). To test a network protocol, the network packets are treated as inputs. To test a daily user application like the word processor, the input is either by UI (User Interface) or XML (eXtended Markup Language) documents. For validating the observed behavior of the software to be tested, a test case is formed using the input values and a test oracle, which requires an output value. This may be the expected value returned by a function or an output file, or a network packet, as the case may be. A test suite or a test set comprises the selected test cases.

To test the software, a series of tasks are performed by a test engineer. The process of testing requires the following steps:

- Identify an objective for testing.
- Selection of Inputs.
- Compute the expected outputs corresponding to the inputs selected.
- Set up the correct environment for testing.
- Execute the software system with the selected inputs.
- Analyze the results of execution and generate a test report.

Software testing can be done manually, but it is largely being anticipated to automate it. The advantages of automation include the ability to test the execution many times as desired. It reduces the human error of repeated execution while saving a lot of time. To automate the testing process, test cases are executed using a test driver, considering the system under test (SUT) under certain conditions. It applies to the input and verifies the output using the test oracle [4].

Testing is needed at different levels involving system parts or system software as a whole. The levels of software testing based on software activity [5] are as follows:

- Acceptance Testing – validating the SUT with respect to the requirements.
- System Testing – verifying the SUT with respect to its architectural design.
- Integration Testing – evaluating the SUT with respect to the subsystem design.
- Module Testing – checking and testing the detailed design of the SUT.
- Unit Testing – assessing the SUT with respect to its implementation.

Testing the software completely is an impossible task. The testing principle looks simple, but effective testing is a tedious task [6].

Testing rules are, thus, needed to define a criterion that the test data must satisfy, helping the tester in the selection of appropriate test inputs and helps in determining when to stop testing [5]. The next subsection details the various categories of coverage criteria for testing.

TEST COVERAGE AND ADEQUACY PRELIMINARIES

The software cannot be tested with every possible input, so test coverage criteria can be helpful for deciding which test inputs should be selected. The research on software testing largely reflects that the effective usage of the coverage criteria makes it more probable that the testers will locate faults in the SUT and increase the reliability and assurance of the correct functioning of the software.

Goodenough and Gerhart [7] brought up two key questions in software testing:

a. "What are the testing criteria?" or "what constitutes an adequate test suite?", and.
b. "How to generate a finite test suite that satisfies the adequacy criteria?".

Structural Testing

Structural testing techniques (well-known as White-box testing techniques) require knowledge of the structure of the SUT or its internal implementation. It is also known as clear box testing, glass box testing, path driven testing, open box testing, or logic driven testing. The coverage criteria here are mainly covered under the following categorization:

- Program based testing.
- Specification based testing.

Program Based Testing

The program-based structural adequacy criteria can be divisible into two groups: control-flow-based and data-flow-based criteria [8]. These two categories collectively form dependence coverage criteria. The program-based criteria mainly focus on the flow-graph model of the program structure. Although, some control flow-based criteria use program text to define the test requirements instead of using an abstract model of the structure of SUT. Control flow deals with the flow of control from one instruction or a set of instructions to another. This flow of control from instruction to instruction can be carried out in a number of ways. It can be in the form of one instruction appearing after another or through a function calls or maybe through message passing or even interrupts. The usage of conditional statements alters the sequential flow of control in a program. The term "Data-flow" refers to the transmission of values from one variable or constant to another variable. The data flow aspect is determined by the definition and use of variables in a program. The flow graphs associate an edge with each possible branch or path in the program. Its sequence of statements is represented as a node.

A coverage criterion is defined as a rule or set of rules that inflict test requirements on the test set. For program-based specifications in control flow-based testing, the following coverage criteria are defined:

- **Statement coverage criterion**: this requires coverage of all statements in the program by the test cases.
- **Branch coverage criterion:** this requires coverage of all edges in the flow graph by the test cases.
- **Path coverage criterion:** this requires coverage of all execution paths in the flow graph by the test cases.
- **Cyclomatic complexity criterion:** this requires the coverage of independent paths in the flow graph, where the independent paths(v) are given by $v = e - n + 2P$ where 'e' refers to the number of edges in the flow graph, 'n' refers to the number of nodes in the flow graph and 'P' refers to the number of disconnected components in the flow graph of the SUT.
- **Multi-condition coverage criterion**: this requires coverage of the multiple conditions imposed by the tester such that there is a test case corresponding to each of the stated conditions.

These coverage criteria are conceptually very strong. However, since the real software is large in size, there are many infeasible paths.

These criteria have been modified by many researchers working in the area of software testing to make this type of testing feasible.

The data flow-based testing investigates the flow of data, *i.e.*, the values of the variables used in the program and how it changes with its execution. This is accomplished by focusing on the definition and use of the value of the variables. The aim behind this is to ensure that the variables are created and manipulated or used correctly in the program.

The coverage criteria based on data flow testing as used by the researchers are as follows:

- **The all-definitions criterion** [9]: It requires an adequate test set to cover all definition occurrences such that the testing paths should cover, for each definition occurrence, the path from its definition to its use (some use).
- **The all-use criterion** [10]: It requires the test set to cover each path from the definition of the variable to all its uses.
- **The interaction between variables criterion** [11]: It requires the test set to cover the interactions between variables of the program.

Specification-based Testing

The specification-based testing [12] deals with two things:

1. Provides a way to verify the correctness of the output of the program (also known as the oracle problem).
2. Reveals how to select test data and measure its adequacy.

The idea of designing the coverage criterion is to do input-space partitioning using the domain knowledge of the SUT instead of its implementation. The coverage criterion for specification-based testing is mainly categorized as follows:

- **Model-based Coverage Criterion or Model Based Testing** [13]: Here, the specification of the SUT is expressed using two components: a state model and the operations required on the states of the state model. The state model is mostly an abstraction of the desired behavior of the SUT. The test cases are then derived from this model to check the functionality of the SUT. These test cases are named *abstract test suites* as they possess the same level of abstraction as that of the model. An *executable test suite* for the SUT, thereby, needs to be derived from this abstract test suite. This derivation or mapping is done using the information provided in the model itself. It can also be done by creating method calls or certain statements, specifically by adding to the test suite.
- **Property-based Coverage Criterion** [12]: Property oriented functional specifications require the software functions to possess a certain set of properties as software functions. The testing of the SUT, therefore, requires investigation if

it satisfies all mentioned functional specifications. The adequacy of the test set thus requires coverage of these properties of the SUT.

Both programs-based and specification-based testing individually is not sufficient individually to adequately test the software. Thus, combining both techniques provides a good measure of the adequacy of the test suite.

- **Fault-based Testing**: Fault-based testing [14] aims to ensure that the SUT is free of the prescribed faults. The fault-based adequacy criteria thus, measure the quality of a test set in terms of its effectiveness or ability to detect faults. It can be further categorized as Error seeding, Mutation Testing, and Perturbation Testing.

Error Seeding

This technique implants some random, artificial faults in the code of the SUT [15]. These faults are assumed to be similar to the inherent or plausible faults in the software. The software is then tested to test the artificial faults discovered. The adequacy of the test suite hereby measures the number of artificial faults discovered by the test suite.

The advantage of this technique is that it can be applied to any form of testing. However, the disadvantage is the nature of the artificial faults introduced. These faults may not be similar to the plausible faults resulting in inefficient testing of the software. This limitation is overcome in the process of Mutation Testing in which the faults are generated in a systematic manner.

Mutation Testing

In this technique, faulty versions of the program are created to generate what is known as 'mutants' of the code of the SUT [16]. These mutants are generated systematically from the mutation operators, known to be a highly researched topic in the area. These mutants are then executed on the test cases. This process continues until the stopping criterium is met. The stopping criteria to be stated here can be when all mutants are dead, exceeding the time limits or when the test cases in the test suite are exhausted.

Perturbation Testing

This type of testing deals with considering faults in the "error space". The space can deal with computation errors [17], security flaws [18], or XML messages [19]. This type of testing enables us to discover the faults in a program in terms of the functionality difference between the correct function and its faulty form. This technique bridges fault-based and error-based testing, which is detailed in the next subsection.

Error-based (Infection Based) and Domain Analysis Testing

Error-based testing methods verify the programs by focusing on certain potential error points [20, 21]. The basis of domain testing is partitioning the input and output space of the program into smaller domains. The behavior of the execution of one test case within a smaller domain (or subdomain) is the same for all data within it. The test adequacy criteria require at least one test case for each subdomain. The correctness of the behavior of the software for the test cases in a subdomain reflects that the software should behave correctly for all data within that very subdomain. The probability of error or sub-domain partitioning can be based on the following four criteria.

• Specification-Based Input Space Partition

To create the input space partition, based on the specifications of the SUT, a part of the data is considered as a valid subdomain provided the specification works with the same function on that data. After designing the sub-domain of the input space, the test cases are designed corresponding to each subdomain. The testing is then done on this test suite, thus designed.

- Program-Based Input Space Partition

To separate the input space according to the program, the subdomain constitutes the data that leads to the same functioning or working of the program. The test cases are then designed for these subdomains.

- Boundary Analysis

The boundary analysis considers the N boundaries of the program as sub-domains. Thus, N test cases are created for each boundary of the program and one test case for the "off-the border" condition. This technique was given by White & Cohen [22].

- Functional Analysis

Functional analysis, as given by Howden [23] deals with analyzing the sequence of transformations in the operators, data types, and functions that occur in a subdomain. The test cases can thus be determined from the number of transformations occurring in the functional structure.

STUDY OF MUTATION TESTING

Mutation testing is a fault-based testing technique based on the coverage criterion of "mutation adequacy score". The hints of this technique can be traced from the work of Lipton [24]. The credit for laying the foundation of mutation testing goes to DeMillo *et al.* [25] and Hamlet [26] in the late 1970s.

Traditionally, the concept of mutation testing was laid on the following hypotheses [25].

- *The Competent Programmer Hypothesis (CPH)*: The assumption here is that programmers are usually proficient in the sense that they write codes that are near perfect, and the faults that may be present in the code are usually simple in nature.
- *The Coupling effect Hypothesis (CEH)*: The assumption is that if the test data is capable of detecting simple faults in a program, then the test data can detect complex faults too. Various studies manifested the empirical evaluation [24, 27-29] and theoretical validation [30-32] of CEH.

The Process of Mutation Testing

The process of traditional mutation testing is demonstrated in Fig. (**1**), as derived from the work of Offutt and Untch [33]. The process begins with the creation of mutants of the software under test. The SUT is executed using the test data provided, and the results of the execution are recorded. Then, each of the mutants is executed using the test data. If the result of execution is different from the result of the original program, then the mutant is said to be killed, else the mutant is said to be alive.

The results of this execution are used to evaluate the quality of the test data used. The tester may keep adding test cases to improve the score of mutants killed. There may be some mutants that will not be killed even after execution with all test data provided. These mutants may be alive mutants or "equivalent mutants".

The equivalent mutants are the ones whose execution output is the same as the original program. The techniques for handling the equivalent mutants are discussed in a later section.

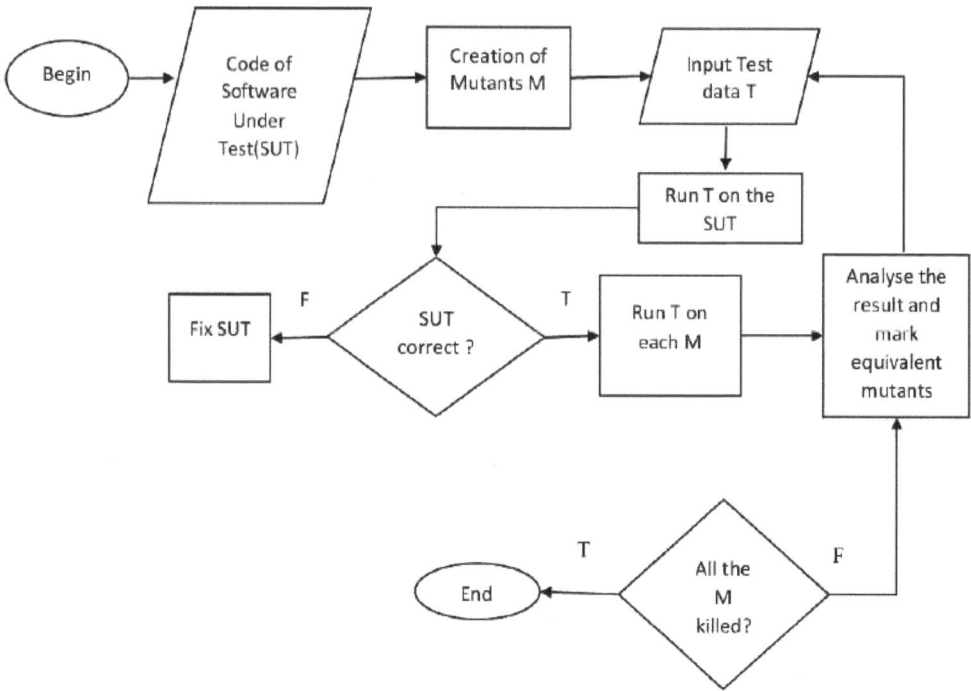

Fig. (1). The traditional process of mutation testing [33].

The process ends by providing the Mutation adequacy Score (MS) of the test set or test suite that is calculated by using the following formula:

$$MS = \text{number of mutants killed} / [\text{Total number of mutants} - \text{number of equivalent mutants}]$$

The value of MS close to 1 indicates that the test suite is an effective one. In essence, the aim here is to obtain a test suite that is able to kill the maximum number of mutants (which is anticipated to expose a maximum number of faults).

The most traditional form of mutation testing, as depicted in Fig. (**1**), is known as strong mutation. The weak mutation testing [34] is when the state of the mutated program is monitored just after the execution of the mutant. There is another variant, known as firmly mutation testing [35], wherein we check the state of the program somewhere between the state of execution of mutants and the appearance of the final output. The advantage of these variants of mutation testing is that they require less computational costs. However, the strong mutation is considered the most effective compared to firm and weak mutation testing [36].

Mutant Operators

The mutants here are created using a mutation operator (also known as a mutant operator, mutation rule, mutagenic operators, or simply as mutagens). These operators are generally simple syntactic changes like modification of expressions or variables. The first set of mutation operators was given by King and Offutt [37] for the FORTRAN Language and named Mothra mutation operators. Table **1** shows the Mothra mutation operators. Table **1** shows a simple example of the application of one of the Mothra Mutation operators to create a mutant.

Table 1. Mothra Mutation operators [37].

Mutation operator	Description
AAR	Array reference for Array reference Replacement
ACR	Array reference for Constant Replacement
ABS	ABSolute value insertion
AOR	Arithmetic Operator Replacement
ASR	Array reference for Scalar variable Replacement
CAR	Constant for Array Reference replacement
CNR	Comparable array Name Replacement
CSR	Constant for Scalar variable Replacement
CRP	Constant RePlacement
DER	Do statement End Replacement
DSA	Data Statement Alterations
GLR	Goto Label Replacement
LCR	Logical Connector Replacement
ROR	Relational Operator Replacement
RSR	Return Statement Replacement
SAN	Statement ANalysis
SAR	Scalar variable for Array reference Replacement
SCR	Scalar for Constant Replacement
SDL	Statement DeLetion
SRC	Scalar Constant Replacement
SVR	Source Variable Replacement
UOI	Unary Operator Insertion

Applications of Mutation Testing

Mutation testing has been applied to both the source code and specifications of the software under test. Mutation testing, when applied to the source code, is named Program Mutation [39]. It is a structural or white box technique as the mutants are created using the source code of the SUT. Mutation testing, when applied to the specifications, is named Specification Mutation [40], which is the black box technique and the mutants here are created using the program specifications at the design level.

A set of five mutant operators was empirically evaluated to be almost equally efficient as the 22 Mothra mutation operators provided by Offutt *et al.* [38]. The five-operator set is shown in the following Table **3**. An example of AOR application is set in Table **2** to create a mutant.

Table 2. An example of the application of AOR to create a mutant.

Original Program	A Mutant using AOR operator
.... A= S + C; printf ("%d", A);	.... A= S / C; printf("%d", A); ....

Table 3. The Five Mutation operators was set by Offutt *et al.* [38].

Mutation operator	Description
ABS	Absolute Value Insertion
AOR	Arithmetic Operator Replacement
LCR	Logical Connector Replacement
ROR	Relational Operator Replacement
UOI	Unary Operator Insertion

Program Mutation

Mutation Testing has been used at the unit level as well as the integration level by Program Mutation. At the unit level, program mutation refers to the most traditional form of testing, as given by Demillo *et al.* [25] wherein the mutants are created using the code of a unit of the SUT. At the integration level, the mutants of the program are created to represent the plausible faults during combining the units of the software. This was introduced by Delamaro *et al.* [41] and is also known as Interface Mutation Testing. Program Mutation has been used for testing software developed in numerous programming languages. The applicability is feasible and successful due to the availability of various tools that automate the process of the generation of mutants and their execution. The various mutation testing tools for popular programming languages are listed in Table **4**. The table mentions the year of the advent of the tool, and the reference section mentions the source of its introduction or significant usage. As is evident from Table **4**, many tools are available for C and Java languages, but there are tools available for other languages as well.

Table 4. Tools developed for Program Mutation in various languages.

Language	Tools Available	Year	Reference
FORTRAN	PIMS	1977	[42, 43]
	EXPER	1979	[44]
	FMS.3	1981	[45]
	Mothra	1987	[46]
C	Proteum 1.4	1993	[47]
	TUMS	1995	[48]
	Insure++	1998	[49]
	Proteum	2001	[50]
	MUTGEN	2003	[51]
	Plextext	2005	[52]
	Certitude	2006	[53]
	ExMAn	2006	[54]
	CSAW	2007	[55]
	ESPT	2008	[56]
	MUFORMAT	2008	[57]
	MILU	2008	[58]
	SMT-C	2012	[59]
	CCMUTATOR	2013	[60]
	MuVM	2016	[61]

(Table 4) cont.....

Language	Tools Available	Year	Reference
JAVA	Jester	2001	[62]
	JavaMut	2002	[63]
	MuJAVA	2004	[64]
	BYTEME	2006	[65]
	Jumble	2007	[66]
	Testooj	2007	[67]
	JAVALANCHE	2009	[68]
	PIT	2010	[69]
	MutMut	2010	[70]
	JUDY	2010	[71]
	BACTERIO	2010	[72]
	Evosuite	2011	[73]
	MAJOR	2011	[74]
	Paraµ	2011	[75]
	CoMUTATION	2013	[76]
	LittleDarwin	2017	[77]
AspectJ	AjMutator	2009	[78, 79]
	HOMAJ	2014	[80]
SQL	SQLMutation	2006	[81]
	MUSIC	2008	[82]
	JDAMA	2009	[83]
.Net	GenMutants	2010	[84]
Python	Pester	2001	[62]
	MutPy	2014	[85]
MATLAB	MATmute	2008	[86]
C#	ILMutator	2011	[87]
Javascript	Mutandis	2013	[88, 89]
Ruby	MuRUBY	2012	[90, 91]
	Heckle	2007	[92]

Specification Mutation

Gopal and Budd [93, 94] introduced the idea of Specification Mutation by applying the concept of generating mutants of software specifications at the design level. Specification mutants are created by seeding faults into logic expressions or the state machine. If the output condition is false for the specification, then the mutant is said to be killed. Specification Mutants are capable of finding faults like the misinterpretation of a specification or missing functionality [95]. At the design level, mutants have been created from different specifications like formal specifications, including mutants created using relational calculus, expression, faults representative of the states, events, and outputs in a Finite State Machine (FSM), Statecharts, or Petri Nets. Other specifications include the mutants for the final target environment of the SUT. Specification Mutants have also been created for XML data, network protocols, and security policies used in web services. Some of the representations of such specifications are shown in Table **5**, along with the corresponding seminal work.

Table 5. Seminal work in the area of specification mutation.

Representation of specification used for Mutation	Seminal work Reference
Relational Calculus Expression	Budd & Gopal [94]
	Woodward [96]
Finite State Machine	Fabbri *et al.* [97]
	Heirons & Merayo [98, 99]
Statechart	Fabbri *et al.* [100]
	Yoon *et al.* [101]
Petri Nets	Fabbri *et al.* [102]
Target Environment	Spafford [103]
	Du & Mathur [104]
XML Data in Web services	Offutt & Xu [105]
	Xu *et al.* [106]
Network Protocol	Sidhu & Leung [107]
	Probert & Guo [108]
Security Policy	[109-114]

Problems in Mutation Testing

Although mutation testing has been efficiently applied to various programming languages, it invariably suffers from certain shortcomings. The problems are described as follows:

1. High computational cost due to a huge number of mutants. The high cost incurred in the execution of a large number of mutants with the test cases is the major drawback associated with Mutation Testing. This restricts the use of

Mutation Testing as a practical approach in the software industry. A large number of mutants are created corresponding to even very small programs, and then executing the candidate test cases with each of the test cases leads to too much computational effort and time. There are, however, many techniques proposed to overcome this limitation. The techniques proposed by researchers to overcome the high computational cost problem are discussed in the next sub-section.

2. Equivalent and trivial mutants. If the behaviour of the mutated version of the program is the same as the original program, then that mutant is said to be an equivalent mutant. The evaluation of mutants to check their equivalence to the original program requires human effort. These mutants act as false negatives in the evaluation of the mutation score. Trivial mutants are those that are generated by very syntactical changes, easily getting killed by the simplest test cases. These mutants don't add much to the quality assessment of the test cases. The detail of equivalent mutants and the proposed solutions available in the literature are described in the next sub-section.

Solutions to Problems in Mutation Testing

It is impossible to get rid of the problems associated with Mutation Testing, but there have been substantial efforts to substantially resolve these problems. This subsection discusses the significant solutions proposed by various researchers in the area. Broadly, the cost reduction techniques are classified as Cost Reduction Techniques, Equivalent Mutant Reduction Techniques, and Search-based Mutation Testing.

Cost Reduction Techniques

The high computation cost in Mutation Testing incurred due to the execution of mutants generated from each of the test cases inhibits its application in the software industry. There are, thus, many endeavors by researchers working in the area to find a solution to this problem. The cost reduction techniques available in the literature can broadly be categorized, as shown in Fig. (**2**). The details on the techniques available for each subcategory are elaborated in this subsection.

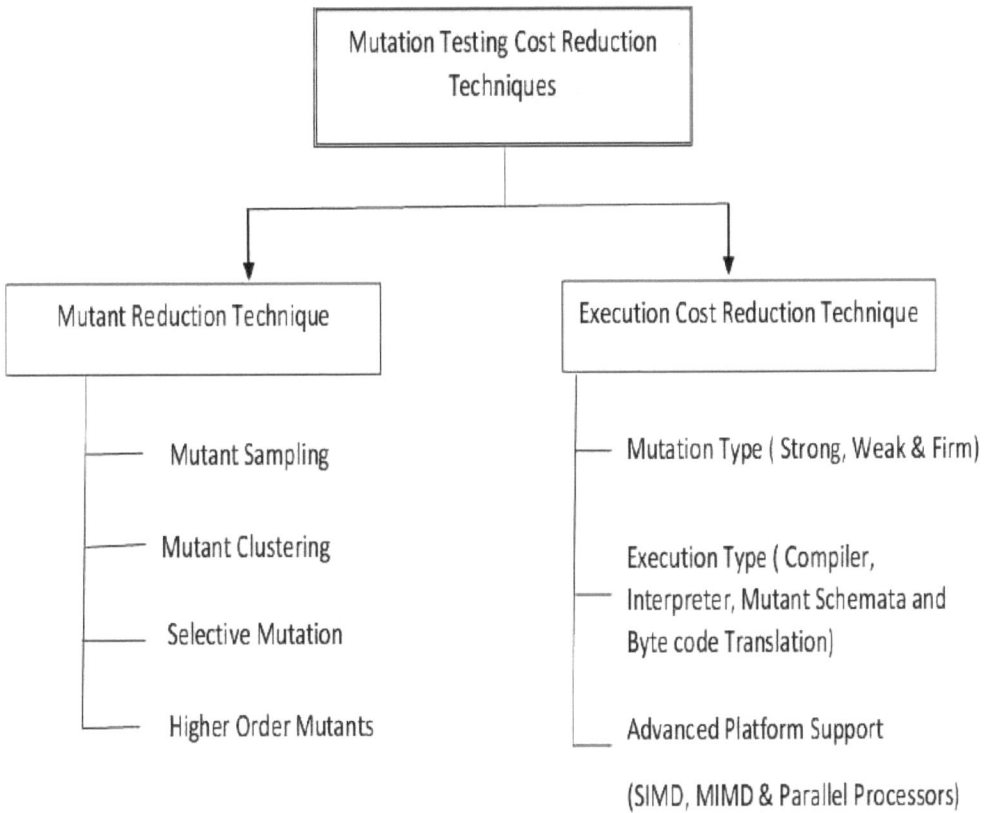

Fig. (2). Categorization of Mutation Testing Cost Reduction Techniques.

The details of the techniques for mutant reduction technique and execution cost reduction technique are discussed below:

Mutant Reduction Techniques

Even very small programs can have a large number of mutants. Thus, the cost of executing each mutant on each of the test cases incurs a high computational cost. Therefore, minimizing the number of mutants of the SUT without substantial loss in the test suite effectiveness is a significant research problem in the community of Mutation Testing researchers.

Mutant Sampling

Mutant sampling means a random selection of mutants from the total set of mutants generated. Acree [115] and Budd [116] proposed the idea of mutant sampling in their Ph.D. thesis. Their empirical investigation reported that even 10% sampling of mutants could achieve high effectiveness of the test suite. This empirical investigation was further supported by Wong & Mathur [117]. Sahinoglu & Spafford [118] gave a systematic method of sampling mutants using Bayesian statistical procedure. This model is more sensitive and efficient as it adjusts the mutant sampling rate according to the test data available. Zhang *et al.* [119] compared the mutant operator selection with the mutant sampling method and found that even as low as 5% of mutants can achieve a high mutation score (as well as 99%). Derezińska *et al.* [120] evaluated the mutant sampling method for mutation testing of object-oriented programs. Gopinath *et al.* [121] investigated the mutant reduction strategies both theoretically as well as empirically concluding the pure random sampling approach is the best approach for generic projects.

Mutant Clustering

Instead of applying a random sampling approach to mutant reduction, an alternative approach of creating clusters of mutants was proposed [122] by applying clustering approaches, namely K-means and agglomerative clustering. Ji *et al.* [123] gave a method of mutant clustering using the concept of domain analysis. Derezińska [124] proposed three metrics for the clustering of mutants, namely, the usefulness of the mutants generated by different mutation operators, their frequency, and their dependability. These metrics were empirically evaluated and gave promising results. Ma & Kim [125] gave a technique of mutant clustering based on weak mutations and compared the proposed approach with two mutant filtering approaches [126, 127].

Selective Mutation

Reduction in mutants can also be made by limiting the number of mutant operators used to create the mutants. This technique was introduced by Mathur [128] and was successfully improved and applied by Offutt *et al.* [129]. The successive development of selective mutation is shown in the following (Fig. **3**). The first block in the Figure shows the technique, and the consecutive block gives the result of the application of selective mutation with the percentage of mutants reduced and the percentage of the mutation score achieved.

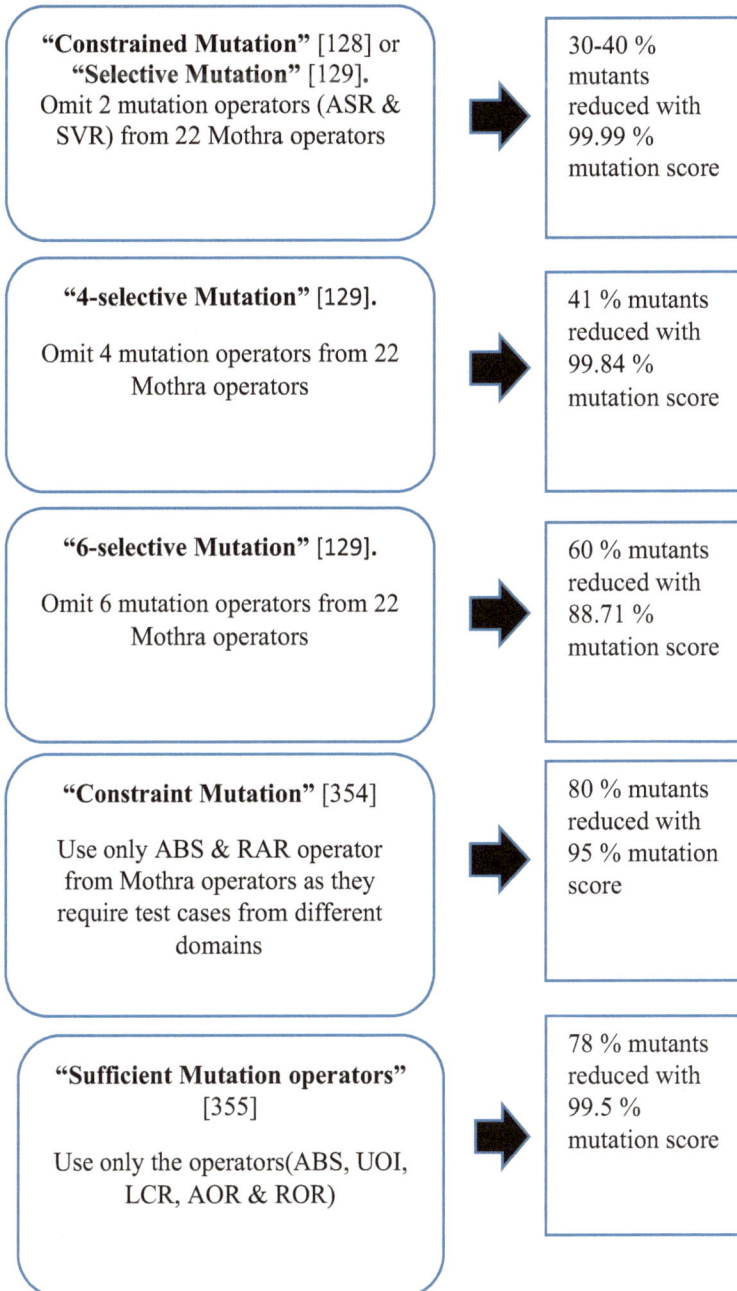

Fig. (3). Development of Selective Mutation.

Another strategy was used by Mresa & Botacci [130] to reduce the cost of mutation testing. They considered the mutation score and cost of each mutant operator to determine the selection of mutant operators. The cost here is determined by considering the time of generation of test cases and the time needed to examine mutants to find the equivalent mutants. This technique was successful in maintaining the efficiency of the test suite along with the determination of equivalent mutants by selective mutation. Barbosa *et al.* [131] used selective mutation to find a set of mutant operators from the Proteum's 77 mutation operators for C Language. Namin & Andrews [132] used a linear statistical approach to find a sufficient subset of mutation operators for C language. From the 108 mutation operators of C Language, they found a set of 28 operators, which they claim to be sufficient and resulted in a 92% reduction in the total number of mutants.

A recent paper depicted the relevance of selective mutation in real-life projects at Google [133]. Guizzo *et al.* [134] recently did an extensive study along with empirical analysis on selective mutation and reported pieces of evidence of a potential threat to the validity of using a number of mutants instead of the actual time of generating and executing mutants in the available literature.

Higher-order Mutants

Higher-order Mutant (HOM) is a relatively new concept given by Jia & Harman [135]. They stated that the mutants in traditional mutation testing that are generated by applying the mutation operator are often trivial with ease of destruction. These mutants, therefore, do not add much quality to the test suite generated. The HOMS are those that are created by applying mutation operators more than once. They called the mutants generated 'Subsumed HOMs (SHOMs)' generated from multiple first-order mutants and are harder to kill than the corresponding first-order mutants. This leads to a reduction in the number of mutants. They also gave the concept of 'Strongly SHOMs (SSHOMs)', and empirically evaluated its effectiveness [136].

Polo *et al.* [137] used the concept of HOMs to create second-order mutants to decrease the cost of mutation testing. They stated that they were able to kill mutants by up to 40%, and the equivalent mutants were also reduced by using the second-order mutants. Nguyen & Madeyski [138] applied multiobjective optimization algorithms to generate, search, and evaluate HOMs. They stated that they were able to generate 70% fewer mutants (HOMs) of high quality than the corresponding first-order mutants, as shown in Fig. (**3**). The concept of HOMs has proved to be ideal in dealing with mutation testing problems.

Execution Cost Reduction Techniques

The other way to reduce the overall cost of mutation testing is to reduce the cost of executing the mutants. The technique available in the literature to reduce the execution cost are divisible into three major categories, as described below:

Mutation Type

The most traditional form of mutation testing, as depicted in Fig. (**1**), is known as the *strong mutation*. The weak mutation testing [34] is when the program state is monitored just after the execution of the mutant. There is another variant, known as *firmly mutation testing* [35], wherein we check the state of the program somewhere between the state of execution of mutants and the appearance of the final output. The advantage of these variants of mutation testing is that they require less computational costs. However, the strong mutation is considered the most effective compared to firm and weak mutation testing [36]. Although, empirical studies [139-142] show that weak mutation testing should be used as it is computationally less expensive and can, in some cases, be almost as efficient as the strong mutation testing. A Parallel form of firmly mutation was proposed by Woodward [143].

Execution Type

One of the optimization techniques available in the literature is the interpreter-based technique by Offutt and King [37, 144]. Their technique converted the original code of the SUT into an intermediate form. This intermediate form was mutated and interpreted. This proved efficient for the small program but failed to do so for larger programs. The Compiler based techniques [145], however, are quite useful and highly applicable for program mutation. Here, the mutants are first compiled, which are then made to execute with different test cases. This approach proved to be much faster than interpretation techniques. This technique suffers from speed limits due to a high compilation cost incurred. DeMillo *et al.* [146] gave a solution to this problem by providing a Compiler-Integrated Technique. The details of use and implementation can be traced from Krauser's PhD thesis [147]. Another optimization approach available in literature is the Mutant Schematum Approach [148, 149]. This technique generates a metaprogram or a 'supermutant', which can be used to represent all mutants possible. This needs only a one-time compilation for all mutants. Untch *et al.* [149] developed a prototype tool named TUMS using mutant schemata and stated that it is significantly faster than interpreter-based techniques. The details of this can be traced from Untch's Ph.D. report [150]. Mutaion based approach for optimization proposed by R. Khan *et al.* [151]. In this technique, the mutants are generated using the compiled code and not the source code of the SUT. This can thus, be executed directly without having to compile it. This technique can also be applied to software whose source code is not available. This technique has been applied to Java Programs. Another approach by Bogacki and Walter [152, 153] named Aspect-oriented mutation is also a useful attempt to reduce the compilation cost.

Advanced Platform Support

Additional approaches to optimization of mutation testing costs available in the literature deal with advanced computer architecture techniques aiming to parallelize the process by distributing it among various processors. Mathur and Krauser made the first such attempt [154] by using a vector processor system. Krauser *et al.* [155] later gave an approach to concurrently execute mutants using SIMD machines. Fleyshgakker and Weiss [156] gave an effective algorithm that was able to parallelize the Mutation Testing process. Choi & Mathur [157] and Offutt *et al.* [158] used MIMD machines to distribute the computation process. Zapf [159] used a network for the independent and distributed execution of mutants.

Equivalent Mutant Handling Technique

In the process of mutation testing, some mutants may never be killed or will remain alive even after adding more and more test cases to the test set. This is because the syntactic change has altered the original program, but the output of the mutant execution is the same as the original program.

An example of such a mutant is explained in Table **6**, where the mutagen has altered the program statement, but the resultant output of its execution will remain the same as the original program. Such mutants are known as equivalent mutants. In Table **6**, the usage of AOR operator has created a mutant, but the execution of this mutant will always remain the same as the original program. Automatic Detection of all equivalent mutants is an impossible task [160, 161]. The equivalent mutants thus need human intervention. Researchers have found through empirical evaluations that equivalent mutants can range from 10% to 40% of the total mutants generated by the software under test [160, 162]. This is a major drawback in the process of mutation testing. Nonetheless, there have been many attempts to deal with the problem of equivalent mutants. Significant efforts by researchers to handle equivalent mutants' problems are mentioned in Table 7.

Table 7. Solutions provided by researchers to deal with the equivalent mutant problem.

S. No.	Solution provided/ Technique used	Source
1.	Designed Compiler optimization rules for the detection of equivalent mutants.	Baldwin & Sayward [163]
2.	Formulated the equivalent mutant problem as a constraint satisfaction problem and labelled a mutant as equivalent if the constraint is unsatisfiable.	Offutt & Pan [160, 164]
3.	Program slicing method for detecting equivalent mutants.	Harman *et al.* [165], Hierons *et al.* [166]
4.	Co-evolutionary approach to detect equivalent mutants.	Adamopoulos *et al.* [167]
5.	Studied impact of mutants by measuring the code coverage, and hence the mutants with less impact are likely to be equivalent.	Grün *et al.* [168]
6.	Studied the impact of mutants by measuring the code coverage, impact on the value returned, and impact on invariants. Hence, the mutants with less than 10% are likely to be equivalent.	Schuler *et al.* [169]
7.	Used Trivial Compiler Equivalence method to detect equivalent mutants.	Papadakis *et al.* [170], Kintis *et al.* [171]
8.	Introduced Memory Mutation operators to target the most common memory faults along with dealing with the equivalent and duplicate mutants.	Wu *et al.* [172]

Search-Based Mutation Testing

Search-Based Software Testing [173] makes use of the meta-heuristic or search-based techniques as an optimizing search technique, like the Genetic Algorithm, for the task of automating or partially automating a testing task that otherwise requires a lot of human effort. The objective is to obtain the right solution to the problem in a reasonable time. Search-Based Mutation Testing (SBMT) works by formulating optimization problems in software testing, such as test data generation/optimization and mutant optimization problems as search problems, and applies metaheuristic techniques to solve them in the context of Mutation Testing [174].

Application of Mutation Testing for Handling the Test Suite

Mutation testing has been intensely applied for software quality assurance [175]. Mutation testing also finds application in processes related to handling the test suite like generation, minimizing, and even prioritizing the test suite. Fig. (4) below gives a detailed view of the process of using mutation testing for test data handling. This process is an extended form of the modern Mutation Testing process detailed by Papadakis *et al.* [36].

Test Case Generation Techniques

Mutation based test case generation involves the automatic generation of test cases that are able to detect (or kill) the maximum number of mutants. One of the earliest works on test data generation using Mutation Testing represented mutant killing as constraints, and the process of generating test data that satisfied these constraints. They called it 'Constraint based Testing (CBT)' [176]. They developed a toolset named Godzilla, which generates constraints automatically, using them for creating test cases to be used for the unit as well as module testing. The tool Godzilla was integrated with the Mothra testing system to use it as an effective way to the generation of test data able to kill mutants of the program under test. They used path coverage and symbolic execution for test data generation along with mutation testing.

Offutt & Pan [177] gave three conditions (namely, Reachability, Necessity, and sufficiency) that a mutant must satisfy to be killed. To overcome the limitations of Constraint-based testing, including the inability to handle loops, nesting of expressions and composite data structures like arrays, Offutt *et al.* [178] used a Dynamic Domain Reduction technique. Liu *et al.* [179] proposed a further cost-effective improvement of the CBT technique. Dynamic Symbolic Execution (DSE) has been used by Zhang *et al.* [84] and Papadakis & Malveris [180]. Both these studies use program transformation by augmenting the program with conditional statements and path coverage for the generation of test data for mutation testing. Search based technique is another way of automating the process of data generation. Botacci was the first to propose [181] the use of search-based techniques for the generation of test data for Mutation Testing. The proposed model is shown in Fig. (**4**). Ayari *et al.* [182], Fraser & Zeller [183], Baudry *et al.* [184] also used search-based techniques for mutation-based test data generation of Java Programs. All the above approaches use weak mutation for the generation of test data. Chapter 2 discusses details of the use of search based techniques for test data generation using Mutation Testing. Harman *et al.* [185] used Higher Order Mutants for the generation of test data. They also used a search-based technique and DSE for automating the process of data generation. This was the first approach to target strong mutation adequacy. A survey on mutation-based test data generation [186] lists various publications in the area.

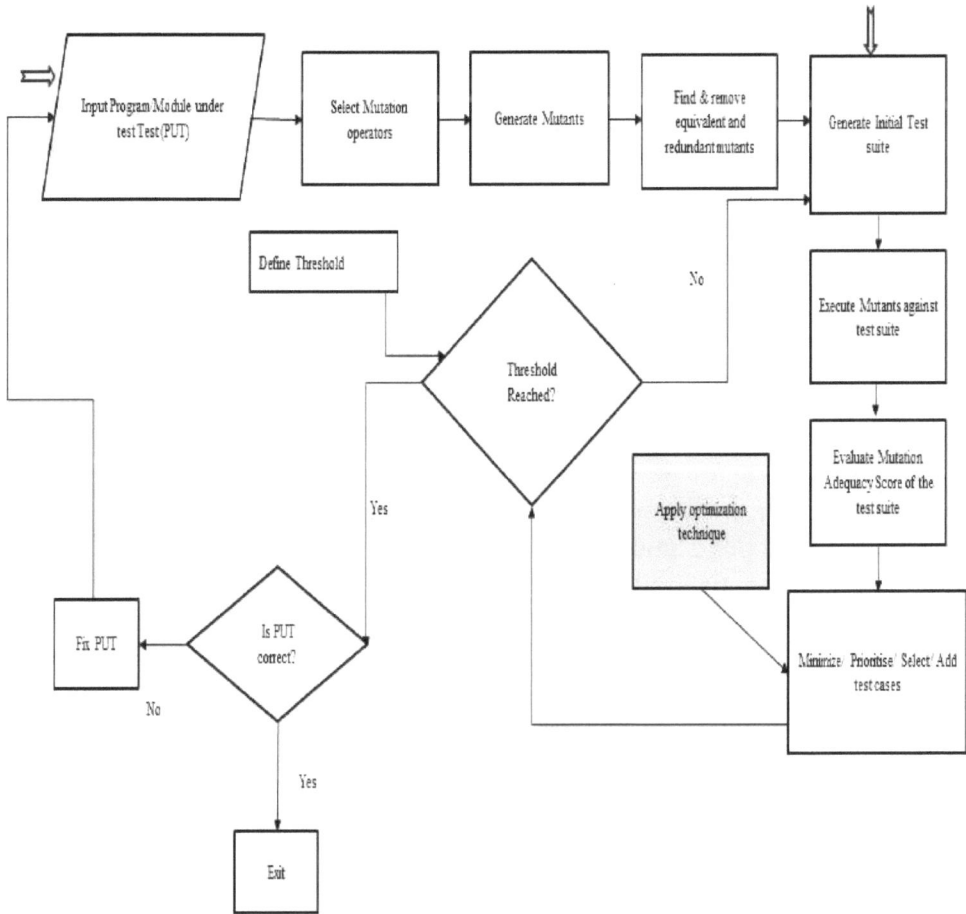

Fig. (4). Process of using mutation testing for test data generation/minimization/selection or prioritization. This process is an extended form of the Modern Mutation Testing Process detailed by Papadakis *et al.* [36].

Test Case Selection and Minimization Techniques

Test suite minimization or selection technique aims to reduce test execution cost by eliminating the redundant test cases from the test suite. Mutation testing can aid in locating the redundant test suite. This can be done by checking the mutants already covered by the test cases in the test suite. If the test case does not kill a new mutant, it can be considered redundant. Although limited literature is available on using mutation testing for test case selection or minimization, relevant publications are briefed here. Offutt *et al.* [187] gave a proof-of-concept (named Ping-Pong) by conducting an empirical test suite minimization to assist regression testing. The minimization process finds a subset of test data having the highest mutation score based on the coverage criteria. They were able to effectively reduce the size of the test suite by 33%. On similar lines, Wong *et al.*

[188] minimized the size of the test suite using the fault detection effectiveness. They empirically concluded that the test cases that do not add to coverage might not further add to fault detection. Rani and Suri [189-191] gave an approach for test data generation using a Genetic Algorithm and deleted Mutation Analysis. Ahmed [192] used a combinatorial approach and a search-based approach along with Mutation Testing to minimize the test cases effectively. Wei *et al.* [193] introduced a multi-objective Mutation Testing based approach for minimization of the test suite. They used three objective criteria (less computational time, high coverage, and high fault detectability) and applied six different evolutionary algorithms to find an efficient minimized test suite.

Test Case Prioritization Techniques

Test case prioritization using Mutation Testing deals with prioritizing test cases based on their effectiveness in the mutant killing. Do, and Gregg [65, 194] conducted a controlled experiment on Java programs by creating their mutants using their bytecode. Their analyses reveal that test case prioritization has the ability to improve the rate of fault detection when measured in relation to mutation faults. These results may vary with the number of mutation faults and with the fault detection capability of the test suite. Just *et al.* [195] gave a scalable approach to Mutation Testing by first using a reduced, yet sufficient mutation operator to create mutants and thereby presented and experimentally evaluated an optimized approach to exploit the redundancies and difference in execution time of the test cases for reordering and splitting the corresponding test suite to prioritize the test cases in the corresponding test suite. Zhang *et al.* [196, 197] also gave a technique for reduction and prioritization of the test suites using Mutation Testing.

CONSENT OF PUBLICATION

Not applicable.

CONFLICT OF INTEREST

The author declares no conflict of interest, financial or otherwise.

ACKNOWLEDGEMENTS

Declared none.

REFERENCES

[1]   A. Pope, *The complete poetical works of Alexander Pope.*, Houghton Mifflin, 1903.

[2]   B. Beizer, *Software Testing Techniques.*, 2nd ed.,Van Nostrand Reinhold Co.: New York, USA, 1990.

[3]   R.N. Charette, "Why software fails", *IEEE Spectr,* vol. 42, no. 9, pp. 42-49, 2005.
[http://dx.doi.org/10.1109/MSPEC.2005.1502528]

[4]   G. Fraser, and J.M. Rojas, "Software Testing", *Handbook of Software Engineering,* Springer: Cham,
pp. 123-192, 2019.
[http://dx.doi.org/10.1007/978-3-030-00262-6_4]

[5]   P. Ammann, and J. Offutt, *Introduction to Software Testing,* Cambridge University Press, 2008.

[6]   P.S. May, "Test Data Generation: two Evolutionary Approaches to Mutation Testing", In: *Doctoral
Dissertation.* Computing Laboratory, 2007.

[7]   J.B. Goodenough, and S.L. Gerhart, "Toward a theory of test data selection", *IEEE Trans. Softw. Eng,*
vol. 2, no. 2, pp. 156-173, 1975.
[http://dx.doi.org/10.1109/TSE.1975.6312836]

[8]   M. Hutchins, H. Foster, T. Goradia, and T. Ostrand, "Experiments on the effectiveness of dataflow-
and control-flow-based test adequacy criteria", *16th International Conference on Software
Engineering.,* 1994.
[http://dx.doi.org/10.1109/ICSE.1994.296778]

[9]   P.G. Frankl, and E.J. Weyuker, "An applicable family of data flow testing criteria", *IEEE Trans.
Softw. Eng,* vol. 14, no. 10, pp. 1483-1498, 1998.
[http://dx.doi.org/10.1109/32.6194]

[10]   P.M. Herman, "A data flow analysis approach to program testing", *Aust. Comput. J.,* vol. 8, no. 3, pp.
92-96, 1976.

[11]   S.C. Ntafos, "On required element testing", *IEEE Trans. Softw. Eng,* vol. 6, no. 6, pp. 795-803, 1984.
[http://dx.doi.org/10.1109/TSE.1984.5010308]

[12]   H. Zhu, P.A. Hall, and J.H. May, "Software unit test coverage and adequacy", *ACM Comput. Surv,*
vol. 29, no. 4, pp. 366-427, 1997. [csur].
[http://dx.doi.org/10.1145/267580.267590]

[13]   G. Fraser, A. Gargantini, and F. Wotawa, "On the order of test goals in specification-based testing", *J.
Log. Algebraic Program,* vol. 78, no. 6, pp. 472-490, 2009.
[http://dx.doi.org/10.1016/j.jlap.2009.01.004]

[14]   L.J. Morell, "A theory of fault-based testing", *IEEE Trans. Softw. Eng,* vol. 16, no. 8, pp. 844-857,
1990.
[http://dx.doi.org/10.1109/32.57623]

[15]   B. Meek, and K.K. Siu, "The effectiveness of error seeding", *SIGPLAN Not,* vol. 24, no. 6, pp. 81-89,
1989.
[http://dx.doi.org/10.1145/71052.71064]

[16]   Y. Jia, and M. Harman, "An Analysis and Survey of the Development of Mutation Testing", *IEEE
Trans. Softw. Eng,* vol. 37, no. 5, pp. 649-678, 2010.
[http://dx.doi.org/10.1109/TSE.2010.62]

[17]   S.J. Zeil, "Perturbation testing for computation errors", *7th international conference on Software
engineering,* 1984.

[18]   W. Du, and A.P. Mathur, "Testing for software vulnerability using environment perturbation", *Qual.
Reliab. Eng. Int,* vol. 18, no. 3, pp. 261-272, 2002.
[http://dx.doi.org/10.1002/qre.480]

[19]   W. Xu, J. Offutt, and J. Luo, "Testing web services by XML perturbation", *16th IEEE International
Symposium on Software Reliability Engineering (ISSRE'05),* p. 10, 2005.

[20]   K.A. Foster, "Error sensitive test cases analysis (ESTCA)", *IEEE Trans. Softw. Eng,* vol. 3, no. 3, pp.
258-264, 1980.

[http://dx.doi.org/10.1109/TSE.1980.234487]

[21]   G. J. Myers, *The Art of Software Testing,* John Wiley and Sons Ltd, 1979.

[22]   L.J. White, and E.I. Cohen, "A domain strategy for computer program testing", *IEEE Trans. Softw. Eng,* vol. 3, no. 3, pp. 247-257, 1980.
[http://dx.doi.org/10.1109/TSE.1980.234486]

[23]   W.E. Howden, "A functional approach to program testing and analysis", *IEEE Trans. Softw. Eng,* vol. 10, no. 10, pp. 997-1005, 1986.
[http://dx.doi.org/10.1109/TSE.1986.6313016]

[24]   R. Lipton, Fault Diagnosis of Computer Programs. *Student Report,* Carnegie Mellon Univ., 1971.

[25]   R.A. DeMillo, R.J. Lipton, and F.G. Sayward, "Hints on Test Data Selection: Help for the Practicing Programmer", *Computer,* vol. 11, pp. 34-41, 1978.

[26]   R.G. Hamlet, "Testing Programs with the Aid of a Compiler", *IEEE Trans. Softw. Eng,* vol. 3, no. 4, pp. 279-290, 1977.
[http://dx.doi.org/10.1109/TSE.1977.231145]

[27]   L. Morell, *Theory of error-based testing.* PhD thesis, Univ. of Maryland: College Park, 1984.
[http://dx.doi.org/10.21236/ADA143533]

[28]   A. Offutt, "The Coupling Effect: Fact or Fiction", *Softw. Eng. Notes,* vol. 14, no. 8, pp. 131-140, 1989.
[http://dx.doi.org/10.1145/75309.75324]

[29]   A. Offutt, "Investigations of the Software Testing Coupling Effect", *ACM Trans. Softw. Eng. Methodol,* vol. 1, no. 1, pp. 5-20, 1992.
[http://dx.doi.org/10.1145/125489.125473]

[30]   C. Jing, Z. Wang, X. Shi, X. Yin, and J. Wu, "Mutation Testing of Protocol Messages Based on Extended TTCN-3", *Advanced Information Networking and Applications.,* 2008.
[http://dx.doi.org/10.1109/AINA.2008.98]

[31]   K. Wa, "A Theoretical Study of Fault Coupling", *Softw. Test. Verif. Reliab,* vol. 10, no. 1, pp. 3-46, 2000.
[http://dx.doi.org/10.1002/(SICI)1099-1689(200003)10:1<3::AID-STVR196>3.0.CO;2-P]

[32]   K. Wah, "An Analysis of the Coupling Effect I: Single Test Data", *Science of Computer Programming,* vol. 48, no. 2-3, pp. 119-161, 2003.

[33]   A.J. Offutt, and R.H. Untch, "Mutation 2000: Uniting the Orthogonal", *Proceedings of the 1st Workshop on Mutation Analysis (MUTATION'00),* 2000.

[34]   W. Howden, "Weak Mutation Testing and Completeness of Test Sets", *IEEE Trans. Softw. Eng,* vol. 8, no. 4, pp. 371-379, 1982.
[http://dx.doi.org/10.1109/TSE.1982.235571]

[35]   M. Woodward, and K. Halewood, "From Weak to Strong Dead or Alive? An Analysis of Some Mutationtesting Issues", *Second Workshop Software Testing, Verification, and Analysis,* 1988.
[http://dx.doi.org/10.1109/WST.1988.5370]

[36]   M. Papadakis, M. Kintis, J. Zhang, Y. Jia, Y. Le Traon, and M. Harman, "Mutation testing advances: an analysis and survey", *Adv. Comput,* vol. 112, pp. 275-378, 2019.
[http://dx.doi.org/10.1016/bs.adcom.2018.03.015]

[37]   K.N. King, and A.J. Offutt, "A Fortran Language System for Mutation-Based Software Testing", *Softw. Pract. Exper,* vol. 21, no. 7, pp. 685-718, 1991.
[http://dx.doi.org/10.1002/spe.4380210704]

[38]   A.J. Offutt, A. Lee, G. Rothermel, R.H. Untch, and C. Zapf, "An experimental determination of sufficient mutant operators", *ACM Trans. Softw. Eng. Methodol,* vol. 5, no. 2, pp. 99-118, 1996.
[TOSEM].

[http://dx.doi.org/10.1145/227607.227610]

[39] R. DeMillo, Program mutation: an approach to software testing. *Technical Report, Georgia Inst. of Technology*, 1983.

[40] A. Gopal, and T. Budd, Program Testing by Specification Mutation. *Technical Report TR 83-17*, Univ. of Arizona, 1983.

[41] M.E. Delamaro, J.C. Maldonado, and A.P. Mathur, "Integration testing using interface mutation", *7th International Symposium on Software Reliability Engineering ISSRE'96*, 1996.
[http://dx.doi.org/10.1109/ISSRE.1996.558719]

[42] T.A. Budd, and F.G. Sayward, Users guide to the pilot mutation system*techreport 114*, Yale University: New Haven, Connecticut, 1977.

[43] T.A. Budd, R.J. Lipton, R. DeMillo, and F. Sayward, "The design of a prototype mutation system for program testing", *International Workshop on Managing Requirements Knowledge*, 1978.

[44] T.A. Budd, R. Hess, and F.G. Sayward, "EXPER implementor's guide", *Technique Report*, Yale University: New Haven, Connecticut, 1980.

[45] A. Tanaka, Equivalence Testing for FORTRAN Mutation System Using Data Flow Analysis.*(No. GIT-ICS-82/10)*, Georgia Inst. of Tech Atlanta School of Information and Computer Science, 1981.
[http://dx.doi.org/10.21236/ADA118840]

[46] R.A. DeMillo, D.S. Guindi, W.M. McCracken, A.J. Offutt, and K.N. King, "An extended overview of the Mothra software testing environment", *Second Workshop on Software Testing, Verification, and Analysis*, 1988.
[http://dx.doi.org/10.1109/WST.1988.5369]

[47] M.E. Delamaro, Proteum-A MutatioAnalysis Based Testing Environmen," Master's thesis, Univ. of São Paulo., 1993.

[48] R.H. Untch, A.J. Offutt, and M.J. Harrold, "Mutation analysis using mutant schemata", *Proceedings of the 1993 ACM SIGSOFT international symposium on Software testing and analysis*, 1993.

[49] http://www.parasoft.com/jsp/products/home.jsp? product=Insure

[50] M.E. Delamaro, J.C. Maldonado, and A.M.R. Vincenzi, *Proteum/IM 2.0: An integrated mutation testing environment*, 2001.

[51] J.H. Andrews, and Y. Zhang, "General test result checking with log file analysis", *IEEE Trans. Softw. Eng*, vol. 29, no. 7, pp. 634-648, 2003.
[http://dx.doi.org/10.1109/TSE.2003.1214327]

[52] http://www.itregister.com.au/products/plextest.htm

[53] http://www.certess.com/product/

[54] J.S. Bradbury, J.R. Cordy, and J. Dingel, "ExMAn: A generic and customizable framework for experimental mutation analysis", *Second Workshop on Mutation Analysis (Mutation 2006-ISSRE Workshops)*, 2006.
[http://dx.doi.org/10.1109/MUTATION.2006.5]

[55] http://www.skicambridge.com/papers/Csaw v1 files.html

[56] X. Feng, S. Marr, and T. O'Callaghan, "ESTP: An experimental software testing platform", *Testing: Academic & Industrial Conference-Practice and Research Techniques (taic part 2008)*, 2008.
[http://dx.doi.org/10.1109/TAIC-PART.2008.8]

[57] H. Shahriar, and M. Zulkernine, "Mutation-based testing of format string bugs", *11th IEEE High Assurance Systems Engineering Symposium*, 2008.

[58] Y. Jia, and M. Harman, "MILU: A customizable, runtime-optimized higher order mutation testing tool for the full C language", *Practice and Research Techniques, 2008. TAIC PART '08*, Windsor: Testing:

Academic & Industrial Conference, pp. 29-31, 2008.
[http://dx.doi.org/10.1109/TAIC-PART.2008.18]

[59] H. Dan, and R.M. Hierons, "SMT-C: A semantic mutation testing tools for C", *Fifth International Conference on Software Testing, Verification and Validation,* 2012.
[http://dx.doi.org/10.1109/ICST.2012.155]

[60] M. Kusano, and C. Wang, "CCmutator: A mutation generator for concurrency constructs in multithreaded C/C++ applications", *28ʰ IEEE/ACM International Conference on Automated Software Engineering (ASE),* 2013.
[http://dx.doi.org/10.1109/ASE.2013.6693142]

[61] S. Tokumoto, H. Yoshida, K. Sakamoto, and S. Honiden, "MuVM: Higher order mutation analysis virtual machine for C", *IEEE International Conference on Software Testing, Verification and Validation (ICST),* 2016.
[http://dx.doi.org/10.1109/ICST.2016.18]

[62] I. Moore, *Jester and Pester,* 2001. http://jester.sourceforge.net/

[63] P. Chevalley, and P. Thevenod-Fosse, "A mutation analysis tool for Java programs", *Int. J. Softw. Tools Technol. Transf,* vol. 5, no. 1, pp. 90-103, 2003.
[http://dx.doi.org/10.1007/s10009-002-0099-9]

[64] Y.S. Ma, J. Offutt, and Y.R. Kwon, "MuJava: an automated class mutation system", *Softw. Test. Verif. Reliab,* vol. 15, no. 2, pp. 97-133, 2005.
[http://dx.doi.org/10.1002/stvr.308]

[65] H. Do, and G. Rothermel, "On the use of mutation faults in empirical assessments of test case prioritization techniques", *IEEE Trans. Softw. Eng,* vol. 32, no. 9, pp. 733-752, 2006.
[http://dx.doi.org/10.1109/TSE.2006.92]

[66] Source Forge "Jumble", http://jumble.sourceforge.net/

[67] M. Polo, S. Tendero, and M. Piattini, "Integrating techniques and tools for testing automation: Research Articles", *Softw. Test. Verif. Reliab,* vol. 17, no. 1, pp. 3-39, 2007.
[http://dx.doi.org/10.1002/stvr.348]

[68] D. Schuler, V. Dallmeier, and A. Zeller, "Efficient mutation testing by checking invariant violations", *eighteenth international symposium on Software testing and analysis,* 2009.
[http://dx.doi.org/10.1145/1572272.1572282]

[69] H. Coles, T. Laurent, C. Henard, M. Papadakis, and A. Ventresque, "Pit: a practical mutation testing tool for java", *25ʰ International Symposium on Software Testing and Analysis,* 2016.
[http://dx.doi.org/10.1145/2931037.2948707]

[70] M. Gligoric, V. Jagannath, and D. Marinov, "MuTMuT: Efficient exploration for mutation testing of multithreaded code", *Third International Conference on Software Testing, Verification and Validation,* 2010.
[http://dx.doi.org/10.1109/ICST.2010.33]

[71] L. Madeyski, and N. Radyk, "Judy-a mutation testing tool for Java", *IET Softw,* vol. 4, no. 1, pp. 32-42, 2010.
[http://dx.doi.org/10.1049/iet-sen.2008.0038]

[72] P.R. Mateo, M.P. Usaola, and J. Offutt, "Mutation at system and functional levels", *Third International Conference on Software Testing, Verification, and Validation Workshops,* 2010.
[http://dx.doi.org/10.1109/ICSTW.2010.18]

[73] G. Fraser, and A. Arcuri, "Evosuite: automatic test suite generation for object-oriented software", *19ʰ ACM SIGSOFT symposium and the 13ʰ European conference on Foundations of software engineering,* 2011.
[http://dx.doi.org/10.1145/2025113.2025179]

[74] R. Just, "The Major mutation framework: Efficient and scalable mutation analysis for Java", *International Symposium on Software Testing and Analysis,* 2014. [http://dx.doi.org/10.1145/2610384.2628053]

[75] P. Madiraju, and A.S. Namin, "Paraµ--A Partial and Higher-Order Mutation Tool with Concurrency Operators", *Fourth International Conference on Software Testing, Verification and Validation Workshops,* 2011.

[76] M. Gligoric, L. Zhang, C. Pereira, and G. Pokam, "Selective mutation testing for concurrent code", *International Symposium on Software Testing and Analysis,* 2013.

[77] A. Parsai, A. Murgia, and S. Demeyer, "Littledarwin: a feature-rich and extensible mutation testing framework for large and complex java systems", *International Conference on Fundamentals of Software Engineering,* 2017. [http://dx.doi.org/10.1007/978-3-319-68972-2_10]

[78] R. Delamare, B. Baudry, S. Ghosh, and Y. Le Traon, "A test-driven approach to developing pointcut descriptors in aspectj", *International Conference on Software Testing Verification and Validation,* 2009. [http://dx.doi.org/10.1109/ICST.2009.41]

[79] R. Delamare, B. Baudry, and Y. Le Traon, "Ajmutator: A tool for the mutation analysis of aspectj pointcut descriptors", *International Conference on Software Testing, Verification, and Validation Workshops,* 2009. [http://dx.doi.org/10.1109/ICSTW.2009.41]

[80] E. Omar, S. Ghosh, and D. Whitley, "HOMAJ: A tool for higher order mutation testing in AspectJ and Java", *Seventh International Conference on Software Testing, Verification and Validation Workshops,* 2014. [http://dx.doi.org/10.1109/ICSTW.2014.19]

[81] J. Tuya, M.J. Suarez-Cabal, and C. De La Riva, "SQLMutation: A tool to generate mutants of SQL database queries", [http://dx.doi.org/10.1109/MUTATION.2006.13]

[82] H. Shahriar, and M. Zulkernine, "MUSIC: Mutation-based SQL injection vulnerability checking", *The Eighth International Conference on Quality Software,* 2008.

[83] C. Zhou, and P. Frankl, "Mutation testing for java database applications", *International Conference on Software Testing Verification and Validation,* 2009. [http://dx.doi.org/10.1109/ICST.2009.43]

[84] L. Zhang, T. Xie, L. Zhang, N. Tillmann, J. De Halleux, and H. Mei, "Test generation via dynamic symbolic execution for mutation testing", *IEEE International Conference on Software Maintenance.* [http://dx.doi.org/10.1109/ICSM.2010.5609672]

[85] A. Derezińska, and K. Hałas, "Analysis of mutation operators for the python language", *The Ninth International Conference on Dependability and Complex Systems DepCoS-RELCOMEX,* 2014. [http://dx.doi.org/10.1007/978-3-319-07013-1_15]

[86] *M.A. Tmute,* 2008. Availabe at: https://sourceforge.net/projects/matmute/

[87] A. Derezinska, and K. Kowalski, "Object-oriented mutation applied in common intermediate language programs originated from c", *IEEE Fourth International Conference on Software Testing, Verification and Validation Workshops,* 2011. [http://dx.doi.org/10.1109/ICSTW.2011.54]

[88] S. Mirshokraie, A. Mesbah, and K. Pattabiraman, "Efficient JavaScript mutation testing", *IEEE Sixth International Conference on Software Testing, Verification and Validation,* 2013.

[89] S. Mirshokraie, A. Mesbah, and K. Pattabiraman, "Guided mutation testing for javascript web applications", *IEEE Trans. Softw. Eng,* vol. 41, no. 5, pp. 429-444, 2014.

[http://dx.doi.org/10.1109/TSE.2014.2371458]

[90]   M. Schirp, "Mutation Testing for rubY", https://github.com/mbj/mutant

[91]   N. Li, M. West, A. Escalona, and V.H. Durelli, "Mutation testing in practice using ruby", *Eighth International Conference on Software Testing, Verification and Validation Workshops (ICSTW)*, 2015. [http://dx.doi.org/10.1109/ICSTW.2015.7107453]

[92]   http://seattlerb.rubyforge.org/heckle/

[93]   A.S. Gopal, and T.A. Budd, Program Testing by Specification Mutation.*Technical Report TR 83-17*, University of Arizona: Tucson, Arizona, 1983.

[94]   T.A. Budd, and A.S. Gopal, "Program Testing by Specification Mutation", *Comput. Lang,* vol. 10, no. 1, pp. 63-73, 1985. [http://dx.doi.org/10.1016/0096-0551(85)90011-6]

[95]   V. Okun, *Specification Mutation for Test Generation and Analysis.* University of Maryland Baltimore County: Baltimore, Maryland, 2004.

[96]   M.R. Woodward, "OBJTEST: an experimental testing tool for algebraic specifications", *IEE Colloquium on Automating Formal Methods for Computer Assisted Prototyping.,* 1992.

[97]   S.P.F. Fabbri, M.E. Delamaro, J.C. Maldonado, and P.C. Masiero, "Mutation analysis testing for finite state machines", *International Symposium on Software Reliability Engineering,* 1994.

[98]   R. M. Hierons, and M. G. Merayo, "Mutation testing from probabilistic finite state machines", *Testing: Academic and Industrial Conference Practice and Research Techniques-MUTATION (TAICPART-MUTATION 2007),* 2007. [http://dx.doi.org/10.1109/TAIC.PART.2007.20]

[99]   R.M. Hierons, and M.G. Merayo, "Mutation testing from probabilistic and stochastic finite state machines", *J. Syst. Softw,* vol. 82, no. 11, pp. 1804-1818, 2009. [http://dx.doi.org/10.1016/j.jss.2009.06.030]

[100]   S.P.F. Fabbri, M.E. Delamaro, J.C. Maldonado, and P.C. Masiero, "Mutation analysis testing for finite state machines", *IEEE International Symposium on Software Reliability Engineering,* 1994.

[101]   H. Yoon, B. Choi, and J.O. Jeon, "Mutation-based inter-class testing", *Asia Pacific Software Engineering Conference (Cat. No. 98EX240),* 1998.

[102]   S.C.P.F. Fabbri, J.C. Maldonado, P.C. Masiero, and W.E.W.M.E. Delamaro, "Mutation Testing Applied to Validate Specifications", *IFIP TC6 8th International Conference on Formal Description Techniques VIII,* 2009.

[103]   E.H. Spafford, "Extending Mutation Testing to Find Environmental Bugs", *Softw. Pract. Exper,* vol. 20, no. 2, pp. 181-189, 1990. [http://dx.doi.org/10.1002/spe.4380200205]

[104]   W. Du, and A.P. Mathur, "Vulnerability testing of software system using fault injection", *Technique Report Coast TR,* Purdue University: West Lafayette, Indiana, pp. 98-02, 1998.

[105]   J. Offutt, and W. Xu, "Generating test cases for web services using data perturbation", *Softw. Eng. Notes,* vol. 29, no. 5, pp. 1-10, 2004. [http://dx.doi.org/10.1145/1022494.1022529]

[106]   W. Xu, J. Offutt, and J. Luo, "Testing web services by XML perturbation", *International Symposium on Software Reliability Engineering (ISSRE'05),* 2005.

[107]   D. Sidhu, and T.K. Leung, "Fault coverage of protocol test methods", *7th Annual Joint Conference of the IEEE Computer and Communcations Societies (INFOCOM'88),* 1998.

[108]   R. Probert, and F. Guo, "Mutation testing of protocols: Principles and preliminary experimental results", *Workshop on Protocol Test Systems,* 1991.

[109] Y. Le Traon, T. Mouelhi, and B. Baudry, "Testing security policies: going beyond functional testing", *IEEE International Symposium on Software Reliability (ISSRE'07)*, 2007.
[http://dx.doi.org/10.1109/ISSRE.2007.27]

[110] E. Martin, and T. Xie, "A fault model and mutation testing of access control policies", *16th international conference on World Wide Web*, 2007.
[http://dx.doi.org/10.1145/1242572.1242663]

[111] T. Mouelhiv, F. Fleurey, and B. Baudry, "A generic metamodel for security policies mutation", *International Conference on Software Testing Verification and Validation Workshop*, 2008.
[http://dx.doi.org/10.1109/ICSTW.2008.2]

[112] T. Mouelhi, Y. Le Traon, and B. Baudry, "Mutation analysis for security tests qualification", *Testing: Academic and Industrial Conference Practice and Research Techniques-MUTATION (TAICPART-MUTATION 2007)*, 2007.
[http://dx.doi.org/10.1109/TAIC.PART.2007.21]

[113] A. Pretschner, T. Mouelhi, and Y.L. Traon, "Model-Based Tests for Access Control Policies", *1st International Conference on Software Testing, Verification, and Validation (ICST '08)*, 2008.

[114] J. Hwang, T. Xie, F. Chen, and A.X. Liu, "Systematic structural testing of firewall policies", *Symposium on Reliable Distributed Systems*, 2008.

[115] J.A.T. Acree, "On mutation", *PhD thesis (No. GIT-ICS-80/12).*, Georgia Inst of Tech Atlanta School of Information and Computer Science: Atlanta, 1980.

[116] T.A. Budd, "Mutation analysis of program test data", *PhD Thesis, AAI8025191*, New Haven: CT, USA, 1980.

[117] A.P. Mathur, and W. Wong, "Reducing the cost of mutation testing: An empirical study", *J. Syst. Softw*, vol. 31, no. 3, pp. 185-196, 1995.
[http://dx.doi.org/10.1016/0164-1212(94)00098-0]

[118] M. Sahinoglu, and E. Spafford, "A Bayes Sequential Statistical Procedure for Approving Software Products", *IFIP Conference on Approving Software Products (ASP'90)*, 1990.

[119] L. Zhang, M. Gligoric, D. Marinov, and S. Khurshid, "Operator-based and random mutant selection: Better together", *IEEE/ACM International Conference on Automated Software Engineering*, 2013.
[http://dx.doi.org/10.1109/ASE.2013.6693070]

[120] A. Derezińska, and M. Rudnik, "Evaluation of mutant sampling criteria in object-oriented mutation testing", *Federated Conference on Computer Science and Information Systems (FedCSIS)*, 2017.
[http://dx.doi.org/10.15439/2017F375]

[121] R. Gopinath, I. Ahmed, M.A. Alipour, C. Jensen, and A. Groce, "Mutation reduction strategies considered harmful", *IEEE Trans. Reliab*, vol. 66, no. 3, pp. 854-874, 2017.
[http://dx.doi.org/10.1109/TR.2017.2705662]

[122] S. Hussain, "Mutation Clustering", *Master's thesis*, King's College: London, 2008.

[123] C. Ji, Z. Chen, B. Xu, and Z. Zhao, "A Novel Method of Mutation Clustering Based on Domain Analysis", *SEKE*, vol. 9, pp. 422-425, 2009.

[124] A. Derezińska, *Toward generalization of mutant clustering results in mutation testing*, Soft Computing in Computer and Information Science, pp. 395-407, 2015.
[http://dx.doi.org/10.1007/978-3-319-15147-2_33]

[125] Y.S. Ma, and S.W. Kim, "Mutation testing cost reduction by clustering overlapped mutants", *J. Syst. Softw*, vol. 115, pp. 18-30, 2016.
[http://dx.doi.org/10.1016/j.jss.2016.01.007]

[126] S. David, and Z. Andreas, "Javalanche: efficient mutation testing for Java", *7th Joint Meeting of the European Software Engineering Conference and the International Symposium on Foundations of*

Software Engineering., Amsterdam, 2009.

[127] S. Kim, Y. Ma, and Y. Kwon, "Combining weak and strong mutation for a noninterpretive Java mutation system", *Softw. Test. Verif. Reliab,* vol. 23, no. 8, pp. 647-668, 2013.
[http://dx.doi.org/10.1002/stvr.1480]

[128] A. P. Mathur, "Performance, effectiveness, and reliability issues in software testing", *The Fifteenth Annual International Computer Software & Applications Conference,* 1991.
[http://dx.doi.org/10.1109/CMPSAC.1991.170248]

[129] A.J. Offutt, G. Rothermel, and C. Zapf, "An experimental evaluation of selective mutation", *15th International Conference on Software Engineering,* 1993.

[130] E.S. Mresa, and L. Bottaci, "Efficiency of mutation operators and selective mutation strategies: An empirical study", *Softw. Test. Verif. Reliab,* vol. 9, no. 4, pp. 205-232, 1999.
[http://dx.doi.org/10.1002/(SICI)1099-1689(199912)9:4<205::AID-STVR186>3.0.CO;2-X]

[131] E.F. Barbosa, J.C. Maldonado, and A.M.R. Vincenzi, "Toward the determination of sufficient mutant operators for C", *Softw. Test. Verif. Reliab,* vol. 11, no. 2, pp. 113-136, 2001.
[http://dx.doi.org/10.1002/stvr.226]

[132] A. Namin, J. Andrews, and D. Murdoch, "Sufficient mutation operators for measuring test effectiveness", *ACM/IEEE 30th International Conference on Software Engineering,* 2008.

[133] G. Petrović, and M. Ivanković, "State of mutation testing at google", *40th international conference on software engineering: Software engineering in practice.,* 2018.
[http://dx.doi.org/10.1145/3183519.3183521]

[134] G. Guizzo, F. Sarro, and M. Harman, "Cost measures matter for mutation testing study validity", *Proceedings of ESEC/FSE,* 2020.
[http://dx.doi.org/10.1145/3368089.3409742]

[135] Y. Jia, and M. Harman, "Constructing subtle faults using higher order mutation testing", In: *Eighth IEEE International Working Conference on Source Code Analysis and Manipulation,* 2008.
[http://dx.doi.org/10.1109/SCAM.2008.36]

[136] M. Harman, Y. Jia, P. Reales Mateo, and M. Polo, "Angels and monsters: An empirical investigation of potential test effectiveness and efficiency improvement from strongly subsuming higher order mutation", In: *29th ACM/IEEE international conference on Automated software engineering,* 2014.
[http://dx.doi.org/10.1145/2642937.2643008]

[137] M. Polo, M. Piattini, and I. García-Rodríguez, "Decreasing the cost of mutation testing with second-order mutants", *Softw. Test. Verif. Reliab,* vol. 19, no. 2, pp. 111-131, 2009.
[http://dx.doi.org/10.1002/stvr.392]

[138] Q.V. Nguyen, and L. Madeyski, "Empirical evaluation of multiobjective optimization algorithms searching for higher order mutants", *Cybern. Syst,* vol. 47, no. 1-2, pp. 48-68, 2016.
[http://dx.doi.org/10.1080/01969722.2016.1128763]

[139] M.R. Girgis, and M.R. Woodward, "An integrated system for program testing using weak mutation and data flow analysis", *Proceedings of the 8th international conference on Software engineering,* 1985.

[140] J.R. Horgan, and A.P. Mathur, "Weak mutation is probably strong mutation", *Technical Report SERC-TR-83-P,* Purdue University: West Lafayette, Indiana, 1990.

[141] B. Marick, "The weak mutation hypothesis", *Proceedings of the symposium on Testing, analysis, and verification,* 1991.
[http://dx.doi.org/10.1145/120807.120825]

[142] M. Papadakis, N. Malevris, and M. Kintis, "Mutation Testing Strategies-A Collateral Approach", *ICSOFT (2),* 2010.

[143] D. Jackson, and M.R. Woodward, "Parallel firm mutation of Java programs", In: *Mutation testing for*

the new century. MA: Boston, 2001.
[http://dx.doi.org/10.1007/978-1-4757-5939-6_10]

[144] A. Offutt, and K. King, "A Fortran 77 Interpreter for Mutation Analysis", *SIGPLAN Not,* vol. 22, no. 7, pp. 177-188, 1987.
[http://dx.doi.org/10.1145/960114.29669]

[145] M.E. Delamaro, J.C. Maldonado, and A.P. Mathur, *Proteum-a tool for the assessment of test adequacy for c programs user's guide,* vol. Vol. 96, PCS, pp. 79-95, 1996.

[146] R. A. DeMillo, E. W. Krauser, and A. P. Mathur, "Compiler-integrated program mutation", *The Fifteenth Annual International Computer Software & Applications Conference.,* 1991.
[http://dx.doi.org/10.1109/CMPSAC.1991.170202]

[147] E.W. Krauser, "Compiler-integrated software testing", In: *Doctoral dissertation, PhD Thesis.* Purdue University: West Lafyette, 1991.

[148] R.H. Untch, "Mutation-based software testing using program schemata", *30th annual Southeast regional conference.,* 1992.
[http://dx.doi.org/10.1145/503720.503749]

[149] R. H. Untch, A. J. Offutt, and M. J. Harrold, "Mutation analysis using mutant schemata", *ACM SIGSOFT international symposium on Software testing and analysis.,* 1993.
[http://dx.doi.org/10.1145/154183.154265]

[150] R.H. Untch, *"Schema-Based Mutation Analysis: A New Test Data Adequacy Assessment Method",* PhD thesis, Clemson Univ, 1997.

[151] R. Khan, and M. Amjad, "Mutation-based genetic algorithm for efficiency optimisation of unit testing", *International Journal of Advanced Intelligence Paradigms,* vol. 12, no. 3-4, pp. 254-265, 2019.
[http://dx.doi.org/10.1504/IJAIP.2019.098563]

[152] B. Bogacki, and B. Walter, "Evaluation of test code quality with aspect-oriented mutations", In: *International Conference on Extreme Programming and Agile Processes in Software Engineering.* Heidelberg: Berlin, 2006.
[http://dx.doi.org/10.1007/11774129_26]

[153] B. Bogacki, and B. Walter, "Aspect-oriented response injection: an alternative to classical mutation testing", In: *Software Engineering Techniques: Design for Quality.* MA: Boston, 2006.

[154] A. Mathur, and E. Krauser, "Mutant Unification for Improved Vectorization", *Technical Report SERC-TR-14-P,* Purdue University, 1988.

[155] E. Krauser, A. Mathur, and V. Rego, "High Performance Software Testing on SIMD Machines", *IEEE Trans. Softw. Eng,* vol. 17, no. 5, pp. 403-423, 1991.
[http://dx.doi.org/10.1109/32.90444]

[156] V. N. Fleyshgakker, and S. N. Weiss, "Efficient mutation analysis: A new approach", *ACM SIGSOFT international symposium on Software testing and analysis,* 1994.

[157] C. Byoungju, and A.P. Mathur, "High-performance mutation testing", *J. Syst. Softw,* vol. 29, no. 2, pp. 135-152, 1993.
[http://dx.doi.org/10.1016/0164-1212(93)90005-I]

[158] A.J. Offutt, R.P. Pargas, S.V. Fichter, and P.K. Khambekar, "Mutation Testing of Software Using MIMD Computer", *Int'l Conf. Parallel Processing,* 1992.

[159] C. Zapf, "A Distributed Interpreter for the Mothra Mutation Testing System", In: *Master's Thesis.* Clemson University, 1993.

[160] A.J. Offutt, and J. Pan, "Automatically Detecting Equivalent Mutants and Infeasible Paths", *Softw. Test. Verif. Reliab,* vol. 7, no. 3, pp. 165-192, 1997.
[http://dx.doi.org/10.1002/(SICI)1099-1689(199709)7:3<165::AID-STVR143>3.0.CO;2-U]

[161] T.A. Budd, and D. Angluin, "Two Notions of Correctness and Their Relation to Testing", *Acta Inform,* vol. 18, no. 1, pp. 31-45, 1982.
[http://dx.doi.org/10.1007/BF00625279]

[162] A.J. Offutt, and W.M. Craft, "Using Compiler Optimization Techniques to Detect Equivalent Mutants", *Softw. Test. Verif. Reliab,* vol. 4, no. 3, pp. 131-154, 1994.
[http://dx.doi.org/10.1002/stvr.4370040303]

[163] D. Baldwin, and F.G. Sayward, "Heuristics for Determining Equivalence of Program Mutations", *Research Report 276.,* Yale University: New Haven, Connecticut, 1979.
[http://dx.doi.org/10.21236/ADA071795]

[164] A.J. Offutt, and J. Pan, "Detecting Equivalent Mutants and the Feasible Path Problem", *Annual Conference on Computer As Surance.,* Gaithersburg, Maryland, 1996.
[http://dx.doi.org/10.1109/CMPASS.1996.507890]

[165] M. Harman, R. Hierons, and S. Danicic, "The relationship between program dependence and mutation analysis", *In Mutation testing for the new century,* Boston, MA, 2001.
[http://dx.doi.org/10.1007/978-1-4757-5939-6_4]

[166] R. Hierons, M. Harman, and S. Danicic, "Using program slicing to assist in the detection of equivalent mutants", *Softw. Test. Verif. Reliab,* vol. 9, no. 4, pp. 233-262, 1999.
[http://dx.doi.org/10.1002/(SICI)1099-1689(199912)9:4<233::AID-STVR191>3.0.CO;2-3]

[167] K. Adamopoulos, M. Harman, and R.M. Hierons, "How to overcome the equivalent mutant problem and achieve tailored selective mutation using co-evolution", *In Genetic and evolutionary computation conference,* Berlin , Hei, 2004.
[http://dx.doi.org/10.1007/978-3-540-24855-2_155]

[168] B.J. Grün, D. Schuler, and A. Zeller, "The impact of equivalent mutants", *International Conference on Software Testing, Verification, and Validation Workshops,* 2009.
[http://dx.doi.org/10.1109/ICSTW.2009.37]

[169] D. Schuler, V. Dallmeier, and A. Zeller, "Efficient mutation testing by checking invariant violations", *The eighteenth international symposium on Software testing and analysis,* 2009.
[http://dx.doi.org/10.1145/1572272.1572282]

[170] M. Papadakis, Y. Jia, M. Harman, and Y. Le Traon, "Trivial compiler equivalence: A large scale empirical study of a simple, fast and effective equivalent mutant detection technique", *IEEE/ACM 37th IEEE International Conference on Software Engineering,* vol. 1, IEEE., pp. 936-946, 2015.
[http://dx.doi.org/10.1109/ICSE.2015.103]

[171] M. Kintis, M. Papadakis, Y. Jia, N. Malevris, Y. Le Traon, and M. Harman, "Detecting trivial mutant equivalences via compiler optimisations", *IEEE Trans. Softw. Eng,* vol. 44, no. 4, pp. 308-333, 2017.
[http://dx.doi.org/10.1109/TSE.2017.2684805]

[172] F. Wu, J. Nanavati, M. Harman, Y. Jia, and J. Krinke, "Memory mutation testing", *Inf. Softw. Technol,* vol. 81, pp. 97-111, 2017.
[http://dx.doi.org/10.1016/j.infsof.2016.03.002]

[173] P. McMinn, "Search-based software testing: Past, present and future", *IEEE Fourth International Conference on Software Testing, Verification and Validation Workshops,* 2011.
[http://dx.doi.org/10.1109/ICSTW.2011.100]

[174] N. Jatana, B. Suri, and S. Rani, "Systematic literature review on search based mutation testing", *e-Informatica Software Engineering Journal,* vol. 11, 2017.

[175] Q. Zhu, A. Panichella, and A. Zaidman, "A systematic literature review of how mutation testing supports quality assurance processes", *Softw. Test. Verif. Reliab,* vol. 28, no. 6, p. e1675, 2018.
[http://dx.doi.org/10.1002/stvr.1675]

[176] R.A. DeMillo, and A.J. Offutt, "Constraint-Based Automatic Test Data Generation", *IEEE Trans.*

Softw. Eng, vol. 17, no. 9, pp. 900-910, 1991.
[http://dx.doi.org/10.1109/32.92910]

[177] A.J. Offutt, and J. Pan, "Detecting equivalent mutants and the feasible path problem", *11th Annual Conference on Computer Assurance. COMPASS'96,* 1996.
[http://dx.doi.org/10.1109/CMPASS.1996.507890]

[178] A.J. Offutt, Z. Jin, and J. Pan, "The dynamic domain reduction procedure for test data generation", *Softw. Pract. Exper,* vol. 29, no. 2, pp. 167-193, 1999.
[http://dx.doi.org/10.1002/(SICI)1097-024X(199902)29:2<167::AID-SPE225>3.0.CO;2-V]

[179] M. H. Liu, Y. F. Gao, J. H. Shan, J. H. Liu, L. Zhang, and J. S. Sun, "An approach to test data generation for killing multiple mutants", *IEEE International Conference on Software Maintenance.,* 2006.
[http://dx.doi.org/10.1109/ICSM.2006.13]

[180] M. Papadakis, and N. Malevris, "Automatic mutation test case generation via dynamic symbolic execution", *21st International Symposium on Software Reliability Engineering,* 2010.
[http://dx.doi.org/10.1109/ISSRE.2010.38]

[181] L. Bottaci, "A genetic algorithm fitness function for mutation testing", *8th Wrokshop on Software Engineering using Metaheuristic (SEMINAL'01),* 2001.

[182] K. Ayari, S. Bouktif, and G. Antoniol, "Automatic Mutation Test Input Data Generation via Ant Colony", *Genetic and Evolutionary Computation Conference (GECCO'07),* 2007.
[http://dx.doi.org/10.1145/1276958.1277172]

[183] G. Fraser, and A. Zeller, "Mutation-Driven Generation of Unit Tests and Oracles", *IEEE Trans. Softw. Eng,* vol. 38, no. 2, pp. 278-292, 2012.
[http://dx.doi.org/10.1109/TSE.2011.93]

[184] B. Baudry, V.L. Hanh, J-M. Jézéquel, and Y.L. Traon, "Trustable Components: Yet Another Mutation-Based Approach", *Proc. First Workshop Mutation Analysis,* 2001.

[185] M. Harman, Y. Jia, and W.B. Langdon, "Strong higher order mutation-based test data generation", *19th ACM SIGSOFT symposium and the 13th European conference on Foundations of software engineering,* 2011.
[http://dx.doi.org/10.1145/2025113.2025144]

[186] H.L.T. My, B.N. Thanh, and T.K. Thanh, "Survey on mutation-based test data generation", *Iran. J. Electr. Comput. Eng,* vol. 5, no. 5, 2015.

[187] J. Offutt, J. Pan, and J.M. Voas, "Procedures for reducing the size of coverage-based test sets", *Proceedings of the 12th International Conference on Testing Computer Software,* New York, 1995.

[188] W.E. Wong, J.R. Horgan, S. London, and A.P. Mathur, "Effect of test set minimization on fault detection effectiveness", *Softw. Pract. Exper,* vol. 28, no. 4, pp. 347-369, 1998.
[http://dx.doi.org/10.1002/(SICI)1097-024X(19980410)28:4<347::AID-SPE145>3.0.CO;2-L]

[189] S. Rani, and B. Suri, "An approach for test data generation based on genetic algorithm and delete mutation operators", *Second International Conference on Advances in Computing and Communication Engineering,* Dehradun, 2015.
[http://dx.doi.org/10.1109/ICACCE.2015.145]

[190] S. Rani, H. Dhawan, G. Nagpal, and B. Suri, Implementing Time-Bounded Automatic Test Data Generation Approach Based on Search-Based Mutation Testing*in Progress in Advanced Computing and Intelligent Engineering. Advances in Intelligent Systems and Computing,* vol. Vol. 714, Springer, 2019.

[191] S. Rani, and B. Suri, "Adopting Social Group Optimization Algorithm Using Mutation Testing for Test Suite Generation: SGO-MT", *International Conference on Computational Science and Its Applications,* 2019.
[http://dx.doi.org/10.1007/978-3-030-24305-0_39]

[192] B.S. Ahmed, "Test case minimization approach using fault detection and combinatorial optimization techniques for configuration-aware structural testing", *Engineering Science and Technology, an International Journal,* vol. 19, no. 2, pp. 737-753, 2016.
[http://dx.doi.org/10.1016/j.jestch.2015.11.006]

[193] Z. Wei, W. Xiaoxue, Y. Xibing, C. Shichao, L. Wenxin, and L. Jun, "Test suite minimization with mutation testing-based many-objective evolutionary optimization", *International Conference on Software Analysis, Testing and Evolution(SATE),* 2017.
[http://dx.doi.org/10.1109/SATE.2017.12]

[194] H. Do, and G. Rothermel, "A controlled experiment assessing test case prioritization techniques via mutation faults", *21st IEEE International Conference on Software Maintenance (ICSM'05),* 2005.
[http://dx.doi.org/10.1109/ICSM.2005.9]

[195] R. Just, G.M. Kapfhammer, and F. Schweiggert, "Using non-redundant mutation operators and test suite prioritization to achieve efficient and scalable mutation analysis", *23rd International Symposium on Software Reliability Engineering,* 2012.
[http://dx.doi.org/10.1109/ISSRE.2012.31]

[196] L. Zhang, D. Marinov, L. Zhang, and S. Khurshid, "Regression mutation testing", *ISSTA,* 2012.
[http://dx.doi.org/10.1145/2338965.2336793]

[197] L. Zhang, D. Marinov, and S. Khurshid, "Faster mutation testing inspired by test prioritization and reduction", *International Symposium on Software Testing and Analysis,* 2013.
[http://dx.doi.org/10.1145/2483760.2483782]

Multimodal Genetic Optimized Feature Selection for Online Sequential Extreme Learning Machine

Archana P. Kale[1,*], Shefali P. Sonavane[1], Shashwati P. Kale[1] and **Aditi R. Wade[2]**

[1] *Department of Computer Engineering, Modern Education Society's College of Engineering, SPPU Pune, India*

[2] *Department of Information Technology, Walchand College of Engineering Sangli, The Bishops Education Society, Pune, The Kaushalya Academy, Latur, India*

Abstract: Extreme learning machine (ELM) is a rapid classifier evolved for batch learning mode unsuitable for sequential input. Retrieving data from the new inventory leads to a time-extended process. Therefore, online sequential extreme learning machine (OSELM) algorithms were proposed by Liang *et al.*. The OSELM is able to handle the sequential input by reading data 1 by 1 or chunk by chunk mode. The overall system generalization performance may devalue because of the amalgamation of the random initialization of OS-ELM and the presence of redundant and irrelevant features. To resolve the said problem, this paper proposes a correspondence multimodal genetic optimized feature selection paradigm for sequential input (MG-OSELM) for radial basis function by using clinical datasets. For performance comparison, the proposed paradigm is implemented and evaluated for ELM, multimodal genetic optimized for ELM classifier (MG-ELM), OS-ELM, MG-OSELM. Experimental results are calculated and analysed accordingly. The comparative results analysis illustrates that MG-ELM provides 10.94% improved accuracy with 43.25% features compared to ELM.

Keywords: Classification Problem, Feature Selection problem, Genetic Algorithm, Online sequential Extreme Learning Machine.

INTRODUCTION

Nowadays, artificial intelligence is a growing and critical area [1]. Feature subset selection (FSS) is an intricate procedure in the fields of artificial intelligence and machine learning. The prime objective of feature selection is to adopt the optimal features for further evaluation. The features which are relevant and non-redundant are called optimal features. It is entangled to decide the significance of features.

---

* **Corresponding author Archana P. Kale**: Department of Computer Engineering, Modern Education Society's College of Engineering, SPPU Pune, India; E-mail: archana.kale@mescoepune.org

Rijwan Khan, Pawan Sharma, Sugam Sharma and Santosh Kumar (Eds.)

[2]. To enhance the system generalization performance, it is necessary to search and finalize only the optimal features.

Various FSS algorithms like Half selection, Neural Network for threshold, Mean Selection, *etc.*, are used for FSS. These are random searched optimization techniques useful for selecting the optimal feature subsets [3]. The big search space is handled by GA very effectively [4] and has the maximum chance of a globally optimal solution.

Extreme Learning Machines are rapid classifiers with various advantages like good generalization performance, high speed, less training time, *etc.* ELM is primarily designed for batch mode, in which all data is available before training. However, it is not suitable for sequential input [5]. Therefore, OS-ELM is designed by Liang *et al.* for sequential input. Zhu *et al.* developed Evolutionary ELM [6] and Han *et al.* developed the particle swarm optimization-based Evolutionary ELM [7]. In many papers, for ELM sig activation function is used [8, 9]. Huang *et al.* designed Incremental – ELM [10]. ELM is also used to solve real-time applications like medical data classification [11], universal approximation [12], and big data [13].

The original Extreme learning machine (ELM) is primarily designed for batch mode. Nan-Ying *et al.* [5] emerged online sequential – ELM (OS-ELM) for linear, incremental, or sequential input. ELM and OS-ELM calculate the input to hidden layer neurons by randomly assigning the specified input weights and biases. The target output is calculated [14, 15] by analytically evaluating the weights between the hidden layers resulting in the layer as shown in Fig. (**1**). Therefore, the generalization performance of the system may deteriorate due to the random initialization. One of the most significant steps is required, *i.e.*, optimal feature subset selection.

The key intent of the paper is the innovative use of a genetic algorithm with a multimodal optimization approach for OS-ELM (MG-OSELM) for clinical datasets. In various papers, authors evaluated OSELM only by changing hidden nodes, but extensive literature breaks down to recognize the changes in the inceptive training data (block) according to the quantity of hidden nodes.

The structure of the paper is organised as follows: The detailed structure of the proposed methodology of MG-OSELM with the aid of the paradigm is detailed in Section 2. Innovative results and a comparison of results are mentioned in Section 3. The future work, in combination with the conclusion, is described in Section 4.

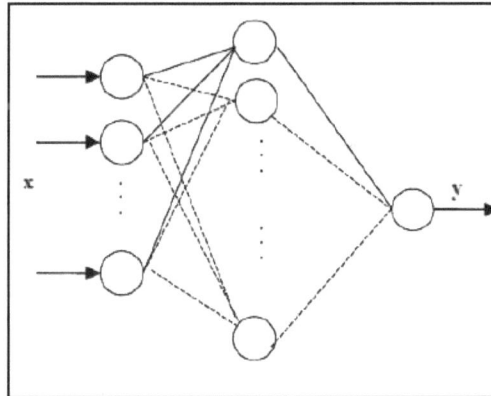

Fig. (1). Basic ELM Architecture

PROPOSED MG-OSELM APPROACH

The paradigm of the proposed MG-OSELM approach is as shown in Fig. (**2**), which is categorized into threefold subsystems – a. Pre-processing subsystem, b. FSS subsystem 3. Classification Subsystem.

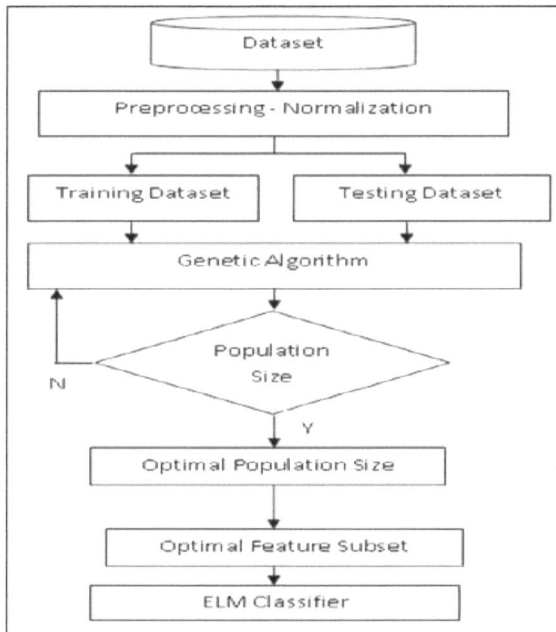

Fig. (2). Proposed MG-OSELM Paradigm.

Datasets

The various datasets like Pima, Indian Diabetes (PID), Stat, log heart disease (SHD), Breast Cancer (BC), and Australian (AS) [16, 17] are used. The dimensional scope of these datasets is from 8 to 36. Most of the considered datasets are clinical datasets which are standard UCI repository datasets. PID, SHD, BC, and AS datasets contain 8, 13, 10, 14 attributes and 768, 270, 699, 690 instances, respectively.

Preprocessing Subsystem

Data Normalization is used in preprocessing subsystem. Data normalization is an intricate preprocessing method useful for various artificial intelligence and machine learning algorithms [13]. The features present in the dataset are of different scales. Therefore, it becomes very critical to handle such a type of vector space as it contains the maximum account of a vital task to convert all vector spaced features to unit space features resulting between zero and one.

After normalization, all datasets are further divided into duplet parts, *i.e.*, the training set in which 70% of instances are considered and the remaining 30% are considered for the testing set. For example, the total number of instances present in the PID dataset is 768, which are further divided into 538 instances that are used as a training set and 230 instances used for the testing set. Same for the SHD dataset, the total number of instances present in the SHD dataset is 270, which are further divided into 189 instances used as a training set and 81 instances used for the testing set. For the BC dataset, the total number of instances present is 699, which are further divided into 490 instances used as training set and 209 instances used for the testing set. For AS dataset, the total number of instances presented is 690, which are further divided into 483 instances used as the training set and 207 instances used for the testing set.

Feature Subset Selection Subsystem

Thousands of features are present in the high-dimensional dataset. For classification, all features are not required as it may be the presence of nonoptimal features, *i.e.*, irrelevant and redundant features. These features act as noise which degrades the predictive accuracy.

Genetic Algorithm (GA) is a relevant technique for selecting ideal features. GA contains the population which is a collection of a set of possible solutions to solve the problem [18]. Three steps like, selection, evaluation, and recombination, are executed in every iterative step. Selection, Crossover, and Mutation are the genetic operators mainly used in GA. The number of iterations is depended on the condition of termination. Based on the quality, the fitness function is evaluated. Moreover, based on the evaluated fitness value, the strings are selected for the new generation, which is comparatively superior to those other strings. From the population, the points are eliminated in which a moderate fitness value is present.

For exploration, especially mutation and crossover are utilized to obtain new solutions [19]. The mutation is the major contributor to changing part genetics randomly. Crossover is used to incorporate the fittest members of genetic material from populations.

GA provides different results of feature subsets as per the changes in population size. In the literature surveys, various authors use 50 and 70 as the population size. However, the vast literature survey has disadvantaged that proper selection of population size is absent. Therefore, a multimodal genetic optimized feature selection paradigm is proposed for batch input as well as for sequential input in the context of this paper. Here, the feature subset is finalised by considering the various population sizes from 10:10:90. Thus, the total number of feature subsets evaluated is 9. One feature subset is selected for further experimentation as an ideal feature subset that provides maximum accuracy.

Classification Subsystem

By using the optimal features, OS-ELM is evaluated. The initialization and sequential learning phase are the two major phases of OS-ELM. In the initialization phase, various parameters are executed like the number of data required to fill up, the number of hidden nodes, defining the chunk size, *etc*. The target class is decided based on the initialized data and newly arrived chunk data in the sequential learning phase [20, 21].

EXPERIMENTAL RESULTS

Related experimentation has been conducted in MATLAB© R2014a. The two activation functions, sigmoidal and radial basis activation function (rbf), are used for simulation. For evaluation, in the literature survey, various authors consider only the quantity of hidden nodes in OS-ELM [5, 14, 15]. However, the initial block size is not considered for evaluation. By virtue of the experiment, it is observed that the initial training data is much more important. Therefore, in every step of the hidden layer, the training data (n) also changes with the number of hidden nodes (j) like j to n with incremental I value. The output results are calculated using a fixed chunk size (1or 20) or randomly changing the chunk size between 10 to 30.

Accuracy is a part of the evaluation measurement. The performance metrics are computed by evaluating the values of false negatives and positives both as well as true negatives and positives also [22]. Equation 1 shows the formula for the calculation of accuracy.

$$Accuracy = \frac{TP + TN}{TP + FP + TN + FN} \tag{1}$$

As experimental results of ELM and OS-ELM by using all features for binary classification problems are given in Table **1**. The evaluation performance is compared in three different ways - 1. MG-ELM and ELM 2. MG-OSELM and OS-ELM.

Table 1. Experimental results of ELM and OSELM on Binary classification application.

Dataset	Act. Fun.	Algorithm	Learning Mode	Accuracy		Node	Initial Block Size
PID	Sig	ELM	Batch	87.91	81.3	50	-
-	-	OSELM	1-by-1	88.29	82.6	115	465
-	-	-	20-by-20	87.36	82.17	25	175
-	-	-	10,30	83.82	83.04	15	65
-	Rbf	ELM	Batch	88.66	81.73	157	-
-	-	OSELM	1-by-1	87.17	82.17	80	180
-	-	-	20-by-20	87.91	82.17	80	180
-	-	-	10,30	81.59	83.47	45	245
SHD	Sig	ELM	Batch	99.47	88.88	17	-
-	-	OSELM	1-by-1	99.47	88.88	25	125
-	-	-	20-by-20	99.47	88.88	20	70
-	-	-	10,30	99.47	91.35	30	30
-	Rbf	ELM	Batch	99.47	86.41	89	-
-	-	OSELM	1-by-1	96.29	87.65	50	100
-	-	-	20-by-20	98.41	88.88	30	30
-	-	-	10,30	98.94	90.12	20	20

MG-ELM and ELM

To enhance the efficiency and effectiveness of the MG-ELM paradigm, the clinical datasets are used for experimentation using an ELM classifier. Table **2** indicates GA results changing with the size of the population. Total 9 feature subsets are evaluated by varying population sizes. Out of all these subsets, one subset is finalized, with maximum occurrence as an optimal subset as shown in the second last column in Table **2**. For example, for the PID dataset the accuracy is calculated by differentiating the value of the population. For each subset, the accuracy is shown. From all these subsets, one subset needs to be finalized which produced maximum accuracy. For PID dataset optimal feature subset is {2,5,6} with accuracy 77.82%. ELM classifier is a source for the computation of classification accuracy. Comparative result analysis of ELM and MG-ELM is shown in Table **3**. With the result analysis, it is observed that MG-ELM has success in achieving 10.94% improved classification accuracy over a 56.75% reduction in features as in ELM.

Table 2. MG-ELM for binary classification problem for clinical dataset.

Population Size											Optimal	ELM
-											Subset	Accuracy
Data	All	10	20	30	40	50	60	70	80	90	-	-
Set	-	-	-	-	-	-	-	-	-	-	-	-
PID	69.56	2,4,8	2,5,6 2,5,6	2,5,6 2,5,6	2,5,8	2,5,6	2,5,6	2,5,6	2,5,6	2,5,6	2,5,6	77.82
SHD	77.77	3,8,9,	2,3,10,	1,2,3,	1,2,3,	3,8,9,	1,2,3,	1,2,3,	1,2,3,	1,2,3,	1,2,3,	83.95
-	-	10,13	12,13	7,12,13	7,12,13 9,12	10,13	9,12	9,12	9,12	9,12	9,12	-
BC	85.16	2,7,8,	2,7,8,	2,7,8,	2,7,8,	2,3,4,	2,3,4,	2,3,4,	2,3,4,	2,3,4,	2,3,4,	99.52
-	-	9	9	9	9	5,6,7,	5,6,7,	5,6,7,	5,6,7,	5,6,7,	5,6,7,	-
-	-	-	-	-	-	10	10	10	10	10	10	-
AS	73.91	3,4,8,	3,5,8,	5,7,8,	3,5,8,	3,5,8,	3,5,8,	3,5,8,	3,5,8,	3,5,8,	3,5,8,	88.88
-	-	9,11	9	10,11	9	9	9	9	9	9	9	-

Table 3. Comparative analysis of ELM and MG-ELM.

Dataset	ELM (%)	MG-ELM(%)	Accu-racy(%)	All Features	Feature Subset	Reduction %	Used Features
PID	69.56	77.82	8.26	8	3	63	37
SHD	77.77	83.95	6.18	13	5	62	38
BC	85.16	99.52	14.36	10	7	30	70
AS	73.91	88.88	14.97	14	4	72	28
Average	76.6	87.54	10.94	-	4.75	56.75	43.25

MG-OSELM and OSELM

The experimental results are calculated by using optimal features for ELM and OS-ELM as shown in Table **4**. The comparative performance between OS-ELM and MG-OSELM is shown in Table **4** by calculating the average sequential mode (1-by-1, 20-by-20, and [10,30]). Table **4** indicates the detailed comparative analysis of OSELM and MG-OSELM by using both activity functions like sig and rbf.

Table 4. Experimental Results of MG-ELM and MG-OSELM on classification.

Dataset	Act. Fun.	Algorithm	Learning Mode	Accuracy		Node	Initial Block Size
				Training	Testing		
PID	Sig	MG -ELM	Batch	87.36	81.73	43	-
-	-	MG -OSELM	1-by-1	83.27	81.73	20	20
-	-	-	20-by-20	82.71	81.73	55	205
-	-	-	[10,30]	81.41	82.6	55	55
-	Rbf	MG -ELM	Batch	82.89	81.73	12	-
-	-	MG -OSELM	1-by-1	83.64	81.3	40	290
-	-	-	20-by-20	83.64	81.3	45	395
-	-	-	[10,30]	81.41	82.6	55	305
SHD	Sig	MG -ELM	Batch	99.47	83.95	91	-
-	-	MG -OSELM	1-by-1	87.83	83.95	10	10
-	-	-	20-by-20	89.41	83.95	10	40
-	-	-	[10,30]	89.41	86.41	10	14
-	Rbf	MG -ELM	Batch	99.47	85.18	36	-
-	-	MG -OSELM	1-by-1	87.3	85.18	20	30
-	-	-	20-by-20	87.3	85.18	15	33
-	-	-	[10,30]	88.88	86.41	15	29

CONCLUSION

Genetic Algorithm is a top priority-based optimization algorithm that is to classify the best optimal feature subset. However, GA varies its result as per the changes in the population. To solve this problem, in this paper multimodal genetic optimized feature selection paradigm is proposed for sequential input (MG-OSELM) by using clinical datasets. The proposed paradigm is accomplished to handle the dimensionality reduction and optimization problems for sequential input. OS-ELM algorithm is used for sequential input training only new arrival data instead of the whole training dataset, which saves the computational cost. In order to prove the importance and strength of the MG-OSELM, a comparative study of results for ELM, OS-ELM, MG-ELM is carried out. Here, the MG-OSELM paradigm is evaluated for the binary classification problem. The work can be extended by using archetypes for multiclass classification problems and improved shuffled frog leaping algorithm [23] which may support inclusive clear insight and direction regarding future improvements.

CONSENT OF PUBLICATION

Not applicable.

CONFLICT OF INTEREST

The author declares no conflict of interest, financial or otherwise.

ACKNOWLEDGEMENTS

I gratefully acknowledge the Modern Education Society's College of Engineering (MESCoE), Pune, for the support. I am extremely thankful to Dr. S. S. Sarawade, Principal, MESCOE, for his moral support. I am indebted to Dr. A. J. Hake, Secretary, MESCoE, Pune, for his enriching advice and strong support. I am thankful to Dr. Sampada Joshi, Chief Finance Officer, MESCoE, Pune, for her encouragement. I also wanted to thank all the people who helped us in a direct or indirect way.

REFERENCES

[1]   E. Cambria, G-B. Huang, L.L.C. Kasun, H. Zhou, C.M. Vong, J. Lin, J. Yin, Z. Cai, Q. Liu, K. Li, V.C.M. Leung, L. Feng, Y-S. Ong, M-H. Lim, A. Akusok, A. Lendasse, F. Corona, R. Nian, Y. Miche, P. Gastaldo, R. Zunino, S. Decherchi, X. Yang, K. Mao, B-S. Oh, J. Jeon, K-A. Toh, A.B.J. Teoh, J. Kim, H. Yu, Y. Chen, and J. Liu, "Extreme learning machines [trends & controversies]", *IEEE Intell. Syst.,* vol. 28, no. 6, pp. 30-59, 2013.
[http://dx.doi.org/10.1109/MIS.2013.140]

[2]   L. Yu, and L. Huan, "Efficient feature selection via analysis of relevance and redundancy", *J. Mach. Learn. Res.,* vol. 5, no. Oct, pp. 1205-1224, 2004.

[3]   G. Pahuja, and T.N. Nagabhushan, "A novel GA-ELM approach for Parkinson's disease detection using brain structural T1-weighted MRI data", In: *2016 Second International Conference on Cognitive Computing and Information Processing (CCIP)* IEEE, 2016.
[http://dx.doi.org/10.1109/CCIP.2016.7802848]

[4]   L. Mao, L. Zhang, X. Liu, C. Li, and H. Yang, "Improved extreme learning machine and its application in image quality assessment", *Math. Probl. Eng.,* vol. 2014, p. 2014, 2014.
[http://dx.doi.org/10.1155/2014/426152]

[5]   N-Y. Liang, G.B. Huang, P. Saratchandran, and N. Sundararajan, "A fast and accurate online sequential learning algorithm for feedforward networks", *IEEE Trans. Neural Netw.,* vol. 17, no. 6, pp. 1411-1423, 2006.
[http://dx.doi.org/10.1109/TNN.2006.880583] [PMID: 17131657]

[6]   Q-Y. Zhu, A.K. Qin, P.N. Suganthan, and G-B. Huang, "Evolutionary extreme learning machine", *Pattern Recognit.,* vol. 38, no. 10, pp. 1759-1763, 2005.
[http://dx.doi.org/10.1016/j.patcog.2005.03.028]

[7]   F. Han, H-F. Yao, and Q-H. Ling, "An improved evolutionary extreme learning machine based on particle swarm optimization", *Neurocomputing,* vol. 116, pp. 87-93, 2013.
[http://dx.doi.org/10.1016/j.neucom.2011.12.062]

[8]   X Zhixiang, "A modified extreme learning machine with sigmoidal activation functions", *Neural Computing and Applications,* vol. 22.3-4, pp. 541-550, 2013.

[9]   D. Nguyen, and B. Widrow, "Improving the learning speed of 2-layer neural networks by choosing initial values of the adaptive weights", In: *1990 IJCNN International Joint Conference on Neural Networks.* IEEE, 1990.
[http://dx.doi.org/10.1109/IJCNN.1990.137819]

[10]   Guang-Bin Huang, and Lei Chen, "Enhanced random search based incremental extreme learning machine", *Neurocomputing,* vol. 71.16-18, pp. 3460-3468, 2008.
[http://dx.doi.org/10.1016/j.neucom.2007.10.008]

[11]   C.V. Subbulakshmi, and S.N. Deepa, "Medical dataset classification: a machine learning paradigm integrating particle swarm optimization with extreme learning machine classifier", *Scientific World Journal,* vol. 2015, p. 418060, 2015.
[http://dx.doi.org/10.1155/2015/418060] [PMID: 26491713]

[12]   R. Zhang, Y. Lan, G.B. Huang, and Z.B. Xu, "Universal approximation of extreme learning machine with adaptive growth of hidden nodes", *IEEE Trans. Neural Netw. Learn. Syst.,* vol. 23, no. 2, pp. 365-371, 2012.
[http://dx.doi.org/10.1109/TNNLS.2011.2178124] [PMID: 24808516]

[13]   A. Akusok, K-M. Bjork, Y. Miche, and A. Lendasse, "High-performance extreme learning machines: a complete toolbox for big data applications", *IEEE Access,* vol. 3, pp. 1011-1025, 2015.
[http://dx.doi.org/10.1109/ACCESS.2015.2450498]

[14]   S.Y. Wong, K.S. Yap, H.J. Yap, and S.C. Tan, "A truly online learning algorithm using hybrid fuzzy ARTMAP and online extreme learning machine for pattern classification", *Neural Process. Lett.,* vol. 42, no. 3, pp. 585-602, 2015.
[http://dx.doi.org/10.1007/s11063-014-9374-5]

[15]   Yeng Chai Soh Lan Yuan, and Guang-Bin Huang, "Ensemble of online sequential extreme learning machine", *Neurocomputing 72,* vol. 13-15, pp. 3391-3395, 2009./

[16]   A. Asuncion, and D. Newman, *UCI Machine Learning Repository,* 2007.

[17]   J. Li, and H. Liu, *Kent ridge bio-medical data set repository.,* 2002.http://sdmc. lit. org

[18]   L. Zhuo, "A genetic algorithm-based wrapper feature selection method for classification of hyperspectral images using support vector machine", In: *Geoinformatics 2008 and Joint Conference on GIS and Built Environment: Classification of Remote Sensing Images.* vol. 7147. International Society for Optics and Photonics, 2008.
[http://dx.doi.org/10.1117/12.813256]

[19]   Y. Fei, and H. Min, "Simultaneous feature with support vector selection and parameters optimization using GA-based SVM solve the binary classification", *2016 First IEEE International Conference on Computer Communication and the Internet (ICCCI),* 2016.
[http://dx.doi.org/10.1109/CCI.2016.7778958]

[20]   G-B. Huang, P. Saratchandran, and N. Sundararajan, "An efficient sequential learning algorithm for growing and pruning RBF (GAP-RBF) networks", *IEEE Trans. Syst. Man Cybern. B Cybern.,* vol. 34, no. 6, pp. 2284-2292, 2004.
[http://dx.doi.org/10.1109/TSMCB.2004.834428] [PMID: 15619929]

[21]   G-B. Huang, P. Saratchandran, and N. Sundararajan, "A generalized growing and pruning RBF (GGAP-RBF) neural network for function approximation", *IEEE Trans. Neural Netw.,* vol. 16, no. 1, pp. 57-67, 2005.
[http://dx.doi.org/10.1109/TNN.2004.836241] [PMID: 15732389]

[22]   K.B. Nahato, N.H. Khanna, and A. Kannan, "Hybrid approach using fuzzy sets and extreme learning machine for classifying clinical datasets", *Informatics in Medicine Unlocked,* vol. 2, pp. 1-11, 2016.
[http://dx.doi.org/10.1016/j.imu.2016.01.001]

[23]   B. Hu, Y. Dai, Y. Su, P. Moore, X. Zhang, C. Mao, J. Chen, and L. Xu, "Feature selection for optimized high-dimensional biomedical data using an improved shuffled frog leaping algorithm", *IEEE/ACM Trans. Comput. Biol. Bioinformatics,* vol. 15, no. 6, pp. 1765-1773, 2018.
[http://dx.doi.org/10.1109/TCBB.2016.2602263] [PMID: 28113635]

CHAPTER 16

A New Non-Stigmergic-Ant Algorithm to Make Load Balancing Resilient in Big Data Processing for Enterprises

Samia Chehbi Gamoura[1,*]

[1] *EM Strasbourg Business School, Strasbourg University, HuManiS (UR 7308),Strasbourg, France*

Abstract: Due to the continuous evolution of the Big Data phenomenon, data processing in Business Big Data Analytics (BBDA) needs new advanced load balancing techniques. This chapter proposes a new algorithm based on a non-stigmergic approach to address these concerns. The algorithm imitates a specific species of ants that communicate by the acoustics in situations of threats. Besides, the research methodology in this study presents a methodic filtration of the relevant metrics before carrying out the benchmarking trials of several ant-colony algorithms (*i.e.*, makespan, response time, throughput, memory and CPU utilization, *etc.*). The experimentations' outcomes show the effectiveness of the proposed approach that might empower the research efforts in big data analytics, business intelligence, and intelligent autonomous software agents. The main objective of this research is to contribute to reinforcing the resilience of the Big Data processing environment for enterprises.

Keywords: Big Data processing, Business Big Data Analytics, Load balancing, Swarm intelligence, Workload Management.

INTRODUCTION

With the advent of Big Data, enterprises continuously need to extract more and more value from accumulated data in their Information Systems (IS). Companies then adopt high-frequency parallel data processing as a new compulsory economic model [1]. In such complex platforms, workload management and load balancing become essential in maintaining resilient business activity [2].

In the new research community, the paradigm "Big Valuable Data" is an emerging topic that triggers several challenges, including load balancing

---

* **Corresponding author Samia Chehbi Gamoura:** EM Strasbourg Business School, Strasbourg University, HuManiS (UR 7308), Strasbourg, France; E-mail: samia.gamoura@em-strasbourg.eu

Rijwan Khan, Pawan Sharma, Sugam Sharma and Santosh Kumar (Eds.)

management in high-frequency parallel environments [3]. Such large-scale computation systems include dedicated distributed Big Data processing using MapReduce® programming models such as Hadoop® [4], and distributed databases in clusters such as Cassandra® [4]. Such technologies can handle a massive amount of data, along with some difficulties and challenges. Hadoop®, for instance, is designed to parallelize large-scale computations; however, these computations often attain peaks of high latency because of workload issues [5].

With the incessant urge to extract valuable patterns from volatile data, workload management has stepped to the head of research concerns in business and management engineering [6]. One of the most challenging topics is the resilient management of wide-ranged workload types in real-time and with very complex inter-dependencies systems [7]. Resilient management includes a robust load balancing system, which means a pilot process that supports assigning tasks to avoid unavailability and unexpected cuts of services [8]. The main role of load balancing policies is to accelerate software execution by using limited resources where workload fluctuates irregularly [9].

Accordingly, providing an effective load balancing algorithm is vital to perform well in such a challenging environment. Several algorithms and heuristics have been proposed in the academic literature, particularly after the advent of the Big Data and Cloud computing paradigms. Authors [10 - 12] classified these algorithms into static and dynamic approaches. Static algorithms are widely used in the standard Cloud and Grid Computing environments, such as Round Robin Algorithm [13], Min-Min Algorithm [14], Max-Min Algorithms [15], and Throttled Algorithm (TA) [16]. These algorithms are based on two main characteristics: procedural, following immovable rules, and completing preliminary information about the system without the flexibility to change [10]. Dynamic algorithms, on the contrary, are characterized by their ability to decide based on the changing state with the capacity of flexibility [12]. They cover different sub-categories, including agent-based algorithms [17], application-based algorithms [18], workflow-based algorithms [19], and nature-based algorithms [20].

The last sub-category (nature-based) is one of the most prolific due to the abilities of the algorithms to solve complex problems compared to three other sub-categories [11]. These techniques have the particularity of miming the natural phenomena and behaviors and are also clustered into three classes: the Bio-Inspired Algorithms (BIA), and the Physics-Chemistry-inspired Algorithms (PCA), and others.

In the class of physics-chemistry-inspired heuristics, the natural chemical and physical transformations and interactions form the foundation of inspiration, such as some specific mechanical laws and organic movements [21]. For instance, the well-known Osmotic Load Balancing Algorithm (OLBA) imitates the osmosis self-regulatory phenomenon where liquids interchange through semi-permeable membranes [22].

The other class of bio-inspired algorithms forms the branch of Swarm Intelligence (SI), where the miming behavior can be extracted through five ways to assist in load balancing:

a. Swarming behavior is inspired by insects, particles, birds, bacteriological organisms, and vegetation [23]. These techniques are predominantly used in load balancing for optimization purposes and resource migrations strategies. Examples are Particle Swarm Optimization (PSO) [24], Bat-Inspired Algorithm (BIA) [25], and Artificial Bee Colony (ABC) [26].

b. Foraging behavior is replicated in some species of insects and animals like ants and bees. These algorithms are mainly applied to searching for available resources and allocation optimization in load balancing. Examples are the Ant Colony Optimization (ACO) [27] by imitating the trailed pheromone in searching for food, and the Honey Bee Foraging (HBF) algorithm [28] by reproducing the hunting process of bees in computing the distance between the hive and food sources.

c. Evolution behavior is based on Darwin's theory of natural organisms' survivorship, where critters can be preserved via three processes (reproduction, mutations, and cross-over [29]. These algorithms constitute the sub-class of Evolutionary Computation Algorithms (ECA). They are mainly applied in load balancing for workflow and node management. Well-known Genetic Algorithms (GE) are employed to ease operative resource exploitation and attain improved performances in nodes [30].

d. Breeding behavior mimicked some animals like birds and body cells [31]. The breeding-inspired algorithms are primarily applied to resource scheduling and optimal node selection in load balancing. Examples are the Cuckoo Optimization Algorithm (COA) [32].

e. Self-learning behavior is emulated from the learning ability of the human brain [33]. Artificial Neural Networks (ANN) are the most commonly known in this sub-category. They are helpful in load balancing for inferring optimal configurations and forecasting purposes due to their robustness in heterogeneous and large-scale infrastructures [34, 35].

In addition to these popular algorithms, there exist an extensive number of hybrid natural-inspired algorithms that have been developed for load balancing, such as ACO-ABC [36], HBA-G A [37], ANN- Cuckoo [38] and HD-PSA [39]. Other algorithms are less popular but have proved their efficacy in load balancing issues like Frog Leaping Algorithm (FLA) [40], Invasive Weed Optimization (IWO) [41], Fish Swarming Algorithm (FSA) [42], Artificial Immune System (AIS) [43], Fireflies Algorithm (FA) [44], and many others.

Like these research works, the present chapter offers a new load-balancing algorithm based on an ant-inspired behavior. The approach is based on a search procedure labeled PB-DNA as "Propagation and Back-Propagation Diffusion through Neighborhoods Algorithm." In the research process, the approach adopts a meta-clustering technique for partitioning the space into a combination of clusters (also called meta-nodes) by using the neighborhood relationships.

In the remaining parts, the chapter is structured as follows: Section 2 includes two sub-parts of related works on workload management and swarm intelligence. Section 3 describes the proposed approach and research methodology. Experimental settings, implementation, and empirical results are presented in Section 4. Finally, conclusions with open views are provided in Section 5.

RELATED WORKS AND PROBLEM STATEMENT

The area of parallel processing related to the Big Data environment for enterprises, and the possibility to design resilient load balancing, has immersed the consideration to advanced approaches such as Artificial Intelligence (AI), Machine Learning (ML), Computational Intelligence (CI), Statistics, Swarm Intelligence (SI) among others.

Business Big Data Processing, Workload Management, and Load Balancing

In the current era of Big Data, distributed systems offer a technical panel to allow the organizations to assimilate their Business Processes (BP) robustly. They ensure the ability to incorporate massive data acquisition, transaction, and transformation [45]. Such systems are currently used to integrate end-to-end BPs in a single central view that ensures that information can be shared through all management and IT infrastructure levels [46]. The primary purpose is to place a juxtaposition with all the traditional ISs for enterprises: The Enterprise Resource Planning (ERP), the Customer Relationship Management (CRM), the Supplier Relationship Management (SRM), the Supply Chain Management (SCM), the Human Capital Management (HCM), the Product Lifecycle Management (PLM) [47], and so forth.

In recent years, massive data is continuously accumulated and stored in manifold and massive data centers worldwide. The primary causes are the low costs of storage, advanced communications networking, and the competitive business environment [3]. IT infrastructures in these platforms combine sub-systems for ruling, finding, merging, and analyzing with many servers operating in parallel distributions [5]. Parallel data processing is being used in high-performance computing to meet scalability and fault tolerance [1]. The distributed data processing systems can be -roughly- classified according to two main sub-processes: The Parallel Complex Event Processing (PCEP) to handle massive event streams flexibly, and the Parallel Data Processing (PDP) to compute the data batches powerfully [6] (Fig. **1**).

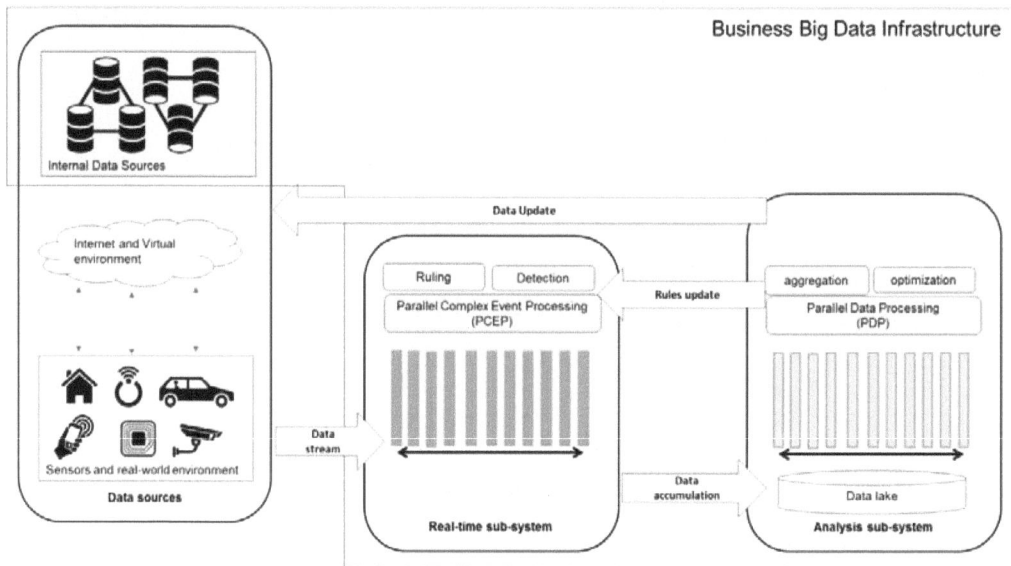

Fig. (1). Distributed parallel data processing sub-systems in business big data infrastructures.

In any system operating in parallel, Workload Management (WM) is the core process of distributing tasks to provide optimal performance [45]. Technically, a WM system is implemented through a Load Balancing (LB) algorithm.

Researches in workload management and load balancing in Big Data processing are emergent, while the Cloud Computing and Software-Defined Network (SDN) environments bias the prevalence [48]. Still, most of them are trying to improve performance metrics by reusing the same classic policies of non-scalable environments (for example, the significant reuse of the FIFO job scheduler in MapReduce® [9]. A few researchers have attempted to propose a new load balancing approaches, such as the TOLHIT approach [49], and the TWO-PASS algorithm [50]. That is probably due to the Big Data systems' complexity and heterogeneity [1] because improving the availability of charges in highly scalable, real-time, and elastic architectures is highly challenging [2]. Some other algorithms originate from classic algorithms but are improved to support complex and heterogeneous environments, such as the approximation-based load-balancing algorithm named ALB [5]. The algorithm creates and manages the incoming requests in classes dynamically by using an admission controller system according to their durations for each class and each node capacity. The algorithm process seems potentially interesting. However, it may suffer from latency in a big data environment due to the complexity and length of execution.

From the academic literature analysis of Big Data high-frequency platforms, we found that the existing load balancing policies demonstrate their deficiency in guaranteeing resilience. We also observed the use of Swarm Intelligence (SI) algorithms emerging, promising where the well-known algorithms fail [3].

Swarm Intelligence for Load Balancing

For the past twenty years, a growing consideration has focused on the distributed Swarm Intelligence approaches to deal with complex resource allocation problems [6], particularly in parallel processing management [51]. The best known are the Artificial Bee Colony (ABC) algorithm [9], Ant Colony Optimization-ACO [9], Multi-Agent Systems-MAS, and many others. This popularity is motivated by their potential to unravel composite problems, their flexibility, their incoordination ability, and their facility to support large-scalable systems [3].

Swarm intelligence is a sub-field of Artificial Intelligence (AI) that denotes a class of problem-solving capability that occurs from the interactions of simple software units [52]. The expression "swarm" advocates "multiplicity" with "haphazardness" and "self-organization," and the expression "intelligence" represents complex problem-solving [53]. The software units that constitute the swarm can imitate the behaviors of birds, bugs, bees, ants, sheep, or human beings. They can be abstract models, mathematical elements, software bots, or standalone terminals [54].

Employing swarm intelligence techniques in workload management to deal with scheduling and load balancing challenges is not first-hand in academic research. In a study [55], many works exist: authors highlighted an original technique based on Particle Swarm Optimization (PSO) for task scheduling in the large-scaled cloud. However, as with all PSO approaches, the main weakness is that performance is problem-dependent. Besides, the authors [56] presented a statistical approach to workload traces with prioritization by using the Agent-based Hybrid Priority Scheduling (AHS) [57]. This approach seems simple to implement, though convergence does not guarantee convergence when applied to large-scale environments. Authors [58] proposed an ACO algorithm capable of providing the near-optimum. The approach might be performant in a Big Data large-scaled environment, even if the load degree has been left unexplored and unaddressed in the original research.

More than the superficial investigation of the academic literature, swarm-based techniques are presently gaining popularity in industrial applications [1]. That is due to their simplicity, swiftness, and high efficiency in solving large-scale and dynamic problems [9].

PROPOSED APPROACH

Key Concepts

Concept of Neighborhood and Meta-Clustering

In a servers-clustered environment, nodes are distributed and identified by distinctive identifiers (ID) and may be grouped to form gatherings or meta-clusters (clusters of clusters) through neighborhoods. In a meta-cluster, we define meta-nodes as independent clusters where two meta-nodes are defined as neighbors when each node is aware of the existence of the other (Fig. **2**).

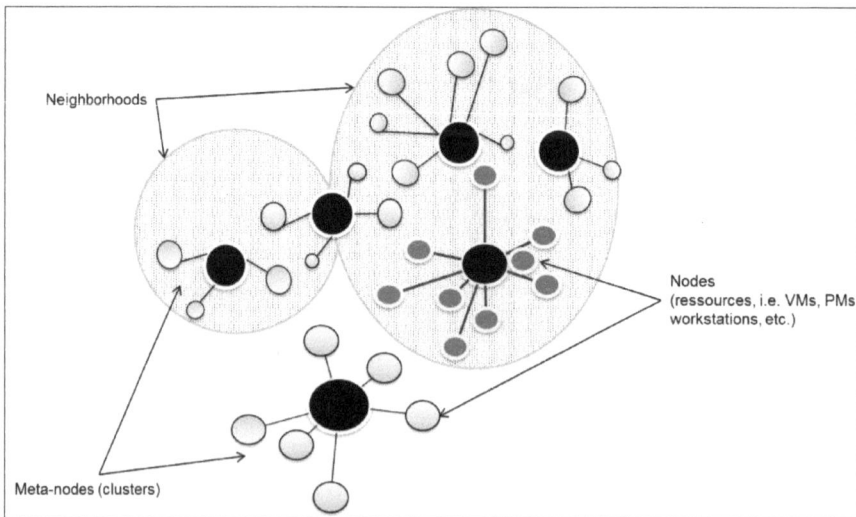

Fig. (2). Neighborhood concept in the proposed approach.

The neighborhood relationship between nodes is based on the concept of acquaintances in the environment. Some primary research facing the problem of identifying clusters and communities is similar to neighborhood identification. In this nature of problem, two different kinds of data can be used for identification (neighborhood) (Gonzalez-Pardo, Jung and Camacho n.d.):

- The data about the information available in the different nodes where each node contains information about the properties of the other recorded nodes;
- The data about the information can be mined from the network linkages among the different characteristics.

Concepts of Inner and Outer Load Balancing

Typically, in a Big Data high-computational system, what happens if there is no resource available in the cluster when a failure occurs? Today, there is no concrete answer to this question apart from increasing scalability by adding additional servers (nodes) [59], for instance, the elastic solution of Amazon MapReduce EMR® [60]. However, this workaround is overpriced with accumulated delay in nodes because of the complexity of implementations in Big Data environments for enterprises [61].

This research study adopts a new load distribution strategy in which we distinguish between the 'inner load balancing' inside a cluster (intra-cluster) and the 'outer load balancing' (inter-clusters) to avoid clusters failure. This strategy performs the 'outer load balancing' part in complementing the traditional load balancing policy in the inner balancing (Fig. **3**).

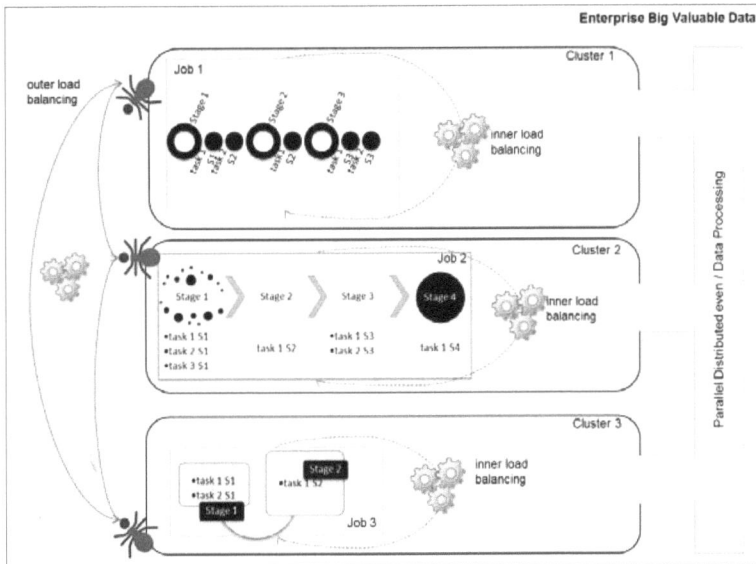

Fig. (3). Outer load balancing in the proposed approach.

PB-DNA Algorithm

Life-science researchers are aware that ants communicate by stigmergy through biochemical substances named pheromones [6]. The stigmergic mode is known as the indirect communication mode first observed in social insects. However, this communication channel is not the exclusive mode, as some ants lack pheromone substance. Experiments proved that some species of ants, including the well-known "red fire ants" (Solenopsis Invicta), use acoustic calls (alarm stridulating) as a non-stigmergic communication instead of diffusing pheromone in situations of threats [62] (Fig. **4**).

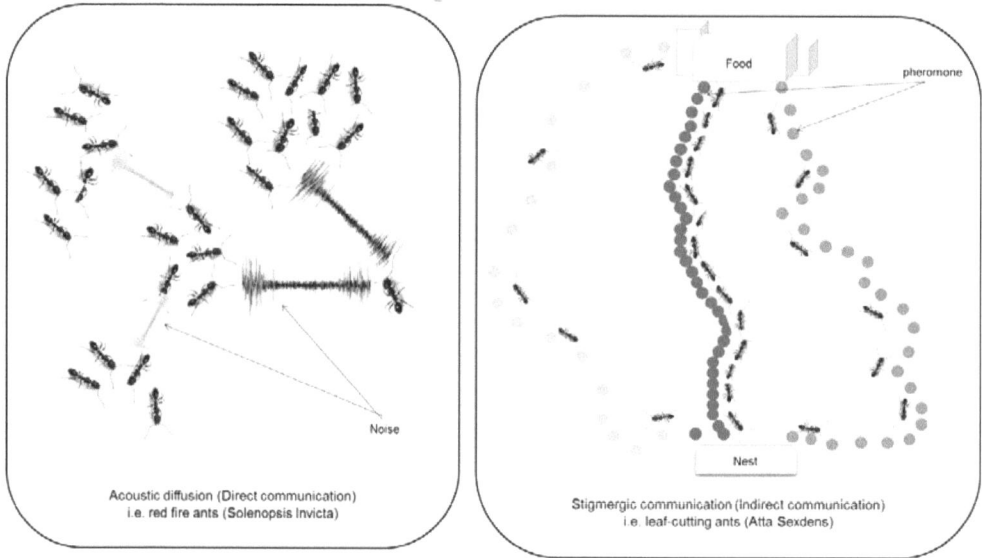

Fig. (4). Stigmergic *vs.* non-stigmergic communication modes in swarms of ants.

The non-stigmergic communication mode has also been confirmed later in the publication of the same author in [63] and then in Leonhardt *et al.* [64]. Contrasting many other ant-inspired algorithms that emit stigmergic coordination of pheromone as ACO [65]; we propose PB-DNA, which is based on direct acoustic communication (one-to-one) of red fire ants (Solenopsis Invicta). The algorithm is somehow close to the SDS (Stochastic Diffusion Search) algorithm of Bishop [66]. SDS uses the 'tandem calling' mechanism of 'Leptothorax Acervorum' ants, where PB-DNA is inspired by the 'attack calling' behavior of 'Solenopsis Invicta' ants [62] (Fig. **5**).

(b)

(a)

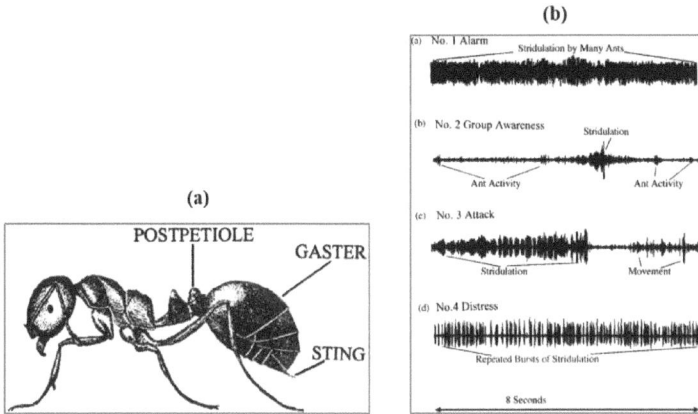

Fig. (5). (a) The stridulatory organ (Gaster). **(b)** The Pressure-time traces of stridulatory signals (images taken from [62] about the acoustic communication in the colonies of red fire ant workers).

Formulation and Settings

The proposed system performs load balancing by coupling the propagation and the backpropagation. In the proposed model, the system consists of a finite set C of $N + 1$ clusters (meta-nodes):

$$C = \{c_n\}_{n\in\{0,1,\ldots,N\}} \tag{1}$$

An ant-agent symbolizes each meta-node. Suppose a finite set A of $N + 1$ ant-agents:

$$A = \{a_n\}_{n\in\{0,1,\ldots,N\}} \tag{2}$$

We name 'ant-agent initiator' the meta-node that inaugurates the process of the outer load balancing. There is only one agent initiator in the system (a_o).

$$\exists\, a_0 \; ant\text{-}agent \; initiator, \; \forall\, n \in N, \; a_n \neq a_0 \tag{3}$$

Each ant-agent (named 'guest agent') can have 0, 1, or more neighbors (named 'host agents'). For an ant-agent a_n there is a set $H(a_n)$ of V neighbors:

$$\forall a_n \in A, \; \exists H(a_n) = \left\{h_v^{a_n}\right\}_{v\in\{0,1,\ldots,V\}} \quad or \quad \exists H(a_n) = \emptyset \tag{4}$$

Each ant-agent has its information (parameters and values). The agent can transmit the information partially (local information) by direct diffusion (emulating the acoustic communication) to the other agents in its neighborhood. The set of parameters in the local information of each ant-agent are the following:

- Reference constraints: A set of biased constraints that are the minimum requirements in the resource to allow allocating the failed task. For example, vCPU power, the capacity of vRAM, Operating System (OS), *etc*. For each ant-agent a_n, consider a set R^a_n reference constraints:

$$\forall a_n \in A, \ \exists R^{a_n} = \left\{ r_k^{a_n} \right\}_{k \in \{0,1,...,K\}} \tag{5}$$

- Weights of the reference constraints: Each constraint ($r_k^{a_n}$) must be biased by a preferential coefficient. For example, for a highly calculation-consuming task, the heavier weight is given to vCPU rather than vRAM. For the set R^a_n, consider the finite set Λ^{a_n} of K weights:

$$\forall a_n \in A, \ \exists \Lambda^{a_n} = \left\{ \begin{matrix} \lambda_k^{a_n}; 0 \le \lambda_k^{a_n} \le 1; \\ \sum_1^K \lambda_k^{a_n} = 1 \end{matrix} \right\}_{k \in \{0,1,...,K\}} \tag{6}$$

If no preferences are known, all weights are set to an equal value 1/K (Fig. **6**).

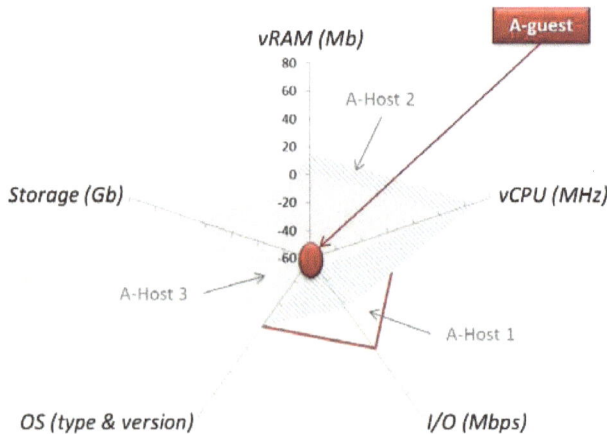

Fig. (6). Preferences of the ant-guest and the ant-hosts agents in the proposed algorithm.

- Ultimate propagation level: The maximum level of exploration must limit the exploration with a threshold. For example, suppose that the failed task to migrate requires a constraint of I/O transactions. In that case, the ant-agent initiator must determine the ultimate level with a lesser value to avoid balancing the task to a distant location. Besides, the threshold level can prevent divergence and the combinatory explosion of the algorithm.

We define the ultimate propagation level Uan as following:

$$\forall a_n \in A, \exists U^{a_n} \tag{7}$$

- Utility function: This parameter stores the value of the local minima known by the ant-agent. Accordingly, all the ant-agents do not have the same utility function value as they do not share the same information. For each ant-agent an, suppose the utility function Fan:

$$\forall a_n \in A, \exists F^{a_n} \tag{8}$$

- Identifier of the local minima: For each ant-agent an, suppose the identifier Ian:

$$\forall a_n \in A, \exists I^{a_n} \tag{9}$$

- Current exploration level: Does the agent reach the level during exploration. The ant-agent initiator is supposed to be at level 1. In every progress step, this parameter is incremented. For each ant-agent an suppose the current exploration level Lan:

$$\forall a_n \in A, \exists L^{a_n} \tag{10}$$

Suppose the propagation matrix Pan:

$$\forall a_n \in A, \exists P^{a_n} = \begin{bmatrix} F^{a_n} & r_1^{a_n} & \lambda_K^{a_1} \\ I^{a_n} & r_2^{a_n} & \lambda_K^{a_2} \\ L^{a_n} & \dots & \dots \\ U^{a_n} & r_K^{a_n} & \lambda_K^{a_n} \end{bmatrix} \tag{11}$$

- Maximum available values of constraints: The set of available meta-nodes that are candidates to allocate the failed task in migration. For each ant-agent an, suppose the finite set Qan of the maximum available values for the K criteria:

$$\forall a_n \in A - \{a_0\}, \ \exists Q^{a_n} = \left\{q_k^{a_n}\right\}_{k \in \{0,1,...,K\}} \tag{12}$$

- Backpropagation markers vector: This vector stores a Boolean value for each neighbor (set of markers) to trace the list of visited neighbors in exploration. For each ant-agent an, suppose the vector Tan of V backpropagation markers tvan:

$$\forall a_n \in A, T^{a_n} = \left[t_v^{a_n}\right]_{v \in \{0,1,...,V\}}; \ t_v^{a_n} \in \{0,1\} \tag{13}$$

Suppose the backpropagation vector Xan (with tvan set to 1):

$$\forall a_n \in A, \ X^{a_n} = \left[t_v^{a_n}{}_{\{=1\}} \quad F^{a_n} \quad I^{a_n}\right] \tag{14}$$

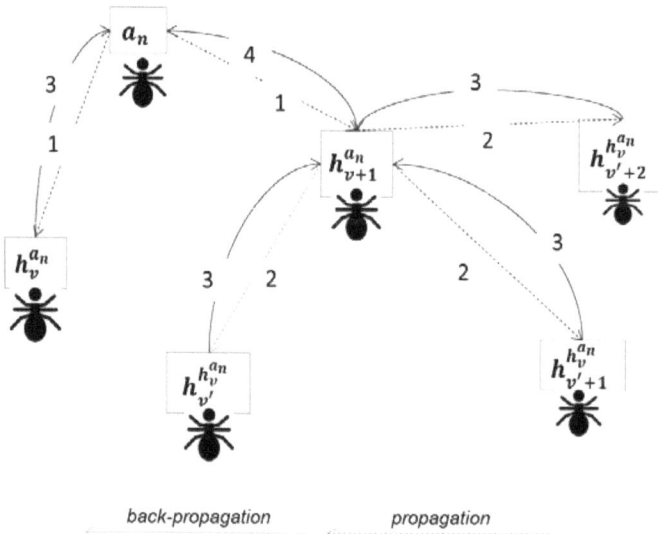

Fig. (7). Propagation and Backpropagation mechanisms in the proposed algorithm.

Phase 1: Propagation of Constraints

When a new request for task migration occurs, the ant-agent initiator triggers the propagation phase by sending the P^{a0} Matrix to the neighbors. Once the matrix P^{a0} received, each neighbor a_n computes the utility function F^{an} based on the available resources Q^{an}. This process is repeated until the maximum level of exploration is reached L^{an} or in case there are no more new neighbors to visit $H(a_n) = \emptyset$ (Fig. **7**).

The propagation phase follows automatically and sequentially the following steps:

- Step P1.1: Each ant-agent an (ant-guest) propagates the constraints to the agents-hosts by sending a REQUEST message with the Pan the matrix in the content:

$$\forall a_n \in A, H(a_n) \neq \emptyset \;\Rightarrow\; \forall h_v^{a_n} \in H(a_n), \; a_n \xrightarrow{\;send:\,REQUEST.Msg(P^{a_n})\;} h_v^{a_n} \quad (15)$$

- Step P1.2: Each host hvan receives the REQUEST message with Pan matrix, and then extracts the information of the content for update:

$$\forall h_v^{a_n} \in H(a_n), \quad \begin{cases} F^{h_{v_l}^{a_n}} \leftarrow F^{a_n} \\ I^{h_v^{a_n}} \leftarrow I^{a_n} \\ L^{h_v^{a_n}} \leftarrow L^{a_n} \\ U^{h_v^{a_n}} \leftarrow U^{a_n} \\ R^{h_v^{a_n}} \leftarrow R^{a_n} \\ \Lambda^{h_v^{a_n}} \leftarrow \Lambda^{a_n} \end{cases} \quad (16)$$

- Step P1.3: Each host hvan calculates the vector Ähvan of the weighted quantified differences hvan. The hvan values represent the distances between the references of the ant-agent guest Rhvan and the internal values of the ant-host agent Qhvan:

$$\forall h_v^{a_n} \in H(a_n), \; \Delta^{h_v^{a_n}} = \left\{ \delta_v^{h_v^{a_n}} = \lambda_k^{h_v^{a_n}} \cdot \left(q_k^{h_v^{a_n}} \Delta \, r_k^{h_v^{a_n}} \right) \right\}_{k \in \{0,1,\dots,K\}} \quad (17)$$

- Step P1.4: The host hvan checks if all the weighted differences hvan.are positive. If that is the case, the host computes the sum function Shvan of the quantified differences Ähvan:

$$\forall h_v^{a_n} \in H(a_n), \forall k \in \{1, \dots, K\}; \; \delta_v^{h_v^{a_n}} \geq 0 \Rightarrow S_v^{h_v^{aa_0}} = \sum_{k=1}^{K} L_v^{h_v^{a_n}} \cdot \lambda_k^{h_v^{a_n}} \cdot \quad (18)$$

$$\left(q_k^{h_v^{a_n}} \Delta \, r_k^{h_v^{a_n}} \right)$$

Otherwise, the corresponding difference hvan is negative. Accordingly, the agent assigns a MAX value to the sum function Shvan to eliminate the agent from the list of candidates:

$$\forall \, h_v^{a_n} \in H(a_n), \forall k \in \{1, \dots, K\}; \; \delta_v^{h_v^{a_n}} < 0 \Rightarrow S_v^{h_v^{aa_0}} = MAX \qquad (19)$$

- Step P1.5: The host calculates the local minima's new values, the utility function, and the identifier. If the sum function Shvan is smaller than the known utility function Fhvan, this host itself becomes the new local minimum. In this case, the agent informs the guest with an INFORM message with the two new computed values:

$$\forall h_v^{a_n} \in H(a_n), S_v^{h_v^{a_n}} < F_v^{h_v^{a_n}} \Rightarrow \begin{cases} F_v^{h_v^{a_n}} = S_v^{h_v^{a_n}} \\ I_v^{h_v^{a_n}} = h_v^{a_n} \\ h_v^{a_n} \xrightarrow{\;send:\,INFORM.Msg\left(F_v^{h_v^{a_n}}, I_v^{h_v^{a_n}}\right)\;} a_n \end{cases} \qquad (20)$$

- Step P1.6: When receiving the INFORM message, the agent updates the internal parameters and then diffuses the new values to all the neighbors:

$$\forall a_n \in A, \begin{cases} F^{a_n} = F_v^{h_v^{a_n}} \\ I^{a_n} = I_v^{h_v^{a_n}} \\ \forall h_v^{a_n} \in H(a_n) - \left\{ I_v^{h_v^{a_n}} \right\}, a_n \xrightarrow{\;send:\,INFORM.Msg(F^{a_n}, I^{a_n})\;} h_v^{aa_0} \end{cases} \qquad (21)$$

- Step P1.7: The neighbors receive the new INFORM message and thus update their information. At this last step, all ant-agents that belong to the same neighborhood share the same information:

$$\forall h_v^{a_n} \in H(a_n) - \left\{ I_v^{h_v^{a_n}} \right\}, \begin{cases} F_v^{h_v^{a_n}} = F^{a_n} \\ I_v^{h_v^{a_n}} = I^{a_n} \end{cases} \qquad (22)$$

These seven steps are repeated until each exploration line reaches its leaf. The leaf is the last meta-node with one of the two following cases:

- The exploration of a neighborhood queue has achieved the ultimate level of propagation Uan,
- The ant-guest agent does not have more neighbors to explore.

$$\forall a_n \in A, \begin{cases} L^{a_n} = U^{a_n} \\ \qquad \vee \\ H(a_n) \neq \emptyset \end{cases} \Rightarrow a_n \ is \ a \ leave \tag{23}$$

This outcome of the propagation phase is a tree of local minima with the ant-agent initiator (first meta-node) as a root and all the neighborhoods of the last visited levels as the leaves.

$$\forall a_n \in A, \ H(a_n) \neq \emptyset \Rightarrow a_n \ is \ a \ leave \tag{24}$$

The tree of local minima has to be explored to extract the global minimum. That constitutes the second phase of backpropagation.

Phase 2: Backpropagation of Local Minima

The phases of backpropagation and propagation progress in parallel. However, in each outlet (propagation track), the backpropagation process must be triggered automatically after the propagation process by ascending the tree. Two steps are enumerated in this phase:

- Step P2.1: At the end of the propagation process, each ant-host hvan replies to the ant-guests with a REPLY message to diffuse the backpropagation vector Xan. This operation is triggered following two conditions:
  - The host is a leaf. This marks the end of the descending branch,
  - The host is not a leaf, but all the neighbors have already replied (all markers of the backpropagation vector are set to 1)

$$\forall h_v^{a_n} \in H(a_n), \quad \begin{cases} L^{h_v^{a_n}} = U^{h_v^{a_n}} \\ \lor \\ H\left(h_v^{a_n}\right) = \emptyset \\ \lor \\ \forall t_v^{h_v^{a_n}} \in T^{h_v^{a_n}}, t_v^{h_v^{a_n}} = 1 \end{cases} \Rightarrow h_v^{a_n} \xrightarrow{\ send:\ REPLY.Msg(X^{a_n})\ } a_n \quad (25)$$

- Step P2.2: The ant-guest catches the vector Xan, then extracts and updates parameters as follows:
  - ○ The marker tvan in the vector Tan, is updated as it is a visited node (value set to 1),
  - ○ According to the extracted utility functions, the ant-agent updates the value Fan and the local minima identifier Ian is computed:

$$\forall a_n \in A, \quad \begin{cases} t_v^{a_n} \mid = 1 \\ F^{h_v^{a_n}} < F^{a_n} \Rightarrow \begin{cases} F^{a_n} = F^{h_v^{a_n}} \\ I^{a_n} = I^{h_v^{a_n}} \end{cases} \end{cases} \quad (26)$$

Steps P2.1 and P2.2 go up from the leaves to the root, where each neighborhood diffuses the local minima and updates the local information. In the end, the global minimum is elected (the most suitable meta-node) (Ia0 with Fa0) (Fig. **8**).

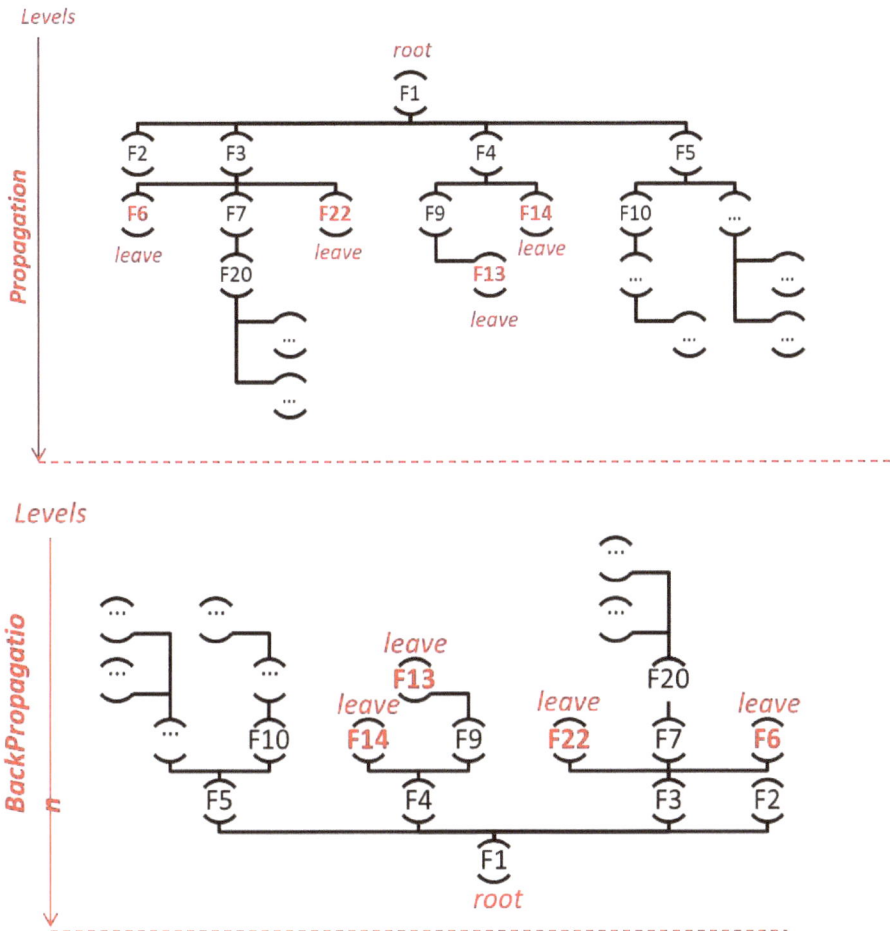

Fig. (8). Exploration of the propagation/backpropagation tree of nodes in the proposed algorithm.

Methodology and Simulation Settings

The methodology we propose is applied in an environment emulated as a Big Data infrastructure with parallel processing. The diagram in Fig. **9**) illustrates the sequential steps of the proposed methodology.

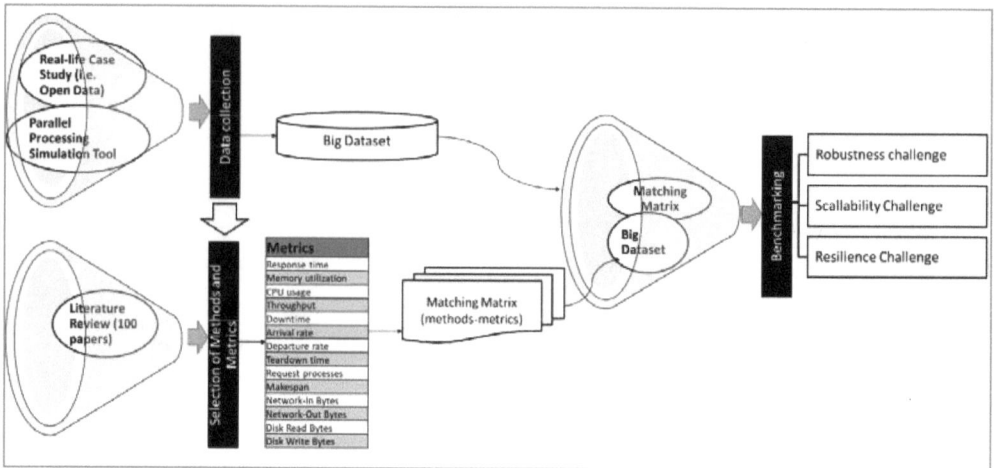

Fig. (9). A simplified model of the proposed methodology.

The model is structured in the following steps:

1st step: Dataset collection

We choose a case study that fits with the addressed issue of parallel processing in a Business Big Data environment. Then we collect data to be used in the parallel processing simulation. The outcome is then selected as the input data for the simulation.

2nd step: Methods and Metrics selection

We analyze the yearly top five most relevant approaches from the reactive and predictive approaches in the literature. We distinguish two sub-steps, A and B:

B. Literature Synthesis

We pick the method and the metrics used in the proposed approach to constitute a matching matrix from each reference. We conducted an in-depth analysis of the classification of the academic literature since the year 2010 from the online journal databases (Elsevier, Springer, and Taylor & Francis) since 2010. Table **1** synthesizes the yearly top five main load-balancing approaches with the classification related to the infrastructures (Software-Defined Network (SDN), Cloud Computing (CC), Grid Computing (GC), Big Data (BD), Edge Computing (EC), and Fog Computing (FC)). Table **2** illustrates the outcome matrix that includes the methods selected in Table **1** with a new classification associated with the modes (predictive/reactive) and the load balancing metrics.

Table 1. The yearly top 5 relevant publications about load balancing matching with the infrastructure types (review).

Method / Algorithm / Heuristic for load balancing	Reference Code *	Approach **	Response time	Memory utilization	CPU usage	Throughput	Downtime	Arrival rate	Departure rate	Teardown time	Request processes	makespan	Network-In Bytes	Network-Out Bytes	Disk Read Bytes	Disk Write Bytes
Real-time logs analysis	[01]	P*	•	x	x	x	x	x	x	x	x	x	x	x	x	x
Distributed Balancing	[02]	R*	x	x	x	x	x	•	x	x	x	•	x	x	x	x
Task-parallel algorithm	[03]	R*	x	•	•	x	x	x	x	x	x	x	x	x	x	x
Ant theory load balancing	[04]	P*	•	x	x	x	•	x	x	x	x	x	x	x	x	x
Approximation-based Algorithm	[05]	R*	•	x	x	•	•	x	x	x	x	x	x	x	x	x
Machine Learning xx	[06]	P*	x	•	•	x	x	x	x	x	x	x	x	x	x	x
linear and Queuing Model	[07]	P*	•	x	x	x	x	x	x	x	x	x	x	x	•	x
Data-Mining Algorithms	[08]	P*	x	x	x	x	x	•	•	•	x	x	x	x	x	x
Functional buffer	[09]	R*	•	x	x	x	x	x	x	x	•	•	x	x	x	x
Secure Socket Distributed	[10]	R*	•	x	x	x	•	x	x	x	x	x	x	x	x	x
Proximity Load Balancing	[11]	R*	x	x	x	x	x	x	x	x	x	•	x	x	x	x
Queue-Based provisioning	[12]	P*	x	x	x	•	x	x	x	x	•	x	x	x	x	x
Clustering Based HEFT	[13]	R*	x	x	•	x	x	x	•	x	x	x	x	•	x	•
Stochastic Hill Climbing	[14]	R*	•	x	x	x	x	x	•	x	x	x	x	x	x	x
Swarm intelligent balancing	[15]	P*	•	x	x	x	x	x	x	x	x	x	x	x	x	x
Policy-Based Provisioning (PBP*)	[16]	P*	•	•	•	x	x	x	x	x	x	x	x	x	x	x
Machine Learning-Linear regression (MLL*)	[17]	P*	•	x	•	•	x	x	x	x	x	x	x	•	x	x
Prior Balance List	[18]	R*	x	•	•	x	•	x	x	x	x	x	x	x	x	x
Neural Network Load balancing	[19]	P*	x	•	x	x	x	x	x	•	x	x	x	x	x	x
Lazy Migration algorithm	[20]	R*	•	x	•	x	x	x	x	x	x	x	x	x	x	x
ARIMA model	[21]	P*	x	x	x	•	x	•	•	x	•	x	x	x	x	x
Random Scheduling Algorithm (RSA*)	[22]	R*	x	x	x	x	•	x	x	x	x	•	x	x	x	x
Biased Random Sampling	[23]	P*	•	x	x	x	x	x	x	x	x	x	x	x	x	x
Online Resource Scheduling	[24]	R*	•	•	•	x	•	x	x	x	x	x	x	x	x	x
Power optimization algorithm	[25]	R*	x	x	x	•	x	x	x	x	x	x	x	•	•	•
Big Data DIRAC algorithm	[26]	R*	•	x	x	x	x	x	x	x	•	x	x	x	x	•
Policy-based provisioning	[27]	P*	x	x	x	•	x	x	x	x	x	x	x	x	x	x
Round Robin Algorithm (RRA*)	[28]	R*	x	x	x	x	•	x	x	x	x	x	x	x	x	x
Agent-based load balancing	[29]	R*	x	•	•	x	x	•	•	x	x	x	x	x	x	x
Data Sharing Load Balancing	[30]	P*	•	x	x	x	•	x	x	x	x	x	x	x	x	x
Max Min algorithm	[31]	R*	x	x	x	x	x	x	x	x	x	•	x	x	x	x
Predictive Resource approach	[32]	P*	x	•	•	x	x	x	x	x	•	x	•	•	•	•
Autonomous Agent-Based	[33]	R*	x	x	x	x	x	x	x	x	x	•	x	x	x	x
Dynamical Load Balancing	[34]	R*	•	x	x	x	•	x	x	x	x	x	x	x	x	x
Path Neural Network	[35]	P*	x	x	•	•	x	x	x	x	x	x	•	•	x	•
Cross-region load balancing	[36]	P*	•	x	x	•	x	x	x	x	x	x	x	x	x	x
Ant colony optimization	[37]	P*	x	x	x	x	x	x	x	x	x	•	x	x	x	x
Holistic approach	[38]	R*	•	•	x	x	x	x	x	x	x	•	x	x	x	x

(Table 1) cont.....

ethod / Algorithm / Heuristic for load balancing	Reference Code *	Approach **	Response time	Memory utilization	CPU usage	Throughput	Downtime	Arrival rate	Departure rate	Teardown time	Request processes	makespan	Network-In Bytes	Network-Out Bytes	Disk Read Bytes	Disk Write Bytes
Load Balancing Decision	[39]	R*	•	x	x	x	x	x	x	x	x	•	x	x	x	x
Load Balancing for SaaS	[40]	R*	x	x	•	•	x	x	x	x	x	x	x	x	x	x
ACO allocation-based algorithm	[41]	P*	•	•	•	x	•	x	x	x	x	x	x	x	x	x
Joint Load and Offloading	[42]	R*	x	•	x	x	x	x	x	x	x	x	•	•	x	x
Dynamic migration algorithm	[43]	P*	x	•	x	•	•	x	x	x	x	x	x	x	x	x
Multi-Level Real-Time	[44]	R*	x	x	x	•	x	•	•	•	x	x	x	x	x	x
Fault-Tolerant Global Balancing	[45]	R*	•	x	x	•	•	x	x	x	x	x	x	x	x	x
Max-Min fairness algorithm	[46]	R*	•	x	x	x	x	x	x	x	x	x	x	x	x	x
Localized Fault Tolerant	[47]	R*	x	x	x	x	•	x	x	x	x	x	x	x	x	x
Pattern-Based Load Balancing	[48]	R*	•	x	x	•	x	x	x	x	•	x	x	x	x	x
Markov chain model balancing	[49]	P*	•	x	x	x	•	x	x	x	x	x	x	x	x	x
Optimized dynamic algorithm	[50]	P*	•	x	x	•	x	x	x	x	x	x	x	x	x	x
Network Weak Load Balancing	[51]	R*	•	x	x	•	x	x	x	x	x	x	x	x	x	x
Optimization reinforcement	[52]	P*	•	x	x	•	•	x	x	x	•	•	x	x	x	•
Harris Hawks Optimization	[53]	R*	x	x	x	•	x	x	x	x	x	•	x	x	x	x
Co-operative Load balancing	[54]	R*	•	x	x	x	•	x	x	x	x	•	x	x	x	x
Fuzzy inference load balancing	[55]	P*	•	•	•	x	x	x	x	x	x	x	x	x	x	x

Note: Reference Code *: referred to Table 1. Approach**: Reactive Approaches (R*), Predictive Approaches (P*).

Table 2. The matching matrix with the classification by mode and metrics in load balancing.

chronology	Reference Code	Reference	infrastructures					
			Software-Defined Network	Cloud Computing	Grid Computing	Big Data	Edge Computing	Fog Computing
2010	[01]	(Iqbal, Dailey and Carrera 2010)	•	•	x	x	x	x
	[02]	(Fang, Wang and Ge 2010)	x	•	x	x	x	x
	[03]	(Kim, *et al.* 2010)	•	x	x	x	x	x
	[04]	(Etoundi, *et al.* 2010)	•	x	x	x	x	x
	[05]	(Sharifian, Motamedi *et al.* Akbari 2010)	•	•	x	x	x	x

(Table 2) cont.....

chronology	Reference Code	Reference	infrastructures					
			Software-Defined Network	Cloud Computing	Grid Computing	Big Data	Edge Computing	Fog Computing
2011	[06]	(Xiong, *et al.* 2011)	x	●	x	x	x	x
	[07]	(Shi, Jiang and Ye 2011)	x	●	x	x	x	x
	[08]	(Doumith, *et al.* 2011)	x	●	x	x	x	x
	[09]	(Ma, *et al.* 2011)	x	x	●	x	x	x
	[10]	(Kungumaraj and Ravichandran 2011)	●	x	x	x	x	x
2012	[11]	(Solar, Suppi and Luque 2012)	●	●	x	x	x	x
	[12]	(Ali-Eldin 2012)	x	●	x	x	x	x
	[13]	(Abdelkader and Omara 2012)	●	x	x	x	x	x
	[14]	(Mondal 2012)	x	●	x	x	x	x
	[15]	(El-kenawy, El-Desoky *et al.* Al-rahamawy 2012)	x	x	x	●	x	x
2013	[16]	(Elprince 2013)	●	x	x	x	x	x
	[17]	(Bankole and Ajila 2013)	●	●	x	x	x	x
	[18]	(Liu *et al.* Xu 2013)	x	x	x	●	x	x
	[19]	(Al Sallami *et al.* Al Alousi 2013)	●	●	x	●	x	x
	[20]	(Zhang, *et al.* 2013)	x	●	x	●	x	x
2014	[21]	(Calheiros 2014)	x	●	x	x	x	x
	[22]	(Xu, *et al.* 2014)	●	x	x	x	x	x
	[23]	(Wen *et al.* Chang 2014)	●	●	x	●	x	x
	[24]	(Xu *et al.* Tian 2014)	x	●	x	x	x	x
	[25]	(Sharma *et al.* Singh 2014)	x	●	x	x	x	x

(Table 2) cont.....

chronology	Reference Code	Reference	Software-Defined Network	Cloud Computing	Grid Computing	Big Data	Edge Computing	Fog Computing
			infrastructures					
2015	[26]	(Fernández 2015)	x	x	x	●	x	x
	[27]	(Kouki 2015)	x	●	x	x	x	x
	[28]	(Yussof et al. Ezanee 2015)	●	x	x	x	x	x
	[29]	(Gutierrez-Garcia 2015)	x	●	x	x	x	x
	[30]	(Pradeepa et al. Priyadarsini 2014)	x	●	x	x	x	x
2016	[31]	(Shanmugam 2016)	x	●	x	x	x	x
	[32]	(Balaji 2016)	x	●	x	x	x	x
	[33]	(Singh 2016)	x	●	x	x	x	x
	[34]	(Ma, et al. 2016)	●	x	x	x	x	x
	[35]	(Chen-Xiao and Ya-Bin 2016)	●	x	x	x	x	x
2017	[36]	(Sekaran et al. Krishna 2017)	●	x	x	x	x	x
	[37]	(Gupta et al. Garg 2017)	x	●	x	x	x	x
	[38]	(Lin et al. Lin 2017)	x	x	x	●	x	x
	[39]	(Dhari et al. Arif 2017)	x	●	x	x	x	x
	[40]	(Jassar 2017)	x	●	x	●	x	x
2018	[41]	(Xu, et al. 2018)	x	●	x	x	x	x
	[42]	(Dai, et al. 2018)	x	x	x	x	●	x
	[43]	(Cui 2018)	x	●	x	●	x	x
	[44]	(Elsharkawey et al. Refaat 2018)	x	●	x	x	x	●
	[45]	(Posner et al. Fohry 2018)	●	●	●	●	x	x
2019	[46]	(Lin, et al. 2019)	●	x	x	x	x	x
	[47]	(Munir, et al. 2019)	●	x	x	x	x	x
	[48]	(Gasmelseed et al. Ramar 2019)	●	●	x	x	x	x
	[49]	(Ledmi, Bendjenna et al. Mounine 2018)	x	●	x	x	x	x
	[50]	(Zhang and Wang 2018)	●	●	x	●	x	x

(Table 2) cont.....

				infrastructures					
chronology	Reference Code	Reference	Software-Defined Network	Cloud Computing	Grid Computing	Big Data	Edge Computing	Fog Computing
2020	[51]	(Shu and Zhu 2020)	x	x	x	x	•	x
	[52]	(Talaat, *et al.* 2020)	x	x	x	•	•	•
	[53]	(Zhang, Zhou *et al.* Shih 2020)	•	•	x	x	x	x
	[54]	(Kim and Kwon 2020)	•	x	x	x	x	x
	[55]	(Fouad, Saleh and EL-Rahamawy n.d.)	x	x	x	x	x	•

C. Methods and metrics extraction

Using a data clustering tool, we extracted the top 2 of the most used predictive methods, the top 2 of the most used reactive methods, and the top 6 of the most selected metrics used in reactive and predictive methods types.

3rd step: Benchmarking

This final step is used to experiment with the proposed method by comparing the other techniques afore-selected from the 2nd step and referring to the set of afore-picked metrics. Three benchmarking trials were conducted in the experimental benches of this research, as illustrated in Table **3**.

Table 3. The experiments benches in the benchmarking of the proposed algorithm with the other approaches.

BENCHMARKING CHALLENGE	COMPARED APPROACHES			METRICS
	PB-DNA	Reactive approaches	Predictive approaches	
ROBUSTNESS CHALLENGE	✓	✓	✓	All metrics
SCALABILITY CHALLENGE	✓		✓	number of jobs
RESILIENCE CHALLENGE	✓	✓		number of iterations

EXPERIMENTATION AND RESULTS

For validation purposes, two experimental tools were developed:

a. Big Data Processing Simulation tool: an experimental prototype based on CloudSim 3.0.1® to emulate the parallel clusters in our experimentation.
b. Data Visualization Apps.® tool [67]: an interactive software based on Oracle JET 2.0® [68], to make a straightforward analysis of our experimental outputs.

Dataset Collection and Case Study

Table **4** summarizes the parameters of simulation as configured in CloudSim®. Table **5** lists the input values as extracted from the open data available on [69]. The company is a French public railways' Company and one of Europe's significant railway organizations Europe [70].

Table 4. Parameters of simulation.

TYPE	PARAMETERS	VALUE
CLUSTERS INSTANCES (ESX)	Number of clusters (meta-nodes)	49
	Number of cloudlets (jobs) per cluster	1
	Number of tasks per cloudlet	12-24
	Number of instructions per cloudlet (length)	2000-3400

Table 5. Input Data as extracted from the Open Data available on [69].

Host ID	guest ID	Name in CloudSim	vRAM (Gb)	vCPU (GHz)	I/O (Mbps)	Storage (Gb)	OS (name, version)
3451	-	Ant-INIT	1024	258	150	658	Win5.1, Win6.0, Win6.1, Ubunto14.04
3526	3451	Ant-A	131072	5326	250	310	Win6.1
3309	3451	Ant-B	8192	372	425	533	Debian6.0.10
5498	3451	Ant-C	131072	3082	355	1054	Win6.0
7109	3309	Ant-E	512	303	879	985	Linux Mint17.3
3253	7109	Ant-G	8192	675	844	342	Win6.2
6253	3253	Ant-D	16384	900	340	425	Win6.1
9843	7109	Ant-F	1024	322	234	695	Mandriva5.1
1987	9843	Ant-J	256	334	234	142	Mageia3
2074	1987	Ant-H	2048	198	900	98	Win5.1
1074	1987	Ant-Q	262144	10267	100	98	MVS
4362	7109	Ant-I	2048	239	765	4152	z/OS
5246	2074	Ant-L	32768	1516	435	1024	Debian6.0.9
1222	5246	Ant-K	1024	322	235	675	Ubunto14.04

(Table 5) cont.....

Host ID	guest ID	Name in CloudSim	vRAM (Gb)	vCPU (GHz)	I/O (Mbps)	Storage (Gb)	OS (name, version)
1251	7109	Ant-M	16384	550	436	980	Win6.3
4303	1251	Ant-O	512	426	109	512	Mandriva5.1
7421	1987	Ant-N	65536	1660	156	287	Win5.1
7263	7421	Ant-Z	65536	1616	399	2048	Win5.1
3220	7263	Ant-AB	65536	2884	80	6523	MaxOSX
1431	3721	Ant-AC	8192	331	546	125	Win6.2
4912	3220	Ant-P	32768	906	234	87	Win6.1
9867	3721	Ant-AK	2048	281	234	15	Win6.1
9536	9867	Ant-AL	2048	402	432	952	Debian7.1
2624	4303	Ant-AN	4096	437	987	100	MVS
8788	2624	Ant-AM	131072	2990	432	614	Mandriva5.1
1427	2624	Ant-AU	2048	281	543	621	Win6.1
3310	9098	Ant-AP	2048	484	129	315	Ubunto15.90
4170	9098	Ant-AV	32768	949	340	479	Debian7.1
4234	9098	Ant-AQ	65536	2792	224	883	Mageia3
1744	4234	Ant-AS	512	206	345	904	Win6.3
9806	4234	Ant-AR	16384	550	213	124	Win2.10
5512	5498	Ant-R	4096	325	123	12	MVS
2153	5512	Ant-S	65536	2884	89	742	Ubunto15.04
8464	5512	Ant-T	2048	360	213	921	Win6.1
8095	3244	Ant-X	1024	217	342	317	Win4.0
1099	3244	Ant-W	1024	176	123	644	Win6.2
2985	1099	Ant-Y	3072	432	542	314	Madela3
6776	1099	Ant-AE	12288	984	100	325	Ubunto15.90
2115	5512	Ant-AG	2048	1098	211	143	Debian7.1
5251	6776	Ant-AF	14336	102	304	315	Win6.2
6673	2115	Ant-AH	22528	921	209	314	Win2.10
4224	2115	Ant-AI	12288	90	521	941	MacOSX
1443	4224	Ant-AJ	44032	132	532	15	MVS
3721	7263	Ant-AA	14336	207	120	231	Ubunto15.90
9098	2624	Ant-AO	22528	566	432	247	Ubunto14.04
5356	8464	Ant-U	18432	421	106	754	Win6.2
8364	6776	Ant-AD	10240	98	312	731	Win5.1

Fig. (**10**) illustrates the mechanism of propagation and backpropagation between the nodes of the simulated environment based on the parameters of Tables 4 and 5 in the proposed Big Data Processing Simulation tool (a).

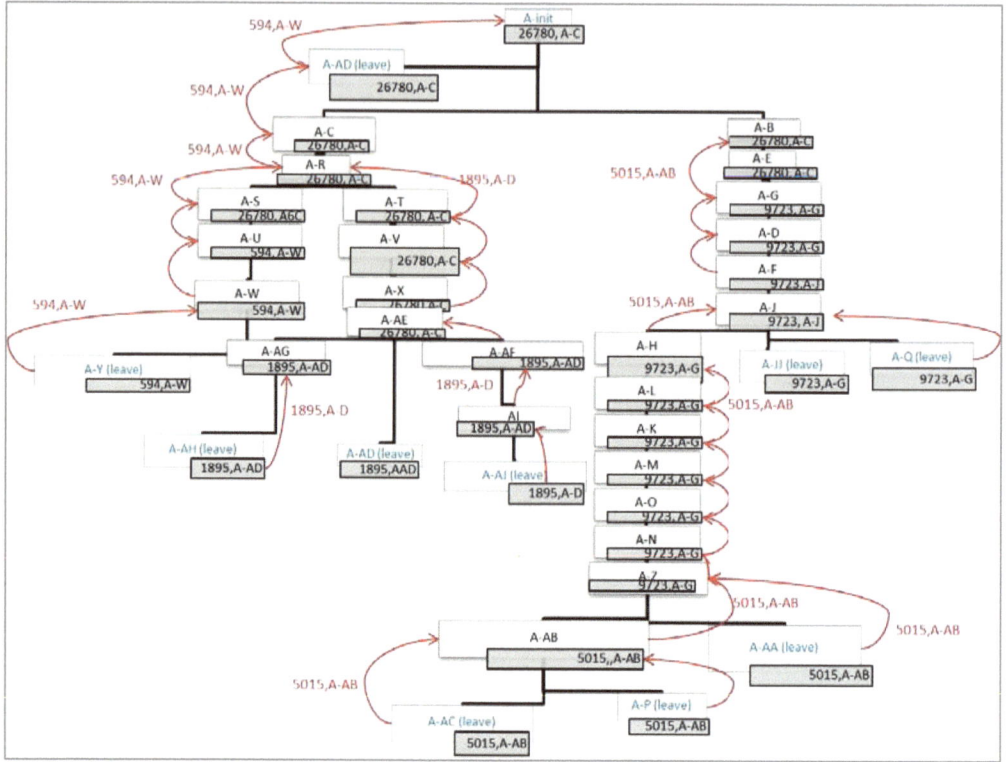

Fig. (10). Mechanism of the proposed algorithm in the simulation.

Data Visualization

Based on an Oracle database, we pictured data and clustered it using the Data Visualization Apps.® tool [67] based on the selected Dataset (Fig. **11**).

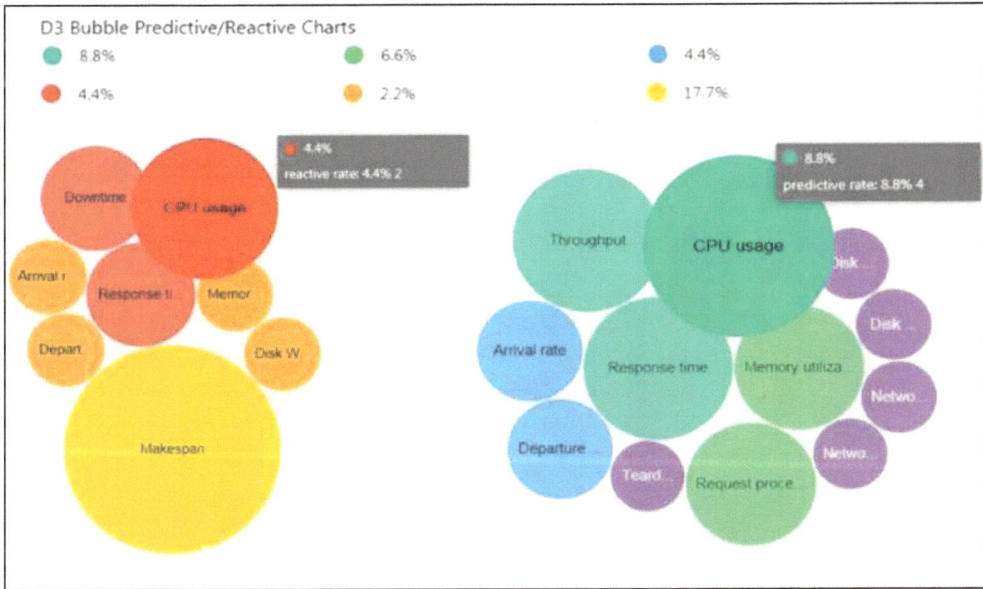

Fig. (11). Screenshot from Data visualization Apps.® [67].

From the bubble-clustering chart of Fig. (**11**), the set of selected methods comprises the top 2 most used predictive methods (MLL* and PBP' from Table **2**), the top 2 most used reactive methods (RSA* and RRA* from Table **2**), and the top 6 selected metrics (CPU usage, memory utilization, downtime, makespan (completion time), response time, and throughput).

Benchmarking n°1: PB-DNA Vs. Predictive and Reactive Methods (Robustness Challenge)

The Bar-charts of Fig. (**12**) illustrate the speedup gained in using our algorithm for each metric by comparing the selected reactive and predictive approaches.

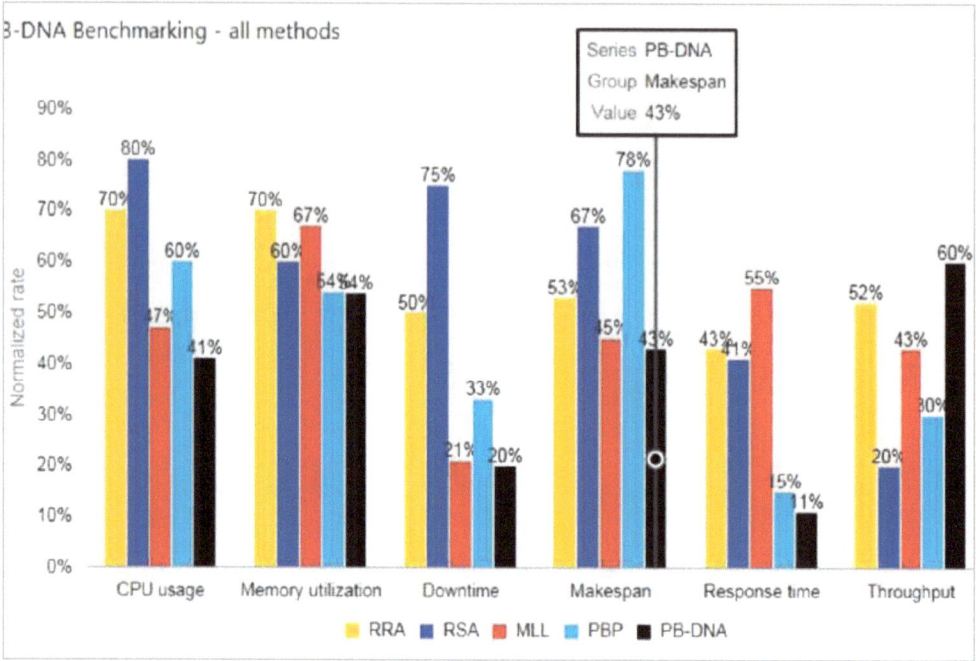

Fig. (12). PB-DNA benchmarking with PBP, MLL, RSA, RRA algorithms concerning the selected metrics (Screenshot from Data visualization Apps.® [67]).

The illustration in Fig. (**12**) makes the reactive methods (RRA* and RSA*) less performing than the PB-DNA. The job distributions reveal the unpredictable behavior due to a lack of real-time knowledge about the actual status in clusters, where predictive methods (MLL* and PBP*) show better performances but remain less efficient than PB-DNA. The proposed algorithm realizes the best robustness regarding all the metrics.

Benchmarking n°2: PB-DNA *Vs.* Predictive Methods (Scalability Challenge)

The experimental bench illustrates the scalability challenge (interpreted by the increasing number of jobs) for PB-DNA. The algorithm is compared with two predictive methods (MLL* and PBP*). The Lines-charts shown in our tool of Data Visualization Apps.® (Fig. **13**) demonstrate the advantage of PB-DNA in the performance of CPU usage metrics.

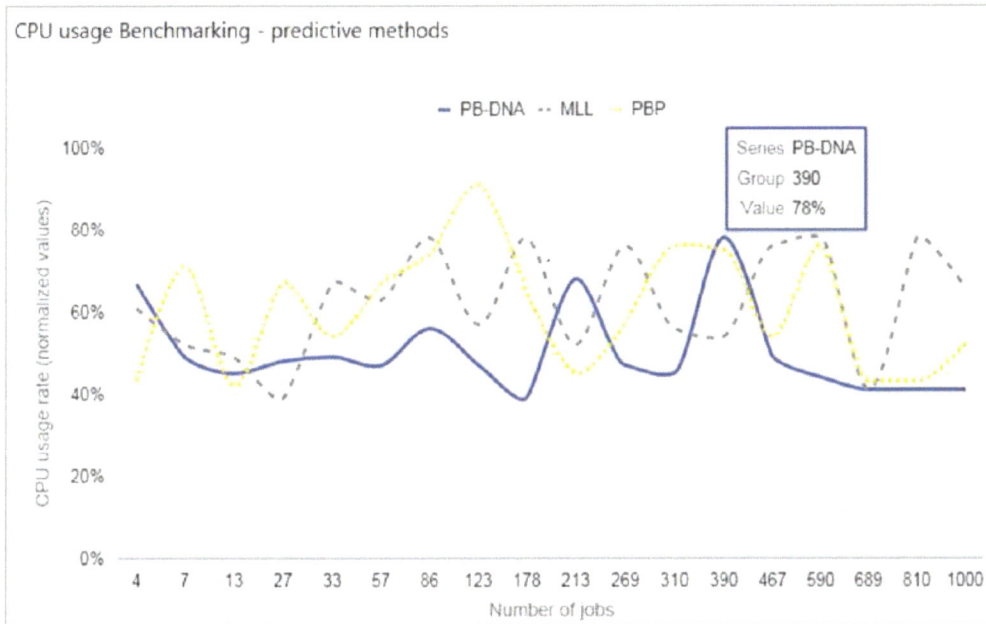

Fig. (13). PB-DNA is benchmarking with predictive methods MLL and PBP (scalability challenge) (Screenshot from Data visualization Apps® [67] illustrated in Fig. (**13**), the PB-DNA is more tolerant to scalability than the predictive methods. The two consecutive peaks of the CPU usage rate appear at 213 and 390 but do not exceed 78%. That is probably due to the unsuccessful propagation phase where the algorithm implies more interactions and increases the communication time in exchanging between the ant-agents. Despite this phenomenon, a good average performance is observed opposing to the other methods. As a result, the PB-DNA ensures more scalability and availability of services).

Benchmarking n°3: PB-DNA *vs.* other Reactive Methods (Resilience Challenge)

In the third case, the resilience is measured (represented by the downtime metric), referring to the incremental iterations comparing PB-DNA with the two other reactive methods (RRA* and RSA*). The Bar-charts in our Data Visualization Apps.® (Fig. **14**) indicate that the proposed algorithm causes less downtime during iterations.

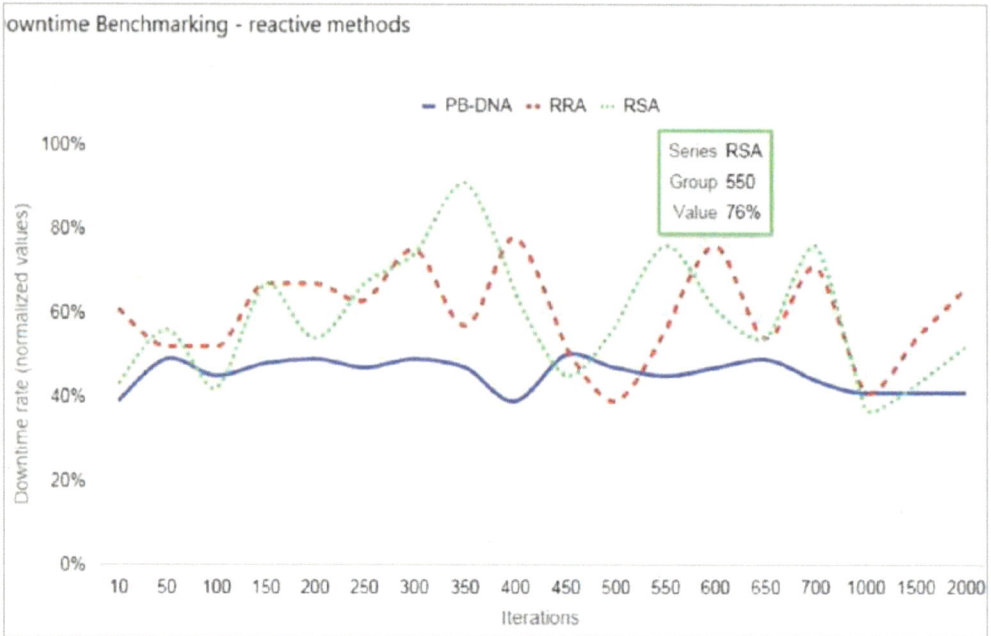

Fig. (14). PB-DNA benchmarking with other reactive methods RRA and RSA (resilience challenge) (Screenshot from Data visualization Apps.® [67]).

The Line-curves chart in Fig. (**14**) illustrates the optimal solution regarding the sensitivity to the iterations. For the PB-DNA, we observe it is nearly unchanging (~ 40%). However, RRA* and RSA* show irregular behavior and attain ~ 90% of downtimes because of the bottlenecks. The proposed algorithm proves robustness in reducing the failures compared to other reactive methods.

CONCLUSION AND FUTURE WORKS

Even with the spectacular expansion of Big Data processing in the modern parallel infrastructures for enterprises, the research works with traditional load balancing methods still in the early stages. This chapter proposes a new workload balancing approach to prove resilience. The proposed algorithm (called PB-DNA as the Propagation and Back-propagation Diffusion through Neighborhoods Algorithm) goes with the class of ant-inspired heuristics. This chapter includes the structure of our approach methodology with the simulation benches and the data visualization tools set up from a real dataset for experimentations.

The results achieved in these experiments are promising to continue the prototype in a natural production environment. We also think that the reliability of the proposed approach can increase by introducing a machine learning prediction such as Q-learning. Likewise, using an open meta-clustering organization may cause potential security issues for further research gaps and open discussions.

CONSENT OF PUBLICATION

Not applicable.

CONFLICT OF INTEREST

The author declares no conflict of interest, financial or otherwise.

ACKNOWLEDGEMENTS

Declared none.

REFERENCES

[1]   R. Sahal, J.G. Breslin, and M.I. Ali, "Big data and stream processing platforms for Industry 4.0 requirements mapping for a predictive maintenance use case", *J. Manuf. Syst.,* vol. 54, pp. 138-151, 2020.
        [http://dx.doi.org/10.1016/j.jmsy.2019.11.004]

[2]   G. Morana, R. Mikkilineni, and S. Keshan, "Cognitive workload management on globally interoperable network of clouds", *Int. J. Grid Util. Comput.,* vol. 10, no. 6, pp. 586-592, 2019.
        [http://dx.doi.org/10.1504/IJGUC.2019.102707]

[3]   S.P.M. Ziyath, and S. Senthilkumar, "MHO: Meta heuristic optimization applied task scheduling with load balancing technique for cloud infrastructure services", *J. Ambient Intell. Humaniz. Comput.,* pp. 1-10, 2020.

[4]   Apache Software Foundation. Apache, Available from: http://hadoop.apache.org/

[5]   M. Hanine, and E.H. Benlahmar, "A load-balancing approach using an improved simulated annealing algorithm", *J. Inf. Process. Syst.,* vol. 16, no. 1, pp. 132-144, 2020.

[6]   S. Chehbi-Gamoura, "Smart workload automation by swarm intelligence within the wide cloud computing", *Int. J. Mech. Eng.,* vol. 3, pp. 2163-2405, 2016.

[7]   Y. Ping, "Load balancing algorithms for big data flow classification based on heterogeneous computing in software definition networks", *J. Grid Comput.,* vol. 18, no. 2, pp. 275-291, 2020.
        [http://dx.doi.org/10.1007/s10723-020-09511-5]

[8]   H.A. Khattak, H. Arshad, S. Islam, G. Ahmed, S. Jabbar, A.M. Sharif, and S. Khalid, "Utilization and load balancing in fog servers for health applications", *EURASIP J. Wirel. Commun. Netw.,* vol. 2019, no. 1, p. 91, 2019.
        [http://dx.doi.org/10.1186/s13638-019-1395-3]

[9]   A. Akbar Neghabi, N. Jafari Navimipour, M. Hosseinzadeh, and A. Rezaee, "Nature-inspired meta-heuristic algorithms for solving the load balancing problem in the software-defined network", *Int. J. Commun. Syst.,* vol. 32, no. 4, p. e3875, 2019.
        [http://dx.doi.org/10.1002/dac.3875]

[10]   E.J. Ghomi, A.M. Rahmani, and N.N. Qader, "Load-balancing algorithms in cloud computing: A survey", *Journal of Network and Computer Applications,* 2017.

[11]   G. Rastogi, and R. Sushil, "Analytical literature survey on existing load balancing schemes in cloud computing", *2015 International Conference on Green Computing and Internet of Things (ICGCIoT),* 2015

[http://dx.doi.org/10.1109/ICGCIoT.2015.7380705]

[12]   N.K. Mishra, and N. Mishra, "Load balancing techniques: need, objectives and major challenges in cloud computing-a systematic review", *International Journal of Computer Applications*, 2015.

[13]   M.M. Abed, and M.F. Younis, "Developing load balancing for IoT-cloud computing based on advanced firefly and weighted round robin algorithms", *Baghdad Sci. J.,* no. 1, p. 16, 2019.

[14]   A. Abdulrahman, "An extended min-min scheduling algorithm in cloud computing", *I-manager's Journal on Civil Engineering,* vol. 5, no. 2, pp. 20-26, 2018.

[15]   P.P. Kumar, and V.K. Devi, "Efficiënt load balancing by optimized flexi max-min algorithm", *J. Phys. Conf. Ser.,* vol. 012051, no. 1, p. 1716, 2020.

[16]   G. Ramadhan, T.W. Purboyo, and R. Latuconsina, "Experimental model for load balancing in cloud computing using throttled algorithm", *Int. J. Appl. Eng. Res.,* vol. 13, no. 2, pp. 1139-1143, 2018.

[17]   K. Hanada, T. Wada, I. Masubuchi, T. Asai, and Y. Fujisaki, "Multi-agent consensus for distributed power dispatch with load balancing", *Asian J. Control,* vol. 23, no. 2, pp. 611-619, 2021. [http://dx.doi.org/10.1002/asjc.2257]

[18]   B. Mukhopadhyay, R. Bose, and S. Roy, "A novel approach to load balancing and cloud computing security using SSL in IaaS environment", *Int. J.,* no. 2, p. 9, 2020.

[19]   A. Kaur, B. Kaur, and D. Singh, "Meta-heuristic based framework for workflow load balancing in cloud environment", *Int. J. Inf. Technol.,* vol. 11, no. 1, pp. 119-125, 2019. [http://dx.doi.org/10.1007/s41870-018-0231-z]

[20]   V. Arulkumar, and N. Bhalaji, "Performance analysis of nature inspired load balancing algorithm in cloud environment", *J Amb. Intel. Hum. Comp.,* vol. 12, no. 3, pp. 3735-3742, 2021.

[21]   A.N. Ismael, M.A.A. Al-Asady, and H.A.A. Al-Asadi, "A Critical Comparative Review of Nature-Inspired Optimization Algorithms (NIOAs)", *International Journal of Simulation Systems Science & Technology,* no. 3, p. 21, 2020.

[22]   M. Gamal, R. Rizk, H. Mahdi, and B.E. Elnaghi, "Osmotic bio-inspired load balancing algorithm in cloud computing", *IEEE Access,* vol. 7, pp. 42735-42744, 2019.

[23]   A.A.S. Farrag, S. A. Mohamad, and M. El Sayed, "Swarm Intelligent Algorithms for solving load balancing in cloud computing", *Egyptian Computer Science Journal,* vol. 43, no. 1, pp. 45-57, 2019.

[24]   A. Yousefipour, A. Rahmani, and M. Jahanshahi, "Improving the load balancing and dynamic placement of virtual machines in cloud computing using particle swarm optimization algorithm", *International Journal of Engineering,* vol. 34, no. 6, pp. 1419-1429, 2021.

[25]   A. Ullah, N.M. Nawi, and M.H. Khan, "BAT algorithm used for load balancing purpose in cloud computing: An overview", *International Journal of High Performance Computing and Networking,* vol. 16, no. 1, pp. 43-54, 2020. [http://dx.doi.org/10.1504/IJHPCN.2020.110258]

[26]   A.R.I.F. Ullah, "Artificial bee colony algorithm used for load balancing in cloud computing: Review", *IAES International Journal of Artificial Intelligence (IJAI),* vol. 8, no. 2, p. 156, 2019. [http://dx.doi.org/10.11591/ijai.v8.i2.pp156-167]

[27]   V.V. Bhavya, K.P. Rejina, and A.S. Mahesh, "An intensification of honey bee foraging load balancing algorithm in cloud computing", *International Journal of Pure and Applied Mathematics,* vol. 114, no. 11, pp. 127-136, 2017.

[28]   S. Asghari, and N. J. Navimipour, "Cloud service composition using an inverted ant colony optimisation algorithm", *Int. J Bio.-Inspir. Com.,* vol. 13, no. 4, pp. 257-268, 2019. [http://dx.doi.org/10.1504/IJBIC.2019.100139]

[29]   A.C. Adamuthe, and J.T. Patil, "Differential evolution algorithm for optimizing virtual machine placement problem in cloud computing", *Int. J. Intell. Syst. Appl.,* no. 7, p. 10, 2018.

[http://dx.doi.org/10.5815/ijisa.2018.07.06]

[30]   S. Sandhya, and N.K. Cauvery, "Dynamic Load Balancing Based on Genetic Algorithm", *Int. J. Innov. Technol. Explor. Eng.*, vol. 176-179, no. 11, p. 8, 2019.

[31]   G. Kiruthiga, and S. M. Vennila, "Bio inspired optimization algorithms for scheduling task in cloud environment", *International Journal of Future Generation Communication and Networking,* vol. 13, no. 3, pp. 666-674, 2020.

[32]   A.A. Tadi, and Z. Aghajanloo, "Load Balancing in Cloud Computing using Cuckoo Optimization Algorithm", *Journal of Innovative Research in Engineering Sciences,* no. 4, p. 4, 2018.

[33]   V. Punitha, and C. Mala, "Traffic classification for efficient load balancing in server cluster using deep learning technique", *J. Supercomput.*, vol. 77, no. 8, pp. 8038-8062, 2021.
         [http://dx.doi.org/10.1007/s11227-020-03613-3]

[34]   S. Moreno-Alvarez, J. M. Haut, M. E. Paoletti, J. A. Rico-Gallego, J. C. Diaz-Martin, and J. Plaza, "Training deep neural networks: A static load balancing approach", *The Journal of Supercomputing,* vol. 76, no. 12, pp. 9739-9754, 2020.
         [http://dx.doi.org/10.1007/s11227-020-03200-6]

[35]   N. Al Sallami, and S. Al Alousi, "Load balancing with neural network", *Int. J. Adv. Comput. Sci. Appl.,* no. 10, p. 4, 2013.

[36]   R. Kumar, and T. Prashar, "A bio-inspired hybrid algorithm for effective load balancing in cloud computing", *International Journal of Cloud Computing,* vol. 5, no. 3, pp. 218-246, 2016.
         [http://dx.doi.org/10.1504/IJCC.2016.080047]

[37]   M. Ahmad, A. Hameed, F. Ullah, I. Wahid, S.U. Rehman, and H.A. Khattak, "A bio-inspired clustering in mobile adhoc networks for internet of things based on honey bee and genetic algorithm", *J. Ambient Intell. Humaniz. Comput.,* pp. 1-15, 2018.

[38]   P. Lajevardy, F. A. Parand, H. Rashidi, and H. Rahimi, "A hybrid method for load forecasting in smart grid based on neural networks and cuckoo search optimization approach", *International Journal of Renewable Energy Resources,* vol. 5, no. 1, pp. 13-20, 2017.

[39]   B.A. Mahafzah, and B.A. Jaradat, "The hybrid dynamic parallel scheduling algorithm for load balancing on chained-cubic tree interconnection networks", *The Journal of Supercomputing,* vol. 52, no. 3, pp. 224-252, 2010.
         [http://dx.doi.org/10.1007/s11227-009-0288-3]

[40]   D.R. Edla, A. Lipare, R. Cheruku, and V. Kuppili, "An efficient load balancing of gateways using improved shuffled frog leaping algorithm and novel fitness function for WSNs", *IEEE Sensors Journal,* vol. 17, no. 20, pp. 6724-6733, 2017.
         [http://dx.doi.org/10.1109/JSEN.2017.2750696]

[41]   S. Yu, K. Li, and Y. Xu, "A DAG task scheduling scheme on heterogeneous cluster systems using discrete IWO algorithm", *Journal of computational science,* vol. 26, pp. 307-317, 2018.
         [http://dx.doi.org/10.1016/j.jocs.2016.09.008]

[42]   H. Shen, H. Zhao, and Z. Yang, "Adaptive resource schedule method in cloud computing system based on improved artificial fish swarm", *Journal of Computational and Theoretical Nanoscience,* vol. 13, no. 4, pp. 2556-2561, 2016.
         [http://dx.doi.org/10.1166/jctn.2016.4617]

[43]   V.S. Bhadoria, N.S. Pal, and V. Shrivastava, "Artificial immune system based approach for size and location optimization of distributed generation in distribution system", *International Journal of System Assurance Engineering and Management,* vol. 10, no. 3, pp. 339-349, 2019.
         [http://dx.doi.org/10.1007/s13198-019-00779-9]

[44]   M.S. Vivek, and P. Manohar, "A load balancing model using bio inspired firefly algorithm in cloud computing", *IACSIT Int. J. Eng. Technol.,* vol. 7, pp. 671-674, 2017.

[45]　S. Chehbi-Gamoura, "Cross-management of risks in big data-driven industries by the use of fuzzy cognitive maps", *Logistique & Management,* vol. 28, no. 2, pp. 155-166, 2020.
[http://dx.doi.org/10.1080/12507970.2019.1686437]

[46]　M.A. Elsharkawey, and H.E. Refaat, "MLRTS: Multi-level real-time scheduling algorithm for load balancing in fog computing environment", *International Journal of Modern Education and Computer Science,* vol. 11, no. 2, p. 1, 2018.
[http://dx.doi.org/10.5815/ijmecs.2018.02.01]

[47]　S. Chehbi-Gamoura, R. Derrouiche, D. Damand, and M. Barth, "Insights from big Data Analytics in supply chain management: an all-inclusive literature review using the SCOR model", *Prod. Plann. Contr.,* vol. 31, no. 5, pp. 355-382, 2020.
[http://dx.doi.org/10.1080/09537287.2019.1639839]

[48]　K. Kungumaraj, and T. Ravichandran, "An efficient load balancing algorithm for a distributed computer system", *International Journal of Computer Technology and Applications,* vol. 2, no. 6, 2011.

[49]　M. Brahmwar, M. Kumar, and G. Sikka, "Tolhit – A scheduling algorithm for hadoop cluster", *Procedia Comput. Sci.,* vol. 89, pp. 203-208, 2016.
[http://dx.doi.org/10.1016/j.procs.2016.06.043]

[50]　E.D. Raj, and L.D.D. Babu, "A two pass scheduling policy based resource allocation for mapreduce", *Procedia Comput. Sci.,* vol. 46, pp. 627-634, 2015.
[http://dx.doi.org/10.1016/j.procs.2015.02.110]

[51]　A.M. AbdelAziz, K.K.A. Ghany, T.H.A. Soliman, and A.A.E.M. Sewisy, "A parallel multi-objective swarm intelligence framework for big data analysis", *Int. J. Comput. Appl. Technol.,* vol. 63, no. 3, pp. 200-212, 2020.
[http://dx.doi.org/10.1504/IJCAT.2020.109342]

[52]　L. Brezočnik, I. Fister, and V. Podgorelec, "Swarm intelligence algorithms for feature selection: A review", *Appl. Sci. (Basel),* vol. 8, no. 9, p. 1521, 2018.
[http://dx.doi.org/10.3390/app8091521]

[53]　X.S. Yang, S. Deb, Y.X. Zhao, S. Fong, and X. He, "Swarm intelligence: Past, present and future", *Soft Comput.,* vol. 22, no. 18, pp. 5923-5933, 2018.
[http://dx.doi.org/10.1007/s00500-017-2810-5]

[54]　A. Chakraborty, and A.K. Kar, "Swarm intelligence: A review of algorithms", In: *Nature-Inspired Computing and Optimization* Springer: Cham, Switzerland, 2017, pp. 475-494.

[55]　B. Liu, J. Li, W. Lin, W. Bai, P. Li, and Q. Gao, "K☐PSO: An improved PSO☐based container scheduling algorithm for big data applications", *Int. J. Netw. Manage.,* p. e2092, 2020.

[56]　A. Asghari, M.K. Sohrabi, and F. Yaghmaee, "Task scheduling, resource provisioning, and load balancing on scientific workflows using parallel SARSA reinforcement learning agents and genetic algorithm", *J. Supercomput.,* pp. 1-29, 2020.

[57]　S. Chehbi-Gamoura, "A cloud-based approach for cross-management of disaster plans: Managing risk in networked enterprises", In: *In Emergency and Disaster Management: Concepts, Methodologies, Tools, and Applications, by Information Resources Management Association.* IGI Global, 2019, pp. 857-881.
[http://dx.doi.org/10.4018/978-1-5225-6195-8.ch040]

[58]　H.R. Boveiri, "A novel ACO-based static task scheduling approach for multiprocessor environments", *International Journal of Computational Intelligence Systems,* vol. 9, no. 5, pp. 800-811, 2016.
[http://dx.doi.org/10.1080/18756891.2016.1237181]

[59]　M.A. Fardbastani, and M. Sharifi, "Scalable complex event processing using adaptive load balancing", *J. Syst. Softw.,* vol. 149, pp. 305-317, 2019.
[http://dx.doi.org/10.1016/j.jss.2018.12.012]

[60] J. Eckroth, "A course on big data analytics", *J. Parallel Distrib. Comput.,* vol. 118, pp. 166-176, 2018.
[http://dx.doi.org/10.1016/j.jpdc.2018.02.019]

[61] D. Medhat, A.H. Yousef, and C. Salama, "Cost-aware load balancing for multilingual record linkage using MapReduce", *Ain Shams Eng. J.,* vol. 11, no. 2, pp. 419-433, 2020.
[http://dx.doi.org/10.1016/j.asej.2019.08.009]

[62] R. Hickling, W. Wei, and L. Lambert, "Acoustic communication by imported fire ants", *J. Acoust. Soc. Am.,* vol. 99, no. 4, pp. 2557-2574, 1996.
[http://dx.doi.org/10.1121/1.415201]

[63] R. Hickling, and R.L. Brown, "Analysis of acoustic communication by ants", *J. Acoust. Soc. Am.,* vol. 108, no. 4, pp. 1920-1929, 2000.
[http://dx.doi.org/10.1121/1.1290515] [PMID: 11051518]

[64] S.D. Leonhardt, F. Menzel, V. Nehring, and T. Schmitt, "Ecology and evolution of communication in social insects", *Cell,* vol. 164, no. 6, pp. 1277-1287, 2016.
[http://dx.doi.org/10.1016/j.cell.2016.01.035] [PMID: 26967293]

[65] H. Fahmi, M. Zarlis, E.B. Nababan, and P. Sihombing, "Ant Colony Optimization (ACO) algorithm for determining the nearest route search in distribution of light food production", *J. Phys. Conf. Ser.,* vol. 1566, no. 1, p. 012045, 2020.
[http://dx.doi.org/10.1088/1742-6596/1566/1/012045]

[66] H. Williams, and M. Bishop, "Stochastic diffusion search: A comparison of swarm intelligence parameter estimation algorithms with ransac", *Algorithms,* vol. 7, no. 2, pp. 206-228, 2014.
[http://dx.doi.org/10.3390/a7020206]

[67] Data Visualization Apps, Available from: https://sites.google.com/site/publicationsresults/

[68] Oracle Inc, Available from: https://apex.oracle.com/en/

[69] SNCF Open Data, Available from: https://data.sncf.com

[70] M. Bensalah, A. Elouadi, and H. Mharzi, "Building information modeling & sustainability in railway", *International Congress on Modeling, Optimization and Planning,* 2019pp. 16-20

CHAPTER 17

Computational Algorithms and Study of Elastic Artery and their Applications

Anil Kumar[1,*]

[1] Department of Mathematics, Swami Vivekananda Subharti University, Meerut (UP), India

Abstract: The concept of computational algorithmic and sustainable elastic artery evaluation and its impact on different variables such as structural and morphological variations and its applications are explored in this chapter. The Crank-Nicolson approach has solved the mathematical goal of the equation. The result is explained in the case of blood supply in elastic vessels while the electromagnetic effect is established. In this computational analysis, the discrepancy between the arteries and veins attached to the elastic arteries in the blood vessel is easier than determining the presence or absence of the elastic layer within the vessel. The obtained results in the analysis are in relatively accurate compliance with the computational findings in this chapter. The findings may be applicable to cases of pulmonary edema, *etc.*

Keywords: Blood flow, Computational algorithm, Crank- Nicolson scheme, Elastic artery, Shear rate, Vessels.

INTRODUCTION

The renal cortex of an elastic artery (conducting artery or conduit artery) includes numerous collagen and elastin filaments, enabling it to stretch in response to each pulse. The Windkessel effect results from this elasticity, which effectively prevents the pressure in the arteries from being relatively constant despite the pulsating nature of the blood flow. The largest arteries in the body, those proximal to the heart, are elastic arteries. They give rise to distributing arteries that are medium-sized vessels (or muscular arteries). The body's elastic artery system consists of the pulmonary arteries, the aorta, and branches. In recent years, researchers have investigated the physiology of laminated composite materials from the context of continuous bio-mechanics. Elastic arteries are already adapted to receive blood throughout the outflow region of the heart at relatively high pressure. For example, for the measurement of friction and flow waves along with

---

* **Corresponding author Anil Kumar**: Department of Mathematics, Swami Vivekananda Subharti University, Meerut (UP), India; E-mail: dranilkumar73@rediffmail.com

Rijwan Khan, Pawan Sharma, Sugam Sharma and Santosh Kumar (Eds.)

an artery, the magnificent area of the aorta, pulmonary artery, and aorta is validated. Over the past few decades, the significance of arterial flow phenomena such as secondary flow, recirculation and instability, flow separation movement, low and oscillatory wall shear intensity, and long particle residence duration for the development of atherosclerosis has become glaringly evident.

Some scientific research papers have discussed algorithmic and sustainable blood assessment through elastic arteries. Thurston [1] profounded the thermal behaviour of blood using non-Newtonian, poroelastic, and rheology models and their applications. Liepsch and Moravec [2] examined the simulated fluid flow and discovered the change in pressure velocity to the measured velocity of a Newtonian fluid with the simulated fluid's high shear rate viscosity. Both experimental and numerical, the two-dimensional steady state and pulsatile flow developed by Rindt *et al.* [3] were considered.

Nazemi *et al.* [4] made a major contribution to the discovery of atherosclerosis. Rodkiewicz *et al.* [5] reported two significant non-Newtonian blood designs in predicting the heart rate, including the heart rate, including the aorta. They found that blood yield stress has no effect on the allocation of velocity or wall shear tension. Chaturani and Palanisamy [6] examined the pulsatile flow of blood into a rigid artery under the influence of tissue displacement of a Newtonian fluid.

In straight and curved rigid arterial models under established oscillating flow conditions, a study [7] used renal blood to examine the relationships between haematocrit concentrations and wall shear rate patterns.

The results revealed that the improved viscosity of the aqueous glycerol solution created the wall cut-rate waveform. Initial blood enhanced by haematocrit has the same size and shape. It is concluded that the change in shear stress is mainly due to a viscosity improvement rather than a blood elasticity change. The blood flow was described by Perktold *et al.* [8] in a stenosis vessel as an inviscid laminar flow in a flexible tube. Sharma and Kapoor [9] used the finite element process to scientifically analyse the blood circulation through the artery and their applications.

Dutta and Tarbell [10] explored two hemorheological models that demonstrate the effects of shear-thinning viscosity and oscillating flow viscoelasticity [11] and found their structural and physical adaptation models of arteries. Based on the principle of the layer boundary layer, two methods were used by Botnar *et al.* [12] to explore the specifics of the influence of different flow patterns on the initiation and amplification of atherosclerotic plaque deposition based on the correspondence between estimations of Ultrasound speed and theoretical predictions. Sharma *et al.* [17] used the finite element Galerkin method to analyse the mathematical flow of blood through the artery. Kumar *et al.* [18] developed the design and analysis of elastic arterial supply. These models are used in accordance with the Newtonian model to study the sine-wave movement of rigid and elastic straight arteries. Bazilevs *et al.* [13] founded a computer model for the modelling of cerebellar embolism implementations precise to physicians and also explained a novel paradigm for blood algorithm prestress of the vessel tissue. Yang and Murfee [14] discovered that the angular shape modifications are much more complicated than just channel depletion in adult rat herniation frameworks obtained from spontaneous hypertensives. High blood pressure networks contained an excessive level of blood vessel interactions compared with cerebral perfusion systems, which would diminish channel sensitivity via limited pathways from either low or high closer to zero sides of the system.

Bianchi *et al.* [15] have concentrated on certain experimental mechanical studies in order to challenge the model. The results obtained by computation using finite element simulation have been correlated. Impact of viscous dissipation on magneto-hydro-dynamics unsteady motion across longitudinal transparent media through persistent suction [11]. Kumar [19] has analytical results for a porous consequence on oscillatory blood flow that acts as a Newtonian flow to fully appreciate the irregular flow conditions of blood in a locally constricted blood vessel. Kumar [20] investigated a Mathematical and Mechanical Analysis of Arterial Blood Flow with Porous Effects. Kumar and Agarwal [21] have two different non-Newtonian models for blood flow. One displays only shear-thinning viscosity while the other displays both shear-thinning viscosity and oscillating flow viscous-elasticity.

In recent research, we are interested in understanding blood flow in an elastic artery in the electromagnetic effects. We use the appropriate finite difference approach to measure the effects of shear-thinning viscous-elasticity of blood on the flow phenomenon in the electromagnetic effects in large elastic arteries to extend the local flow estimation to include non-Newtonian for hemorheology.

DYNAMICAL STUDY OF PULSATILE FLOW

In a rigid artery, circulatory flow builds, and the fluid fluctuates in volume. r is, a uniform increase and decrease in the velocity flow pattern for multiple places along the vessel appear with each heartbeat introduced to the fluid. As discussed before, to regulate heart production, the distance across an artery is regulated. In this way, it has been described that the concern of exhibiting artery flow has been limited to the region of the blood vessel where there is no significant stable shrinkage and no fanning or existence of vasodilatation.

PERFORMANCE OF PULSATILE FLOW IN ELASTIC ARTERIES

The main effects of tube elasticity are as follows:

a. With the exception of the axial direction, from all the arterial wall deflection, the velocity vector has a radial direction.
b. The pressure moves in an axial direction, and the shape of the pressure-time curve can modify with z, but there is also a radial direction in the pressure gradient.
c. They must describe and integrate the elastic equations for wall deformation.

Shear and elastic material continuity at the point of intersection must be generated by the boundary conditions. We assume, using condition (1), we get

$$v_r = v_r(r,z,t), \; v_\theta = 0 \, ;$$
$$v_z = v_z(r\,z\,t), \; p = p(r,z,t) \tag{1}$$

The above equations (1) simplify the continuity equations and then the motion equation would be given as if the inertial terms were disregarded:

$$\frac{\partial v_r}{\partial t} = -\frac{1}{\rho}\frac{\partial p}{\partial r} + \frac{\mu}{\rho}\left(\frac{\partial^2 v_r}{\partial r^2} + \frac{1}{r}\frac{\partial v_r}{\partial r} - \frac{v_r}{r} + \frac{\partial^2 v_r}{\partial z^2}\right) \tag{2}$$

$$\frac{\partial v_z}{\partial t} = -\frac{1}{\rho}\frac{\partial p}{\partial r} + \frac{\mu}{\rho}\left(\frac{\partial^2 v_z}{\partial r^2} + \frac{1}{r}\frac{\partial v_z}{\partial r} - \frac{v_z}{r} + \frac{\partial^2 v_z}{\partial z^2}\right) \tag{3}$$

$$\frac{\partial}{\partial r}(v_r r) + \frac{\partial v_z}{\partial z} = 0 \tag{4}$$

Then, reduced equation are

$$\rho_w \frac{\partial^2 u_r}{\partial t^2} = G\left(\frac{\partial^2 u_r}{\partial r^2} + \frac{1}{r}\frac{\partial u_r}{\partial r} - \frac{u_r}{r} + \frac{\partial^2 u_r}{\partial z^2}\right) - \frac{\partial \Omega}{\partial r} \tag{5}$$

$$\rho_w \frac{\partial^2 u_z}{\partial t^2} = G\left(\frac{\partial^2 u_z}{\partial r^2} + \frac{1}{r}\frac{\partial u_z}{\partial r} + \frac{\partial^2 u_z}{\partial z^2}\right) - \frac{\partial \Omega}{\partial z} \tag{6}$$

$$\frac{\partial}{\partial r}(u_r r) + \frac{\partial u_z}{\partial z} = 0 \tag{7}$$

In deriving [5] and [6] by using the above equation we get

$$\rho_w \frac{\partial^2 u_r}{\partial t^2} = \frac{\partial \tau_{rr}}{\partial r} + \frac{\partial \tau_{rz}}{\partial z} + \frac{\tau_{rr} - \tau_{\theta\theta}}{r} \tag{8}$$

$$\rho_w \frac{\partial^2 u_z}{\partial t^2} = \frac{\partial \tau_{zr}}{\partial r} + \frac{\partial \tau_{zz}}{\partial z} + \frac{\tau_{rz}}{r} \tag{9}$$

$$\tau_{ij} = 2G\varepsilon_{ij} - \Omega\delta_{ij}$$

$$\varepsilon_{rr} = \frac{\partial u_r}{\partial r}, \; \varepsilon_{rz} = \frac{1}{2}\left(\frac{\partial u_r}{\partial z} + \frac{\partial u_r}{\partial r}\right) = \varepsilon_{zr}$$

$$\varepsilon_{\theta\theta} = \frac{\partial u_r}{\partial z}, \; \varepsilon_{r\theta} = 0 = \varepsilon_{\theta r} \tag{10}$$

$$\varepsilon_{zz} = \frac{\partial u_z}{\partial z}, \; \varepsilon_{z\theta} = 0 = \varepsilon_{\theta z}$$

The boundary conditions are as given below:

(i) Here the velocity profile symmetry is

$$v_r = 0, \; v_z' = 0 \quad \text{for r} = 0 \tag{11}$$

(ii) The continuity of movement in the fluid's interaction is provided by

$$v_r = \frac{\partial u_r}{\partial t}, v_z = \frac{\partial u_z}{\partial t} \quad \text{at r} = a \tag{12}$$

(iii) The continuity of shear stress and radial stress on the interior layer are given by

$$\mu\left(\frac{\partial v_r}{\partial z}+\frac{\partial v_z}{\partial r}\right)=G\left(\frac{\partial u_r}{\partial z}+\frac{\partial u_z}{\partial r}\right) \text{ at } r=a$$

(13)

$$-p+2\mu\frac{\partial v_r}{\partial r}=-\Omega+2z\left(\frac{\partial u_r}{\partial r}\right) \text{ at } r=a$$

(iv) The outer wall basic assumption is constrained, allowed radially and axially by

$$G\left(\frac{\partial u_r}{\partial z}+\frac{\partial u_z}{\partial r}\right)=0, \quad -\Omega+2G\frac{\partial u_r}{\partial r}=0 \text{, at } r=b$$

(14)

Although the inner wall is disturbed, we have assumed that the disturbance is very small, and boundary conditions can be applied to the undisturbed inner artery wall. We assume that the outer wall is constrained in the radial and axial directions, and the same condition [16] is applied to the undisturbed radius of the outer wall. To solve equations (5,6) through trivial solutions, we assume the form:

$$v_r=v_1(r)e^{-iy_n z}e^{inwt}$$

$$v_z=v_2(r)e^{-iy_n z}e^{inwt}$$

(15)

$$p=P(r)e^{-iy_n z}e^{inwt}$$

Putting all these value in equation (5-7), we get

$$\frac{d^2v_1}{dr^2}+\frac{1}{r}\frac{dv_1}{dr}-\frac{v_1}{r^2}-y_n^2 v_1-\frac{P}{\mu}inwv_1=\frac{1}{\mu}\frac{dP}{dr}$$

(16)

$$\frac{d^2v_2}{dr^2}+\frac{1}{r}\frac{dv_2}{dr}-\frac{v_1}{r^2}-y_n^2 v_2-\frac{P}{\mu}inwv_2=-\frac{iy_n P}{\mu}$$

(17)

$$- iv_2 y_n + \frac{dv_1}{dr} + \frac{v_1}{r^2} = 0$$

(18)

$$\text{Setting} \quad k_n{}^2 = \frac{inw}{\gamma} + y_n{}^2$$

Then reduced to these equations as given below:

$$-\frac{d^2 v_1}{d\, r^2} + \frac{1}{r}\frac{dv_1}{dr} - (k_n{}^2 + \frac{1}{r^2})v_1 = \frac{1}{\mu}\frac{dP}{dr} \qquad -\frac{d^2 v_2}{d\, r^2} + \frac{1}{r}\frac{dv_2}{dr} - k_n{}^2 v_2 = -\frac{iy_n P}{\mu}$$

(19)

$$-\frac{d}{dr}(rv_1) = iy_n rv_2$$

Now expressions are as given below:

$$X = \alpha_1 J_1(iy_n r) + \alpha_2 J_1(ik_n r)$$

(20)

$$\text{and} \quad Y = \beta_1 J_0(iy_n r) + \beta_2 J_0(ik_n r)$$

Satisfy the equations (20)

$$\frac{d^2 X}{d\, r^2} + \frac{1}{r}\frac{dX}{dr} - (k_n{}^2 + \frac{1}{r^2})X = -\frac{iwn}{\gamma}\alpha_1 J_1(iy_n r)$$

(21)

$$-\frac{d^2 Y}{d\, r^2} + \frac{1}{r}\frac{dY}{dr} - k_n{}^2 Y = -\frac{iwn}{\gamma}\beta_1 J_0(iy_n r)$$

From equation 16-21, we get

$$v_1(r) = -i[A_1 y_n J_1(iy_n r) + A_2 y_n J_1(ik_n r)]$$

$$v_2(r) = -i[A_1 y_n J_0(iy_n r) + A_2 y_n J_0(ik_n r)] \qquad (22)$$

$$P(r) = -A_1 inwP J_0(iy_n r)$$

Since our basic equation is linear, the general solutions are

$$v_r(r) = -\sum_{n=0} i[A_1 y_n J_1(iy_n r) + A_2 y_n J_1(ik_n r)]e^{(inwt - iy_n z)}$$

$$v_z(r) = -\sum_{n=0} i[A_1 y_n J_0(iy_n r) + A_2 y_n J_0(ik_n r)]e^{(inwt - iy_n z)} \qquad (23)$$

$$p = -\sum_{n=0} iA_1 \rho nwP J_0(iy_n r)e^{(inwt - iy_n z)}$$

The volumetric flow rate for n^{th} harmonic is given by

$$Q_n = \int_0^a 2\pi r v_z dr = -2\pi a[A_1 J_1(iy_n a) + A_2 J_1(ik_n a)]e^{(inwt - iy_n z)} \qquad (24)$$

$$Z_n = \frac{-(inw\rho)[iy_n a J_n(iy_n a)]A_1}{2\pi a[A_1 J_1(iy_n a) A_2 J_1(ik_n a)]} \qquad (25)$$

The previous discussion shows that although we have considered the material as Hooke's elastic material, the problem of pulsating flow in an elastic tube is complex.

PERFORMANCE OF WAVE REFLECTIONS BRANCHING AND TETHERING

The above computational model does not fully illustrate the real physical flow of arteries because there are too many simplifications. Reflex is an important factor affecting the pulse flow in the veins. Since the pulsating flow spreads downward into the general cylinder in the form of waves, any obstacles will appear in the cylinder. For example, when the vein branches into two smaller routes, it will reflect the movement of the wave. The reflected wave and the forward wave mix together to form an incredible flow field.

Combining these wave elements into the above dialogue, you can get a numerical model that can properly collect pulsatile pulse blood flow. Clinical imaging can be used to determine clear stretch structures in the supply route. From these pictures, models can be inferred to predict blood flow, especially in fan-shaped structures. These models can better understand blood flow components and blood flow abnormalities, such as atherosclerosis.

COMPUTATIONAL TECHNIQUES FOR BLOOD FLOW

With the popularization of high-speed digital computers, the recent development of computational fluid dynamics has flourished. When possible, analytical solutions will produce closed-form expressions that provide continuous changes in the dependent variable throughout the domain (called grid points). But these solutions are not always feasible. This is why digital methods must be used. With the development of high-speed access, in the continuous development in the past, people are urgently discovering fluid dynamics.

Reasonable arrangements (if imaginable) will produce closed structural connections that will continue to provide various regional factors throughout the area (called grid points). Nevertheless, these arrangements are not always conceivable. This is why a digital strategy is needed.

Finite Difference Technique

The finite difference method is widely used and perhaps the oldest method. For example, if $z_{i,j}$ represents the value of the dependent variable z at the point (i,j) with the coordinate axis (xi, yj), where g can be the velocity component of fluid, temperature, or any other dependent variable, then by using series expansion, we get

$$z_{i+1,j} = z_{i,j} + \left(\frac{\partial z}{\partial x}\right)_{i,j} \Delta x + \left(\frac{\partial^2 z}{\partial x^2}\right)_{i,j} \frac{(\Delta x)^2}{L2} + \left(\frac{\partial^3 z}{\partial x^3}\right)_{i,j} \frac{(\Delta x)^3}{L3} + - - - - - - \quad (26)$$

The geometrical structure of finite difference grid is in Fig. (**1**). The equation (26) is second-order accurate if the second-order small terms and higher-order small terms are neglected. In that case, (26) becomes,

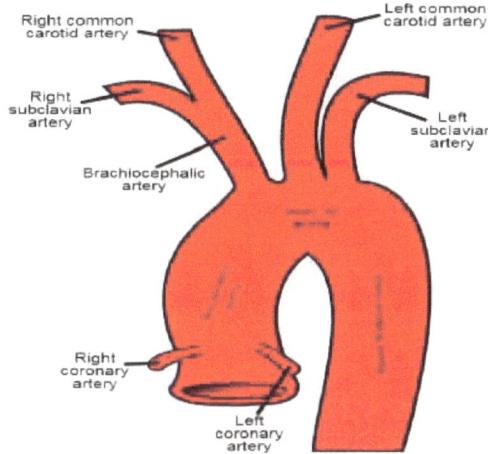

Fig. (1). Aorta the elastic arteries of physiology diagram.

$$z_{i+1,j} = z_{i,j} + \left(\frac{\partial z}{\partial x}\right)_{i,j} \Delta x$$

$$\left(\frac{\partial z}{\partial x}\right)_{i,j} = \frac{z_{i+1,j} - z_{i,j}}{\Delta x} + O(\Delta x)$$

(27)

The equation (27) is first-order forward approximation formula. Similarly, first-order backward difference formula can be written as,

$$\left(\frac{\partial z}{\partial x}\right)_{i,j} = \frac{z_{i,j} - z_{i-1,j}}{\Delta x} + O(\Delta x) \quad (28)$$

From equations (27) and (28) we have

$$\left(\frac{\partial z}{\partial x}\right)_{i,j} = \frac{z_{i+1,j} - z_{i-1,j}}{2\Delta x} + O(\Delta x)^2 \tag{29}$$

Equation (29) is second order central difference formula for the derivative $\left(\dfrac{\partial z}{\partial x}\right)$ at grid point (i, j). Similarly, the formula for $\left(\dfrac{\partial^2 z}{\partial x^2}\right)_{i,j}$ is,

$$\left(\frac{\partial^2 z}{\partial x^2}\right)_{i,j} = \frac{z_{i+1,j} - 2z_{i,j} + z_{i-1,j}}{(\Delta x)^2} + O(\Delta x)^2 \tag{30}$$

Equation (30) is known as second –order central second difference approximation.

The finite difference expression for the mixed derivative $\left(\dfrac{\partial^2 z}{\partial x\, \partial y}\right)$ at grid point (i, j) is given below,

$$\left(\frac{\partial^{22} z}{\partial x\, \partial y}\right)_{i,j} = \frac{1}{4\Delta x \Delta y}\left[z_{i+1,j+1} + z_{i-1,j-1} - z_{i+1,j-1} + z_{i-1,j+1}\right] + O\left[(\Delta x)^2, (\Delta y)^2\right] \tag{31}$$

Many other difference approximations can be obtained for derivatives of even higher order. A numerical solution is one in which all error components are bounded. A numerical solution is said to be convergent if the discretization error approaches zero, as the mesh is refined.

Crank –Nicolson Scheme

Partial differential equations are decomposed in the sense of a finite difference procedure. At only discrete points in the domain, the numerical solutions would bring attention, called grid points. Examine the performance, partial differential equation as given below,

$$\frac{\partial v}{\partial t} = \frac{\partial^2 v}{\partial x^2} \tag{32}$$

In computational fluid dynamics, the index for a time typically occurs as a subscript here n represents values at a time (t), and n+1 represents values at (t+Δt). For one spatial dimension considered here, the subscripts also denote the position of the grid scheme.

$$\frac{v_i^{n+1} - v_i^n}{\Delta t} = \frac{1}{2}\left[\begin{array}{l} v_{i+1}^{n+1} + v_{i+1}^n - \\ 2v_{i+1}^n - 2v_i^n + v_{i-1}^{n+1} + v_{i-1}^n \end{array} \right] \tag{33}$$

The Crank-Nicolson technique of a given partial differential equation is known as equation (33). The unknown v_i^{n+1} can be represented at the time index n by the known quantity. A solution of v_i^{n+1} cannot lead to the grid point i itself. 1. The algebraic equation system can find the unknown v_i^{n+1} and simultaneously help to solve all i.

There are some other technical solutions besides finite differences, but we only use the above solutions in the above work to find the Navier-Stokes equation solution involved in the model considered.

BASIC EQUATION OF BLOOD FLOW

The basic equation of whole blood has been proposed as follows:

$$\tau^{1/2} = \eta_c \gamma^{1/2} + \tau_y^{1/2}; \qquad |\tau| > \tau_y \tag{34}$$

$$\gamma = 0, \qquad |\tau| < \tau_y \tag{35}$$

The reduce to Power law model is

$$\tau = k\gamma^n \tag{36}$$

The model parameters have been generated through experimental viscosity measurement and viscous-elastic data of 43 percent haematocrit anti-coagulated human blood. The model of the governing equation is described as [Thurston (1)]

$$\tau_p + T_p \frac{\partial \tau_p}{\partial t} = \frac{\eta_{0,p}}{1+(\gamma T_p)^2} \gamma \tag{37}$$

$$\tau = \sum_{p=1}^{6} \tau_p + \eta_\infty \gamma \tag{38}$$

Where n_∞ is the finishing statement of intent viscosity, t_p is the pth material's shear stress. Geometrical structure of elastic and muscular arteries in Fig. (2).

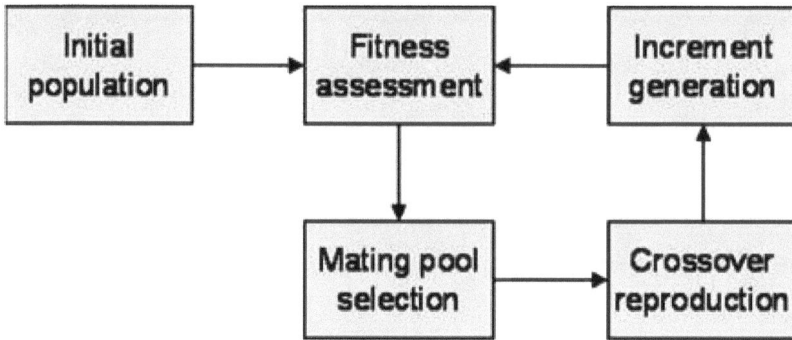

Fig. (2). Flowchart for blood flow of arterial behavior for genetic algorithm.

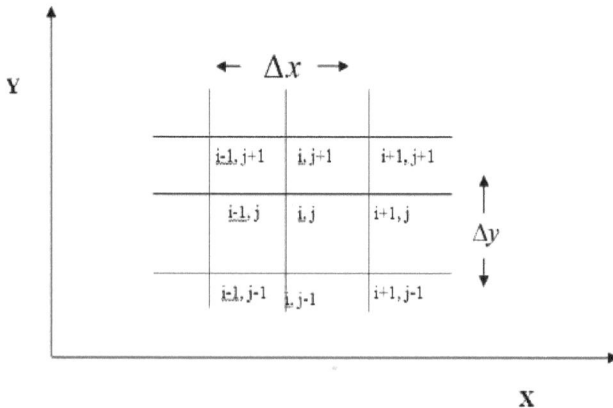

Fig. (3). Geometrical structure of finite-difference grid in a two-dimensional region.

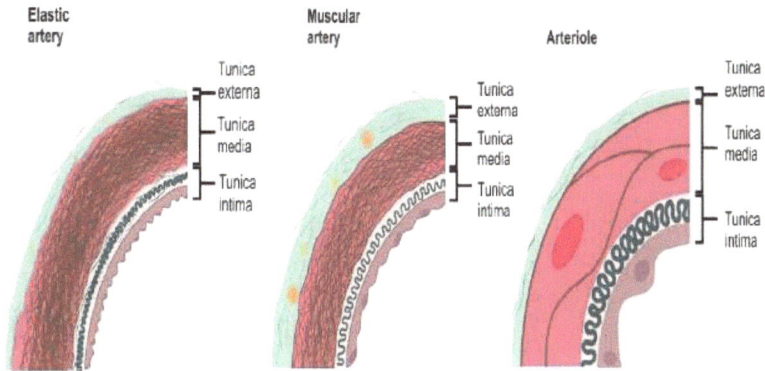

Fig. (4). Geometrical structure of elastic and muscular arteries.

DESCRIPTION OF MATHEMATICAL MODEL

In this investigation, the electromagnetic effects of non-Newtonian fluid in the epithelial fluid flow through elastic arteries. It is possible to escape the electromagnetic field which is formed. In cylindrical coordinates, the governing momentum equation and the continuity equation are, as shown below:

$$\frac{\partial w}{\partial t} + u\frac{\partial w}{\partial r} + w\frac{\partial w}{\partial z} = -\frac{1}{\rho}\frac{\partial P}{\partial z} - \frac{1}{\rho r}\frac{\partial}{\partial r}(r\tau) - Mw \tag{39}$$

$$\frac{\partial p}{\partial r} = 0 \tag{40}$$

and

$$\frac{\partial}{\partial r}(ru) + \frac{\partial w}{\partial z} = 0 \tag{41}$$

In the elastic model by [Milnor (1989)]:

$$R=R(p) \tag{42}$$

Here

$$w_r = 0 \quad \text{u is zero, for} \quad r = 0, \tag{43}$$

and

$$w = 0, \quad u = R_t \quad \text{for} \quad r = R \tag{44}$$

Put $\xi = \dfrac{r}{R(t,z)}$, then reduced equations are [Milnor(1989)].

$$\frac{\partial w}{\partial t} + (\frac{u}{r} - \frac{\xi}{R})\frac{\partial w}{\partial \xi} - \frac{w}{R}(\frac{\partial u}{\partial \xi} + \frac{u}{\xi}) = -\frac{1}{\rho}\frac{\partial P}{\partial z} - \frac{1}{\rho R}\frac{\partial \tau}{\partial \xi} - \frac{\tau}{\rho R \xi} - Mw,$$

$$\tag{45}$$

$$\frac{\partial w}{\partial t} = -\frac{1}{\rho}\frac{\partial P}{\partial z} - \frac{1}{\rho R}\frac{\partial \tau}{\partial \xi} - \frac{\tau}{\rho R \xi} + (\frac{\xi}{R}\frac{\partial R}{\partial t} - \frac{u}{r})\frac{\partial w}{\partial \xi} + \frac{w}{R}(\frac{\partial u}{\partial \xi} + \frac{u}{\xi}) - Mw,$$

Boundary condition are:

$$w_\xi = 0, \quad u = 0 \quad \text{for} \quad \xi = 0, \tag{46}$$

$$w = 0, \quad u = R_t \quad \text{for} \quad \xi = 1, \tag{47}$$

Now, equation (36) is

$$\tau = -k\left|\frac{\partial w}{\partial r}\right|^{n-1}\frac{\partial w}{\partial r}, \tag{48}$$

Then Power law is

$$\tau = -\frac{k}{R}\left|\frac{\frac{\partial w}{\partial \xi}}{R}\right|^{n-1}\frac{\partial w}{\partial \xi}, \tag{49}$$

$$\tau = \sum_{p=1}^{6} \tau_p + \eta_\infty \gamma \tag{50}$$

And

$$\frac{\partial P(t)}{\partial z} = \overline{K} + k \, \cos(\omega t) \tag{51}$$

$$R(t) = \overline{R}(1 + k_R \cos(\omega t - \phi)) \tag{52}$$

$$Q(t) = \overline{Q}(1 + k_\theta \cos(\omega t - \theta)) \tag{53}$$

COMPUTATIONAL ALGORITHM

Each great application is established upon a decent calculation. Calculations are the basic pieces of any application. In this part, you can locate a concise introduction of the principle calculations used for separating and putting away planned highlights of histology pictures. The discrete spatial form of the governing equation may still be obtained using the Crank-Nicholson scheme. The time index is widely chosen as a subscript in computational fluid dynamics, where n describes the time condition (t), and (n + 1) describes the next time stage condition. Its equation for semi-discrete control is shown below.

$$\frac{w_i^{n+1} - w_i^n}{\Delta t} = \frac{1}{\rho_i^n} \frac{P_i^{n+1} - P_i^n}{\Delta z} - \frac{1}{\rho_i^n R_i^n} \frac{\tau_i^{n+1} - \tau_i^n}{\Delta \xi} \tag{54}$$

$$- \frac{\tau_i^n}{\rho_i \, \xi_i^n R_i^n} + [\frac{\xi_i^n}{R_i^n} (\frac{R_i^{n+1} - R_i^n}{2\Delta t}) - \frac{u_i^n}{R_i^n}] \frac{w_i^{n+1} - w_i^n}{\Delta \xi}$$

Where

$$+ \frac{w_i^n}{R_i^n} \{(\frac{u_i^{n+1} - u_i^n}{\Delta \xi}) - \frac{u_i^n}{\xi_i^n}\} - M_i^n w_i^n \tag{55}$$

The conditions of discretized boundary are

$$(\frac{\partial w}{\partial \xi})_i = \frac{w_i^{n+1} - w_i^n}{\Delta \xi} + O(\Delta \xi)^2 = 0, \ at \ \xi = 0 \tag{56}$$

$$w = 0, \ u = (\frac{\partial R}{\partial t})_i = \frac{R_i^{n+1} - R_i^{n}}{\Delta t} \ , \ at \ \ \xi = 1 \quad\quad (57)$$

In order to ensure that the convection and diffusion terms have accurate second-order solutions in time and space, this method is used for temporary discretization.

RESULTS AND DISCUSSION

In this section, the computational algorithmic and reliable sustainable assessment of elastic artery is taken into consideration along with electromagnetic effects to evaluate wall shear stress, flow rate, and velocity profile. Fig. (**5**) found that the average wall shear friction of all the models considered is the same. For the distinct characteristics of the P-Q reflection coefficient, Fig. (**6**) illustrates the correlation between the variables flow velocity and the average pressure gradient at 1.9 cm. Fig. (**7**) stated that non-effect directly impacts the swell.

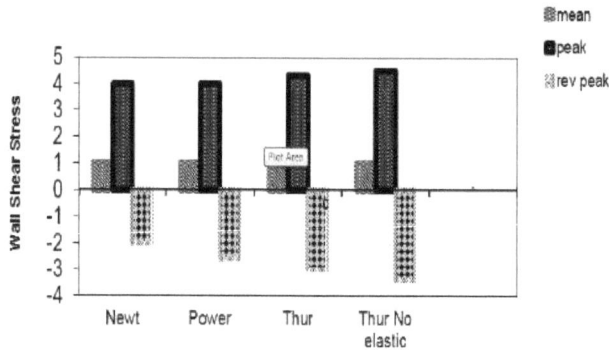

Fig. (5). Relation of the wall shear stress with the electromagnetic effects of a specific pressure gradient amplitude of the multiple rheological models in rigid arteries.

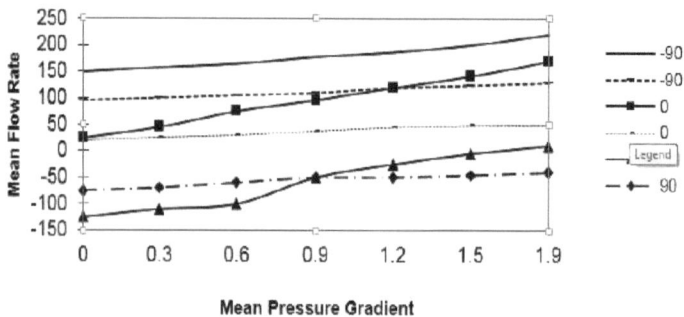

Fig. (6). Average flow rate vs mean gradient of pressure in elastic arteries.

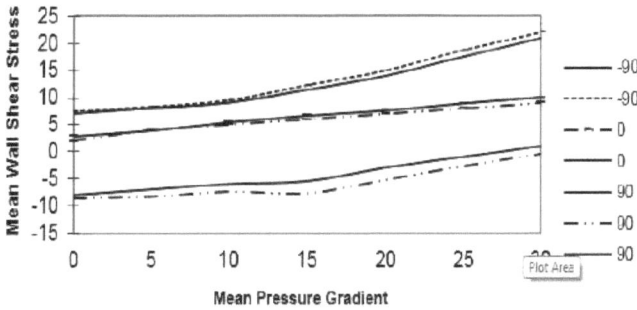

Fig. (7). For varying factors versus a mean pressure gradient, reasonable shear stress in an elastic vessel.

There is little consequence of the wall shear friction on the shear thinning conduct. In Fig. (**8**), the average wall shear stress and average flow velocity are shown. In reference to electromagnetic effects to measure the mean wall shear stress in the elastic artery, the average flow velocity instead of the average pressure gradient is used.

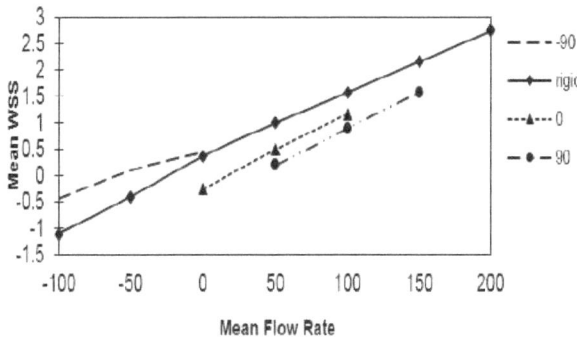

Fig. (8). For the Power law model shear stress against the normal flow rate.

The magnitude of the first harmonic flow rate scaled against the average pressure gradient is shown in Fig. (**9**). In Fig. (**10**), the wall shear pressure amplitude limitations are shown on the average pressure gradient at a fixed pressure gradient amplitude.

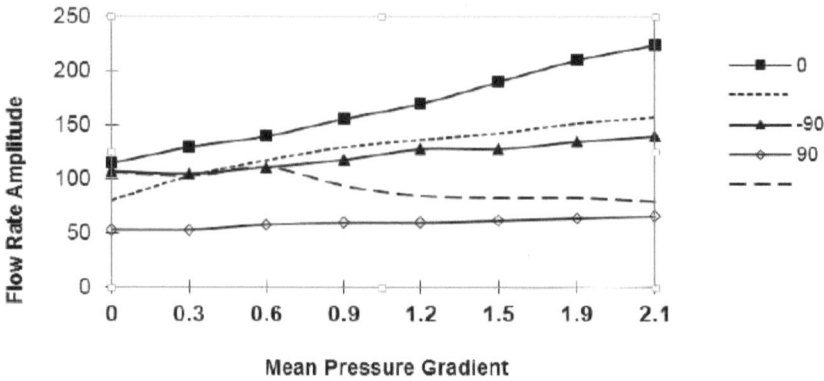

Fig. (9). The flow rate vs. the mean continuum of stress and the elastic arteries.

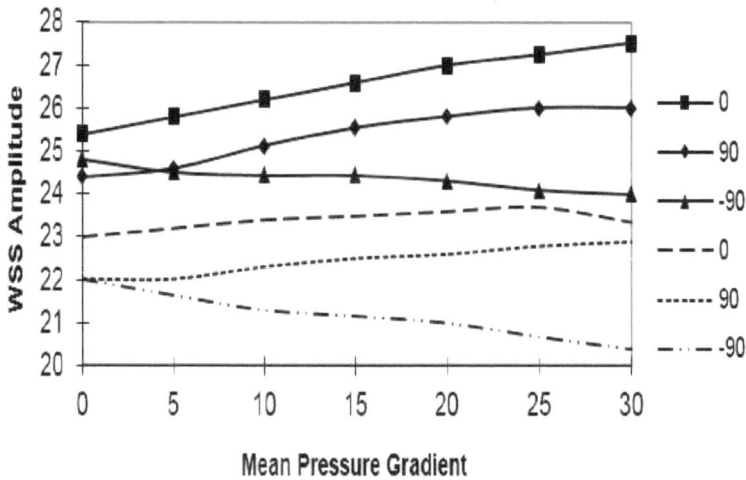

Fig. (10). Wall shear stress amplitude and phase vs standard flow velocity in an elastic artery.

The effect of rheology on the wall shear tension waveform after patching the flow waveform is demonstrated in Fig. (**11**). Especially in comparison with Newtonian fluids, the average wall shear stress of power-law fluids increases, and its constant value is constant for rigid tubes with the transverse magnetic field of Newtonian fluids.

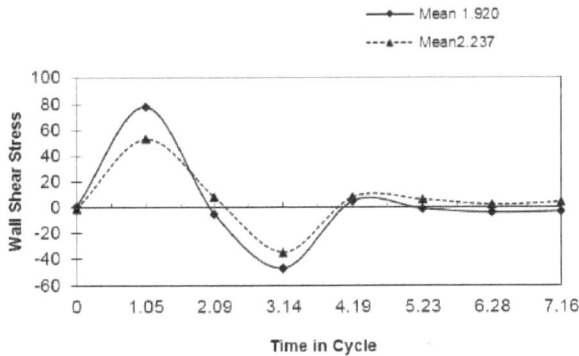

Fig. (11). For an elastic artery model, wall shear stress waveforms.

These are in line with the pulmonary flow simulation. Under the same pressure gradient, in particular sine flow simulation, the wall shear stress amplitude of the power law fluid is smaller than that of the Newtonian Fluid (Fig. 5)

CONCLUSION

Blood flow has been studied, and the electromagnetic effects of blood flow through the elastic artery have been analysed for the effects of various factors such as geometry and surface irregularities. The electromagnetic effects change the flow field inside the tube. The flow rate and wall shear stress estimate improved greatly when the fluid variable was removed from the viscoelastic model to result in an oscillatory model.

The governing equation has also been solved by Crank-Nicolson technique. In the case of blood in elastic arteries, while preserving the electromagnetic effect, this consequence is described. The average wall shear stress of the Power law model for the biological fluid flow in the aorta will increase, but the peak wall shear stress will decrease. However, the development of a Newtonian fluid will also fit the flow rate curve. As a result, the proposed algorithms can be used to generate more complex blood flow in elastic arteries while also enhancing computing performance.

APPLICATIONS

In this chapter, developing computational algorithmic and reliable methods for sustainable assessment of elastic arteries has many important applications. Elastic materials are composed of elastomers, collagen and smooth muscles with different elastic properties, and the condition of the outer wall is not realistic enough. We can foresee that further complications may occur. In this communication, we focus on the mathematical modelling of the three-dimensional layering of composite materials. In particular, we study the anatomy (destruction) of the arterial layer caused due to non-physiological loads (for example, mechanical operations). A simplified two-dimensional example was calculated to test the proposed calculation technique, including some important features of biomechanical applications. The first example is a flow in an elliptical cavity, and the second example is a flow through a channel with elastic walls. Obtaining an effective mathematical model for the branch structure of the arterial network allows virtual investigations. Through simulation, local fluid diseases can be better understood. Similarly, flow shear stress, and other flow dynamics can be approximated to determine the specifications of artificial blood vessel grafts and other biomedical materials. The pulsed ultrasonic flowmeter can be used to verify the mathematical model of the blood flow distribution on a specific artery cross-section. Perhaps more exciting is that the laser Doppler flowmeter can help you understand the hemodynamics of capillaries. The model of elastic arterial flow will provide insight into the transport of oxygen and nutrients to tissue cells. This creates a significantly higher resistance and further hinders blood flow.

CONSENT FOR PUBLICATION

Not applicable.

CONFLICT OF INTEREST

The author confirms that this chapter's contents have no conflict of interest.

ACKNOWLEDGEMENTS

The authors express their appreciation to the Swami VivekanandaSubharti University, Meerut (UP), India, for providing facilities and support for the completion of this work. The related authors are grateful to the learned ones and the referees for their fruitful ideas for the reformation of this work.

REFERENCES

[1]   G.B. Thurston, "Rheological parameters for the viscosity viscoelasticity and thixotropy of blood", *Biorheology,* vol. 16, no. 3, pp. 149-162, 1979.
[http://dx.doi.org/10.3233/BIR-1979-16303] [PMID: 508925]

[2]   D. Liepsch, and S. Moravec, "Pulsatile flow of non-Newtonian fluid in distensible models of human arteries", *Biorheology,* vol. 21, no. 4, pp. 571-586, 1984.
[http://dx.doi.org/10.3233/BIR-1984-21416] [PMID: 6487768]

[3]   C. C. M. Rindt, F. N., Van de Vosse, Van, A. A. Steenhoven, J. D, Janssen and RS Reneman,, " A numerical and experimental analysis of the human carotid bifurcation", *J. Biomech.,* vol. 20, pp. 499-509, 1987.
[http://dx.doi.org/10.1016/0021-9290(87)90250-8]

[4] M. Nazemi, C. Kleinstreuer, and J.P. Archie Jr, "Pulsatile two-dimensional flow and plaque formation in a carotid artery bifurcation", *J. Biomech.*, vol. 23, no. 10, pp. 1031-1037, 1990.
[http://dx.doi.org/10.1016/0021-9290(90)90318-W] [PMID: 2229086]

[5] C.M. Rodkiewicz, P. Sinha, and J.S. Kennedy, "On the application of a constitutive equation for whole human blood", *J. Biomech. Eng.*, vol. 112, no. 2, pp. 198-206, 1990.
[http://dx.doi.org/10.1115/1.2891172] [PMID: 2345451]

[6] P. Chaturani, and V. Palanisamy, "Pulsatile flow of power-law fluid model for blood flow under periodic body acceleration", *Biorheology*, vol. 27, no. 5, pp. 747-758, 1990.
[http://dx.doi.org/10.3233/BIR-1990-27510] [PMID: 2271765]

[7] R. K. Saket, "Reliability of convective diffusion process in porous blood vessels", *International Journal of Chemical Product and Process Modelling*, vol. 3, . Article (25), Canada 2008.

[8] K. Perktold, E. Thurner, and T. Kenner, "Flow and stress characteristics in rigid walled and compliant carotid artery bifurcation models", *Med. Biol. Eng. Comput.*, vol. 32, no. 1, pp. 19-26, 1994.
[http://dx.doi.org/10.1007/BF02512474] [PMID: 8182957]

[9] G.C. Sharma, and J. Kapoor, "Finite element computations of two-dimensional arterial flow in the presence of a transverse magnetic field", *International J. for Numerical Methods in Fluid Dynamics*, vol. 20, pp. 1153-1161, 1995.
[http://dx.doi.org/10.1002/fld.1650201004]

[10] A. Dutta, and J.M. Tarbell, "Influence of non-Newtonian behaviour of blood on flow in an elastic artery model", *J. Biomech. Eng.*, vol. 118, pp. 111-119, 1996.
[http://dx.doi.org/10.1115/1.2795936] [PMID: 8833082]

[11] S.P. Agarwal, and A. Kumar, "Effect of Viscous Dissipation on MHD Unsteady Flow through Vertical Porous Medium with Constant Suction", *Advances in Mathematics: Scientific Journal 9*, no. 9, pp. 7065-7073, 2020.

[12] R. Botnar, G. Rappitsch, M.B. Scheidegger, D. Liepsch, K. Perktold, and P. Boesiger, "Hemodynamics in the carotid artery bifurcation: a comparison between numerical simulations and in vitro MRI measurements", *J. Biomech.*, vol. 33, no. 2, pp. 137-144, 2000.
[http://dx.doi.org/10.1016/S0021-9290(99)00164-5] [PMID: 10653026]

[13] Y. Bazilevs, M.C. Hsu, Y. Zhang, W. Wang, T. Kvamsdal, S. Hentschel, and J.G. Isaksen, "Computational vascular fluid-structure interaction: methodology and application to cerebral aneurysms", *Biomech. Model. Mechanobiol.*, vol. 9, no. 4, pp. 481-498, 2010.
[http://dx.doi.org/10.1007/s10237-010-0189-7] [PMID: 20111978]

[14] M. Yang, and W.L. Murfee, "The effect of microvascular pattern alterations on network resistance in spontaneously hypertensive rats", *Med. Biol. Eng. Comput.*, vol. 50, no. 6, pp. 585-593, 2012.
[http://dx.doi.org/10.1007/s11517-012-0912-x] [PMID: 22562369]

[15] D. Bianchi, C. Morin, and P. Badel, "Morin, C and Badel, P: Computational modelling of arterial tissues: coupling multi scale homogenization strategies and finite element formulation", *Comput. Methods Biomech. Biomed. Engin.*, vol. 22, no. sup1, pp. S22-S24, 2020.
[http://dx.doi.org/10.1080/10255842.2020.1713464]

[16] D. Tang, C. Yang, Y. Huang, and D.N. Ku, "Wall stress and strain analysis using a three-dimensional thick wall model with fluid-structure interactions for blood flow in carotid arteries with stenoses", *Comput. Struc.*, vol. 72, pp. 341-377, 1999.
[http://dx.doi.org/10.1016/S0045-7949(99)00009-7]

[17] G.C. Anil Kumar, "Sharma and Madhu Jain: Finite element Galerkins approach for a computational study of arterial flow", *Appl. Math. Mech.*, vol. 22, no. 9, pp. 1012-1018, 2001.
[http://dx.doi.org/10.1007/BF02438319]

[18] A. Kumar, C.L. Varshney, and G.C. Sharma, "Computational technique for flow in blood vessels with porous effects", *Appl. Math. Mech.*, vol. 26, no. 1, pp. 63-72, 2005.

[http://dx.doi.org/10.1007/BF02438366]

[19]   A. Kumar, "Mathematical model for porous influence through mild stenosis thrombosis over delivery of oxygen and nutrients arteries", *Advances in Mathematics: Scientific Journal,* vol. 10, no. 1, pp. 463-469, 2021.

[20]   "Mathematical and Mechanical Analysis of Arterial Blood Flow with Porous Effects", *International Journal of Computational Modeling and Physical Sciences,* vol. 1, no. 1, 2020.

[21]   A. Kumar, and S.P. Agrawal, "Computational study of blood flow through elastic arteries with porous effects", *3rd Soft Computing for Problem Solving (Soc Pros 2013),* vol. 1, pp. 1-10, 2013.

CHAPTER 18

Performance Analysis of CCS on Inclined Plane using Fuzzy-PID Controller

Saty Prakash Yadav[1,*] and **Amit Kumar Singh**[1]

[1] *Department of Instrumentation and Control Engineering, Dr. B.R. Ambedkar NIT Jalandhar, India*

Abstract: Nowadays, in the automation industries, the Cruise Control System (CCS) is one of the essential aspects, and it is necessary to have a well-designed controller that can suit a new improvement in innovation. The CCS is a very famous and important model in control system engineering. The fundamental objective of CCS is to regulate vehicle speed depending upon the chosen speed. The CCS is an example of a close loop control system. Speedometer is utilized in the feedback path for measurement of the speed. This is a simple model used to solve the many problems of drivers like road accidents, weariness, *etc*. In this paper, we analyze the performance of different controllers such as Proportional-Integral-Derivative (PID) controller, the fuzzy logic controller (FLC) and the fuzzy-PID (F-PID) controller in the different situations on the road, such as friction, road grad, or angle of inclination to attain the chosen speed of the vehicles. The tuning of PID parameters is done using the method of Ziegler-Nichols, and FLC uses the gaussian Membership Function (MF) in this paper. The MF is a graph that lies between zero and one. It indicates the mapping of every point in the input state and the values of MF. The mathematical model of this system is considers the road grad and the friction. Finally, in this paper, we see the response of models with and without a controller in different situations on the road.

Keywords: CCS, Fuzzy, Fuzzy-PID controller, PID controller.

INTRODUCTION

In many countries, CCS is also known as Tempomat Control System (TCS) or Speed Control System (SCS), which automatically controls the speed of any vehicle. The main objective of this system is to regulate the speed of the vehicle that depends upon the desired speed. The speed can be measured with the help of a speed sensor like a speedometer. The CCS uses a servomechanism (the close loop system and converts the mechanical motion into power) that uses a choke into the motor to provide a fixed speed as set by the drivers. These types of

* **Corresponding author Satya Prakash Yadav:** Department of Instrumentation and Control Engineering, Dr. B.R. Ambedkar NIT Jalandhar, India; E-mail: satyprakash13ei46@gmail.com

Rijwan Khan, Pawan Sharma, Sugam Sharma and Santosh Kumar (Eds.)

systems are used to solve the huge problems that are faced by the drivers, such as tiredness and road problems, *etc.,* [1 - 3]. The basic operation of this system has many steps. First, the sensors sense the vehicle's speed and then speed is measured. Now, the error detectors compared this speed with the standard speed that is provided by the drivers. After that, it is decided whether the car will be accelerated or deaccelerated, depending on the error value.

The speed measurement sensor is connected to the feedback path, and this sensor is known as the speed sensor or speedometer. Due to the feedback path, it is a closed-loop system. The CCS can be performed only with velocity control [4]. The performance of the normal CCS for passenger cars is not good due to the traffic density, road condition, *etc.* At present, this type of system minimizes the working of the drivers as stabling gear-pedal and the continuity seeing the needle of the speedometer. This system is not suitable when the speed suddenly changes, and it is the major disadvantage of CCS [3 - 5].

In the SCS, the decision of many controls can be improved by considering the differences as the mass of the vehicle, friction coefficient, drag coefficient, and the road grade can be estimated. The friction coefficient and the angle of inclination are the main sources of peripheral loading [5]. The internal parameters such as the mass, road grade, and drag coefficient can affect the performance, energy efficiency, ride quality, and handling. The two parameters, road grade and the vehicle's mass, are directly associated with the load that can be estimated accurately and reliably. The mass of Vehicle can be directly related to all normal forces that can affect the lateral forces and the longitudinal forces [6].

The CCS has become a very popular option in many states, where the highways are long, flat, open, have good road conditions, *etc.* There are three main advantages of this system as follows:

1: It maintains a constant speed limit throughout the journey,

2: It increases the driver's comfort for the long-distance trip,

3: It improves fuel efficiency [7].

In 1900, this system was utilized in the autos by the scientist Wilson-Pilcher and followed long term during the 1910s by the scientist Peerless. The scientist James Watt and Matthew Boulton used this model to control the steam engine in 1788 [8]. Ralph Teetor developed the advanced version of CCS, known as the Modern speed control, in 1948 [9]. The M-Sgt Frank J. Riley, the patent for the specific speed, was filed in 1950 [10, 11]. American Motors presented a less-valued programmed auto control framework for the enormous -measured vehicles or engines with the auto transmission in 1965 [12]. In 2009, the advancements of this system forced the drivers for maintaining a significant distance on the roadway. CCS can play the role in speed control [13, 14].

One of the most well-known regards the automation of vehicles is the Automated Highway System (AHS). The advancement of the transmission and highway program has been one of the effective examinations done on the AHS with the help of California Partners. The task was balanced on expressways driving a particular prepared vehicle in a different path from another physically determined vehicle. Many projects are done on the longitudinal and horizontal control of the speed control with the many types of research. In 1997, the highway AHS was effectively shown in tests which are done by San Diego in California [15]. The advanced version of conventional CCS is the ACC system. The conventional CCS keeps up the ideal speed of the vehicle which is given by the driver and the ACC framework additionally keeps up a suitable relative separation to the lead vehicle. If the forward vehicles are recognized to be driven at a slower speed than the ideal speed, the system delays the swarm vehicles and keeps up a suitable relative separation, which relies upon the conditions of the swarm vehicles and nature. The extension version of ACC is the Cooperative ACC (CACC) system. The Stop and go system is excellent in urban driving condition where the ACC can't be effortlessly used [16]. Likewise, in urban areas driving, the conditions are more mind-boggling, and necessities for the stricter sensor data [17]. Since it is relied upon to be functional at low speed in urban driving circumstances, an option for responding to visits is available for removing in and leading vehicles for stopping and going system. The CACC is another upgraded variant of the ACC. Now, the CACC uses correspondence among the vehicles or potentially between vehicles and street structures. This correspondence permits the system on a solitary vehicle to get data about an unfamiliar vehicle in the units. Many research projects are done on the CACC near traffic lights and the communication that shows the CACC can improve the traffic stream [18] and the string constancy [19]. When the spacing error increases, the string stabilities show the major role. An unexpected acceleration or de-acceleration of the primary vehicle of the sub-division unit incorporated a mistake for the following vehicles. The magnitude of the error is increased for a later vehicle if the sub-system is unstable.

The main objective of CACCS is to have vehicle drive in the method platoon-wise, within a small room that lie between the individual vehicles; such a methodology may cause circumstances where combining vehicles won't have the option to discover a hole to converge. Our assumption is that the system is working in an environment where the non-automated and automated vehicles are combined. Our framework should have the option to adapt to non-automation vehicles. After a very long time, many researchers added more functions to this system; therefore speed becomes controllable when combined with an automated and non-automated vehicle system [20].

The CACCS has the benefits of V-to-V communication that permit connected and automated vehicles to frame units and the distance covered within shorter progress between them. When the vehicle's information is shared in a distributed manner, then a connected and automated system has the advantage for short-range communication as follows:

Increases the driver's safety as it takes a shorter time than normal driving.

Due to the minimization of time or distance between the vehicles, the road capacity will be increased;

Due to optimization of velocity and the aerodynamics coefficient, energy consumption and pollutant emissions are reduced.

The most important limitations that the driver must be controlled during free-flow are large traffic on the specific highways and the busy time like the vehicle's speed and the time-progress to the previous vehicles. It is essential to get up-an--go in the safe mode and maintain enough time-progress to the vehicle ahead to avoid a rear-end collision. Lee (1976) examined that the safe time depends upon the speed, visibility, and braking capacity and is generally larger than 2 seconds. Many research works are done to optimize the time, as in 1970 by Treiterer and Nemeth and in 1980 by Von Buseck, Evans et.al. When the speed of the motor was in the range of 40-70 mph, then the chosen time-headway will be kept at 1 second, as examined by Van Winsum and Heino in 1996 [21]. The application of CACCS may be reduced due to the minimum advance time and space [22]. A large number of projects of CACCS are done that depend on the real-time project and simulation are discussed [23 - 25]. The basic three challenges in the operation of CACCS are given blow:

To maintain a certain distance between vehicles, it is essential to share the vehicle's information like acceleration, speed and position. There are necessary to establish a network for communication among vehicles and rode side.

The CACCS interface for the driver must address how a driver will communicate with the CACC framework depending upon the driving conditions and CACCS created guidelines.

Control procedures in the vehicle are important so that communication between vehicles can be coordinated to get suitable activities to keep up safe CACCS tasks

Just as control activities if there should arise an occurrence of CACCS disappointment.

The main objective of this research is to describe the mathematical modelling for CCS on the inclined plane (considering the inclined angle and friction) and study the different types of the controller and designed for the system. After that, the model is simulated on MATLAB software for the performance analysis.

Mathematical Modelling and Controller Design

The study of some real-life problems can be easily done with the help of mathematical modeling. Here, the physical situation is converted into mathematics with some conditions. In the modeling process, we make a model that explains the performances of numerous activities of our problems differently. The physical phenomenon of a system could not describe with the help of a mathematical model. Therefore, a gap occurs between the mathematical model and the actual system. The gap between the actual system and the mathematical model is called the uncertainty. The models used in engineering are usually described as differential equations, difference equations, or statistical data. There are some steps for the mathematical modeling given below:

1. Find the physical problems.

2. Using the help of different physical laws, convert the physical problems into a mathematical model and, according to the requirement, also include some variable parameters.

3. Solve the mathematical problems.

4. Take the original result and compare it with the experimental results.

5. The model is accepted if the result is in good agreement, otherwise requires some modification in the hypothesis/assumptions.

The flow chart of mathematical modeling is given in Fig. (**1**):

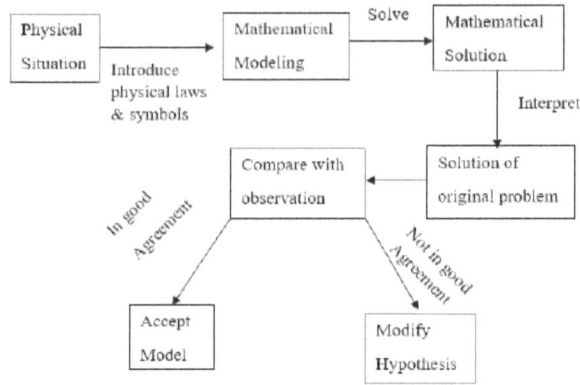

Fig. (1). The flow chart of mathematical modeling.

Mathematical Modelling

The main objective of the CCS is to detect the vehicle's speed and then output speed which is also known as the measured speed, which compares with the reference speed that the driver gives. After comparing both speeds, the requirement driver decides whether it will be accelerated or decelerated. Actually, this system is an example of a Close Loop Control System (CLCS). A speedometer is an example of a speed sensor connected to the feedback path to measure the actual output signal. The block architecture of the CCS is given in Fig. (2) [26].

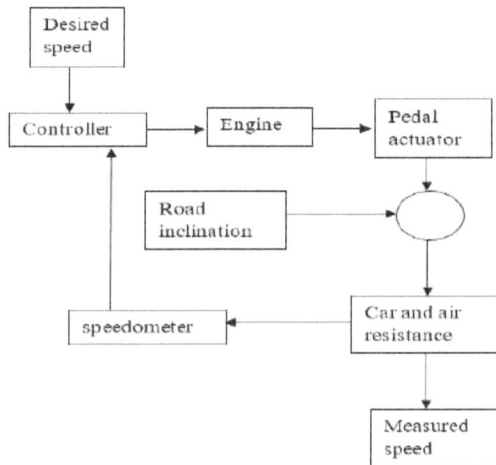

Fig. (2). Block diagram of simple CCS [26].

The difference between the measured signal and the reference signal is known as the error signal. The input signal of the controller is also known as the error signal. Basically, the controller is the combination between the error detector and the amplifier. The controller output signal depends upon the error signal. The throttle range can be changed with the help of a controller because it changes the speed of the vehicle. In the operating process, once the system is set, the system-maintained vehicle's speed is constant until the system is deactivated with the help of a clutch pedal, brake or disconnect the main switch of the plant. If the central switch is turned off, the previous value of speed is stored in the memory. The model of vehicle on inclined plane is given in Fig. (**3**).

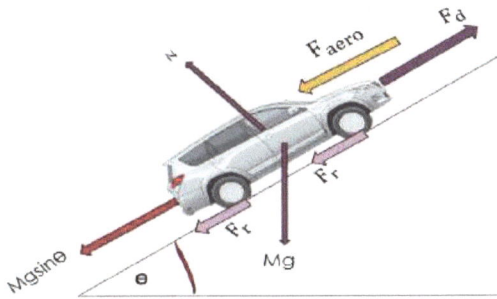

Fig. (3). Diagram of the model on an inclined plane.

The fundamental goal of this system is regulating the vehicle's speed, and the CCS also follows the commands for maintaining the constant speed. The regulation of car speed depends upon the increment or decrement value drive force Fd that is decided with the help of the reference signal and the feedback signal. The feedback signal is given by the speedometer sensor. The longitudinal dynamic model is obtained with the help of force balancing equations.

$$F_d = M\frac{dv}{dt} + F_r + Mgsin\theta + F_{aero} \qquad (1)$$

Where: Fd = Engine force

μ = Friction coefficient

Fr = Friction force

N = Normal force

Faero = Aerodynamic force

$Fr = \mu N$

M = Mass of car and driver

g = Acceleration due to gravity

$N = Mg\cos\theta$

Ca = Aerodynamic coefficient

$Faero = Ca\ V^2$

θ = Road grade

The Engine force depends upon the number of fuels to generate the energy for car. The force generated by air is known as the aerodynamic force, and it depends on many factors such as drag coefficient, speed of car, front areas of the car, and air density. The natural force or the friction force is produced due to the contact of the wheel and road. The model of vehicle's force system and the actuator is done with the help of the time delay function, which is connected in the cascade with the time delay function of the first order.

$$F_d = M\frac{dv}{dt} + \mu Mg\cos\theta + Mg\sin\theta + C_a v^2 \qquad (2)$$

$$\frac{dF_d}{dt} = M\frac{d^2v}{dt^2} + \mu Mg\frac{d}{dt}\cos\theta + Mg\frac{d}{dt}\sin\theta + 2C_a v\frac{dv}{dt} \qquad (3)$$

$$\frac{dF_d}{dt} = M\frac{d^2v}{dt^2} - \mu Mg\sin\theta\frac{v}{R} + Mg\cos\theta\frac{v}{R} + 2C_a v\frac{dv}{dt} \qquad (4)$$

Taking Laplace with the initial condition as zero, we get second-order transfer function as below:

$$\frac{V(s)}{F_d(s)} = \frac{s}{Ms^2 + 2C_a vs + \frac{[Mg\cos\theta - \mu Mg\sin\theta]}{R}} \qquad (5)$$

Where: R = Radius of Wheel.

Now we consider

$$F_d(s) = \frac{ke^{-\alpha}}{1+Ts}U(s) \tag{6}$$

The power series expansion technique can provide the solution only for the initial valve problem, and this type of problem opposesthe boundary problem. The series coefficient will be quantified with the nonlinear recurrence. To find the solution of nonlinear equations, we can simplify it into a linear equation by the Power Series Approximation (PSA) method. At the time of conversion nonlinear equation into linear, all the nonlinear equation must be expressed into the linear simultaneously to combine into one power series. Thus, we expand the exponential function with the help of PSA method as,

$$e^{-\alpha} = \frac{1}{e^{\alpha}} = \frac{1}{1+\alpha s} = \frac{\frac{1}{\alpha}}{1+\frac{1}{\alpha}} \tag{7}$$

$$F_d(s) = \frac{k\frac{1}{\alpha}}{(1+Ts)(1+\frac{1}{\alpha})}U(s) \tag{8}$$

Where: k = Gain of system

T= Time constant

α= Time delay

$$\frac{V(s)}{U(s)} = \frac{\frac{ks}{TM}\alpha}{(s+\frac{1}{T})(s+\frac{1}{\alpha})(s^2+\frac{2Ca\,v}{M}s+\frac{[gcos\,\theta-\mu gsin\theta]}{R})} \tag{9}$$

Finally, the transfer function of our system contains one zero and four poles. The nonlinearity due to the exponential function will become linear with the help of PSA method, but the overall transfer function is not completely linear. Now, we study the function with the simulation performance consisting of the mass, slope, friction coefficient, and aerodynamics coefficient. The value of the constant parameter is used from [58]. A small change can be done in these values because systems often provide different values for the computations.

Controller Design

A controller is a fundamental part of control engineering and uses in all types of complex control systems. It is a mechanism that can use to reduce the difference between the actual values of a system and the desired values of the system. Before ng various controllers in detail that is used in this thesis, it is very important to know the use of the controller in the control systems. The important uses of the controllers include:

1. It improved the steady-state performance through minimized steady-state error.
2. The stability of the system can also improve due to the improvement of steady-state accuracy.
3. It can also help to minimize the unwanted signal, generated through the system.
4. Uses to control overshoots of the system.
5. It uses to reduce the noise signals produced by the system.
6. It can help to speed up the slow response of an overdamped system.

PID CONTROLLER

There are many industries that can use the PID to optimize the performance of a particular control system. This controller is widely used in the industries due to the simple algorithm design. The industries use controller either PID controller or an advance version of PID. There are many types of PID controllers depending on the arrangement series, parallel and mixed controller *etc.* [27, 28]. The algorithm of PID controller is used in the algorithm of velocity, and another name of this algorithm is an incremental algorithm. PID controller methodology is also used in many industries for real-life applications [29, 30].

The output of PID controller provides the combined feature of P, I and D controllers. The response is fast due to the derivative of the controller, the error is minimized due to the integral controller, and the oscillations are minimized due to the proportional controller. In the process industries, PID controller is normally used. More than 95% of the controller are the PID controller are used in the process control application, and single input single output PID controller uses in the maximum pulp and paper industries. The simple architecture of PID controller for the plant is shown in Fig. (**4**) [30]. In this case, the controller output is as:

$$u(t) = K_p * e(t) + K_I * \int e(t) \, dt + K_D * \frac{d}{dt} e(t) \tag{10}$$

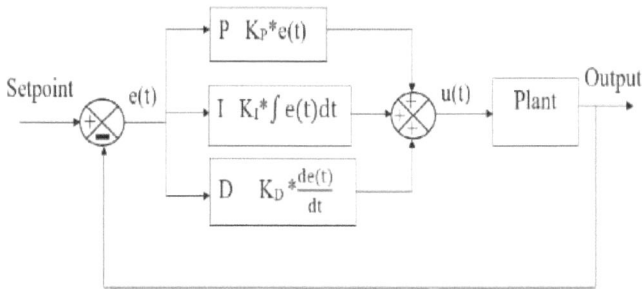

Fig. (4). Simple architecture of PID controller for plant [30].

Where: KP = Proportional constant.

KI = Integral constant.

KD = Derivative constant.

e(t)= Error signal.

u(t)= Controller output signal.

The tuning of PID controller is done with the Ziegler-Nichols Algorithm [31 - 33]. The advanced version of this controller is also discussed in [34 - 36]. The response of PID controller is faster and has a small overshoot.

PID TUNNING: It is a process to find the gain of proportional, integral, and derivative of PID controllers to achieve the desired performance. The popular methods of PID tunning are Adjust and Observed Method and Ziegler-Nichols (Z-N) Method. The Z-N method is classified into two categories as Oscillation Method and Open Loop Method. In this thesis, PID tunning is done with the oscillation method of Z-N method.

PROCEDURE OF PID TUNING WITH OSCILLATION Z-N METHOD

(1) Initialize all the PID constants to zero.

(2) Increase the proportional gain constant (Kp) to the minimum value that will cause the system to oscillate.

(3) Record the value of Kp as ultimate gain (Ku).

(4) Measured the period of oscillation waveform. This period is the ultimate

period (Tu).

(5) Now set the PID constant as the following values.

(i) Kp =0.6Ku

(ii) Ki =2Kp /Tu

(iii) Kd =KpTu /8

ADVANTAGES OF PID CONTROLLER

1. *Steady state error is zero.*
2. *Moderate peak overshoot.*
3. *Moderate stability.*
4. *It can be used for fast and slow process variables.*
5. *Decreased rise time and settling time.*

DISADVANTAGE OF PID CONTROLLER

1. *Cost is high.*
2. *Not optimal for the problems.*
3. *Not dependent on the process.*
4. *Can be unstable unless tuned properly.*

FUZZY LOGIC CONTROLLER (FLC)

In 1965, the fuzzy hypothesis was first developed by L.A. Zadeh. He analyzed that the traditional hypothesis focuses on accuracy as opposed to the simple and productive controlling component. In contrast to old-style sets, the fuzzy set has a specific level of enrolment for every component. The FLC utilized in CCS, framework has the two-input known as the error (e), the rate of change of error d(e), and the single output. FLC framework comprises three fundamental stages the Fuzzification, fuzzy inference framework, and Defuzzification [37 - 39]. The primary stage is used to change the crisp value into the fuzzy rule; the second stage, the controller output, and the input data are computed in the scope with the help of information and the rule bases. The defuzzification interface changes the ends from the interface mechanism into the out of the plant [40]. The simple architecture of the plant with the fuzzy controller is given in Fig. (5) [41].

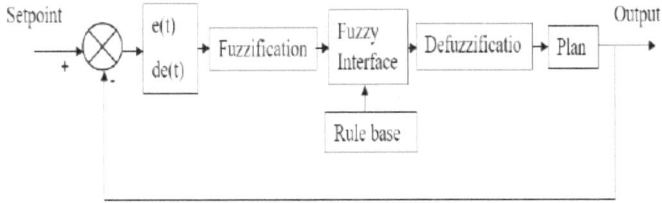

Fig. (5). The simple architecture of the plant with the fuzzy controller [41].

The essential components of FLC are:

1. Fuzzification.

2. Interfacing and rule.

3. Defuzzification.

FUZZIFICATION

The designing of FLC is the most significant phase. The fuzzy rule base utilizes rules on Linguistic Variable (LV). First of all, the numerical input is converted into the linguistic variable. This cycle of changing numerical data into a linguistic variable is known as the process of fuzzification. Error, rate of change of error, or area of error are used as variables. The graphical presentation of the degree of belonging of element to fuzzy sets are known as the membership functions. On the basis of the requirement of precision and accuracy, we use the different membership functions for output and the input. In this model, we use the seven membership functions for all the input and output signals of FLC.

FUZZY RULE INTERFACE (FRI)

There are two methods for fuzzy inference known as Mamdani and Sugeno. The large discussion about Mamdani and Sugeno is done in [42 - 44]. There are three popular fuzzy models like as:

1. Ebrahim Mamdani Fuzzy Models (EMFM).
2. Sugeno Fuzzy Models (SFM).
3. Tsukamoto Fuzzy Models (TFM).

EBRAHIM MAMDANI FUZZY MODEL (EMFM)

This model is developed by Professor Ebrahim Mamdani in 1975. The process of EMFM is completed in four steps:

1. Fuzzification.
2. Rule base.
3. Aggregation of the rule outputs.
4. Defuzzification.

The most common method which is used for the fuzzy interface is Mamdani. It was among the principal control frameworks constructed utilizing the fuzzy set hypothesis. The EMFM expects the output variable into the fuzzy set. EMFM has a large advantage for the use of a single MF of a LV rather than a fuzzy set. When the EMFM is used for the single LV in output is known as the Singleton Output Mechanism. It improves the Defuzzification cycle by rearranging calculation obligatory through a broad EMFM strategy that finds the centroid of the two-dimensional (2-D) function. This model is broadly used for the research and implementation of the system and describes spontaneous expertise.

Sugeno Fuzzy Model (SFM)

This model is just like to the EMFM Mamdani model. This model differs from EMFM through rule consequent but not fuzzy sets. Input variable uses a mathematical function in this model. The SFM is used to model any inference system whose output MF is either constant or linear [44]. The SFM is not used a compositional rule, but EMFM uses a compositional rule. This model is suitable for data-based fuzzy modeling. This method is computationally effective due to optimization and adaptive techniques. The model is very attractive for nonlinear systems. If we consider as the first and second input are P and Q, respectively then the Output O is linear as:

$$O = KP + LQ + M$$

Output is constant for the zero order SFM. The condition of zero order SM is as:

$$K = L = M$$

Tsukamoto Fuzzy Model

In this model, the if-then rule is epitomized by a fuzzy set with a monotonical MF. This model is not used as the Mamdani or Sugeno fuzzy models due to a lack of transparency. The output of this model is taken with the weighted average method of defuzzification to minimize the processing time of defuzzification.

DEFUZZIFICATION

There are many methods for defuzzification given in Fig. (**6**):

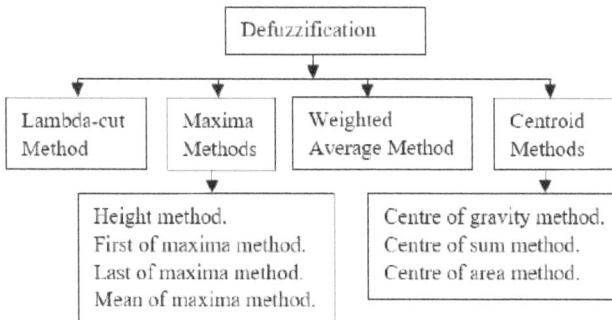

Fig. (6). Block diagram of methods of defuzzification.

The FLC produces an output in the LV form. The best fuzzification method is the Centre of gravity. There are many rules for converting the variables into fuzzy form.

MEMBERSHIP FUNCTION (MF)

The membership function is a graph that lies between 0 and 1 and it indicates the mapping of every point in the input state and values of MF. The MF is the pictorial presentation of the magnitude of each input. When the function is interface, scaled and combined, then it is fuzzified into the output [45].

Types of Membership Functions

The easiest MF is designed with the help of straight lines. Trapezoidal and triangular MF are extensively used in the real-time problem due to simple formulas and computational efficiencies. MF is the combination of straight-line therefore, it is not flat at the bend point [46, 47]. The fundamental MFs are:

1. Gaussian MF (GMF).

2. Triangular MF (TMF).

3. π- Shaped Membership Function (π-MF).

4. Trapezoidal MF.

5. Generalized bell MF (GBMF).

6. S- Shaped Membership Function (SMF).

Formulation and parameterization of some MF have been discussed below:

Triangular MF: The triangular MF is defined by the three parameters {a, b, c}. The mathematical equation and curve of triangular MF are shown in Fig. (**7**).

$$triangle(x; a, b, c) = \begin{cases} 0 & \text{if } x \leq a \\ \frac{x-a}{b-a} & \text{if } a \leq x \leq b \\ \frac{c-x}{c-b} & \text{if } b \leq x \leq c \\ 0 & \text{if } c \leq x \end{cases}$$

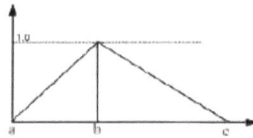

Fig. (7). Triangular MFs.

Trapezoidal MF: The trapezoidal MF is defined by four parameters {a, b, c, d}. The mathematical expression and curve for trapezoidal MF are given in Fig. (**8**).

$$trapeziod(x; a, b, c, d) = \begin{cases} 0 & \text{if } x \leq a \\ \frac{x-a}{b-a} & \text{if } a \leq x \leq b \\ 1 & \text{if } b \leq x \leq c \\ \frac{d-x}{d-c} & \text{if } c \leq x \leq d \\ 0 & \text{if } d \leq x \end{cases}$$

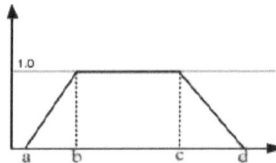

Fig. (8). Trapezoidal MFs.

Gaussian MF: The Gaussian MF is defined with the help of two parameters $\{c, \sigma\}$. The mathematical expression and curve for Gaussian MF are given in Fig. (**9**).

$$\text{gaussian}(x;c,\sigma) = e^{-\frac{1}{2}\left(\frac{x-c}{\sigma}\right)^2}.$$

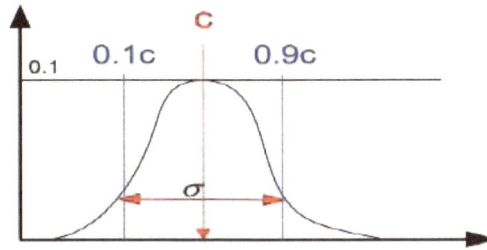

Fig. (9). Gaussian MFs.

Generalized bell: This function is approximately similar to the Gaussian function. There are specified three parameters $\{a, b, c\}$ by which the bell function is defined as in Fig. (**10**).:

$$\text{bell}(x; a, b, c) = \frac{1}{1+\left|\frac{x-c}{a}\right|^{2b}}$$

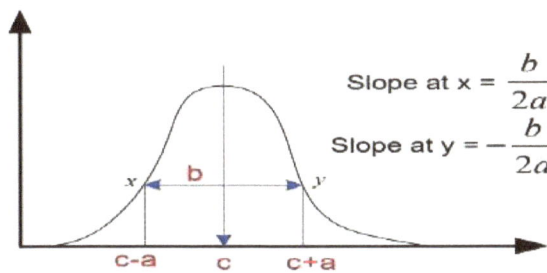

Slope at $x = \dfrac{b}{2a}$

Slope at $y = -\dfrac{b}{2a}$

Fig. (10). Generalized bell MFs.

Sigmoidal MF: This function is defined with two Parameters: $\{a, c\}$. The mathematical expression and the curve of sigmoidal MF are given in Fig. (**11**) where c and a defined as crossover point and slope at c, respectively.

$$Sigmoid(x;a,c) = \frac{1}{1+e^{-[\frac{a}{x-c}]}}$$

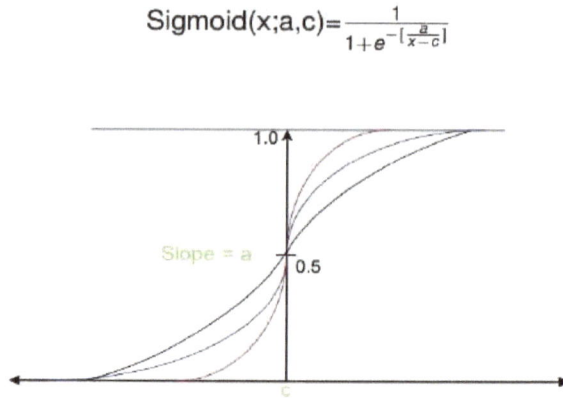

Fig. (11). Sigmoidal MFs.

Any type of continuous probability distribution function (PDF) will be used as MF in the particular situation. The collection of parameters is used to postulate the suitable meaning of MF [48]. The Gaussian membership function is proposed FLC in our model for two input, and the one output is shown in Figs. **(12 - 14)**, respectively. The gaussian and the bell membership function are the famous methods for the fuzzy set due to their smoothness and concise notion.

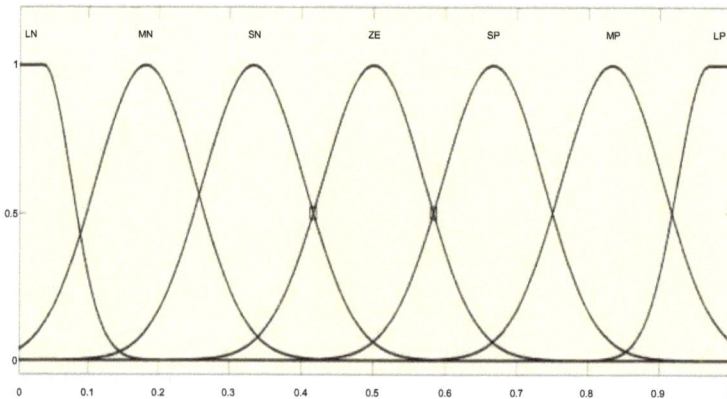

Fig. (12). MF for error.

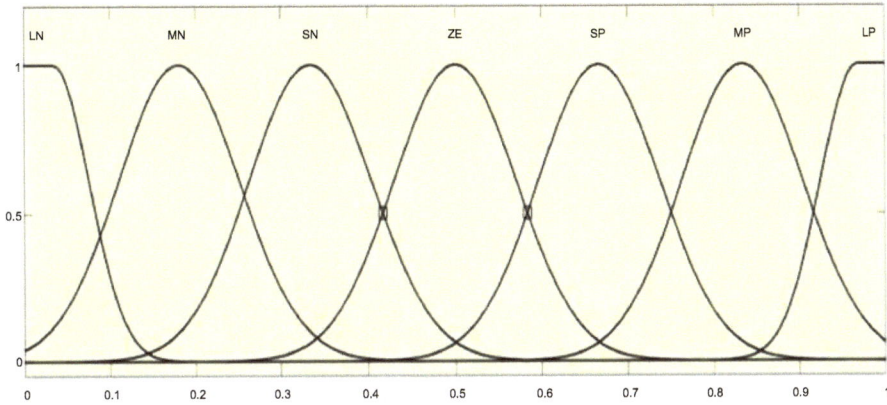

Fig. (13). MF for derivate of error.

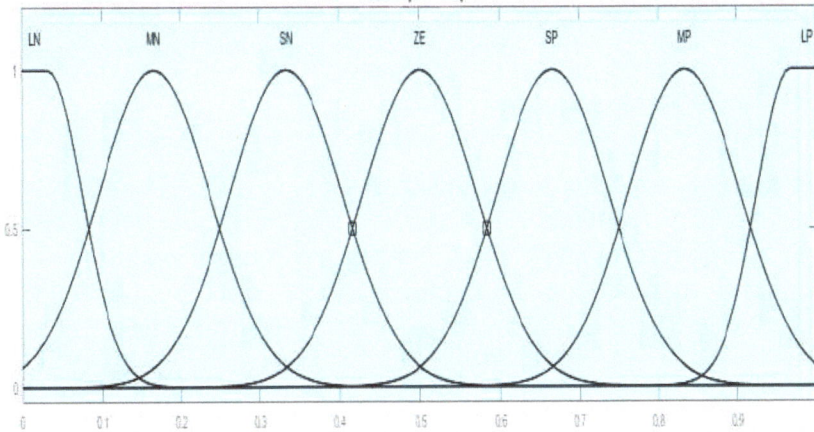

Fig. (14). MF for output actuator control.

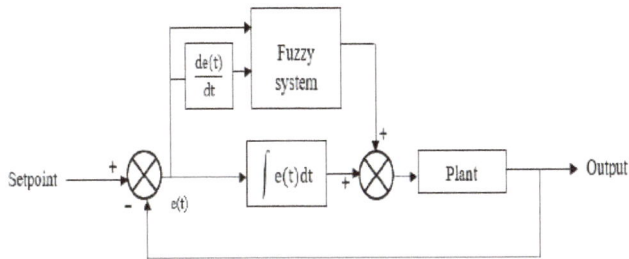

Fig. (15). Fuzzy PID controller (FPD+I) [57].

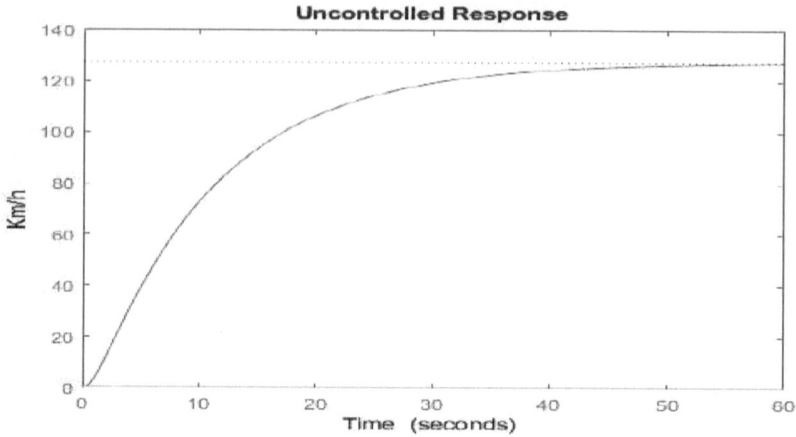

Fig. (16). Performance without friction and the inclination.

The modified fuzzy controller is also discussed in [49, 50]. The rule base is given in Table **1**. This table contains the seven-membership function for the input as error and the derivative of the error. Therefore, a total of forty-nine rules were produced with this membership for output. The range of both input and one output at the different conditions is shown in Table **2**. The corresponding abbreviations are as:

Large negative (LN).

Small negative (SN).

Large positive (LP).

Zero (ZE)

Medium positive (MP).

Small positive (SP).

Medium negative (MN).

The explanation of Table **1** is understood as [51], and I/O in Table **2**:

If the error signal is Large positive (LP) **and** the rate of change of error is Small positive (SP) **then** the output actuator is Medium positive (MP).

If the error is Small positive (SP) **and** the rate of change of error is Medium negative (MN) **then** the output actuator is Small negative (SN).

Table 1. Look up table construction.

Error (e)

Derivative of error (de)		LN	MN	SN	ZE	SP	MP	LP
	LN	LN	LN	LN	LN	MN	SN	ZE
	MN	LN	MN	MN	MN	SN	ZE	SP
	SN	LN	MN	SN	SN	ZE	SP	SP
	ZE	LN	MN	SN	ZE	SP	SP	MP
	SP	MN	SN	ZE	SP	SP	MP	MP
	MP	SN	ZE	SP	MP	MP	MP	LP
	LP	ZE	SP	SP	LP	MP	LP	LP

Table 2. Input and output range of fuzzy control.

Case	Range of error	Range of derivative of error	Range of output actuator
Θ=0, μ=0	-8 to 60	-55 to 5	0 to 0.25
Θ=10°, μ=0	-5 to 60	-85 to 18	0.5 to 1.2
Θ=10°, μ=0.5	-0.5 to 60	-40 to 10	0.025 to 0.035

ADVANTAGE OF FLC

There are many advantages of FLC, therefore, it is considered rather than other controllers. They are [52]:

1. It is easily operated with noisy input.
2. It is also preferable with multiple input and multiple-output (MIMO) system.
3. Easy mathematical analysis.
4. Simple designed.
5. It uses low-precision sensors.

6. It can be easily operated in a nonlinear system.

7. Simple interface.

FUZZY- PID (F-PID) CONTROLLER

This type of controller is related to the nonlinear gain. Due to the nonlinear gain, the F-PID has the possibility to improve and gain better performance rather than normal PID. Theoretically, it is difficult to explain why F-PID provides better performance due to the presence of nonlinearities. Thus, it is significant on the basis of hypothetical and practical perspectives to investigate the properties of nonlinear control of F-PID and discover suitable designed methods. There are different types of F-PID controllers have been proposed [53 - 56]. On the basics of construction F-PID is divided into two categories.

One classification of F-PID controller is the combination of simple PID and mechanism, fuzzy rule [56]. By excellence of the gain properties, the F-PID controller can adjust itself to changes in the environment. The principle trouble in utilizing this class of F-PID controller is examining the problem relating the nonlinearities. Another classification of F-PID controller is built with the set of empirical rules; therefore, the signals are directly presumed from the fuzzy interface and rule base. Designing this type of F-PID controller is easy. The structure analogous of F-PID is similar to conventional PID controllers. The nonlinear assets of F-PID are determined when the structure is fixed. F-PID is the combination of fuzzy and PID controllers. The operation of F-PID is the same based on the reference signal, while the control policy is expressed with fuzzy rules. With the many assumptions according to the shape of MF and the interface method, the F-PID controller is the same as the PID controllers. The input of F-PID controllers depends upon error signal, rate of error and the integration of error. The rules for integral action are not defined simply because the final and the initial value of the integrator action based on the load. In the crisp, the action of integral of PID controller serves its purpose. The architecture of fuzzy PD and the integral controller is shown in Fig. (**15**) [57].

RESULTS AND DISCUSSION

This section discussed the simulation result of the uncontrolled and controlled model. First of all, we discussed the simulation results of the uncontrolled model at all the situations that appeared in Figs. (**16 - 19**). The car is running at speed 60 kilometers per hour. The disturbance of the model is considered as the road grade and friction. If friction is not considered, but road grade is considered, then the TF of our model contains the one zero, and four poles. In this situation, the simulation result of the uncontrol model after compensation the zero is shown in Fig. (**17**). When the road grade and friction appear in the system, then the system also has the one zero and for poles. In this situation, the simulation result of the uncontrol model without compensation of zero is shown in Fig. (**18**), and after the compensation the zero is shown in Fig. (**19**). The simulation performance of the model in all situations is considered not to provide the desired speed as given by the driver. Therefore, we need some controllers for achieving the wanted objective.

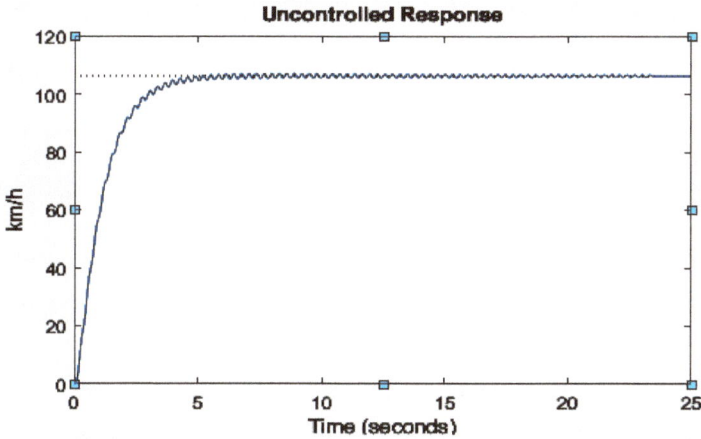

Fig. (17). Performance with road grade after zero compensation.

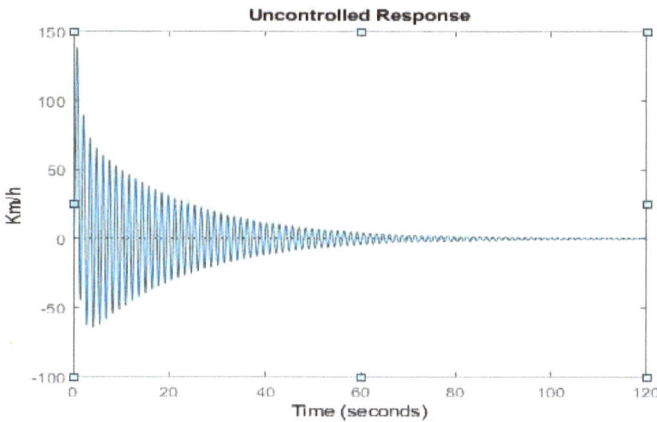

Fig. (18). Performance with friction and road grade but without zero compensation.

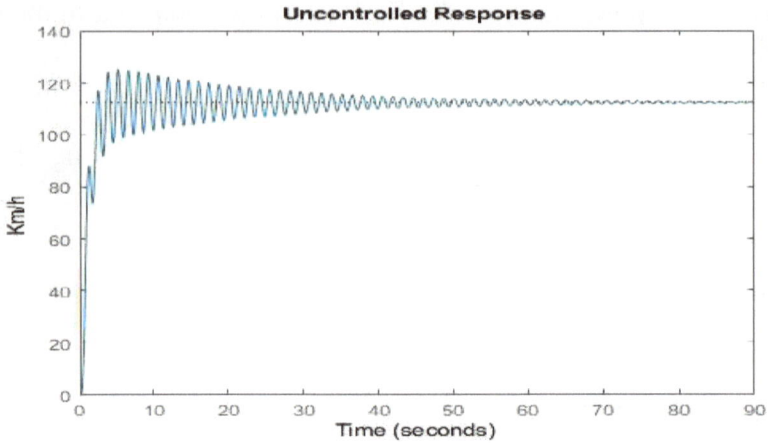

Fig. (19). Performance with friction and road grade but with compensation.

Now, we designed many controllers like PID, Fuzzy, and Fuzzy-PID to get better results. The performance of the model with different controllers in all situations and conditions appear in Figs. (**20 - 22**).

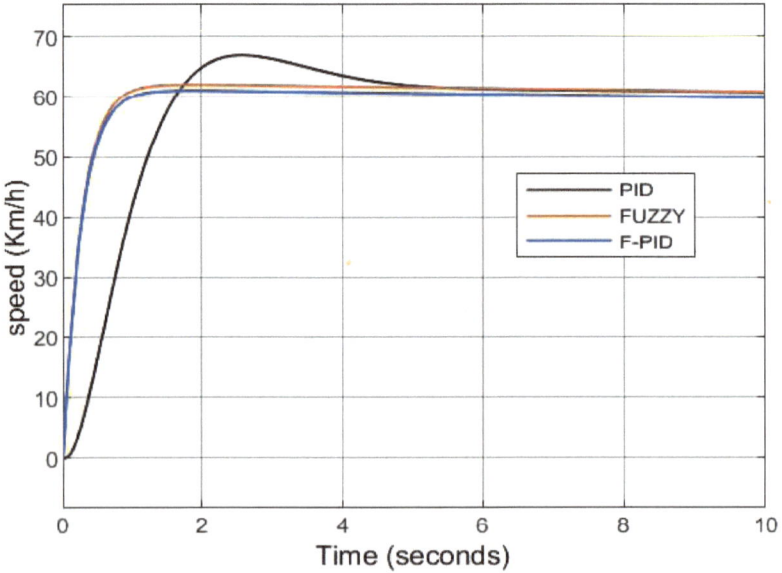

Fig. (20). Performance without inclination and friction.

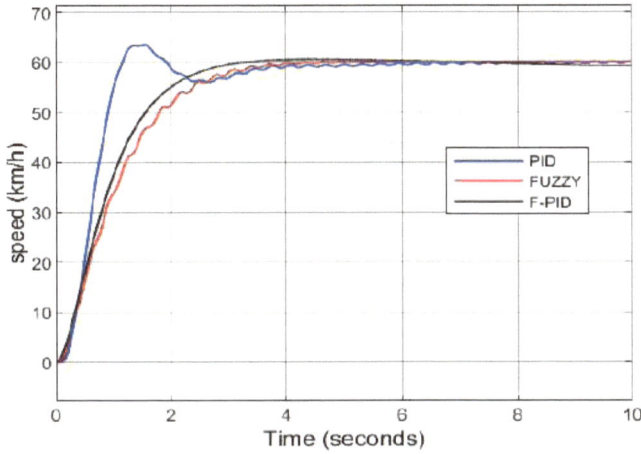

Fig. (21). Performance with the inclination and without friction after zero compensation.

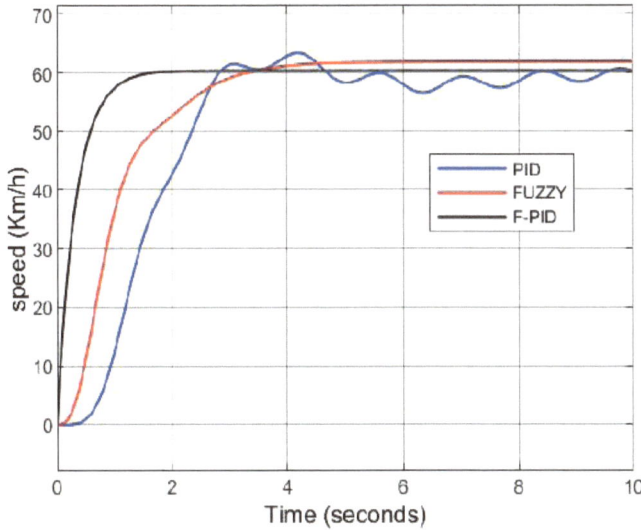

Fig. (22). Performance with inclination and friction after compensating the zero.

The performance can be obtained at the several conditions of friction coefficient and road grad with the different controllers, but we considered the three conditions relating to the friction and the angle.

The first condition, when the friction and the road grad are not considered in model systems, the simulation result of the model with all various controller discussed above is given in Fig. (**20**). The response of PID, fuzzy and fuzzy-PID controller is better than the system's performance without a controller as also in Fig. (**16**). In the second condition, when the system has only road grad, the performance with the various controller is shown in Fig. (**21**). This performance of the CCS is shown after compensating for the zero in the model. The fuzzy controller reduced the oscillation compared with PID controllers, but the F-PID controller approximates the oscillation from the system. Third condition, when road grad and friction are both considered in the system, the model's response with different controllers is shown in Fig. (**22**). FLC provides a better-simulating result as compared to the PID controller. The fuzzy-PID provides the best simulation result compared to all controllers in all situations.

Many parameters (like maximum peak value, maximum peak time, settling time, rise time steady state value, *etc.*) are calculated with response of each controller at each condition. These parameters are shown in Tables **3 - 5** as below.

Table **3** (Compared parameter with the different controller when the friction and angle of inclination is not considered)

We compared this result with the paper [58 - 60], which is better in many situations such as rise time, maximum peak value, settling time, maximum peak time, *etc.* The analysis of the dynamic characteristics of the system is easily done with these parameters. These comparisons of dynamic parameters are in Tables **3 - 5**. From the analysis of these tables, it is concluded that the compensation must be incorporated into the model to achieve the desired objective. The response of the fuzzy controller is better than PID in all situations.

Table 4. Compared parameter with the different controller when the only angle of inclination is considered.

Parameters	PID	FUZZY	FUZZY-PID
Maximum peak value	66.78	61.95	60.97
Maximum peak time (seconds)	2.542	2.05	2.033
Rise time (seconds)	1.16	0.8	0.605
Settling time (seconds)	5.8	5.0	4.5
Steady state value	60.77	60.23	60.04
Steady state error (%)	1.28	0.38	0.06
Oscillation	No	No	No

Table 5. Compared parameter with the different controller when both angles of inclination and friction are considered.

Parameters	PID	FUZZY	FUZZY-PID
Maximum peak value	63.55	60.15	60.22
Maximum peak time (seconds)	1.53	5.24	4.50
Rise time (seconds)	0.69	3.2	1.669
Settling time (seconds)	3.98	5.51	5.3
Steady state value	60.08	60.02	60.02
Steady state error (%)	0.13	0.03	0.33
Oscillation	low	Very low	No

The response of fuzzy-PID controller is best in all these situations compared to these controllers. All the parameters are optimum in the fuzzy-PID controller, and the oscillation is neglected in all the situations. The transient response and the steady-state response are good in all situations. Therefore, we can say that fuzzy-PID controller is the best among these controllers.

CONCLUSION

The modeling of CCS with the friction coefficient and the angle of inclination is done successfully. On the basis of simulation performance, it is analyzed that compensation is the important part of this model to achieve the wanted purposes. The comparative performance of the model with various Controller is discussed in Tables 3 - 5. The comparison of various controllers is made on the basis of various dynamic parameters like rise time, maximum peak value, settling time, maximum peak time, *etc.* The performances of the different controllers have been compared at various values of road grad and friction. The better results and the good stability were obtained with the help of fuzzy-PID controller in all the cases. The CCS can improve the performance of dynamics of the automobile by reducing the effluences and improving the comfortability level of the rider.

Future Developments

(1) The performance can be validated and modified by using some more different techniques and algorithms such as Neural Network (NN), Genetic Algorithms (GA), Particle Swarm Optimization (PSO) algorithm, *etc.*

(2) The extension of this work is in the ACC system. The conventional CCS keeps up the ideal speed of the vehicle, which is given by the driver and the ACC framework additionally keeps up a suitable relative separation to the lead vehicle.

(3) The extension version of the ACC system is the Cooperative ACC (CACC).

(4) The CACC system uses wireless communication to detect the risk situation earlier on the highways, and in addition, more wide-ranging and reliable data of other vehicles' motion is collected to improve the performance of the vehicle control system.

LIST OF ABBREVIATIONS

ABS	Adaptive Broadcast Scheme
ACCS	Adaptive Cruise Control System
AHS	Automated Highway System
CACCS	Co-Operative Adaptive Cruise Control System
CAVs	Connected and Automated Vehicles
CCS	Cruise Control System
DOFx	Self-Organization Network
MCCS	Modern Cruise Control System
MF	Membership Function
PSA	Power Series Approximation
SCS	Speed Control Systems
TCS	Tempomat Control System
SON	Self-Organization Network
TTI	Traffic and Travel Information

CONSENT OF PUBLICATION

Not applicable.

CONFLICT OF INTEREST

The author declares no conflict of interest, financial or otherwise.

ACKNOWLEDGEMENT

The modeling and the simulating results are obtained under the supervision of thesis guide Dr. Amit Kumar Singh.

REFERENCES

[1] S.M. Bharadwaj, and S. Dattawadkar, *Design of Autonomous Cruise Control Unit for Intelligent Vehicles,* vol. 5, no. 6, pp. 313-316, 2015.

[2] P.A. Ioannou, and C.C. Chien, "Autonomous Intelligent Cruise Control", *IEEE Trans. Vehicular Technol.,* vol. 42, no. 4, pp. 657-672, 1993.
[http://dx.doi.org/10.1109/25.260745]

[3] S. E. Shladover, Vehicle System Dynamics : International Journal of Vehicle Mechanics and Mobility Review of the State of Development of Advanced Vehicle Control Systems (AVCS) 2012.

[4] N.C. Basjaruddin, D. Kuspriyanto, D. Saefudin, and I.K. Nugraha, "Saefudin, and I. K. Nugraha, "Developing adaptive cruise control based on fuzzy logic using hardware simulation", *Iran. J. Electr. Comput. Eng.,* vol. 4, no. 6, pp. 944-951, 2014.
[http://dx.doi.org/10.11591/ijece.v4i6.6734]

[5] P. Venhovens, *Stop and go cruise control and vehicle dynamics.pdf,* 1999, pp. 1-42.

[6] R. Rajamani, *Vehicle Dynamics and Control.* Springer Science, 2006.

[7] L. Givens, "A primer on cruise controls", *Automot. Eng.,* no. June, p. 2632, 1975.

[8] R. Rajamani, *Vehicle Dynamics and Control.* Springer Science & Business Media, 2011.

[9] R. Teetor Ralph, "Speed control device for resisting operation of the accelerator", *US-Patent 2519859 A.*

[10] F.J. Riley, "Constant speed regulator", *United States Patent US2714880.*

[11] United States Air Force, *Keesler Air Force Base Housing..*

[12] "1966 american motors", *Car Life.,* vol. 12, p. 46, 1965.

[13] W. Pananurak, S. Thanok, and M. Parnichkun, "Adaptive cruise control for an intelligent vehicle", In: *Proc. of 1998 American Control Conference* vol. 3. , 2009, pp. 1823-1827.
[http://dx.doi.org/10.1109/ROBIO.2009.4913274]

[14] C-Y. Liang, "Traffic-friendly adaptive cruise control design", *Ph.D. dissertation Dept. Mech. Eng., Univ. Michigan, Ann Arbor.,* 2000.

[15] H.S. Tan, R. Rajamani, and W.B. Zhang, "Demonstration of an automated highway platoon system", In: *Proc. of 1998 American Control Conference 3.,* 1998, pp. 1823-1827.

[16] H. Ohtsuka, and L. Vlacic, "Stop & Go vehicle longitudinal model", *IEEE 5th International Conference on Intelligent Transportation Systems,* 2002.

[17] A. Vahidi, and A. Eskandarianm, "Research Advances in Intelligent Collision Avoidance and Adaptive Cruise Control", *IEEE Trans. Intell. Transp. Syst.,* vol. 4, no. 3, pp. 143-153, 2003.
[http://dx.doi.org/10.1109/TITS.2003.821292]

[18] B. Arem, C. Driel, and R. Visser, "The impact of cooperative adaptive cruise control on traffic-flow characteristics", *In: IEEE Transactions on Intelligent Transportation Systems 7.4,* 2006.

[19] G. Naus, V. René, P. Jeroen, V.D.M. René, and S. Maarten, "Cooperative adaptive cruise control, design and experiments", In: *Proceedings of the 2010 American control conference.* IEEE, 2010, pp. 6145-6150.
[http://dx.doi.org/10.1109/ACC.2010.5531596]

[20] Wolterink, K. Wouter, H. Geert, and K. Geert, "Constrained geocast to support cooperative adaptive cruise control (CACC) merging", In: *2010 IEEE Vehicular Networking Conference.* IEEE, 2010, pp. 41-48.

[21] T.J. Ayres, Li. L., D. Schleuning, and D. Young, "Preferred time-headway of highway drivers." In ITSC 2001", *Intelligent Transportation Systems. Proceedings (Cat. No. 01TH8585).,* IEEE, pp. 826-829, 2001.

[22] B. Van Arem, C.J. van Driel, and R. Visser, "The impact of cooperative adaptive cruise control on traffic-flow characteristics", *IEEE Trans. Intell. Transp. Syst.,* vol. 7, no. 4, pp. 429-436, 2006.

[23] J. Vander Werf, S.E. Shladover, M.A. Miller, and N. Kourjanskaia, "Effects of adaptive cruise control systems on highway traffic flow capacity", *Transp. Res. Rec.,* vol. 1800, no. 1, pp. 78-84, 2002.
[http://dx.doi.org/10.3141/1800-10]

[24] B. van Arem, C.M.J. Tampère, and K.M. Malone, "Modelling traffic flows with intelligent cars and intelligent roads", *Proc. IEEE Intell. Veh. Symp.,* 2003pp. 456-461
[http://dx.doi.org/10.1109/IVS.2003.1212954]

[25] P.A. Ioannou, *Automated Highway Systems.,* P.A. Ioannou, Ed., Plenum: New York, NY, USA, 1997.

[26] ME 132 DSF _ Control Theory _ Control System,

[27] G.K.I. Mann, B.G. Hu, and R.G. Gosine, "Time-domain based design and analysis of new PID tuning rules, Proc. Inst. Elect. Eng.—", *IEE Proc. Contr. Theory Appl.,* vol. 148, no. 3, pp. 251-261, 2001.
[http://dx.doi.org/10.1049/ip-cta:20010464]

[28] C. Hang, W.K. Ho, and L.S. Cao, "A comparison of two design methods for PID controllers", In: *Proceedings of the ISA/93 Advances in Instrumentation and Control Conference.* McCormick Place: Chicago, Illinois, 1993, pp. 959-967.

[29] S. Bennett, "The past of PID controllers", In: *Proc. IFAC Workshop on Digital Control: Past, Present and Future of PID Control.* Spain: Terrassa, 2000, pp. 1-11.

[30] K.J. Astrom, and T. Haglund, *PID Controllers: Theory, Design and Tuning.* 2nd ed. Instrum. Soc. Amer.: Research Triangle Park, NC, 1995.

[31] Ch. Bhanu Prakash, and R. Srinu Naik, "Tuning of PID Controller by Ziegler-Nichols Algorithm for Position Control of DC Motor", *International Journal of Innovative Science, Engineering & Technology,* vol. 1, pp. 379-382, 2014.

[32] C.C. Hang, K.J. Astrom, and W.K. Ho, ""Refinements of the Ziegler–Nichols tuning formula," Proc Inst. Elect", *Eng.—Part D: Control Theory and Applications,* vol. 138, no. 2, pp. 111-118, 1991.

[33] A.K. Singh, B. Tyagi, and V. Kumar, "Application of neural network based control strategies to binary distillation column", *Control Eng Appl Informatics,* vol. 15, pp. 47-57, 2013.

[34] K.J. Astrom, and T. Hagglund, *Advanced PID Controller.* Instrument Society of America: Research Triangle Park, North Carolina, 2006.

[35] A. Visioli, "Research Trends for PID Controllers", *Acta Polytechnica,* vol. 52, no. 5, 2012.
[http://dx.doi.org/10.14311/1656]

[36] K.J. Åström, and T. Hägglund, "The future of PID control", *Control Eng. Pract.,* vol. 9, no. 11, pp. 1163-1175, 2001.
[http://dx.doi.org/10.1016/S0967-0661(01)00062-4]

[37] P. Press, G. Britain, and W.I. Controllers, *A Control Engineering Review of Fuzzy Systems.,* 1977.

[38] Li-Xin Wang, "A Course in Fuzzy Systems and Control", *Prentice-Hall International, Inc.,International,* 1997.

[39] A.K. Singh, B. Tyagi, and V. Kumar, "Comparative performance analysis of fuzzy logic controller for the composition control of binary distillation column", *IEEE Recent Adv Intell Comput Syst RAICS,* 2011.
[http://dx.doi.org/10.1109/RAICS.2011.6069365]

[40] Taylor, Publisher. International Journal of General Systems A Review of : ' FUZZY SETS AND FUZZY LOGIC : Theory and Applications ' by George Klir and Bo Yuan , Prentice Hall PTR Upper Saddle River , New Jersey 2014.

[41] Mazin Abed Mohammed, *Design and Implementing an Efficient Expert Assistance System for Car*

Design and Implementing an Efficient Expert Assistance System for Car Evaluation via Fuzzy Logic Controller, 2015.

[42] Mathworks, http://in.mathworks.com/help/fuzzy/types-of-fuzzy-inference-systems.html

[43] Mathworks, http://in.mathworks.com/help/fuzzy/comparison-of-sugeno-and-mamdani-systems.html

[44] Mathworks, http://in.mathworks.com/help/fuzzy/what-is-sugeno-type-fuzzy-inference.html

[45] A. Bagis, "Determining Fuzzy Membership Functions with Tabu Search - an Application to Control", *Fuzzy Sets Syst.,* vol. 139, no. 1, pp. 209-225, 2003.
[http://dx.doi.org/10.1016/S0165-0114(02)00502-X]

[46] J. Geurge, *KlirfBu Yuan," Fuzzy Sets And Fuzzy Logic.* Prentice Hall, 1995.

[47] L-X. Wang, *A Course in Fuzzy Systems and Control.* International Edition. Prentice-Hall International, Inc., 1997.

[48] S.V. Shinde, and U.V. Kulkarni, "Modified Fuzzy Hyperline-Segment Neural Network For Classification With Mixed Attributes", *5th International conference on Computing Communication and Networking Technologies, IEEE,* pp. 1-7, .

[49] R. Muller, G. Nucker, A.G. Daimler-benz, and F. Technik, "Intelligent cruise control with fuzzy logic", *IEEE,* no. 49, pp. 173-178, 1992.
[http://dx.doi.org/10.1109/IVS.1992.252252]

[50] S.V. Shinde, "Modified fuzzy hyperline-segment neural network for classification with mixed attribues", *IEEE,* 2014.

[51] L.T. Koczy, "Fuzzy if. hen rule models and their transformation into one another", *IEEE Trans. Syst. Man Cybern. A Syst. Hum.,* vol. 26, no. 5, pp. 621-637, 1996.
[http://dx.doi.org/10.1109/3468.531909]

[52] S. Antonio, A. Pedro, and O. Manuel, Fuzzy logic controllers and methodology, advantages and drawbacks.

[53] W. Li, "Design of a hybrid fuzzy logic proportional plus conventional integral-derivative Controller", *IEEE Transactions on Fuzzy Systems,* vol. 6, no. 4, pp. 449-463, 1998.

[54] H.A. Malki, H.D. Li, and G.R. Chen, "New design and stability analysis of fuzzy proportional-derivative control system", *IEEE Transactions on Fuzzy Systems,* vol. 2, no. 4, pp. 245-254, 1994.
[http://dx.doi.org/10.1109/91.324804]

[55] S. J. Qin, and G. Borders, *A multiregion fuzzy logic controller for nonlinear process control.,* vol. 2, no. 1, pp. 74-81, 1994.*IEEE Transactions on Fuzzy Systems,* vol. 2, no. 1, pp. 74-81, 1994.
[http://dx.doi.org/10.1109/91.273128]

[56] H. Ying, "The simplest fuzzy controllers using di!erent inference methods are di!erent nonlinear proportional-integral controllers with variable gains", *Automatica,* vol. 29, no. 6, pp. 1579-1589, 1993.

[57] L Fuzzy, and PID Control, Linear Fuzzy PID Control. 2013.

[58] Y.S. Prakash, and S.A. Kumar, Mathematical Modelling and control of Cruise Control System on the Inclined Plane. pp. 431–436, 2020.

[59] O Munyaneza, BB Munyazikwiye, and HR Karimi, Speed control design for a vehicle system using fuzzy logic and PID controller 2018.

[60] A Kumar, P Deoraj, and K Tanti, "Design of different controller for cruise control system", *Int. J. Elect. Electr. Eng.,* vol. 9, no. 2, pp. 60-69, 2017.

SUBJECT INDEX

www.ingramcontent.com/pod-product-compliance
Lightning Source LLC
Chambersburg PA
CBHW050802220326
41598CB00006B/94